NEWSPAPER DESIGN

NEWSPAPER DESIGN

ALLEN HUTT

LONDON
OXFORD UNIVERSITY PRESS
NEW YORK TORONTO
1960

Oxford University Press, Amen House, London E.C.4
GLASGOW NEW YORK TORONTO MELBOURNE WELLINGTON
BOMBAY CALCUTTA MADRAS KARACHI KUALA LUMPUR
CAPE TOWN IBADAN NAIROBI ACCRA

PRINTED IN GREAT BRITAIN

Preface

THIS book is the first attempt to present for Britain the full-scale treatment of newspaper typography and design that has long been available to American newspapermen through the admirable textbooks of the late John E. Allen, Edmund C. Arnold, and others. That it should not appear until 1960 may seem strange, since the typographical transformation of our newspapers during the past thirty years has been perhaps the most radical of any in the world. English empiricism, our traditional aversion to 'theory', is probably to blame. But there can be no question now that rule-of-thumb will not do any longer. While newspaper concern with the problems of graphic design is constantly growing, as the success of the Annual Award for Newspaper Design shows, the extraordinary inequality in the standards of the entries for the Award is enough to demonstrate the need for some serious theory—that is, an exposition of general principles and the mode of their application—to illuminate and improve the practice.

The pages that follow cannot avoid the defects of all pioneer efforts; nor is it pretended for a moment that the treatments here are exhaustive. Some of the subsidiary chapters, notably those on picture-handling and periodicals, do little more than indicate the need for separate studies of their themes; likewise there is no detailed discussion of the significant current developments in editorial presentation and decoration by the artist qualified in graphic design.

On the other hand, it is hoped that this book may help generally in the vocational training of journalists, already developing in this country, though a good deal less advanced than it is in America, or, for that matter, in Russia. The U.S. and the U.S.S.R., both with highly organized Faculties or Departments of Journalism in their universities, compete with each other as the lands of the newspaper-typography textbook. The works of Allen and Arnold find their parallel in those of B. A. Vyazemsky and I. I. Starobogatov; since the war the last-named has produced three major textbooks, of which the latest, *Tekhnika Oformlieniya Gazet'i* (*The Technique of Newspaper Make-up*, Moscow University Press, 1958), is notable alike for its technical common sense and for the fact that it appeared in an edition of 10,000 copies.

While the present work does not purport to be a textbook of journalism, it has been written by a journalist for journalists; and its approach throughout is that newspaper typography and make-up can never be divorced from the journalism of which they are only the vehicle.

By way of a postscript it is worth noting that several newspapers cited in these pages have made improvements in their typography, notably in their title-pieces, since the completion of this text in 1958–9. The *Crawley Courier* (Fig. 147) has given a striking reverse-block treatment to its Times Bold title. The *Richmond and Twickenham Times* (Fig. 167) has abandoned its poor Blackletter title for an admirably adapted rendering in Corvinus Skyline, with a thorough clean-up of the cluttered subsidiary lines. The *Herts and Essex Observer* (Fig. 169) has changed its title from Blackletter to the elegant and unusual Dutch shaded Rosart on going over from broadsheet to tabloid. If other papers mentioned here have likewise since re-dressed themselves, their indulgence is requested; reproduction of a style since abandoned can still prove instructive.

G. A. H.

Camden Town
September 1960

Contents

List of Illustrations

Acknowledgements

THIS book has a long history; in the course of that history its first debt has been to Mr. Stanley Morison, from whom I have learned so much in the past twenty-five years, and who vetted an initial synopsis of mine as long ago as 1947. Many other colleagues and friends have put themselves out to be extremely helpful. Mr. Walter Tracy organized the formidable specimen settings by Linotype & Machinery Ltd., worked tirelessly to improve Chapter 2, and was an invaluable and generous adviser throughout. Mrs. Beatrice Warde similarly organized the specimen settings by the Monotype Corporation Ltd., and Mr. Caspar Mitchell those by Intertype Ltd. The wholehearted co-operation of the concerns named, together with that of Martin J. Slattery and Son Ltd. (for Ludlow) and the Mergenthaler Linotype Company (Brooklyn), made a major contribution to the proper illustration of this book.

To Mr. Edmund C. Arnold, editor of America's *Linotype News*, I owe the inspiration of his *Functional Newspaper Design*, much quoted in these pages, and copies of American local newspapers that would otherwise have been hard to come by. For reading and advising on portions of the book in which they are expert I am indebted to Mr. W. A. Thurman, manager of Odhams Press composing departments, Mr. A. D. B. Jones, advertising manager of the Monotype Corporation Ltd., Mr. L. S. F. Elsbury, manager of Intertype's Fotosetter division (Chapter 2), Mr. Arthur Christiansen (Chapter 3), and Mr. Ruari McLean (Chapter 12).

For permission to make use of my earlier writings I must thank my colleagues of the National Executive Council of the National Union of Journalists (publishers of my booklet *An Outline of Newspaper Typography*), Mr. Allan Delafons and Lund Humphries (*Penrose Annual*), Mr. Robert Harling and Mr. James Shand (*Alphabet & Image*). Mr. Hugh Williamson and the Oxford University Press have been good enough to allow me to reproduce certain line-illustrations from his *Methods of Book Design*.

The editorial and managerial authorities of many newspapers have co-operated in providing illustration material. Among dailies and Sundays my thanks are due to Messrs. Stanley Morison (*The Times*), Henry Clapp (*Daily Mail*), George Abel (Associated Newspapers), Edward Pickering and A. H. Bruce (*Daily Express*), Andrew Mellor (*Daily Herald*), Francis

King (*Daily Mirror* and *Sunday Pictorial*), George Matthews (*Daily Worker*), Norman Cursley (*News Chronicle*), J. C. Dawson (*Evening Standard*), W. R. Richardson (*Reynolds News*), H. C. Hodson (*Sunday Times*), Alastair Dunnett (*The Scotsman*), and Sir Linton Andrews (*Yorkshire Post*). In the weekly field I have to thank Messrs. A. H. d'Avigdor (*Surrey Comet*), R. A. Bale (*North Devon Journal-Herald*), Harvey Benham (*Colchester Gazette*, *Essex County Standard*), G. G. Carter (*Whitehaven News*), Alan Fassam (*West Sussex County Times*), W. C. France (*Bournemouth Times*), M. G. Douglas Graham (*Wolverhampton Chronicle*), C. M. Hobson (*Reading Mercury*), Jon Lander (*Consett Guardian*), A. J. Marshall (*Hastings & St. Leonards Observer*), John H. Maxwell (*Dumfries and Galloway News*), C. P. Maynard (*St. Helens Reporter* group), George Reed (*Hexham Courant*), Ivan W. Smith (*Aldershot News*), Ronald Yates (*Barnsley Chronicle*), and Mrs. Florence K. Clemetson (*Courier* group, Tunbridge Wells).

For the extensive showings of typefounders' display faces in several chapters I am much in the debt of Stephenson Blake, Stevens Shanks, American Typefounders, Amsterdam Typefoundry, Deberny & Peignot, Fonderie Olive, Fonderie Typographique Française, Nebiolo (Turin), Haas (Basle), Bauer (Frankfurt), Berthold (Berlin), Klingspor (Offenbach), Ludwig & Mayer (Frankfurt), Stempel (Frankfurt).

The Oxford University Press has placed me under the obligation sustained by all Press authors, particularly those of complex technical works.

I think it only right to say a final word in memory of the late J. M. Flanagan (Michael MacAlpin), one of the first editorial craftsmen in this country to tackle type seriously—as I well remember, in the mid-1920's—and among my earliest exemplars. Long one of Fleet Street's star sub-editors, he spent his last years conducting the feature page of the *Daily Worker*, so transforming it that it won special praise from the 1956 Newspaper Design Award judges when they placed the *Worker* first in its class. With him I must couple my many friends in many case rooms, Head Printers and compositors alike, members of the London Typographical Society or the Typographical Association, to whom I owe what practical knowledge I have of the central process in newspaper production.

G. A. H.

1 · Introductory: the General Principles

THE graphic design of a newspaper is not a thing in itself. The good newspaperman does not assemble type in a page merely to make an agreeable pattern, or as an exercise in display for its own sake. Typography and make-up in a newspaper are only a vehicle for journalism; and it is journalism that is the most important. If it is poorly presented, however, good journalism loses much of its impact. First-class content, therefore, requires first-class form, and so the proper relationship of *form* and *content* is the central question of newspaper typography. Stanley Morison put the point admirably in the last sentence of his famous book on the evolution of English newspaper typography:

> The community would unquestionably benefit if men of learning would extend their interest to the end that the tranquillity, exactitude, clarity and ease of reading, which have been secured in the English book, may also be obtained in that other category of printing, the fundamental economic character of which is more fully developed, and which is in consequence more widely distributed —the English Newspaper.[1]

More than a quarter of a century has passed since those words were written, and it may be thought that the men of learning (with the exception of Morison himself and his great transformation of *The Times*) have not been forthcoming. Yet during this period, as described in Chapter 3 below, newspaper typography has been substantially revolutionized and the general standards of presentation greatly improved. It was a revolution, however, without any theoretical basis—an empirical, and often imitative, affair whose achievements were unequal precisely because there was no general understanding of the principles that should govern its practice. The grasp of the essential principles of typography, that we now take for granted with compositor and typographer alike in the best book and jobbing offices, is still too often lacking or quite inadequate among newspaper printers and journalists.

For many years the standard of newspaper typography in America—naturally in terms of the formal and well-drilled style of the country—

[1] Stanley Morison, *The English Newspaper* (1932), p. 319.

has been much higher than it is here. The reason is that to the American newspaperman, both editorial and mechanical, typography has long been a subject for serious study; the United States can boast an elaborate and able literature with which there has been nothing comparable in this country. Clearly we have to emulate the Americans, not as regards their style but in their study, if the expertise we need in this field is to be sufficiently increased throughout our newspaper industry. This amounts to saying that a sound appreciation of the theory (or, if you prefer, the general principles) of newspaper typography must march together with its daily practice; which brings us to some further consideration of the relationship between form and content.

Two main points have to be made here. Form, in the primary sense of the type dress of a newspaper, is—or should be—conditioned by content; since there are great differences in content, for instance, between *The Times* and the *Daily Mirror*, or between a metropolitan evening and a county weekly, the appropriate type dress will differ also. Form, in the secondary sense of the actual make-up of a page, is likewise conditioned by content—and content considered from the standpoint both of space and time; in other words, instead of news being tortured and truncated to fit a predetermined and inflexible make-up, the make-up must fit the news, and be capable of instant adaptation to changes in it.

This is the essential framework which determines how we shall achieve Morison's requirements, 'clarity and ease of reading'. At this point, too, newspaper typographers are in general agreement on the nature of the approach; a passage from an earlier essay by the present writer and one from the latest American authority make this plain:

> The basic problem can be expressed not unfairly in terms of salesmanship; it is the problem of the Shop Window and the Package. Any newspaper page, above all the Front Page, is like a shop window in which a variety of wares—the different news-stories or feature articles—are exhibited. The effective sale of these wares depends on their general display and their particular packaging. Or, to break the metaphor down into newspaper terms, on the style and type of the headline display and page make-up as a whole, and on the ease of reading of the text matter.[1]

> The whole newspaper must be packaged for maximum reader appeal and reader comfort. Typography and layout are the tools the editor uses to do this . . . [*the four purposes of layout are*] (1) To increase readability and to attract the reader into the news; (2) to sort the news so that the reader knows at a glance which are the most important stories; (3) to create attractive and interesting pages; (4) to create recognition, to make the reader identify and want your paper as soon as he sees it.[2]

[1] Allen Hutt, *An Outline of Newspaper Typography* (1950), p. 3.

[2] Edmund C. Arnold, *Functional Newspaper Design* (New York, 1956), pp. 4, 5.

This broad approach, however, takes for granted the basic physical characteristics of the newspaper page, and these dictate how typographic principles are to be applied to newspaper design. A newspaper page combines text and display over a larger area than any other piece of printed matter—for a book page is chiefly text, a displayed advertisement chiefly display, and both are normally much smaller than a newspaper page. It is divided into columns whose number and width are mainly determined by the economics of advertising, the long-term tendency having been to increase the number of columns and to reduce their width (measure). The measure of a newspaper column today is usually less than 2 inches (12 ems), averaging $11\frac{1}{4}$ or $11\frac{1}{2}$ ems; in the case of the 'tabloids' it may be as little as 9 ems. These narrow measures prescribe a small-size basic text—7 pt. average, 8 pt. maximum—and make a certain degree of condensation essential in news text-type design. Moreover, the newspaper page includes advertising as well as editorial display, and once again the position, space, and displayed character of the advertising is a question of economics about which there can be little or no editorial argument. However, editorial display, including picture display, on a given page must take account of the display advertising and must be related (even by divergence) to its typographical and pictorial character if the aspect of the page as a whole is to be agreeable. It is worth emphasizing here that this last point is far too often ignored in current newspaper make-up at all levels.

Clearly these fixed physical and dimensional factors determine how the general principles just described can be put into practice. But in addition to the quantitative factors—number and measure of columns, average point-size of basic text, and so forth—an important qualitative factor is also involved. It is difficult to give it a precise definition, but its character is easily understood, and well described in the American book already quoted:

> There is enough latitude within 'looking like a newspaper' to allow for differences in taste of the editor and of his readers, of style and of technique. All newspapers need not look alike.... But they should all look like *news*papers. They must convey an air of immediacy, alertness, importance, interest and invitation. They must communicate. The newspaper designer must be constantly aware that his task is to facilitate and assure communication.[1]

This matter of 'looking like a newspaper' has further implications. It means that readers grow accustomed to newspaper style and as a result of this 'conditioning' process expect their newspaper to conform to the idea of style that they have consciously or subconsciously formed. Of course style is not static. It has its evolutions and sometimes even its revolutions;

[1] Arnold, op. cit., p. 325.

though these last are rare and only successful if they are the result of deliberate and careful planning. A casual or aimless departure from the accepted convention strikes the reader as a solecism and provokes an unfavourable reaction. Convention, it must however be added, is not mere conservatism: a proper regard for the conventions of newspaper style should not be allowed to degenerate into the permanent retention of outmoded methods of presentation. Morison has written authoritatively on this point:

> The physical act of reading can only become tolerable when the deciphering of alphabetical symbols is performed without effort, when it has become, so far as may be, inherent in the mental constitution—in one word, *habit*. The reading habits of the people are based upon physical, ocular laws; and, within those laws, upon the printed matter they experience. A considerable degree of similarity in the typography of newspapers argues originally a partial and, ultimately, a complete consent of readers. First, a new idea in layout is tried by an innovator, and competing papers follow when success rewards the new display with increased circulation or prestige. . . . An old-fashioned layout acts like a tariff against the new readers who must be secured if the wastage of circulation by death of old readers is to be repaired.
>
> Such 'new' readers have to be detached from other papers. In the final analysis, therefore, these young or new readers, with reading habits based upon the typography of the majority of papers, must ultimately prevail over the most rigidly conservative journal—or that journal will slowly but surely lose ground to its rivals. . . . It is axiomatic that no journal, other than a gazette enjoying a privileged and uncompetitive status, can for any length of time isolate itself from the reading habits of prospective readers. When, therefore, *The Times* of the future accepts double-column headlines [*it was to do so within a few months of these lines appearing*] it will indicate its conviction that such headlines have become permanently incorporated into the reading experience of the general public, and into its own particular public's idea of a newspaper.[1]

Enough has already been said to indicate the limitations of the field in which the newspaper typographer has to operate. His special skill lies in creating satisfactory effects within a restricted medium, or, more precisely, with typographic resources restricted by the nature of the medium itself. Nevertheless, within these limits he must apply the broad general principles of typography. For newspaper purposes these may be summarized as follows:

TEXT

(i) The relationship between *measure* and *type-size*. A newspaperman cannot strictly follow the principles of good book-setting and make nine

[1] Morison, op. cit., pp. 318–19.

to ten words to the line the average for reading comfort: he has to take into account the fundamental optical fact that over-wide measure—that is, too many words to a line—is both tiring and confusing, since the eye has too far to travel, and tends to drop to the succeeding line. If on the other hand there are too few words to the line, the effect is jerky and jarring and the eye is constantly brought up short. As a general rule it may be said that in single-column news setting the average number of words per line should not fall below six.

(ii) The importance of *close-setting*. Here again newspaper requirements—the necessity for speed and for narrow measures—militate against the finesse of book-printing, but setting should be kept as close as is reasonably possible. 'Driving out', or over-wide word spacing in a narrow column, not only wastes precious space; it exaggerates the effect of the narrow measure as well. The customary aversion of news compositors and correctors for word-division needs to be overcome, and there is no reason for the usual increase of paragraph and other indention (1 em for single-column, 2 ems for double column, 3 ems for treble column, and so on) in wide measure setting.

(iii) The *suitability of type for process*. Different printing processes require text-types of differing qualities. Usually a type suitable, say, for gravure or offset, or for direct letterpress printing on coated paper, is unsuitable for rotary printing. A news text-type must remain clear and clean, in sizes down to 5 pt. or even less, both after the pressures of stereotyping, and the distortions caused by matrix shrinkage, and when it is run at high speed, with thin inks, on the absorbent surface of newsprint.

DISPLAY

(i) The types used for *headlines* should be fit—but few. Economy of typographical means is essential to well-ordered headlining, since excessive variety produces a pointless patchwork. The first need is an ability to make the most of the simple, basic variations: caps. and lower-case, roman and italic, within a suitable range of sizes.

(ii) Apart from the simple variation of roman and italic a single type family can provide the necessary *variations* of weight (light, bold) and width (condensed, extended).

(iii) *Contrast*, apart from the variants already mentioned, is secured by two means: a light rest for the eye, for example an italic of lighter weight than the basic roman, together with an occasional 'kicker'—a sharply contrasting and strong-coloured heading, particularly a multi-line single-column Sanserif.

MAKE-UP

(i) The proper handling of *white space* is essential. What does not print, namely space, is as important as what does. The correct management of space, over and through headlines, over and under rules and cut-offs, over and under subheadings, and between paragraphs, is therefore a vital element in the appearance of the page.

(ii) Space has to be considered both *horizontally* and *vertically.* In addition to the horizontal space—through headings and through the breaklines of paragraphs—there is the vertical space of the white at the side of the column rule (or the white when column rules are dispensed with), and the white of indentions in text.

(iii) The page must be regarded as a *unit.* Pictures and display advertisements form part of a pattern of which the lower half—that portion of the page below the fold—is as important as the top.

In all sound typographical practice fitness for purpose is of primary importance, and this is particularly true of newspapers. There is no special magic about type as such. Fine types can be misused to make an appalling newspaper page; commonplace types, well employed, can make a perfectly agreeable one. Only at his peril dare the newspaper man cull his passing fancy from the luxuriant display of type faces now available for both hand and machine composition.

What is essential is that a newspaper should stick to its basic style, once this has been chosen: good style can develop within its own framework, but constant chopping and changing from one style to another is a confession of weakness, and newspapers which do so are never successful newspapers.

2 · The Mechanics of Newspaper Production

THE transformation of editorial copy and illustrations into a newspaper printing surface involves first the setting of copy in words, lines, and columns of type by the compositor. Metal type and blocks are then assembled into pages, but before the printed paper reaches the reader's hand various procedures of varying degrees of complexity intervene. These are summarized below, for *letterpress*—that is the production of printed copies by impressing on paper an inked surface bearing letters and pictures in relief, the original form of printing—is still the principal method of newspaper production. It is likely to remain so, even though its technique may eventually be transformed by photographic and/or electronic means, which include typesetting without type (photocomposition or filmsetting) and the ultra-rapid production of large-size letterpress printing plates (the powderless etching process). These modern developments are also outlined in the course of this chapter, together with the two other basic printing processes, *litho-offset* and *gravure*.

TYPE AND ITS TERMINOLOGY

Type is defined as 'a relief cast stamp of metal[1] used in the composition of printed pages' (Fig. 1).[2] Compositors usually call an individual type a 'stamp', while a solid line of letters and spaces cast on a composing machine from assembled matrices is a 'slug'. Collective terms for type are, first, the *fount* (pronounced *font*), which is the collection of matrices or individual types of one size and one design, covering the alphabet, figures, and the usual punctuation points; second is the *series*, or number of founts of different sizes of an identical design (e.g. the Times Roman

[1] Type metal is an alloy of tin, antimony, and lead, the composition varying greatly according to the casting process. For Linotype and Intertype the tin-antimony percentage may be 3–11, for Ludlow 7–14, for Monotype 9–19 or 12–24, for typefounders' casting, up to 20–30. Tin and antimony are the toughening and hardening agents. The metallurgy involved is complicated, and the compositions have to be strictly maintained to ensure uniform quality in the casts.

[2] *Typeface Nomenclature* (British Standards Institution, 1958).

series); third is the *family*, or group of series derived from a basic design, whose name they bear with the addition of a qualifying term indicating their variation by weight, width or special treatment, e.g. the Gill Sans family, which includes Light, Bold, Extra Bold, Condensed, Bold Condensed, Bold Extra Condensed, Shadow, Shadowline, Cameo.

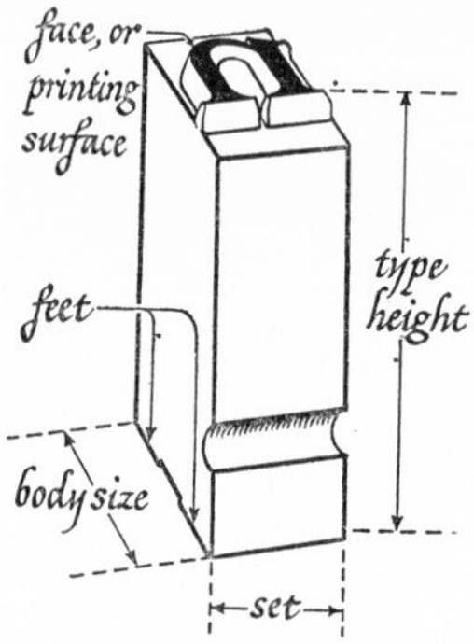

FIG. 1. An individual printing type, technically called a 'stamp'. Standard British type-height is 0·918 in.

The appearance in print of a given type is considerably conditioned by its *weight* (defined as 'degree of blackness') and *width*, or the combination of these two, which determine what is often called its 'colour'. A medley of terms is currently used under both heads; sometimes the same term has different meanings and sometimes different terms have the same meaning, in the case of different types. The British Standard quoted here recommends a list of uniform terms for the future, but the present confusion has to be accepted and the terms memorized as needed. Specially to be noted is the loose use of Bold and Heavy (and the prefixing of Extra- in either case), the use of Black instead of Extra-Bold or Extra-Heavy, the alternation of Wide, Expanded, Extended, and the occasional substitution of Compressed for Condensed. Most confusing of all are the terms not related to weight; thus the fat letter commonly called Ultra-Bodoni (and so named by Monotype, Series 120) is also known as Bodoni Black (Ludlow), Poster Bodoni (Linotype), and Bodoni Modern (Intertype)—Bodoni Modern being the Ludlow designation for its lightest Bodoni.

A normal fount includes both CAPITALS (abbreviated to caps.) and *lower-case* letters; the SMALL CAPS. of the book fount are rare in newspaper work. The old term *upper-* and *lower-case* (abbreviated to U/lc) is still used in marking copy for normal lower-case setting; it derives from the hand-setting practice of mounting the typecase with the caps. on the upper part of the compositor's working frame. Some display founts of caps. only are known as *titling* founts; the actual face of the type usually, but not always, occupies the whole or nearly the whole of the depth of the body. The normal *Roman* fount usually has its *Italic* companion (Fig. 2). The terms are well known; but it should be noted that the true italic is differentiated from its roman mate by details in letter-structure as well as by its slope; an 'italic' which is simply the roman pushed out of the vertical is correctly called a *Sloped Roman*.

ABCDEFGHIJK ABCDEFGHIJKL abcdefghijklm

Abcdefghijk *abcdefghij*

FIG. 2. Settings of type, showing respectively capitals, small capitals, and lower-case (in roman) and a roman with its mated italic.

In addition to its weight and width, an important element in the optical effect of lower-case type is what used to be described as its 'appearing size' or whether, as we still say, it is a 'large' or 'small' face, 'big on the body' or 'small on the body'. It is more correct to define this phenomenon in terms of what is called *x-height*, the actual height of the printing surface of the lower-case letters like *x*, *m*, *n* and so on. The greater the x-height, and therefore the shorter the extending portions of *b*, *d*, *f*, *h*, *k*, *l* (the *ascenders*) and of *g*, *j*, *p*, *q*, *y* (the *descenders*), the larger the type will appear. In text this has an important relation to legibility and in newspaper display it is especially significant; for a 'big' 24 pt. (say, Caslon Heavy) will look as large as a 'small' 30 pt. (say, Bodoni), a fact that a sub-editor needs constantly to bear in mind (Fig. 3).

Newspaper Newspaper

FIG. 3. The difference between 'large face' and 'small face': a 24 pt. Caslon Old Face Heavy and a 30 pt. Bodoni.

THE POINT SYSTEM AND THE PICA EM

The size of type, or more correctly the depth of its body, is measured in points. The British–American *point system*, used in this and most other English-speaking countries,[1] has as its unit the point (0·0138 in.), calculated as one-twelfth of a pica (taken at 0·166 in.) and making approximately 72 to the inch; fractions of a point are used in some newspaper

[1] On the Continent the differently based Didot system is used (the Didot point is 0·0148 in. or 0·38 mm.). Didot sizes thus do not correspond to ours; a number of the display sizes are unusual, e.g. 54 pt. The set-measure is the Cicero (12 pts. Didot). In Belgium the Mediaan point (0·0137 in.) is also used.

text sizes, as follows: $4\frac{3}{4}$, 5, $5\frac{1}{2}$, 6, $6\frac{1}{2}$, $6\frac{3}{4}$, 7, $7\frac{1}{2}$, 8, 9, 10, 12 pt. The 11 pt. size is normally used only in bookwork. The normal run of display sizes is 14, 18, 24, 30, 36, 42, 48, 60, 72 pt.; metal type above 72 pt., i.e. 84, 96, 120 pt., is rarely used here. There are also intermediate sizes, e.g. $9\frac{1}{2}$, 13, 15, 16, 20, 22 pt., mostly intended as two-line initials.

The peculiarities of the point-system's history and practical basis are of no immediate concern to the newspaperman. He should note, however, that some British papers use the old English body names, for newspaper printers were among the last to adopt the point system. With their point equivalents, to which in no case do they precisely correspond, the old bodies are: Pearl (5 pt.), Ruby ($5\frac{1}{2}$), Nonpareil, pronounced *nonprul* (6), Minion (7), Brevier: *breveer* (8), Bourgeois: *burjoyce* (9), Long Primer: *primmer* (10), Pica: *pieker* (12). The written abbreviations are: Nonp., Min., Brev., Bourg. or Bg., L.P.

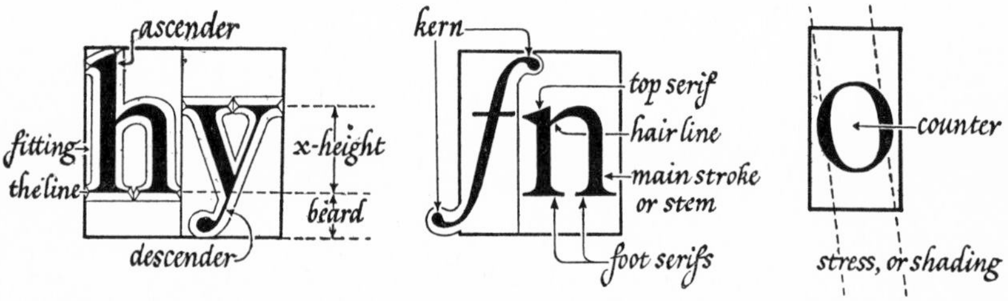

FIG. 4. Principal parts and characteristics of a type face, with their nomenclature.

While type size is expressed in points, the measure to which type is set, or the type area of a page, is not so expressed. The unit of measurement here is the 12 pt. em (i.e. a unit of 12 pts., since the normal letter 'm' has the width of its body depth) or the *pica em*; measures are usually given as so many picas or so many ems, pica being understood. Thus when it is said that a newspaper has an $11\frac{1}{2}$–em column, it always means pica ems; but it should be noted that em, or en[1] (half an em) is used in a different sense when, for example, an instruction is given to 'indent one em (or one en)'; this always means an em or en 'of the body', e.g. in 8 pt. an indention of 8 pts. or 4 pts. respectively.

To avoid confusion the em or en, when used in the sense just mentioned, or when applied to the spaces (quads) of their width, are respectively called *mutton* and *nut*. 'Nut each end', for instance, is a standard indention instruction. Spacing, both in the line and laterally, is commonly expressed in traditional terms, not in points. The usual spaces are hair,

[1] The en, in effect the average-width character, is also used as a measure of output (always quoted in thousands of ens an hour) and as the basis for piecework wages, where these are paid. The London Compositors' Scale, for instance, gives all its piece-rates per 1,000 ens.

thin (one-fifth of an em), mid (one-quarter), thick (one-third), nut quad and mutton quad. The *leads* (pronounced *ledds*) used for spacing between lines—in newspaper work they are usually brasses—are the thin ($1\frac{1}{2}$ pt.) and thick (3 pt.); the 2 pt. lead, a more recent introduction, has no traditional name. The stouter 6 pt. and 12 pt. metal used for whiting-out headings and so on is always referred to as nonpareil or pica.

THE FEATURES OF A TYPE FACE

The term *type face* is used for the actual design of the letter; it is often abbreviated to 'face'. Letter-design is the most complex theme in the entire range of the graphic arts, as a glance at the monumental Berry–Johnson–Jaspert *Encyclopaedia of Type Faces* will show. The newspaperman hardly needs to do more than wet his feet at the shore of this vast ocean. Already three of the elements in the descriptive anatomy of a type face have been explained—ascenders, descenders, and x-height. The other most important ones are the *serifs*, the *mainstroke* or stem, and the *stress* or shading; their drawing largely determines the features of the face. They may be described as follows and it should be borne in mind that they all reflect the calligraphic or engraved origin of printing types:

Serifs: the small terminal strokes at the top or the foot of the mainstroke of a letter. Serifs may be bracketed (that is, rounded-in to the mainstroke) or unbracketed, oblique or horizontal, fine or slab. There can be subsidiary variations, for instance when a bracketed slab serif is given a sharper note by chamfering its ends.

Mainstroke: the thick (with a pen, the down-) stroke of a letter, contrasting with the thin up-stroke.

Stress: this is the direction of the shading, or thickest part of the curved strokes in letters like *o*, *e*, and so on. It may be diagonal, oblique, or vertical.

Further terms to note are: *beard*—the non-printing portion of a type (generically the *shoulder*) which accommodates the descenders; *counter*—the enclosed portion of letters like *p*, *o*, *e*, *a*; *kern*—any part of a letter which overhangs the body, for example in the italic *f* (Fig. 4).

Of the generally accepted broad divisions of type faces the first in historic sequence, the *Venetians*, may be ignored for most newspaper purposes. These strong-coloured, near-monotone, stout-seriffed letters dating from the first half-century of printing in Italy will only occasionally be encountered in modern revivals like Cloister or Eusebius. The *Old Faces* have medium contrast between the thin and mainstrokes, diagonal stress, bracketed oblique serifs, and usually small x-height (Caslon, Garamond, Goudy, Perpetua, Times; note that the x-height of the last-named is large). The *Transitionals* (Baskerville, Bell, Caledonia) move in their stroke contrast, stress, and serifs towards the *Moderns*, with extreme contrast between the thin and mainstrokes, vertical stress, and fine unbracketed horizontal serifs (Bodoni, Modern Roman; Century and Scotch modify the style by bracketing their serifs). The *Sanserifs* are usually monotone (i.e. with no stroke contrast), have no serifs and tend to vertical stress (Grotesque or Grot, Gothic—square, medium or condensed —Doric, Gill, Erbar, Granby, Metro). The *Egyptians*, so named on their appearance in the early part of the nineteenth century because of the contemporary enthusiasm for Egyptian antiquities, are monotone, have unbracketed slab serifs for the most part, vertical stress, and tend to a big x-height (Rockwell, Karnak, Memphis, Beton)[1] (Fig. 5).

These divisions, it must be stressed, are only approximate and many type faces may be described as cross-breeds, combining characteristics of the Old Face and the Modern, or the Modern and the Egyptian, for example. This is notably the case with the modern newspaper text faces like Ionic, Excelsior, Ideal, Jubilee, and Imperial. The *Encyclopaedia of Type Faces* expands the six divisions above into sixteen, and still has a number of anomalies on its hands. Some faces defy classification; for instance Lining, Plate or Engravers' Gothic, a monotone square Sanserif to which beaky little serifs have been strangely added (these are really the mark made by the engraver's tool when cutting a Sans letter, as an alternative to Copperplate Script, for a visiting card); the appearance of this bastard letter as a subsidiary heading type in modern newspapers is to be deplored.

Type classification has long been discussed by experts, and interest in recent years has centred on the scheme of nine divisions proposed by a French typographer, Maximilien Vox. Even this scheme, however, could not classify under a single division each of the 5,000 type faces estimated to exist; a number would require dual classification.

RULES AND BORDERS

The rules, borders, and decorative material required in newspaper work are of the simpler kind. They are referred to in more detail in Chapters 8 and 11. Column rules, formerly of brass, are nowadays mostly cast in lengths in type metal on Monotype Supercaster or on Elrod machines. Strip borders and decorative rules to any length can also be obtained from the Supercaster, or in shorter lengths from the Ludlow, Linotype, or Intertype machines. Decorative items like black or white stars of various sizes, black circles (or focus points) can be similarly cast, or made up to the required measure from individual stamps.

[1] The varied display category of *Scripts* is omitted here; see Chapter 12.

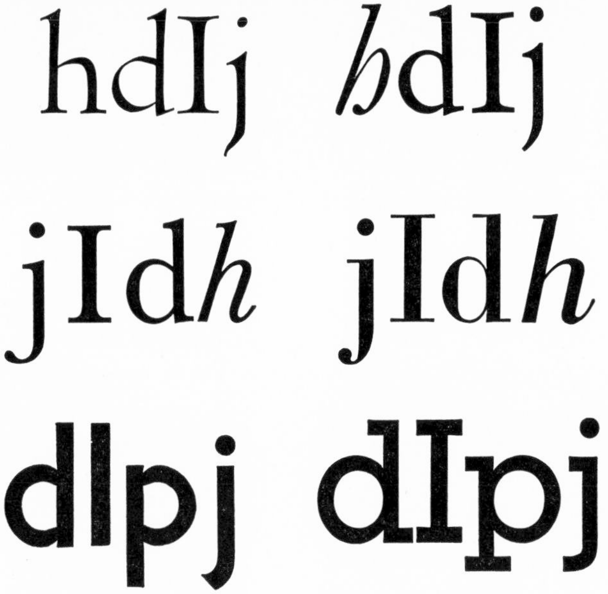

FIG. 5. Specimen letters illustrating the differences between the six approximate divisions of type-design: from left to right, downwards, the Venetians, Old Face, Transitional, Moderns, Sanserifs, Egyptians.

TYPESETTING: 1. TEXT

Newspaper text is mainly set by keyboard-operated composing machines which assemble incised brass matrices and automatically cast from them a solid line or slug of type to the required measure. First of these machines was the *Linotype*, invented by a German–American precision engineer named Ottmar Mergenthaler and perfected some seventy years ago. Later the *Intertype* was introduced, identical in principle and function and with similar merits. The only slug machine on a different principle, the German *Typograph*, is so rarely encountered that it needs no further mention.

The essential principle of the slug machine is the circulating matrix. Matrices of the required letters, figures, and points are keyboard-released from the channels in which they are housed in a flat metal receptacle (the magazine), gravitate to an assembling carriage set to measure, to which they are automatically justified by spacebands (steel wedges with a slide), go forward to face a mould through which a pump injects molten type metal from a heated pot and, as the slug of type is trimmed and ejected, are lifted up to the top of the machine where they travel along a revolving spirally grooved rod (the distributor bar) to drop back into their correct channel according to the way in which, like a Yale-key, they are notched ('combinated' is the technical term).

This schematic description scarcely conveys the mechanical complexity and delicacy of what is still one of the most remarkable contrivances devised by the human mind. It is enough to say that slug machines and their matrices require the highest standards of maintenance and cleanliness: it is thus essential for the trimming knives to be exactly parallel, and for the matrices to be in good condition, for worn matrices begin to show an ugly vertical hairline between letters.

The text range of the slug machine, with double-letter matrices[1] enabling italic or bold to be set with roman, is from 4¾ pt. to 14 pt. Larger display sizes are also keyboarded, as described below, and double-letter matrices are available on the Linotype in certain faces up to 24 pt. The 14 pt. limit still applies to most double-letter matrices, however, and over that size matrices are single-letter, that is, italic or bold require an additional fount of matrices. Measures run up to a normal limit of 30 ems—36 ems if specially equipped—over which settings have to be 'two bars', i.e. continued across two slugs butted end to end.[2] Both body-size and measure are set by the insertion into the mould of steel gauges called liners: the modern machine normally has four operating moulds, though it is possible to have six, giving flexibility and speed in setting varied sizes and measures.

Slug machines fall into five categories: (1) the 'straight' models, mounting from one to four main magazines, each of 90 channels, the normal magazine for text and certain of the smaller display sizes; (2) the side-magazine (SM) models, adding up to four auxiliary magazines, with a separate keyboard, providing a total of eight magazines and enabling the largest display sizes to be accommodated; (3) the 'mixers', which may be either straight or SM, and which can set matrices from any adjoining pair of magazines in the same line—italic and bold as well as roman, for example—distributing them simultaneously to their own magazines (for newspaper work this extra versatility is not usually needed, though in some periodical work it is invaluable); (4) the 72/90 channel models, usually SM as well, which substitute any required number of 72-channel main magazines, up to four, for the normal 90-channel, and thus accom-

[1] Linotype and Intertype matrices will run on each other's machines, provided they are suitably combinated. The only matrices which cannot be interchanged are those punched to 'American depth' (0·043 in.), which is common to many countries as well as the United States, and matrices punched to 'English depth' (0·075 in.), a difference originally arising from differences in stereotyping practice.

[2] Two-bar setting is proportionately slower, to say nothing of the subsequent risk of the joins showing. Where much is done it is wise to use special moulds which cast a tongued end to the slug and ensure a close join with no slipping.

modate larger display sizes in the main; (5) the special high-speed teletypesetter models.

The machines indicated under (4) and (5) are discussed in more detail below, and so is the utility of the 'split' or half-size magazine. The full-length 90-channel main magazine, in text sizes, holds an average fount of 1,200-odd matrices, the remainder of the 1,500-matrix fount being held in a sidecase for insertion by hand; many of these sidecase sorts are foreign accents and what the printer calls 'peculiars', unnecessary for the ordinary run of news work and not ordered by most newspapers. In the large display sizes a matrix fount for a 72-channel main magazine will only total 630 matrices. The cap. matrices for drop letters, cast overhanging the slug, may be inserted by hand from a sidecase or set from a side-magazine.

These items may be noted in conclusion: *space-bands* are supplied extra-thin, thin, or thick—and the thinner the space-band the closer and better the setting; *automatic metal feed*—a specially large ingot suspended over, and automatically fed into the metal pot, thus maintaining even-temperature metal and uniform casting; *Mohr saw*—a built-in saw which cuts slugs to any predetermined measure, and so avoids liner changes; *Thermo-blo*—a cooling device for keeping the mould at an even temperature, which is useful when there is fast or much large-size setting.

The other important method of mechanical composition, the single-type *Monotype* system, has never seriously encroached on the slug-machine's lead in newspaper text composition. *The Times*, which has a large Monotype installation as well as its powerful Linotype-Intertype battery, is a special case. The Monotype, also invented by an American, Tolbert Lanston, is divided into two machines: the keyboard punches a roll of paper and the caster, which is controlled by the perforated roll in the same way as a pianola piano, automatically produces single types and spaces, justified to the required measure, from a die-case containing 225 or 255 matrices. Italic and bold can be mixed with roman. The Monotype is able to cast fully-kerned letters, and thus saves fine designs from the constriction of the vertical matrix. Monotype setting can nearly always be discerned by looking to see whether the 'f', if possible the italic, is kerned.

In this country the Monotype is preferred for bookwork, on account of its repertory of classic and new book faces, its versatility in setting complicated tabular matter, its wide 60-em measure, and its capacity for extremely close spacing. Single type also makes it easier to handle in periodicals which have a good deal of running-round elaborate blocks.

All Monotype faces have a Series number as well as a name, which is necessary for their identification. Throughout this book the Series number is always quoted for Monotype faces, except in certain summary lists when the face has already been identified.

TYPESETTING: 2. HEADLINES

First of the normal ways to set headlines is *by hand* in the usual composing stick from movable type. This may be either founders' type or cast on a Monotype machine (nowadays usually the Supercaster, which provides type up to and including 72 pt., together with rules, borders, leads, and every kind of spacing material). Newspapers with their own Monotype casters enjoy the advantage of the Monotype Corporation's long-standing system of hiring display matrices, and are thus able to cast large display founts (from 14 pt.). For large headings (42 pt. upwards) in wide measures, say a full-page streamer, hand-setting is still the fastest and most flexible method of composition, while Monotype face in these sizes is superior to the larger-sized keyboard or Ludlow product. Distribution, however, has to be considered, kerns break easily and in smaller sizes hand-setting from movable type is outmoded and inefficient.

Next comes *keyboarding* on a Linotype or Intertype machine. As with text, the entire operation of casting and distribution is automatic and the automatic quadding and centring device now available in both mechanical and hydraulic forms saves considerable time in headline composition. By pressing a button the heading can be automatically justified flush left, flush right, or centred. The ease of handling a slug heading, and the elimination of distributing (or 'dissing' as it is usually referred to), are the great advantages of this method, provided the heading keeps within the capacity of the magazine and the maximum measure. In practice this usually means that keyboarded headings above two columns have to be set 'two bar'; hand-justification slows the setting.

The slug machine's size ceiling is 36 pt. in upper- and lower-case, 42 pt. and 48 pt. being available in caps. only (Intertype provides a condensed Sans in 48 pt. lower-case and 60 pt. caps.). In this connexion the following points must be noted:

(i) *Magazine capacity*. The standard 90-channel main magazine only accommodates matrices up to a restricted maximum letter-width, not necessarily related to the body-size; thus an extra condensed 30 pt. may run in the main, while an expanded 18 pt. may not; or the lower-case of a given fount may run in the main, while its caps. will not. The problem is met by use of the 72-channel main magazines (which will take founts up to 36 pt.) and of the side magazines.

(ii) *Magazine layout*. If the required headline range is caps. only, a given machine will accommodate more sizes or styles than it will if the range is in upper- and lower-case. A complete fount of caps. of maximum size and width requires only one side magazine, while two founts of caps. of smaller sizes and widths can be run in a single main magazine—one in the cap. and the other in the lower-case channels. If lower-case is added it will take up either an extra side magazine or half a main magazine, according to the size of the type. Flexibility can be gained by the use of 'split' magazines; these have about half the matrix capacity of a normal magazine, but this is usually enough for headline setting. The extra 'split' magazines have the advantage that they can be stacked beside the machine and changed with relative ease. When display italic is added to a roman, the double-letter display matrices available on the Linotype (with a special mould) in 18 pt. and 24 pt. are essential for conserving magazine accommodation; they cover standard news headings like the Century Bold series and the Bodoni and Metro families. Otherwise all founts of matrices above 14 pt. are single-letter, as already noted, and the addition of italic requires another magazine or magazines.

Last, but most popular of all on the larger newspapers, comes *slug-casting from hand-set matrices* on the Ludlow machine. This combines the flexibility of hand-setting in a precision composing stick with the convenience of new machine-cast slugs. No magazine or mould changes are needed. The machine is simple and compact and a large range of matrix founts takes only a small space. The repertory of faces from 6 pt. to 72 pt., both standard and exclusive to Ludlow, is extensive; larger sizes can be cast up to 144 pt., which is done lengthways on the slug, cut up and hand-assembled. By the use of angle matrices italics retain the effect of their kerned letters. While distribution of the matrices has to be done after casting, this is simpler and speedier than dissing loose type.

The Ludlow casts a standard line of 24 ems, but the slug can always be cut for narrower measures (or a special mould used for any measure below 24 ems, e.g. for many single- or double-column measures), while for wider measures any number of slugs can be pieced together. The cast is made centrally on a 6 pt. or 12 pt. slug, the overhanging face being underpinned by shoulder-high blank slugs. This has the advantage, when underscoring, that by suitable manipulation of the blanks the underscore rule or border can be placed as close as desired to the face, with any descenders breaking the rule. Close 'profiling' of different sizes is also easy. In the larger sizes, and particularly with heavy Sans letter, the quality of the face as cast is not good; the slugs are cast fractionally above normal type height and are put through a surfacing machine.

With the Ludlow should be mentioned its companion machine, the Elrod, which casts rules, borders, blanks, and leads to any length. It is also worth noting that some newspapers contrive a species of 'Ludlow' by stripping an old slug machine down to its casting mechanism, setting display matrices by hand in the assembler, or using a stick like a Ludlow, and casting slugs in the usual fashion. These are called 'Mickey Mouse' machines. Intertype have a composing stick attachment in which matrices can be set and then cast on a normal machine; special series of 48 pt. and 60 pt. display caps. are available. Linotype has a similar device.

A Ludlow-style machine has now been produced by the Società Nebiolo of Turin, the Italian typefounders and printing-machine manufacturers. Called the Nebitype, this machine casts lines from hand-assembled matrices with a size range from 6 pt. to 72 pt. and to a basic measure of 42 ems; a special attachment enables twice this measure to be set. Like the Linotype organization's pre-war display slugcaster the A-P-L (All-Purpose Linotype), not now manufactured, the Nebitype can use either its own matrices, Ludlow matrices, or the matrices of any other slug machine. The machine, first exhibited in 1958, had yet to be generally marketed as these lines were printed (summer 1960).

THE TELETYPESETTER

The initials TTS, standing for Teletypesetter, are the symbols of automation in the composing room and are especially significant in newspaper work. The term autosetting, which is applied to the procedure, perhaps conveys its essence even better; for the central feature is the automatic operation of a slug machine keyboard by perforated tape, which enables the highest manual speeds of setting and casting to be greatly exceeded. TTS, that is to say, is a mode of increasing composing-room productivity by applying the basic principle of high-speed telegraphy—speeding-up the manual operation by limiting it to the keyboard-punching of tape, and using that tape to control a super-fast instrument (in this case a slug-casting machine).

That this system can be used for remote operation, by telegraph or radio, and is substantially so used, is incidental. TTS was perhaps generally regarded as a remote operation system because it was first introduced here in 1934 for that purpose, when *The Scotsman* opened a London–Edinburgh TTS link, to be followed by the *Glasgow Herald* and later *The Times* (from the Houses of Parliament to Printing House Square). In the United States, also, where no fewer than 600 newspapers are now wholly or partly TTS-set, the dominant feature is the TTS service emanating from the national telegraphic news agencies, the Associated Press and United Press-International.

TTS installations in a number of our leading provincial dailies and weeklies are principally employed, with local perforating, as output-boosters. Newspapers carrying extensive classified advertising—like the *Birmingham Mail* with its thirty to forty columns of solid $4\frac{3}{4}$ pt. 'smalls' every day—find TTS of particular convenience and value for this sort of setting; the *Mail* uses six perforators and four high-speed machines.

For TTS operation specially fast slug machines are manufactured, the new Model 79 Linotype and the High Speed Intertype. These machines are geared to run at speeds up to 12 lines set and cast a minute, approximately 20,000 ens an hour, or around three times the average of manual operation. They are cushioned to withstand the vibration. Three of these machines can, it is estimated, cope with the output of four perforators (a fast perforator operator can punch 17,000 ens an hour); and a Pennsylvania newspaper which pioneered TTS reckoned some years ago that its overall slug-machine output had increased by some 23 per cent. Output increases of 50–75 per cent. have been cited.

The agency TTS circuits in America have employed what is known as a 'unit' perforator, requiring the receiving machines to use 'unit' matrices. Briefly, this means restriction to a prescribed single-column measure and a prescribed 'set' of type. The agency prescription was originally '8-set, 12 ems'. The set figure means that all characters in the fount are a prescribed width in relation to the width of the em space of the fount and to the counting mechanism of the perforator and operating unit. An 8-set face requires a lower-case alphabet width of 118·1 pts., whatever the size of the face. Newspapers which were on TTS circuit, even when they were using a 12-em column, were thus at once restricted to such text faces as were 8-set, which varied considerably between the standard 7, 7½, and 8 pt. newspaper texts. Extensive redesigning of faces, condensing and expanding to fit the Procrustean bed of the 'unit', had to be undertaken; and more particularly by those papers already on the new United States 'standard' 11½-em column. Here, for instance, an entirely new Linotype text face, Majestic, was produced, 7·66-set in 8 pt., so that the 12-em service would reproduce line for line in the narrower column.

Elsewhere, including this country, the acute typographic limitations and problems of the 'unit' system are avoided by the use of the 'multiface' perforator. This gives full freedom in choice of matrix and measure (except for display matrices in a 72-channel magazine) and can even be applied to the operation of a mixer machine, with italic and bold as well as roman.

TYPESETTING WITHOUT TYPE

Photocomposition or filmsetting—typesetting, in effect, without type—had passed out of the experimental into the practical stage by the mid-1950's. Not that experiment ceased, or will cease, but there are now (1960) four major filmsetting machines, together with a number of lesser ones, of which note needs to be taken. Of the 350 machines of all types now operating, eleven are in this country—the great majority being in the United States.

All photocomposition has the same aim: to reproduce photographically on film or paper—right-reading, wrong-reading, positive or negative, according to the needs of the ensuing process—justified lines of type characters, just as typographic composing machines produce justified lines of type in hot metal. While the initial purpose was to provide a photographic original to print down direct for gravure or offset plates, cutting out the reproduction proof from set metal type, there were also important implications for letterpress, and these are indicated below.

Of the machines mentioned two make a photographic adaptation of their existing typographic models, two make a radical departure and employ advanced electronic devices. First in the effective field was the Intertype *Fotosetter*, of which some 200 have already been installed, including seven in Britain. The Fotosetter retains the principle of the circulating matrix; in appearance and in fundamental mechanical operation it is a normal slug machine, substituting type-transparency matrices for the incised brass and a photographic apparatus for the metal pot. Keyboard-released from magazines and gravitating to the assembler in the usual way, the matrices are returned to the magazines by the distributor after ascending in succession past the photographing point. Ingenious automatic justification distributes the space required through all letters and spaces; this can produce an effect of microscopic letter-spacing which has been criticized by some, but is in practice scarcely any shortcoming. With four magazines and eight lenses the Fotosetter provides the equivalent of thirty-two founts in sizes ranging from 3 to 54 pt. and in measures from 4 to 51 ems. The camera speed is at the rate of 28,800 characters an hour. Correcting and make-up frames are provided; corrections are stripped into the film after the incorrect lines have been removed.

The Monotype Corporation's *Monophoto* filmsetter retains the normal paper-punching keyboard, the perforated roll then controlling the filmsetter which has been substituted for the caster. The filmsetter operates a matrix case of 255 separate transparency matrices, the mechanical selection of characters being the same as on the caster; the photographic apparatus employs an ingenious system of mirrors and justification, by normal word-spacing, is effected by a complex gearing arrangement. The size-range is 6 to 24 pt. and the measure up to 60 ems. Correction, as with the Fotosetter, is manual. Output is comparable to the hot-metal caster at a rate of 12,000 ens an hour.

Mechanical correction is claimed as an important advantage of the Mergenthaler Linotype Company's *Linofilm*, which had its first European demonstration at Drupa, the international printing exhibition at Düsseldorf, in the spring of 1958. The *corrector* is one of the four units in what is described as 'a complete photocomposition system', which 'gets right away from the familiar limitations imposed by adapting the designs of existing hot-metal machines'. The other three units are: (i) the *keyboard* —an electric typewriter which produces a monitor copy and punches tape to operate (ii) the *photographic unit*; with electronic coding and scanning devices controlling 18 founts of 88 characters each on transparent grids, this can film lines up to 30 ems measure, in from $4\frac{3}{4}$ to 18 pt., at a rate of 15 newspaper lines a minute (this speed means that the unit can cope with the tape from more than one keyboard); (iii) the *composer*—a further photographic apparatus for make-up and enlarging from set film. It produces type characters from 3 to 108 pt. up to 96 ems measure, and can be used to make up a page to full newspaper size as a film positive ready for plate-making.

Also remarkable in its electronic ingenuity is the *Photon*, invented by two French engineers, René Higonnet and Louis Moyroud, and first called the Lumitype, the name its French model retains.[1] It has been developed in the United States by the Graphic Arts Research Foundation and at the beginning of 1958 around forty were reported in operation, all in America. The Photon's electric typewriter keyboard operates two electronic memory devices which signal the character selected and its width to an electronic computer in the photographic unit. Constantly rotating at high speed is a glass master negative disk containing the characters for sixteen different founts arranged in rings. Through the computer control a stroboscopic tube flashes its light at the precise micro-second that the selected character passes the photographic unit. Sizes from 5 to 48 pt. can be set up to 42 ems measure with full mixing and automatic leading. Speed is claimed to be as much as two and a half times that of manual composing machine operation.

Since 1954 the Photon has been partly used in the production of an American local evening newspaper, the *Patriot Ledger* of Quincy (Mass.), which averages 20 pages with a circulation of 40,000. The *Patriot Ledger*'s publisher, Prescott Low, indicated in 1958 that the only portion of the paper then wholly filmset was the display advertising;[2] for this purpose photographic display setting appliances like the *Filmotype* (one of several so far only current in America) were being used as well as the Photon. In American conditions, where many pages of complicated local store display advertising have to be handled daily, filmsetting appears to have an immediate newspaper contribution to make. There are reports of remarkable savings in time by pasting-up large display advertisements from filmset paper positives, and later making a block of the whole, compared with setting and making-up in metal. The Fotosetter is also being used for this

[1] Samuel H. Caldwell, 'Technical Features of the Higonnet-Moyroud Photocomposing Machine' (*Penrose Annual*, 1952).

[2] *Printing News*, 17 July 1958.

purpose; though it should be emphasized that the four photocomposition machines described above are primarily text machines, despite their enlargement capacity—hence the inclusion of the composer in the Linofilm system.

Two smaller and simpler machines are the *ATF Typesetter* (American Type Founders Company), which uses keyboard-punched tape to operate a compact photographic unit having a range of 5 to 14 pt. and an output around fast slug-machine average, or 7,000 ens an hour, and the *Diatyp* (Berthold, the German typefounders), shown at Drupa, which will produce from 6 to 36 pt. at about normal hand-composition speed and is therefore presumably intended mainly for display and jobbing work.

The editor of the *British Printer* recently stressed the need, at this stage in photocomposition, 'for a simple and effective means of applying traditional hand-composing techniques to the production of filmset display matter'.[1] He found an answer in the *Protype*, a desk device introduced by the Linotype organization. This enables the operator to reproduce on the spot, on film or paper, display lines that he has set with the fullest freedom of style, from individual plastic master negatives known as *Profonts*. In more mechanized form there is the Dutch *Hadego Photocompositor*, nicknamed 'the photographic Ludlow'. Like the Ludlow, the Hadego operates from matrices handset and justified in a special stick; from two sizes (20 and 48 pt.) it covers, by enlargement or reduction, a range from 8 to 115 pt. on one model, 4 to 81 pt. on another. By the use of screens and photographic manipulation various shadow, outline, and other effects can be obtained.

In general it will be observed that by freeing type from its metal limitations photocomposition opens the door to all sorts of novelties in setting, of which superimposed or overhanging letters are only the first and most obvious example.

NEW TECHNIQUES IN BLOCKMAKING

The illustration block is a familiar object to every newspaperman, though the techniques of its production are complicated, and the 'process department' has long been an integral part of every newspaper plant of any size. Conventional photo-engraving combines the camera with chemistry to produce a metal printing surface in relief, and to a required size, from an original picture. Briefly, the negative of the original is printed down on sensitized metal (zinc in this case), and the resultant positive is acid-

[1] R. S. Hutchings, 'Protype; a New System of Display Photo-Composition' (*Penrose Annual*, 1957).

etched, acid-resists being used to mask the appropriate portions of the surface, until the required printing depth is obtained. These are the barest principles only of the complex process of producing photo-engraved printing blocks from drawings, maps, diagrams (*line*), or photographs (*half-tone*, often abbreviated to *tone*). The two may be combined as *line-and-tone* when a line of type is reproduced across a photograph. Line blocks may have various shadings or tints mechanically applied during the engraving (mechanical or Ben Day tints).

In newspaper work half-tone blocks are normally 65 screen, if they are to be stereotyped, and up to 85 screen if not; the screen figure represents the number of opaque cross lines per square inch on the glass screen which breaks up the solid tones of the original into the system of graded dots on the printing block; the lower the screen figure the coarser, or more open, the dot system.

Conventional photo-engraving will long remain in newspapers, owing to its flexibility, size range, and the quality inseparable from individual craft finish, notably in the vital factor of depth and angle of etch. But the new electronic engraving machines have made great advances in the newspaper field and need considering in a little more detail. These revolutionary machines cut out camera and chemistry alike; an electronic scanning device follows the original and controls the engraving tool, which produces the completed block automatically in substantially less time than conventional methods. The entire apparatus is contained in one compact cabinet and only a single operator is required.

The two established machines are the German *Klischograph* and the American Fairchild *Scan-a-Graver*; the main difference between them is that the first cuts the block in plastic foil or metal, the second burns it in foil only.[1] The foil blocks are only fully satisfactory for direct printing (they can be stereotyped, though not with the high-temperature hot moulding common in this country). This limits them to flatbed, Cossar, or short-run rotary work, when the block can be directly fixed to the stereotype plate on the press. Over 93 per cent. of the American local dailies using Fairchild Scanplates do this, their short runs only needing one set of plates.

The adaptation of the Klischograph to cut metal, following experiments by *The Times* (which now extensively uses electronically engraved blocks), gives it an obvious advantage for newspaper work. The Klischograph may now be said to be accepted in this country as the newspaper machine. It can cut zinc (*The Times*), which leaves a slight burr, needing removal by a subsequent quick etch, or anodized aluminium (the metal

[1] The Swiss Elgramma electronic engraver also cuts on metal, and can engrave a pre-curved plate. It has not, however, attracted British newspaper attention as has the Klischograph.

now generally recommended), whose extra hard surface requires no further treatment. For line blocks the Klischograph has a different model (the S 240), which uses a chisel-shaped cutter on stereo metal; the scanner can be set to varying degrees of fineness of cut according to the fineness of the line original, and by a simple electrical reversal it is possible to make reverse blocks (black to white).

Both the Klischograph and Fairchild machines were originally limited to making reproductions the same size as the original. Now they have enlarging and reducing models—the Vario and the Scan-a-Sizer. Maximum size on the Vario-Klischograph has also been increased, from 8 by 6 in. to 15·8 by 11·8 in. Both machines have models for the production of colour blocks, which may be of considerable importance in the development of rotary colour.

Like all fully automatic machines, electronic engravers require sensitive skill for their effective exploitation. Their controls—like the controls of a television set—require careful setting in terms of the tonal values of the original, which must have sharp definition and good tonal gradation, avoiding heavy blacks. The electronic engraver cannot produce a satisfactory result from a poor original; but a skilful adjustment of its black and white setting will make as much difference to its rendering of a fair original as good or bad television contrast-setting.

Apart from electronic engraving the major blockmaking development has been the perfecting of the ultra-rapid powderless etching process, to which reference has already been made. The process owes its name to the fact that it eliminates the four successive and time-consuming powderings with acid-resist ('dragon's blood') necessary in conventional etching. It has a mechanical and a chemical aspect. The plate being etched rotates face down in an enclosed machine with paddles dashing the etching solution over it at varying speeds that have to be precisely controlled. The etching solution is an emulsion of the usual nitric acid and filming agents which appears to combine etching and acid-resisting qualities. Half-tone blocks that might conventionally take forty minutes or more can be completed in five minutes.

There are two types of powderless etcher, both American: the Dow (which uses magnesium) and the Dirats (which uses 'fast-etch' zinc, containing very small quantities of magnesium and aluminium). By agreement between the Monotype Corporation and the American interests concerned, a powderless etcher adaptable for either zinc or magnesium, and called the 'Lithotex', is being manufactured in this country by Pictorial Machinery Ltd. (a Monotype subsidiary). Both line and tone work can be done on these etchers. The fast line-etching, particularly good in its sharp reproduction of type, is of course the point where this process links photocomposition with letterpress: the potential, and already in a limited sense the actual, significance of this for newspaper work is evident. American developments in the powderless etching of pre-curved plates may well be out of the experimental stage by the time this book is published.

Still more revolutionary are the prospects of flexible non-metal (plastic) printing surfaces. The Du Pont chemical concern in the United States expected to have its photopolymer plates for rotary printing commercially available by 1960. They were experimentally demonstrated in January 1958, printed down from Fotosetter film together with half-tone blocks. A steel-backed photosensitive plastic plate ⅛ in. thick is exposed through a negative to ultra-violet light, which causes the exposed portion of the plastic to harden throughout its entire depth. An alkaline solution washes out the unexposed and unhardened photopolymer, leaving the printing surface in relief. Curved and suitably mounted, the plate is then ready for the rotary press.

Preparation of these plates takes only some ten minutes; and photopolymerized nylon plates of this sort, developed by the *Time–Life* publishers, have shown that they can stand up to a run of at least half a million.[1]

STEREOTYPING

The *stereotyping* department—familiarly 'the foundry'—is the crucial link in rotary newspaper production. It has to convert the flat forme of type and blocks into a semi-cylindrical printing plate for the rotary press. Without a precise plate, no matter how good the forme and no matter how modern and well managed the rotary, there will be no well-printed paper. Stereotyping falls into two parts:

(i) *Moulding*: a mould or matrix (always shortened to 'mat', and not to be confused with composing machine type 'mats') is taken from the forme by subjecting it to great pressure in contact with a *flong* or sheet of papier-mâché or plastic. The pressure may be applied by passing the forme under a heavy steel cylinder or *mangle* (technically known as 'point' moulding) or by compressing it between the platens of a *hydraulic press*, usually with the simultaneous application of controlled heat. The latter is the usual modern method, particularly favoured because of its superior rendering of half-tones, though some papers claim good half-tone definition, and better control of mat shrinkage, with cold moulding.

While both methods are called 'dry' moulding, to distinguish them from the old-fashioned 'wet-flong' moulding, the flong has, and must have, a high degree of humidity. The constant conditioning of the flong

[1] *Penrose Annual* (1958), pp. xxi–xxiii.

to the correct humidity is vital to good moulding and therefore a principal preoccupation of the efficient foundry.

(ii) *Casting*: after the still damp mould has been thoroughly dried in a drying machine and any low portions (i.e. white areas in the forme) suitably packed with paper felt, it is placed in the curved casting box and molten type metal pumped in (an average percentage for rotary stereo metal is 6 to 8 tin, 13 to 15 antimony, rest lead). With modern Autoplate machinery the ensuing operations of preparing the cast plate for the press —cutting off the blank 'tang' or 'tail' left in casting, boring it internally for even thickness, and cooling—are automatic; the difference between the Pony, Junior, and Automatic Autoplates is in their output, one, two, or four plates a minute.

The casters have to see that the moulds are perfectly dried out before casting, or they will get buckles on the face; that their metal is clean, regularly assayed, and kept at a consistent heat (not above 600° F.); that their casting box is kept hot without overheating, and above all not allowed to cool. 'Sinks' through imprisoned air, and general defects in the face can result without this constant attention.

Shrinkage of the mould in drying is a problem of stereotyping which, when controlled, can be turned to good account. The greatest shrinkage is horizontal; and a reduction say of half an inch in width between the page in the forme and the page in the plate means a corresponding saving in the width of the paper page. The economy in expensive newsprint, most important single item in newspaper budgets, can be imposing for mass-circulation papers. A shrunk page will, of course, show in slightly narrower columns; the column measure of an 11½-em column paper, as printed, will usually gauge around 11 ems, and so on. With very high shrinkage, as in America—where shrinkages of over 1¼ in. across the page are not uncommon—serious distortion of type and half-tones can result; and newspaper text types have had to be designed to overcome this, as mentioned in Chapter 4.

Block-mounting is an important foundry function. In rotary printing, blocks must be mounted on solid metal bases cast and trimmed for size and correct height; absolute accuracy here is essential. Good reproduction of half-tones may involve their mounting fractionally, perhaps 0·003 in. or 0·004 in., above type-height; and there is much argument about the value or otherwise under modern conditions of the traditional practice of 'bumping' blocks, or underlaying them with suitably cut paper to bring the solids up to the indicated three or four thousandths high, maintaining the highlights at normal height. Neither side in this highly technical controversy is wanting for ammunition based on facts.

Foundries are equipped to make flat casts, of advertisements, standing headings, and the like. These are usually in the form of *pica plates*, or casts 12 pts. thick which are suitably mounted, though for some purposes *type-highs*, solid casts sufficiently described by their name, are preferred.

A final point to note is that modern direct-pressure hot moulding, applying 300 tons or more at 200° F., takes a heavy toll of type. Solid slugs, though of inferior metal, stand these pressures better than the single-letter Monotype (unless specially hard metal is used). Kerned letters in movable type will rarely survive a single moulding, though Monotype kerns can and should always be underpinned by an appropriate shoulder-high space. All slug-spacing is automatically shoulder-high; but when movable type is used the more usual low spaces and quads should be replaced throughout by shoulder-high spacing material. This is important not only for protecting kerns but to avoid excessive dip by the mould over white areas.

MACHINING—FLAT AND ROTARY

Small-circulation weeklies may still be printed 'on the flat', i.e. direct from the formes on sheet-fed flatbed presses of the stop-cylinder (Wharfedale) or two-revolution (Miehle) type. The sheets are likely to be hand-fed and the output something over 2,000 copies an hour. Separate folding is necessary.

The next stage is the machine loosely, and quite incorrectly, called the 'flatbed rotary'. It is a flatbed web press, printing direct from the formes and with no rotary action at all; but the paper is fed from reels and the completed copies cut and delivered folded as from a rotary. The universal British machine of this type is the Cossar (in America the Duplex). Output is around 3,600 folded copies an hour, which meets the needs of many papers in the 10,000–30,000 class, according to their edition requirements and the time available for the run. The avoidance of stereotyping is an important technical economy; and direct printing from the originals permits better half-tone work. Cossar presses can also be fitted with a colour device which permits the printing of one or two additional colours. Certain problems peculiar to the Cossar should be noted: the principle of the mechanism makes it a matter of considerable skill to maintain consistent quality of impression and inking; there is a suction effect on the formes which makes extremely accurate lock-up essential, and this involves, according to the manufacturers, the use of grooved brass rule to hold the slugs when running broadsheet papers. The standard Cossar unit is an eight-pager; a page capacity up to twice that of the unit can be obtained by pre-printing and using a re-reeler, which then feeds the pre-printed section through the folder with the later printing.

The rotary, combining the web or reel of paper with a rotating cylindrical printing surface, is the classic high-speed, mass-production newspaper press. Its efficient operation with the maintenance of its inking system, rollers, and cylinder blankets, is one of the more complex sides of the printing art. Rotaries vary greatly in design, capacity, and speed. Their printing units used to be arranged in mounting tiers ('balcony' or 'decker' presses) or at right angles, but nowadays are arranged in lines. Units two pages wide are described as 'single-width', four pages wide as 'double-width'. A standard double-width press produces 8 full-sheet pages (or 16 tabloid) per unit. Folders can be single or double, the last enabling press output to be doubled: e.g. two 12-page papers from one 3-unit 24-page press. Papers can be delivered either fully inset, i.e. the total number of pages in one complete copy, or 'collect', i.e. in sections. Modern presses usually have extended conveyer deliveries direct into the publishing room, with or without devices for the automatic bundling of the 26-copy quires.

A rotary's plate cylinder circumference fixes the paper page-depth of a full-sheet, or page-width of a tabloid, product. This is called the 'cut-off' and may vary, to take two extremes, from 21 to $26\frac{1}{4}$ in. What is now called the 'standard' cut-off, and that most usually met (it was originally the one selected by the *Daily Mail*), is $23\frac{9}{16}$ in., giving a 22-in. column. Reel-width and plate-width can, however, be reduced within certain limits, so that a full-sheet paper can be made narrower and a tabloid shallower. It may be remarked, incidentally, that the terms broadsheet or text are used alike for full-sheet papers, half-sheet or folio for tabloid.

Rotary speeds vary from under 20,000 an hour with very old machines (there is one simpler and more economical modern press, known as the 'columns along' type, constructed specially for local papers, and rating a similar speed) to 36,000 with the between-the-wars vintage, and a nominal 50,000 or even more with the modern super-speed presses. A fast average running speed for a modern machine would be 40,000; the highest speeds, like the rate of fire of a machine-gun, are only intended for short bursts.

Reel changing is manual on old machines, involving stoppage of the press, but the most modern magazine reel stands with automatic or 'flying' pasters enable a new reel to be put on and spliced in without even reducing speed. Colour seal and late news ('fudge') devices are normal on most rotaries; they are dealt with in Chapter 13. The makes of rotary most often met in this country are the Goss, Hoe, Crabtree, and Scott-Vickers; but there are other important manufacturers in America and on the Continent, notably in Germany (M.A.N., Albert, Vomag).

Certain problems that arise in rotary printing call for a brief reference.

On the older machines particularly, there is a marked variation in quality of half-tone reproduction between different pages. Many factors are involved and one press will differ from another, but generally speaking it will be found that the better reproduction is on the 'outer' pages, e.g. on an eight-page paper pp. 1, 3, 6, 8. When this variation, whatever it may be, is known, it has to be taken into account in the placing of half-tones in make-up. Difficulties with set-off and strike-through, the latter increased by the thinner and more porous newsprints of today, are also common.

ROTARY COLOUR PRINTING

Newspaper ROP (run-of-press) colour in this country is a minute fraction of its counterpart in America, where over 800 daily newspapers currently offer advertisers from two to four colours and where between 1951 and 1956 colour advertising in newspapers doubled. Advertising 'spot' colour, i.e. colour requiring no close registration, began to develop in the London nationals before the war, and has been fitfully returning, but labour costs are very high. In 1934 the Glasgow *Daily Record* ran an editorial three-colour half-tone. In 1958 the *Liverpool Daily Post* was the only daily paper providing both editorial and advertising full-colour half-tone (three colours and black).[1]

To secure dead register in rotary colour printing requires the most painstaking precision and control at every stage (not excluding air-conditioning) from the photography and colour separation, the block-making, the moulding, casting, routing out of colour plates, to positioning the colour stages on the machine, and controlling the web tension (in rotary colourgravure this is being done electronically). Making the four-colour blocks for a large advertisement may take from two to three weeks, though the *Daily Post* has found an ingenious way to save time by blowing up proofs from 120 screen electros to double size, thus reducing the screen to 60, the figure they use for rotary half-tones. The development of electronically engraved colour blocks is also expected to save much time.

It may be wondered whether extreme care in accurately reproducing colour photography of pre-1914 Bavarian picture postcard flavour is really adequately exploiting rotary colour. Well before the war the Scandinavians, notably the Copenhagen *Politiken*, demonstrated the real artistry possible with rotary four-colour in line and tint, avoiding over-close register. The achievement of dead register ought not to be regarded

[1] The *Daily Post*'s general manager, James R. Spencer, gave a detailed technical exposition ('Newspaper ROP Colour') in the 1958 *Penrose Annual*, which also reviewed the American experience (Allan Delafons, 'Chromatic Giant'). Other useful references are James Mosley, 'A History of Colour Printing' (*Printing News*, 3 July 1958), and Nils Haglov, 'The Introduction of Colour to Newsprint', discussing web tension control (*Printing News*, 26 June 1958).

as a piece of technical virtuosity apart from the merit of the design or picture reproduced.

There used to be a tendency to add separate colour units to rotary presses; today experts feel this is often unnecessary, since the modern rotary's individual units are reversible for colour, and portable page-wide colour fountains are available to supplement them. Size of run is a concluding factor to note. The *Daily Post* runs under 80,000 nightly; one of the American exemplars, the Rock Hill (S.C.) *Evening Herald*, which works chromatic wonders on a 1910 Goss, has only a 12,000 run.

OFFSET AND GRAVURE

From the newspaper and periodical standpoint the prime virtue of the two non-typographic printing processes, offset and gravure, is their superiority to rotary letterpress in pictorial reproduction, particularly in colour. Gravure has, of course, long been available in full rotary form for full colour, and its speed has been greatly increased, though at an average of 25,000 copies per hour it is only about half the top letterpress pace. Offset has more recently gone rotary: in Australia the now defunct Melbourne *Argus* had a reel-fed offset rotary for colour, with a production speed of 35,000 copies per hour, linked with a letterpress machine for type matter in black; recent experiments in America have registered remarkable results in four-colour rotary offset run on newsprint at 10,000 copies per hour; a German offset rotary supplied to the United States, the Fruehwald and Jaeger, is reported to have a top speed of 32,000 copies per hour.[1]

The reader may be reminded that *offset* is a form of lithography, the planographic or flat-surfaced process which depends on the mutual repulsion of grease and water: the image is offset from the printing plate to a rubber cylinder for transfer to the paper, and the process permits the use of a wide range of papers. The dot-structure in photo-offset blocks is so dense that the effect is one of continuous tone. Offset is an extremely progressive process: the use of bi-metallic or tri-metallic plates, which improve plate ink reception, and the development of the technique of 'dry' offset, which cuts out the waterdamping associated with lithography, are two examples.

Gravure, the principal intaglio or recess process, depends on the transfer to paper of ink deposited in a series of varying cells etched below the surface of the printing cylinder. Highly volatile inks are used, the surplus being removed by a flexible blade, the 'doctor', before the printing con-

[1] See *Penrose Annual*: (1952) W. T. Brown, 'Magazine and News Production by Offset at New High Speeds'; (1958) James W. Marshall and Warren L. Rhodes, 'Colour Web Offset on Newsprint'.

tact. There are several systems of gravure etching, varying from cells of constant area but varying depth, to cells of constant depth but varying area. The delicacy of gravure work may be estimated from the fact that in the first, or 'conventional', system, the depth of the deepest cell, a solid, is only 0·001 in. The transfer of the image to the gravure copper cylinder by fine gelatinized and sensitized paper called carbon tissue is also a highly delicate task; and the laborious and lengthy work of the necessary colour retouching by hand is only beginning to be lightened and speeded up by the introduction of the electronic colour scanner.[1]

While the present principal application of both processes is to magazine and periodical work, and their practical limitations in respect of type faces are thus discussed in the relevant pages below (Chapter 12), the *Daily Herald* has indicated a possible means of using gravure for full-colour advertising in a normal rotary letterpress daily newspaper. Its issue of 10 September 1958 presented a full-page advertisement in four-colour gravure; this was pre-printed on one side and re-reeled at the Watford photogravure plant of Odhams Press, the *Herald*'s controllers; the pre-printed reels were then run through the newspaper rotaries in London and Manchester on edition, the blank verso of the gravure colour page being letterpress-printed from a stereo plate in the ordinary way. To overcome the problems of paper stretch in gravure pre-printing and re-reeling, the colour advertisement was done in continuous pattern or 'wallpaper' style. Electronic web controls obviate this stretch and enable a colour gravure advertisement or editorial picture to be normally positioned on the page. Evidently this ingenious innovation presents important technical, and also economic, problems; it seems feasible only for a newspaper already linked with a large gravure establishment.

THE EDITORIAL AND THE COMPOSING ROOM

The production of a well-made newspaper is impossible without the closest co-operation and mutual understanding between the editorial department and the composing room. To achieve this the editorial man must set himself, in all humility, to learn from the compositors (and in the first place from the overseer, or the Printer as he is called on most dailies). A reasonable editorial mastery of composing-room techniques and procedures is essential if the demands on the compositors are to be so framed that they will secure the fullest response. The journalist who has learnt enough to see the problems of the edition from the compositors' point of view, who understands both the technical limitations and the possibilities of his particular composing room, will always be rewarded by just that

[1] *Preparation of Artwork for Rotary Gravure* (Institute of Practitioners in Advertising, 1958) is a useful technical guide.

extra spurt of skill from his colleagues at case, on the machines, and on the stone, which can turn a fair paper into a first-rate one. Specific items to note include the following:

Copy preparation. All copy must be in the best possible physical state for cleanness, clarity, size of paper; it must be methodically corrected for style; typographical markings and instructions must be plain and legible, always ringed round, and absolutely complete, so that the operator need waste no time in elucidating them.

The basic formula. The number of words per column-inch in the paper's various text sizes should be counted (and in the larger introduction or 'intro' sizes the wordage per double- and treble-column inch). This is the basic formula for casting-off lengths of type matter from copy wordage; without it there can be no accurate or economical page-planning. Obviously the formula should also be prepared for any bastard measure setting (e.g. 1½-column) if the paper regularly uses it. It is useful to recall that normal double-spaced typing on quarto paper, with an inch-plus margin, averages 250 words a side of copy.

The pica gauge. Also called a type gauge, this is the compositor's measuring tool. It is essential for the editorial man who has anything to do with layout or make-up. Graduated in the main body sizes, as well as in inches, the standard pica gauge, usually in polished steel, covers 5, 6, 8, 10, 12 pt. Better for newspapermen is the Monotype Corporation's white plastic gauge, which adds 5½, 7, 9, and 11 pt., the first three being frequent in news work. (The gauge is obtainable from the Corporation's publicity department, 43 Fetter Lane, London, E.C. 4, at 6*s.* 6*d.* post free.)

Proof correction. Editorial corrections on proof should accord strictly with the accepted correctors' style, of which the fullest version is given in the revised British Standard 1219: 1958 (The British Standards Institution, 2 Park Street, London, W. 1: 6*s.*).[1]

[1] On proof correction, and generally on style in copy, see R. A. Hewitt, *Style for Print* (Blandford Press, 1957).

3 · The English Newspaper 1932–60

THE period of 'active headline experiment' by the English newspaper that Stanley Morison correctly foretold in 1932 has amounted to a total revolution in newspaper typography and make-up.[1] The 'decker' headline, with its dashes and dividing rules, was supplanted by the single-deck multi-liner; and in place of the all-caps. style (or at most lower-case for alternate decks) there appeared the all lower-case style. Headlines were increased in size. Standardized arrangements of bold display faces, exploiting the variations of one or two families, took the place of the antiquated and thin news titlings or the unstandardized combinations of often conflicting jobbing letter that had partially ousted the titlings; in these new arrangements italic for the first time took a prominent place.

Where the many decks of the old headline had been written to the rigid prescription 'full out and centred turn', the three- or four-line single-decker was either written flush left with its lines ending unevenly ('streamlined' as the Americans called it) or variously centred, stepped, inverted pyramid. Dashes and dividing rules were discarded, even where a simplified decker style was retained, or restored. Headlines thus became dynamic and lively in a way they had not been before; and they were made up into pages which were also entirely novel in their dynamic and lively look; these pages finally changed the whole stress of make-up from the *vertical* to the *horizontal*. The grim, grey pillars of the newspaper page of tradition, partially broken by the evolution of the decker headline, now vanished for good in an overall, planned pattern where the page was visualized, headlined, and illustrated from top to bottom, and right across its width, as a graphic unit.

Never before had a typographic revolution of the first magnitude been initiated and carried through by the London morning newspapers (the 'nationals'), well known for their conservatism in these matters. In *The English Newspaper* Morison showed how the earlier development of the headline, of the crosshead, of some order in page make-up, was due to the Sunday papers and evening papers like the *Pall Mall Gazette* under

[1] Morison, op. cit., p. 319.

W. T. Stead and the *Star* under T. P. O'Connor, true pioneers of the 'New Journalism'. If Northcliffe was a journalistic revolutionary, he was a typographical conservative, always relying on his Printer for the type style of the *Daily Mail.* While the *Daily Express* signalized its birth in 1901 by the use of bold double-column headlines, the *Mail*, after a couple of imposing but isolated efforts, stuck to its deep single-column deckers. Only the South African War shook it into the emphasis of Sans caps. for alternate decks; thereafter the old-fashioned thin news titlings reigned unchallenged, even the last fateful days of July 1914 producing no more than one incongruous double-column line in De Vinne Condensed caps. leading a single-column titling seven-decker.

THE FIRST WAR AND AFTER

World War I changed all that, its outbreak provoking the *Mail* to a sledge-hammer double column in heavy Doric and Condensed Sans caps. Those climacteric years made general both the double-column headline and the *Express*-pioneered multi-column streamer, usually stretched to a full-page 'banner'. For doublers and streamers alike the jobbing cases were ransacked, Caslon Old Face Heavy mingling with Grot and Cheltenham Bold, with the old titlings still well in evidence. Streamers in particular seemed to be creations of compositorial caprice, set in some weight of Cheltenham Bold (from Condensed to Extended, sometimes even the Outline), in Sans, Hawarden, or a near-eccentric letter like the rough-edged Morland. Occasionally lower-case was used, the size rarely exceeded 36 pt., and the streamer was always cut off from the page, including the story into which it was supposed to lead, by a full double-fine rule.

These styles continued without appreciable change into the Peace. By the end of the 1920's the first introduction of the Ludlow gave currency to some of the American faces better suited to news display, like Caslon Bold and Bold Condensed, and more particularly Century and Century Bold; but these were still used as elements in the dashed-and-ruled decker, all in caps. and with each line sporting the superfluous full point at its end; only the revived *Daily Herald* carried its radical principles into typography, omitting the full point and setting decks in the lower-case of new Monotype faces like Plantin 110.

The long-standing trend to the seven-column page was confirmed, *The Times* so converting all its news pages in 1921 (but retaining the six-column broad gauge on the leader page until World War II). The wider sheet of *The Times* enabled it to run a 14-em column; for the 'populars' the 13½-em column became standard. The half-sheet picture papers adhered to their four-column make-up and made no change in their 15-em measure.

Meantime the great renaissance in typography which was transforming the British book and the British advertisement had had no apparent repercussion in the newspaper field. The year 1929, however, was one of certain signs and portents. In America the late John E. Allen launched a campaign in *Linotype News*, the influential journal of the Mergenthaler Linotype Company, for the 'streamlining' of newspaper headlines by the introduction of the free flush-left style in place of the stiff and formal decker. *The Times* published its most famous *Printing Number*, a remarkable 32-pp. supplement which roused such wide interest that it was

Daily Herald

EVER READY
FOR WIRELESS

Clocks & Watches
CAMERER CUSS

No. 4,395 MONDAY, MARCH 17, 1930 ONE PENNY.

PREMIER WELCOMES THE NEW "HERALD"

HIS MESSAGE TO NATION

Great Day in History of Labour

FORWARD!

Special Visit to Our Offices

MR. MACDONALD'S WISH

PRIME MINISTER'S GREETINGS

HISTORIC HOUR AT NEW OFFICE

SCENES AND INCIDENTS OF HIS TOUR

DON 'ALL OUT' TO-MORROW FOR A SPEED RECORD

PHONE TALK TO THE "DAILY HERALD"

FAITH IN HIS CAR

FOUR MILES A MINUTE —OR MORE?

PRIMO DE RIVERA FOUND DEAD

SURPRISE ARREST OF GIALDINI

PARIS HOTEL DRAMA

LONE PASSING OF THE EX-DICTATOR OF SPAIN

PREMONITION

BALLOON CHASE BY MOTOR-CAR

HEARD OVER 5,000 MILES AWAY

FORD "BABY" CAR FOR £100

MYSTERY HOTEL DEATH

TO-DAY'S 20 PAGES

"SWEATING" IN SHOPS

OUR £10,000 INSURANCE FOR READERS

EVERYDAY RISKS COVERED FOR ALL

REGISTER TO-DAY!

HER MOTHER KNOWS

Experience has taught her Mother that Wincarnis is all that is needed to shorten her daughter's convalescence.

She knows that after any illness, when the tissues and cells need building up, Wincarnis is so constituted that it replenishes through the blood the sugar and revitalising tonics that the body needs.

WINCARNIS

FIG. 6. The first Odhams Press *Daily Herald*, 1930. This Cheltenham typography, with modifications in style and weight, was retained for the first eight years of Odhams conduct of the paper.

promptly reprinted in book form; not least among its features was a critical article by Stanley Morison on newspaper types. Finally the Trades Union Congress that autumn approved, after much heart-searching in some quarters, the transfer of the printing and publishing of the *Daily Herald* to Odhams Press, one of London's best-known newspaper and periodical printing concerns.

THE ODHAMS *HERALD* AND *THE TIMES*

Of these events the Odhams–*Herald* deal was the first, as it was one of the most important, in its impact. The appearance of the new *Herald* in March 1930 was a technical sensation. Fleet Street's backwardness in make-up, text, and machining was exposed by a paper with a consistently planned make-up in the bold variants of one family only (Cheltenham), with a strong-coloured and clear text in the new American Ionic—its first appearance in Britain—and with rotary presswork of a quality only to be compared to that of *The Times.* The reason for this was simple. Odhams had never been newspaper proprietors in the ordinary sense; they were printers who acquired papers in order to print them; and, as printers competing in the contract and general printing market, they were progressive in their equipment and in their technique (Fig. 6).

While the newspaper trade began slowly to digest the lesson of the Odhams *Herald*, Printing House Square was conducting the massive exercise in typographic self-criticism, foreshadowed in Morison's 1929 article, which led to the production of Times New Roman and the complete revolutionizing of the typography of *The Times* in October 1932. An account of the design of Times Roman and the ramifications of its influence will be found below, in Chapter 4; here it is only necessary to emphasize the official P.H.S. view that the really important difference between the old typography and the new lay not in the text, nor in the romanizing of the Gothic title-line, but in the headlines. In their various weights and widths the new heading types, while all derived from the parent design, assured a colour-contrast with the text, and therefore an ease of perception, that the paper had never known in its long history.[1]

The Times style of 1960 is substantially that of 1932; for the new basic style so perfectly fitted the newspaper that, with some additional sizes, it has been able to cope with every development—from the first double-column headline in December 1932 (a style made normal by the war) to the first 'bill' page treble-column in July 1957. Only for the first full banner, over the foreign page round-up on Mr. Khrushchev's 'summit' call of July 1958, was a non-Times face—Monotype Bodoni Bold (Series 260) italic, in 36 pt. lower-case—called upon. The introduction of the remark-

[1] *Printing The Times 1785–1953*, pp. 69–70.

able $4\frac{3}{4}$ pt. Claritas for the small advertisements in 1951 and of the new title-piece in 1953 is mentioned later. Here it is appropriate to note the more flexible treatment now given to the picture page and the appearance of regular literary and feature pages, the latter freely laid out in magazine style, using large sizes of Perpetua (239) and Cochin (165) italic. Wartime newsprint economy dictated a 5 pt. column rule whose lateral constriction of the page was uncomfortable; but to avoid extra paper consumption when it was possible to regain the spaciousness of a wider rule, column measure was cut from 14 to $13\frac{1}{2}$ ems, a gauge still broad enough in these narrow days.

It is time to return to the general field of 1932–3. There was no sign of new ideas on the American model—except the presentation of Ionic as a text face—in the contemporary promotion material issued to newspapers by the Linotype and Monotype organizations. Yet, although any firm evidence seems very elusive, John E. Allen's radical notions must in one way or another have been filtering through; the present writer recollects of this period how, in a first timid attempt to redress the then infant *Daily Worker*, he specified flush-left headings in Caslon Heavy and Bodoni italic lower-case. On one matter, however, the evidence was abundant. The *Herald*'s colourful Ionic text had really shaken its contemporaries; and by the early summer of 1933 they had all followed suit, the *Daily Express* leading the *Daily Mail* and the *News Chronicle*.

CHRISTIANSEN—EDITOR-TYPOGRAPHER

That same year there happened an event in the history of the *Express* more important than the turnover to Ionic. Lord Beaverbrook appointed as its new editor one of his young Manchester executives, twenty-nine-year-old Arthur Christiansen, who was passionately—and, for his generation, unusually—type-conscious. Five years before he had advised a colleague: 'study type. There are too few newspaper journalists who know type.' He had taken his own advice and attended technical courses in general typography. Now he had his chance. Of course he was to do much more than revolutionize the typography and make-up of the *Express*; his brilliant development of the editorial policy described by a critic as 'sophisticated escapism and the bright romantic treatment of news'[1] was to achieve far and away the largest circulation that any broadsheet morning newspaper had ever known. But these considerations lie outside the scope of the present study; they simply have to be noted, as do commercial events like the fantastic free-gift circulation 'war' launched by Odhams to boost the *Herald*, since they played some part in conditioning and stimulating typographic development.

[1] Francis Williams, *Dangerous Estate* (1957), p. 234.

Christiansen's choice of type proved as important as his handling of it. It was inspired, and inspiring; it determined what has since become the characteristic headline typography of the English newspaper, both national and local. For he chose the Century family, principally the Bold (roman and italic) and Bold Extended, as available up to the largest sizes on the

Daily Express

Gordon's is REAL Gin and ITS not coloured

TO-DAY'S WEATHER: Showers; Cold.

Royal Sovereign Pencils

NO. 9,517. MONDAY, NOVEMBER 3, 1930. ONE PENNY.

THUNDERSTORM FREAKS ON SEA AND LAND.

GIANT WAVE STRIKES CHANNEL BOATS.

FOUR PASSENGERS INJURED.

RAIN, HAIL, SNOW AND LIGHTNING.

TWO MEN KILLED.

MOTOR-CARS BLOWN OVER.

LONDON REFLECTIONS in the road near the Law Courts after yesterday's heavy rain.

SOUTHERN ENGLAND and a large part of the midlands were swept yesterday morning by one of the most violent and sudden thunderstorms on record for this time of the year.

It lasted only about half an hour, but during its brief passage several people were struck by lightning, two men being killed, torrential rain fell, and pedestrians and cars were blown over and shop windows smashed.

SHATTERED WINDOWS.

DRIVE THROUGH THE STORM.

FAMOUS BRITISH CAVALRY COMMANDER DEAD.

Lieut.-General Sir Edward Cecil Bethune, the famous cavalry commander, died at his residence, in Eldon-road, Kensington, yesterday. He was seventy-five years of age.

"BETHUNE'S HORSE."

MARQUIS OF WINCHESTER INTERVIEWED.

His Home In An Old French Chateau.

"I AM HERE."

By C. J. KETCHUM. "Daily Express" Special Correspondent.

ABBEVILLE, Sunday, Nov. 2.

A quaint little sixteenth-century chateau, with red-tiled roof and latticed French windows, lying in a deep green valley at the foot of the Quesnoy Mountains, on the southern banks of the Somme —such was the picturesque background in which, late yesterday afternoon, I succeeded in securing a brief interview with the Marquis of Winchester, England's premier marquis, whose position as chairman of various City companies a year ago brought him before the public.

"HIS OWN BUSINESS."

ENGLISH BUTLER.

LOVELY GARDENS.

INDIGNATION.

PAGE TWO, COL. THREE.

IN SPLENDOUR ENTHRONED in the courtyard of his royal palace at Addis Ababa, Ras Tafari, who was yesterday crowned King of Kings and Emperor of Ethiopia, the Lion of Judah. The leopard cub adds to the Arabian Nights appearance of the scene.

ABYSSINIA'S EMPEROR CROWNED AT DAWN.

SCENE OF BARBARIC SPLENDOUR.

CRIMSON ROBE.

PRIESTS IN VELVET AND GOLD.

ADDIS ABABA, Sunday, Nov. 2.

AT 7.30 this morning, in a setting of barbaric splendour that for sheer magnificence of colouring it would be difficult to surpass, Ras Tafari Makonnen was crowned King of Kings and Emperor of Ethiopia in the specially constructed church within the grounds of the Cathedral of St. George here.

THE EMPRESS OF ABYSSINIA.

Ras Tafari.

CORONATION COACH.

CATHEDRAL CEREMONY.

NEW SEARCH FOR LOST VICAR.

WOMAN'S STATEMENT TO POLICE.

SOCIALIST DEFEATS IN ELECTIONS.

92 SEATS LOST: 79 WINS FOR CONSERVATIVES.

DO.X FLIGHT POSTPONED.

HUNTING WOMAN INJURED.

SECRET KINGS OF DRUG TRAFFIC.

TRAITORS DOOMED TO TORTURE AND DEATH.

HUGE FACTORIES.

"Daily Express" Correspondent. PARIS, Sunday, Nov. 2.

Behind the startling announcement recently made by the French Customs authorities at Marseilles that they have in four months—June to September—seized 27cwt. of smuggled drugs from incoming and outgoing ships, compared with roughly 5cwt. during 1929, lies a thrilling romance of a ceaseless struggle against one of the greatest curses of our time.

MYSTERY JAPANESE.

PAGE TWO, COL. ONE.

Pilot Knocks Out A Woman In The Air.

"Daily Express" Correspondent. SYDNEY, Sunday, Nov. 2.

LATE NEWS.

FAMOUS SOLDIER DEAD.

Broadcasting Programmes on Page 15

ADMIRAL TAYLOR IN THE HOUSE TO-DAY.

MR. EVERYMAN

"My wife is my banker Mr. Drage we pay 30/- only on the £75?"

Mr. Drage: That's quite correct. Under my 50 Pay Way Terms.

Mr. Everyman: So I pay just 30/- now and 30/- monthly after for 49 months and £75 worth of fine furniture is delivered at once?

Coupon

DRAGES HIGH HOLBORN · LONDON

FIG. 7. A typical *Daily Express* front page (1930) before the Christiansen revolution. Note the antiquated survival of the full-point at the end of all display lines.

BEAR BRAND'S Slimming Sy-metra

Daily Express

WORLD'S LARGEST DAILY SALE

Thursday, September 29, 1938 One Penny

MADE . . .

PREMIER FLIES TODAY TO LAST-MINUTE PEACE TALK WITH HITLER, DUCE AND DALADIER, TELLS CROWD:

"IT'S ALL RIGHT!"

HITLER POSTPONES HIS MOBILISATION

11th hour message: Now Britain, France and Italy may police Sudetenland

"TOKEN CESSION" PLAN

By GUY EDEN

Daily Express Political Correspondent

THERE IS HOPE—REAL HOPE—OF PEACE. IT CAME THROUGH THE QUIETLY SPOKEN WORDS OF THE PRIME MINISTER, MR. NEVILLE CHAMBERLAIN, IN THE DENSELY PACKED HOUSE OF COMMONS YESTERDAY, WHEN HE ANNOUNCED THAT HERR HITLER HAD AGREED TO SEE

Herr Hitler accepts your proposals.

He will be glad to meet you at Munich tomorrow, together with M. Daladier and Signor Mussolini.

Daily Express reconstruction of the Foreign Office note handed to the Prime Minister in the House of Commons.

"A.R.P. MUST GO ON" —HOME SECRETARY

SIR SAMUEL HOARE, the Home Secretary, issued a message last night urging that the distribution of gas masks, digging of trenches, and organisation of first-aid posts should be pushed rapidly to completion.

Spain, too

'DON'T HOARD FOOD'

THE Board of Trade yesterday asked people not to hoard food. This followed information that there have been increased

LATEST

CENTRAL 8000

Weather: showers (see page 11)

FIG. 8. The Christiansen revolution in full swing, and at its heaviest (the Munich front page, 29 September 1938). Below, eight years later, is the revolution continuing after the war (1946), with the development of the centrally placed single-column Sans 'kicker'. The current style is exemplified in Fig. 88.

DAILY EXPRESS

No. 14,417 Lighting-up: 7.49 pm to 5.54 am FRIDAY SEPTEMBER 27 1946 Weather: Fair, close One Penny

COAL: *Shinwell calls for winter output drive*

EGYPT: *Talks are broken off 'unless British yield'*

GREECE: *Bevin and Byrnes agree on firm policy*

£20,000,000 FOR ROCKETS

Planning Atlantic journeys

RESEARCH STATION NEAR DESERT

From CHAPMAN PINCHER

THE Government is to spend £20,000,000 in building and equipping rocket research stations during the next three years, it was revealed last night.

Annual running costs of the stations are estimated at £10,000,000.

Top priority is to be given to research on guided A.A. missiles and long-range defensive rockets. But considerable sums are earmarked for the development of Transatlantic passenger rockets.

The possibilities of space-ships for inter-planetary travel are to be explored.

By agreement with the Australian Government nearly £6,000,000 will be spent on a rocket testing range in the Central Australian desert.

Shinwell says:— MINES NEED NO EXTRA WORKERS

EGYPT REJECTS OFFER

'Our terms or end the talks'

WANTS SUDAN

Help-Colonies plan starts

HEATH JURY DECIDE IN AN HOUR

One deep breath and then 'Guilty'

From PAUL HOLT

Doreen Marshall: Should she be alive today?

THE POLICE GAZETTE

PUBLISHED BY AUTHORITY.

Special Notice

Picture the newspapers

VICAR CHARGED WITH KIDNAP

After car chase

Explosives in river

Swept away

Strikers riot in Hollywood

Greeks clear king's route

Houses searched

4.30 p.m. LATEST

STAGE EXPLOSION INJURES TWO

CENtral 8000

Ludlow. Bodoni italic provided the secondary contrast. These bold versions of Century immediately showed that they could solve the problem of colour-contrast with the text, in *Express* terms, as successfully as *The Times* titlings had done for that newspaper. The bold Cheltenhams also offered good colour-contrast; but their monotone, blunt-seriffed structure gave an overall effect lacking the crispness and punch of Century, which inherited the sharper serifs and contrast in stroke from its parent Modern Roman. In the Extended versions, invaluable for economical but strong streamer lines in caps., the squat and ugly Cheltenham could not compare with its Century equivalent. Century Bold lower-case had the advantage, particularly for single-column work, of combining condensation with a large x-height in a way done by no other bold roman (except Times Bold).

There were roughly three stages in the transformation of headline styles and make-up, which the *Express* pioneered and its contemporaries followed (Figs. 7, 8). First there was the increasing accent on the horizontal, the multiplication of multi-column headings, notably below the fold. Then the decker style was loosened up, four decks reduced to two and finally to one. Finally large lower-case, in roman and later in italic, was introduced for main headings. By 1936 the basic process was complete; the *Express* had evolved the style which, with appropriate experiment and adaptation, it retains to this day. One subsequent original development, much admired and widely imitated, was the placing of a four-line lower-case Sans top heading around the centre of the front page; against the Century this really kicked right out of the page and came to be called the 'kicker'. It is a most important aid to vigorous make-up and is further discussed in later chapters.

The extent to which Christiansen was inspired by the Americans is debatable, and not of very great importance. The revolutionized *Express* was in any event entirely English, bearing no resemblance to any American model; and John E. Allen's 'streamlining' campaign in the United States did not win a decisive victory until 1937—after the *Express*'s transformation—when the *Los Angeles Times*, restyled on Allen's lines, received the coveted Ayer design award and started a general fashion. By this time inspiration was rather travelling the other way. The Hearst papers, for example, were under orders to study and follow *Express* typography, while American journalism textbooks held up the feature pages of the *Express* and the other Fleet Street 'populars' as models for their students.[1]

All the *Express*'s broadsheet contemporaries began to emulate its new principles of headlining and make-up, though only the *Mail* approxi-

[1] John Rayner, 'Features for Two Millions' (*Typography No. 2*, 1937, p. 13); Vitray, Mills, and Ellard, *Pictorial Journalism* (New York, 1939), p. 303.

NEWS CHRONICLE, Saturday, October 8, 1938.

News Chronicle

No. 28,841 ONE PENNY SATURDAY, OCTOBER 8, 1938

be **sure** to enter the News Chronicle GRACIE FIELDS £1,000 SONGS CONTEST

GERMANY GRANTS TURKEY CREDITS FOR 12 MILLION POUNDS

Bill To Offset Anglo-French Drive in Balkans

BERLIN, Saturday Morning.

It is officially announced that an agreement for a German credit of £12,000,000 has been reached at Ankara between the Reich Minister for Economics, Herr Funk, and the Turkish Minister of National Economy, Shakir Kesebir, at Ankara.

The credit (states B.U.P.) is to be used for paying for German deliveries for Turkish armaments and Turkish industries.

When he arrived in Ankara yesterday Herr Funk declared that Germany was ready to accept Turkish commodities "in the broadest measure" (see Page Two).

Credits of £16,000,000 were recently granted by Britain to assist Turkish rearmament, and British capital has financed much of the development of Turkish heavy industry.

London Balloon Barrage Test Today

London will see its balloon barrage tested for the first time today.

From the forenoon until 6 p.m., the Air Ministry announced last night, balloons will be flown from many points in central and suburban London as a peace-time exercise of the barrage squadrons.

The points include Green Park, Regent's Park, Tower of London, Grosvenor Square, Clapham Common and Temple Lawn.

MERCURY NEARS CAPETOWN—AND 3 RECORDS

Early this morning flares were lit in Table Bay to guide the Mercury, upper component of the pick-a-back plane, which left Dundee on Thursday on a non-stop flight to the Cape, to a safe landing.

This came after news that the Mercury had been seen over Alexander Bay, 380 miles from Capetown.

Mercury reached the half-way stage in her flight early yesterday morning when she passed Kano, radio outpost on the edge of the Sahara. She had then covered a little over 3,000 miles.

Over the Sahara she met with head winds.

£21,158.2.0

was last night's total of the News Chronicle Refugee Fund.

This is magnificent—but more is wanted still.

Contributions to: Czechoslovakia Relief Fund, News Chronicle, Bouverie Street, London, E.C.4.

(Details Page Thirteen)

P.C. CLINGS TO 50 M.P.H. STOLEN CAR

A non-stop car carried a police constable 5 yards on the running-board, knocked down two cyclists and dragged a cycle at 50 m.p.h. half a mile through the main streets of Slough last night.

The police of three counties are searching for the driver.

LATE NEWS

PATROL BOAT EXPLODES IN MID-THAMES

BRITAIN AND RUSSIA SIGN 20-YEAR ALLIANCE

Molotov Flies Here and to U.S.: "Second Front in Europe in 1942"

By E. P. MONTGOMERY, the Diplomatic Correspondent

FOR THE NEXT 20 YEARS, IN PEACE AS IN WAR, GREAT BRITAIN AND RUSSIA WILL BE ALLIES. ON MAY 26 A TREATY OF ALLIANCE AND MUTUAL ASSISTANCE BETWEEN THE TWO NATIONS WAS SIGNED IN LONDON.

And in the course of a dramatic 11,000-mile journey by air made by the Soviet Foreign Minister, V. M. Molotov, to London and Washington, during which the Treaty was concluded, Britain, America and Russia "reached full understanding with regard to the urgent task of creating a second front in Europe in 1942."

At five o'clock yesterday afternoon Mr. Anthony Eden rose from his seat in the House to reveal to the cheering Commons one of the few really well-kept diplomatic secrets of this war—Mr. Molotov's flight from Moscow to Britain and America and the conclusion of a Treaty of Alliance and Mutual Assistance between the United Kingdom and the Union of Soviet Socialist Republics, based on the principles of the Atlantic Charter, which is to endure in war and peace for 20 years to come.

Pact Means A Real New Order For Europe

By VERNON BARTLETT

The document, which bears the names of Mr. Molotov and Mr. Eden, is likely to play an even bigger part in European politics than its parent document, the Atlantic Charter, which bears the names of President Roosevelt and Mr. Churchill.

Mr. Molotov Signs the Treaty

And here he is with the President

How World Greeted the News

Hailed on Soviet Radio and by Allies

Molotov Had Talks With Roosevelt

THE TERROR GOES ON

34 More Deaths for Heydrich's

Prague radio announces the execution of 34 more people in Prague and Brno yesterday.

SUNER FOR PARIS

JAPS REINFORCE

Latest U.S. day raid concentrated on aircraft factories

BRUNSWICK WAS AGAIN MAIN TARGET

By RONALD WALKER

News Chronicle Air Correspondent

Hundreds of bombers and fighters concluded a continuous 48-hour offensive against the Germans in Western Europe when heavies of the United States Strategic Air Force again struck yesterday at military targets in Germany.

American headquarters announced at midnight that "very strong forces of heavy U.S. bombers escorted by almost equally strong formations of fighters attacked aircraft factories at Brunswick and major aerodromes with repair depots in North-West Germany.

The fall in fighters

STREET BATTLES IN KRIVOI ROG

CHANGE IN POLICY TO SLAVS IS

All in 48 hours

In London Tubes last night

Nazi groups cut off at Anzio

COUNTER-ATTACKS BY ALLIED TANKS

British and U.S. armoured units have made penetrations in the Anzio bridgehead area and cut off German battle groups.

This was admitted in a broadcast last night from Berlin by the German war reporter, Lutz Koch.

He added the usual claim that German positions had been restored by counter-attacks.

Nazis were pounded day and night

From NORMAN CLARK

NEW COMB-OUT OF INDUSTRY

PAASIKIVI HAS SOVIET TERMS

—Report

STOCKHOLM, Monday.

Paasikivi is returning to Finland with Russia's armistice demands, it is reported here tonight.

LATE NEWS

LENINGRAD HONOUR

LONDON BLACK-OUT

Fig. 9. The pre-war Granby Sans (Century Bold italic contrast) of the *News Chronicle*, with its wartime Condensed Sans (Gothic) and—from 1944—Bodoni Bold.

Daily Herald

No. 6930 MONDAY, MAY 2, 1938 ONE PENNY

SHERLEY'S 32 PAGE CAT BOOK 2D.

ADDS DISTINCTION TO ANY CAR Bluemel's "FIRMOID" NUMBER PLATES

Goering Snubs Britain And France

A WARNING to Britain and France to "keep out" of the Czechoslovakian problem was delivered in Germany yesterday.

Commenting on the Anglo-French decision to make representations in Berlin over Czechoslovakia, the 'National Zeitung,' known to be the mouthpiece of General Goering declared:

"The Czechoslovakian question does not, in German opinion, need any diplomatic discussions between the Western Powers and the Reich.

STAGE ROMANCE BROKEN

'YOUR FIELD DAY, BUT MY FIELD,' SAID COW

THOUSANDS MARCH FOR SPAIN

By ERNEST E. HUNTER

I HAVE seen May Day demonstrations for more than 30 years. But never have I seen Labour in such mighty numbers, with so much pageantry and enthusiasm, as in Hyde Park, yesterday.

Six great processions marched through London's streets, gay banners waving, bands playing.

Everywhere the tricolour flags of the Spanish Republic

Salvation Army Bandsmen In Sea Rescue

HYTHE, Kent, Salvation Army band was stopped in the middle of a hymn last night by the lifeboat station "ship in distress" maroon.

HUMAN CHAIN UP

GLIDER PILOT 2 AIRMEN KILLED

DAILY HERALD

No. 11162 (D) WEDNESDAY, DECEMBER 19, 1951 PRICE 1½D

LONDON SPECIAL

Vent-Axia

Owbridge's

BRITAIN WILL AID EUROPE'S ARMY

Churchill's promises please the French

From CHARLES LAMBERT PARIS, Tuesday

THE two-day Anglo-French talks have revealed "complete agreement" on all international problems, notably in the Far East, the Middle East and Europe, according to a joint communique issued here this evening.

Mr. Churchill has promised France that Britain will associate herself as closely as possible with the proposed European army.

WHAT THEY SAY ABOUT THE DAY THE EARTH STOOD STILL

Eden talks it over

FATHER AND BABY

Round-world Betty came to London . .

Ocean babes weren't kidnapped —says dad

A BOY aged nine months, and his sister, aged 2½, were last night in mid-Atlantic aboard the New York-bound Queen Mary despite a court order that they must stay in Britain.

MRS. NOREEN BEAUCHEMIN: "We were homesick."

FISHING GROUNDS SHUT TO BRITAIN

DAILY Herald

Friday, July 26, 1957 PRICE 2d. No. 12877 (D)

—Tribunal awards 11/- rise: Owners accept—

BUS STRIKE COULD END ON SUNDAY

By STEPHEN PARKINSON, Industrial Correspondent

THE great strike of 100,000 busmen could be over by Sunday, just a week after it began. A surprise award of 11/- a week increase in pay, recommended by the Disputes Tribunal, is likely to be accepted.

It has already been approved by the employers. Their spokesman said last night:

"The companies accept the award and assume that the unions will now call off the strike and instruct their members to report for duty."

Unions may say Yes tomorrow

SOMETHING TO SING ABOUT

Herald Reporter

Delayed

MAN IN PLANE SHOT HIMSELF FOR £42,000

From JOHN SAMPSON NEW YORK, Thursday

A HOLLYWOOD jeweller insured himself for £42,000, flew to Las Vegas for a night's drinking and gambling, then shot himself on the homeward flight today.

Only casualty

Polio family kept alone on a farm

FIG. 10. An all-Bodoni style as introduced by the *Daily Herald* in 1938, followed by its post-war Sans-Century style, culminating in the full tabloid Sans treatment.

mated to its Century-Bodoni typography, with more play on the Bodoni (in the Bold italic) and the Century in its Bold Extended. Generally the *Mail*'s evolution was slower. It took some time to bring order into a headline chaos where Century and Bodoni fought it out with Cheltenham Bold, Caslon Bold, and even sometimes an old-world Frenchified heavy news titling called Monarch. It also clung to its famous advertising front page, after even the *Daily Telegraph* had gone over to front-page news

Tuesday, August 18, 1936 THE DAILY MIRROR *London Edition* Page 3

BABES-IN-WOOD BOY RUN OVER

AS HE HID IN LEAVES

BY A SPECIAL CORRESPONDENT

WORKMEN were lopping branches from the trees in New Park-road, Brixton, London, S.W., yesterday, to make room for new street lamps, and eleven-year-old Melvin Clack got a great idea for a game.

Finding a pile of leaves on the kerb near his home, he decided to play Babes-in-the-Wood, and told his friend Albert Swift. Albert was busy with a game of his own so Melvin went off alone.

He lay down and covered himself with leaves. The next moment the lorry collecting the leaves drove up—and went right over him.

"Great Fun"

When his companions returned to seek him they found him dead.

With tears streaming down his cheeks, his thirteen-year-old playmate, Albert Swift, told me how he was powerless to prevent the tragedy.

"I was not playing with the others," he said, "but modelling a head in clay. When Mel told me what he was going to do, I thought it was great fun.

"I was too busy with my modelling to watch the end of the game. I heard the lorry driving past, and when I looked up it was just passing over the pile of leaves where Mel was lying.

Awakened from Sleep

"Rushing forward, I parted the leaves, and saw him. . . ."

Poor Albert was too overcome to continue.

Mr. Harry Clack, father of the dead boy—there are five others—who works at night as a garage cleaner, was awakened from his sleep with the news that his boy had met with an accident.

He ran from Lafone-house, his home, to find him dead.

She's Got All Three

Good looks, a sense of humour and outstanding dancing ability. Stanley Lupino's search for a girl with these talents ended when he found Lu Anne Meredith, ex-Dorchester beauty. She's to be his leading lady in the film "Sporting Love."

41,000,000 People

in France call him Monsieur le President Lebrun. His "last word" is law to all of them. But at home he's just "old grandpa" to these three—and it's their word that's law.

THE QUEEN'S HAREWOOD HOLIDAY PLANS CHANGED

Arrangements for the annual visit of Queen Mary to Harewood House, the home of the Princess Royal and the Earl of Harewood, have been altered.

It had been expected that she would go from Sandringham for her ten days' stay on Wednesday, but at Harewood yesterday it was stated that she would not be arriving this week.

It is understood that the Queen will be at Harewood during the first week in September.

WIDOW'S COIN HOARD

A hoard of silver coins of all denominations, worth about £100 and carefully wrapped in small paper packets, was found under the bed and in odd places in a room at Bayham-street, St. Pancras, London, where Mrs. Mary Jewell, aged sixty-five, lived.

She was a widow and an old age pensioner.

It was when she failed to pay her weekly rent at the usual time—a certain hour on one particular day—that her room was entered and she was found dead on the floor.

ISLAND ISOLATED BY CLOSING BRIDGE —SHIPS HELD UP

FROM midnight last night the Isle of Sheppey, off the mouth of the Thames, was cut off from the mainland by the closing for repairs of King's Ferry Bridge to road and rail traffic.

The bridge is the only means of communication with the mainland. To maintain normal living extra food supplies were taken into Sheerness yesterday.

While the bridge is being repaired passengers will be taken in motor-coaches from the stations in the island to the Sheppey end of the bridge. They will be allowed to walk over

Because it is not possible to lift the bridge for vessels to pass through, several ships carrying cargoes are held up.

PIT DISASTERS: MINERS URGE DRASTIC STEPS

The Council of the Yorkshire Miners' Association, at Barnsley yesterday, urged on the responsible authorities the need for a searching inquiry, with a view to drastic steps being taken to prevent the recurrence of such disasters as that at Wharncliffe Woodmoor Colliery.

Little Dr. Tucker Swung for His 'Supper' Too Soon

An old favourite in a new version featuring a New Orleans, Louisiana, doctor, according to an epistle of Reuter.

Little Doctor Tucker
Golfed when work was done.
Entered for a tournament
To hole a ball in one.

He walked out to the contest-hole.
One-sixty yards in length,
Took an iron from his bag
And swung with all his strength.

A ping—the ball flew through the air,
Across the green it stole,
And, to the Doctor's great surprise,
Trickled down the hole

Rushing to the club-house
To claim the winner's "dime,"
He found the competition
Was in a fortnight's time.

B. J. F.

£60,000 MORE EACH WEEK FOR WORKERS

WAGES are rising steadily. How much is revealed in a return issued by the Ministry of Labour last night.

The changes in rates which came into operation in July are estimated to have resulted in an increase of nearly £60,000 in the weekly full-time wages of over a million workpeople—and a decrease of about £3,800 in the pay of 44,000.

Trades Affected

The principal increases affected adult male workers in the engineering industry whose wages were raised by 1s. a week.

Of other increases, the more important affected gas workers, railway shopmen, municipal tramway and omnibus employees in the provinces and pottery workers

Crashed Air Liner Pilot "Best I Knew"

Drowning caused the death of one of the victims of the Cloud of Iona air disaster.

This was decided at the resumed inquest at Jersey yesterday on Ernest James Appleby, a passenger, after a doctor had stated that there was no evidence of injury caused by the crash.

Mr. Louis Greig, director and general manager of Jersey and Guernsey Airways, said that the pilot, Mr. Halmshaw, had joined the company after leaving the Royal Air Force.

"I do not think I ever met a better pilot."

DIED BECAUSE BROTHER WAS ABSENT

BECAUSE his cries for his elder brother went unanswered, twenty-nine-year-old Rochard Vosper, insurance agent, of Weston Mill, Plymouth, died in Plymouth City Hospital yesterday.

Doctors attending Vosper for internal trouble were unable to effect any improvement owing to his insistent calls for his "big brother."

As a last hope they sanctioned a radio SOS for the forty-three-year-old brother, Ernest, a naval pensioner, whose last known home was in Bodmin two years ago.

The SOS failed to reach Ernest—and Richard's parents, who had kept a day-and-night vigil by his bedside, went home broken-hearted.

Mrs. Vosper, mother of the two men, told the *Daily Mirror*:—

"They were great friends. Dick always turned to Ernest in trouble. If Ernest had been able to reach him, I think he would have lived"

MISSING GIRL SEARCH

Police have been asked to assist in the search for a fifteen-year-old girl, Elsie Newman, of Boswell House, Devonshire-street, Holborn, London, who has been missing from her home since August 2.

The girl is described as being 5ft. 2in. in height, with dark brown hair, grey eyes, of sturdy build, and with a round face.

FIG. 11. A *Daily Mirror* inside news page in the early stages of the Bartholomew revolution (1936). Note the make-up of four wide—15-em—columns.

(April 1939). The *News Chronicle*, lacking Ludlow, redressed itself (as advised by Stanley Morison) in type-founder's modern Sans—Granby (with italic) and Granby Bold, using Linotype-set Century Bold italic for contrast (Fig. 9). The *Herald* stuck to its Cheltenham, somewhat lightening the effect by introducing the unusual Medium and Medium Condensed, until May 1938; it then changed over completely to an all-Bodoni dress, in bold and light, each in roman and italic; the streamlining was complete, all heads being single-deck and set flush-left or centred, while instead of a cap. streamer lead to the front page there were three lines across three columns in 72 pt. Bodoni Bold lower-case (Fig. 10).

This was all happening, the reader may be reminded, when a combination of abnormally cheap newsprint and expanding display advertising made large papers (from 24 to 32 pages) normal. In these conditions the main run of news-text was not usually set smaller than 8 pt., and generous whiting of editorial columns was customary.

THE 'TABLOID REVOLUTION'

The *Express* transformation was already in progress when the stage was set for an event in many ways much more startling—the 'tabloid revolution'. It was in 1934 that Harry G. Bartholomew, former process engraver and pioneer art executive of the *Daily Mirror*, succeeded to the editorial direction of that then declining picture paper, seconded by Cecil Harmsworth King of the advertising department (later to oust him from the chairmanship which he attained in 1944). Bartholomew turned the *Mirror* and its companion the *Sunday Pictorial* into tabloids *à l'Américaine*, with poster-size Sans headings, sexy picture spreads, pages of strips, with a combination of strident sensationalism and political and social radicalism —'Forward with The People'—which was to put him well ahead even of the mammoth *Express* in circulation. A recent critical survey of the *Mirror* story said:

> By 1929 the [New York] 'tabloid' formula was set. Mr. Bartholomew's appropriation of it in 1934 was made under the guidance of a powerful American advertising agency at the suggestion of Mr. Cecil King. The agency he selected gave not only counsel, but men who supplied both layout and leader-writing. One of the greatest of British journalistic revolutions was thus initiated, carried through and made successful by men who were not journalists. An art manager and an advertising manager were responsible.[1]

Actually the revolutionary process took much longer to produce the *Mirror* as we know it than might appear from the foregoing. The traditional four 15-em columns of the half-sheet picture paper remained until the

[1] Stanley Morison, 'Picture-printing and Word-printing' (*Penrose Annual*, 1956).

war; the seven 9-em columns now regarded as normal 'national' tabloid practice are a wartime legacy. The new Sans style, as seen in 1936, was modest indeed in comparison with its sledge-hammer sequel; typical inside pages only ran up to 36 pt. and 48 pt. headlines in the caps. of Ludlow Medium and Condensed Gothic (Fig. 11). Yet to come were the double-spreads covering front and back (sometimes printed sideways), the reverse-block front page, the slogan 'the paper with two front pages' (Fig. 69).

EFFECTS OF THE SECOND WAR

Reference to the war's repercussions on newspaper make-up may introduce a more detailed consideration of the important changes brought by newsprint rationing and four-page daily papers, an austerity unbroken until 1946. Almost all these changes have been permanent. First, basic text size dropped from 8 pt. to 7 pt. (there is now a tendency to reverse this) and page format went over from seven to eight columns, initially of 11½ ems but, with the continued post-war rises in newsprint costs, usually dropping to 11¼ ems; the saving of two ems in the width of a page can mean an imposing economy in newsprint with the use of narrower reels. Many provincial papers, both dailies and weeklies, went over to a nine- or even occasionally a ten-column page, with measures of 10 or 10½ ems. Width-saving also induced many papers to adopt 3 pt. column rule, which is too thin for satisfactory working or appearance; this is tacitly admitted nowadays by the three-pointers, who set much of their matter indented each end in order to avoid the overcrowded effect. Fully ruled page folios, which had remained on news pages after the open-top style had been introduced on feature pages, were ousted from news as well. The space-saving virtues of the even lower-case, or 'all down', style for headlines in the new narrower measures brought it into general favour.

As for the typography of individual papers, the Century style of the *Express* and *Mail* proved the most adaptable. Freer handling and the development of straplines over main headings—particularly over the front-page streamer—were the main new features. The *Express* gave a big impetus to the anti-Blackletter movement when it adopted its present hand-lettered roman cap. title-piece in July 1942; headed 'More News', a promotion panel stressed the 'economical design' of the new title. No fundamental change has taken place in the news display typography of either paper up to the present day, save that they are now exclusively Century. After the war the *Mail* deliberately dropped the more sensational handling it had been developing, including the use of large Condensed Gothic lower-case. Both papers demonstrate how freshness can be maintained by the skilful manipulation of an established typographic formula (Figs. 88, 90).

The war and post-war typography of the *News Chronicle* and the *Herald* is a very different story. The *News Chronicle* began well. After seeking to strengthen its Granby style by introducing some sizes of Granby Extra Bold, it evidently concluded that a Sans style fit for wartime must have more impact, implying at once more colour and more condensation. So in July 1940 it went over to typefounders' Medium (Grotesque No. 9) and Condensed Sans, which it learnt to handle most effectively; the substitution in 1942 of the Ludlow versions (Medium and Condensed Gothic) made no difference. The style was apt and presented with skill; there has never been any convincing explanation, other than editorial caprice, of the total change, in February 1944, to an all-Bodoni style; the editor at that time, Sir Gerald Barry, admitted that his associates might think the new style 'too Palladian' (Fig. 9). There then began a protracted struggle to escape from Bodoni, which was first diluted (or adulterated) with various Sans faces, then supplanted by different experimental arrangements of Century, finding their appointed end in the present adaptation of the *Express–Mail* Century style.

The *Herald* did the opposite of the *Chronicle*. In 1940 it scrapped its Bodoni dress for Sans. During the war years that followed it ran the gamut of Ludlow Gothics (Square, Heavy, Medium, Condensed), eventually settling for the more open and legible Square as a lead heading. The Condensed periods, especially since they coincided with the orgy of experimental two-column titles mentioned in Chapter 13 below, produced some extraordinarily dishevelled front pages. After the war the *Herald* showed signs of appreciating the unsuitability of heavy Sans as the permanent headline dress for a broadsheet paper. It adopted—presumably with an imitative eye on the *Express*—an all-Century style, later livening it with Sans 'kickers', *Express*-fashion. But this Century treatment was curiously flat, partly due to the excessive use of Bold Extended for the smaller headings. For a paper that had always been hampered, *vis-à-vis* its contemporaries, by the 2½ inches it lost in page depth through the Odhams 21-inch cut-off, this was an error of typographical judgement. The horizontal spread of the Extended exaggerated the relative squatness of the sheet just as a horizontally striped frock exaggerates the figure defects of a short, stout woman.

In 1951 Sans reappeared as a major ingredient in *Herald* make-up. It began with Tempo Heavy caps. for leads and main stories only; mating well with the Century Bold, this might have been the basis of an effective and flexible style. But Long Acre now had its imitative eye on the immense success of the *Mirror* in winning working-class readers; so the

Herald was forthwith clothed in a complete *Mirror* dress—the first and only time that a broadsheet has been given the full tabloid type treatment. This at least provided a permanent object lesson in the error of such an approach (Fig. 10). Abandoned for a lighter and more varied Sans style following the change in control and editorship of the paper in 1957, it returned in 1959 with the use of specially cut 96 pt. and 120 pt. poster Sans for streamers.

THE DAILY (AND SUNDAY) MAGAZINE

The first number of the *Daily Mail*, in 1896, had given its embryonic feature page the prophetic heading 'The Daily Magazine'. Building what were later to be somewhat unkindly called the 'gaga-maga-zine' pages—first popularized by the mass-sale Sunday papers—into the fabric of the daily paper was an integral part of the *Express* transformation under Christiansen. Free layouts using large display types other than news style (Goudy, Caslon, Garamond, Cameo), bold illustration in varying techniques (photographs, line or wash drawings, scraper board), text set indented with whites instead of column rule and ornamented with fancy drop letters and other decorative devices—these modes of feature page presentation were fully developed by 1936. Nor have they substantially changed since, except perhaps to become a little more 'gaga' with changes in typographic taste and resources, the use of hand-lettering in fancy reverse block headings, and the like.

Historically always an interesting group, the Sundays reacted to their special mid-century problems of super-saturated and unstable circulations with varied typographic formulas. The two 'class'[1] Sundays stood alone, alike for rising sales and repeated award-winning design. The *Observer*'s all lower-case Caslon Heavy and Bodoni style has stood the test of years, while the *Sunday Times*, after experiments with Bodoni deckers and flush-left Century Bold lower-case, has evolved a Century Bold and Extended decker style which has proved fully satisfactory. Both papers, in their extensive feature pages, have settled for straightforward treatments in Perpetua and Perpetua Bold. Of the 'populars' the *Sunday Express* has developed the most distinctive style, a simple Sans treatment mainly in Ludlow Square Gothic, keeping its type tricks (and those reasonably disciplined) for the feature pages. It is perhaps the most effective Sans make-up for a broadsheet yet designed; too monotonous, maybe, for the six days of a daily, but entirely acceptable once a week in a Sunday paper (Fig. 12).

[1] The term 'class' is applied throughout to papers such as *The Times*, the *Manchester Guardian*, the *Observer*, the *Sunday Times* and their provincial 'quality' contemporaries.

The *Express* apart, there has been no effective development of a special Sunday style among its contemporaries. Two may be described as 'tab-loidizers'—the *People* and the *Empire News*—one, the *Sunday Dispatch*, has sought to remodel itself on morning paper Century lines, and *Reynolds News*, the first 'popular' (in its 1936 restyling by the present writer) to show the effectiveness of the large sizes of the Times Bold and Titling range, has descended to a characterless jumble of Grot, Bodoni, Gill, and Goudy Oldstyle. The institutional *News of the World* has abandoned the formalism fitting for an institution; in place of its stiff Latin Elongated deckers it 'streamlines' in a near-Gallic array of heavy Doric (roman and italic), Grotesque No. 9 italic, Clearface Extra Bold, Cheltenham Bold, Winchester Bold italic, Century Bold, Bodoni, Metroblack (roman and italic). To the traditionalist it is not a change for the better.

THE PROVINCIALS AND THE DESIGN AWARD

To attempt a concrete estimate of the effect of Fleet Street's typographic transformations since 1932 upon the provincial Press, both daily and weekly, would go far beyond the possible limits of this chapter. The firm establishment of the Century family, with Bodoni as runner-up (and Sans of the Medium Gothic sort for contrast), may be noted in broad general terms. The wide adoption of Times Roman for text in the provinces, by reason of its space-saving qualities, has been far from an unmixed blessing, for the reasons suggested below in Chapter 4.

The change-over to front-page news has been a continuing feature of the period, both by the leading morning papers (*Yorkshire Post* 1939, *Birmingham Post* 1946, *Manchester Guardian* 1952, *The Scotsman* 1957, *Glasgow Herald* 1958) and by many prominent weeklies, too many indeed to list here. Improvements in typography and make-up have normally accompanied this change-over.

The provincials have so far been the mainstay of the Annual Award for Newspaper Design, whose institution in 1954 on the initiative of *Printing World*, and under the patronage of Linotype and Machinery Ltd., has been a major event in the field of newspaper typography. With the exception of *The Times*, the *Daily Worker*, the *Observer*, and the *Sunday Times* (all repeated prizewinners), most of the 'nationals' have been strangely shy of a contest that has become more than a contest—has become, as its sponsors say, a 'movement to improve newspaper design by promoting a greater interest in it'. Entries grew from 203 in 1954 to 277 in 1959.

Administered by a committee on which representatives of the Newspaper Society (the organization of provincial proprietors), the British Federation of Master Printers, and the Council of Industrial Design join those of the

THE OBSERVER

Established 1791: No. 8,766 — London, Sunday, July 5, 1959 — Price 5d. Postage 2½d. Abroad 3½d.

National Press Gets 3-day Respite

Union Agrees to Ink Pooling: Papers Continue Half-size

No Progress Made at Ministry Talks

By A Staff Reporter

THE national newspapers will continue to publish at least until Wednesday. The National Society of Operative Printers and Assistants, the union concerned, agreed yesterday to allow them to share stocks of printing ink, the redistribution of which will enable them to print small editions to-morrow and for two days after that.

The provincial papers and the printing trade generally were, however, still stopped. The three parties to the dispute which has kept them idle for three weeks met for 3½ hours at the Ministry of Labour yesterday, but did not agree. They left amid recriminations and without arranging to meet again.

THE OBSERVER Notice to Readers

GeorgeBrown Pins Blame on Macleod

THE PEACEFUL PICKETS OF ESSEX ROAD

Pickets equipped with chairs relax outside the printing works of W. R. Royle and Son, Ltd., in Essex Road, Islington, London.

Insistence on Three Points

Bueno Wins Tennis Title in 82 deg.

Demonstrators Barred from Welensky

Bonus Share Issue for Mr. Fraser

By Our Economic Editor

A-Test Experts Still Split

MARSHALL & SNELGROVE

FIG. 12. Contemporary Sunday-newspaper typography exemplified in the 'class' (above) and 'popular' fields (below).

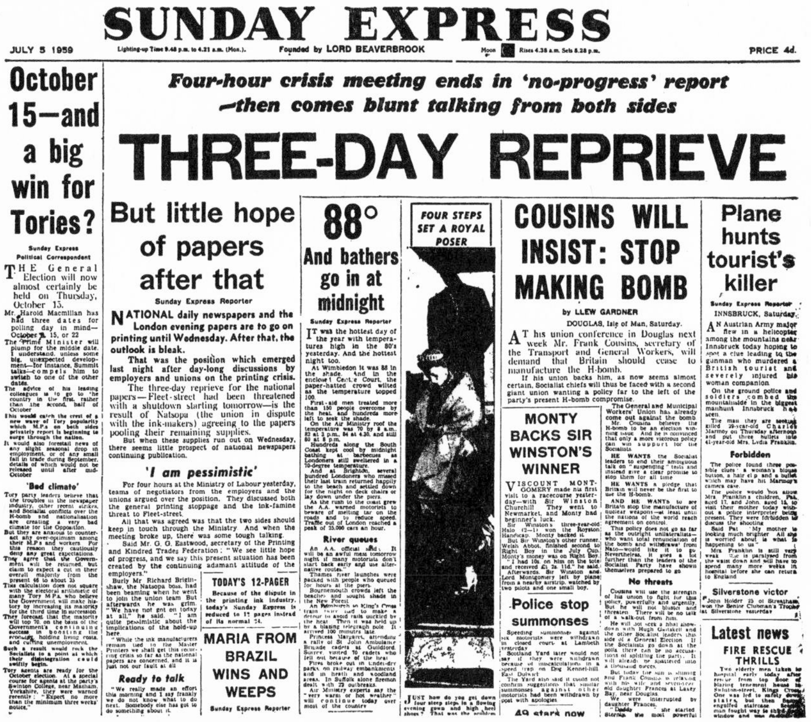

SUNDAY EXPRESS

JULY 5 1959 — Founded by LORD BEAVERBROOK — PRICE 4d.

Four-hour crisis meeting ends in 'no-progress' report —then comes blunt talking from both sides

THREE-DAY REPRIEVE

But little hope of papers after that

Sunday Express Reporter

NATIONAL daily newspapers and the London evening papers are to go on printing until Wednesday. After that, the outlook is bleak.

That was the position which emerged last night after day-long discussions by employers and unions on the printing crisis.

'I am pessimistic'

Ready to talk

TODAY'S 12-PAGER

MARIA FROM BRAZIL WINS AND WEEPS

October 15—and a big win for Tories?

Sunday Express Political Correspondent

THE General Election will now almost certainly be held on Thursday, October 15.

'Bad climate'

88° And bathers go in at midnight

River queues

FOUR STEPS SET A ROYAL POSER

COUSINS WILL INSIST: STOP MAKING BOMB

by LLEW GARDNER

DOUGLAS, Isle of Man, Saturday.

AT his union conference in Douglas next week Mr. Frank Cousins, secretary of the Transport and General Workers, will demand that Britain should cease to manufacture the H-bomb.

MONTY BACKS SIR WINSTON'S WINNER

Police stop summonses

No threats

Plane hunts tourist's killer

INNSBRUCK, Saturday.

Forbidden

Silverstone victor

Latest news

FIRE RESCUE THRILLS

initiating trade paper and the patron, the award is in the hands of three judges. These, selected annually by the committee, are one, a printer; two, a typographer; three, an eminent layman with some interest in general design. The paper judged the best designed of the year becomes the holder of a bronze plaque. First and second places, and three high commendations, are then awarded in each of three classes: (1) Mornings and Sundays; (2) Evenings; (3) Weeklies.

The Award is becoming the British counterpart of the long-established and influential Ayer Award in the United States. Each year the judges' reports have been instructive and stimulating documents. Their quality is typified in the opening sentences of the first report: 'a well-designed paper explains itself at a glance. The typographical treatment distinguishes different kinds of news stories, and separates news from features. Further, it maintains interest throughout. There should be a dynamic quality right through the issue and covering each page.' The 1954 judges went on:

> Among the qualities they looked out for were lucid and orderly layout of news and features; good choice of types and intelligent use of type variation to provide emphasis and differentiate between kinds of matter; appropriate use of white space in the display headings and elsewhere; absence of visual confusion between editorial and advertising matter; good use of pictures; high standard of reproduction of pictures; efficient and even machining; good taste in the display of front page titles and special headings; a pleasant and intelligible appearance generally, giving an impression of easy readability.

That is as sound a general directive for good newspaper typography and design as has ever been written; and with it may be cited the committee's briefing of the 1958 judges, which notably instructs them to 'pay due regard to the *nature of the readership*' in each case, and concludes: 'They will not place undue merit on rare typography or typographical refinements that cannot be seen to serve some practical purpose; neither will they penalise any entry that departs from accepted typographical practice in order to serve its readers' interests more fully.'

4 · Text Types and Text Setting

AN American newspaper management once vividly expressed a great truth about text types when they said 'people are tired of type that mumbles'. They were announcing an increase in the size of their journal's body type. Size alone does not, however, determine readability,[1] or general ease of reading, especially in terms of quantity of narrow-column matter. The relationship of type size to measure has already been touched on in Chapter 1.

Other factors are (i) *reproduction*: the type must print clearly even when stereotyped and rotary-machined, which means that it has to have a clean and open cut; (ii) *colour*: the drawing of the letter should be strong enough to avoid greyness, even with thin inks at high speeds, while retaining sufficient contrast between the thick and thin strokes to break monotony; (iii) *proportion*: the height/width relationship should be oblong, not square, and the body of the type (x-height) must not seriously encroach on the ascenders, those upper distinguishing strokes which perform an essential optical function.

By the 1920's the first two of these factors were telling heavily against the Modern Romans which, in their many variations, had been the normal newspaper text letter since John Bell introduced the first (French-inspired) 'modern' at the end of the eighteenth century. The light-faced Moderns, with their weak serifs and tendency to cramp and enclose in the details of their design (creating 'ink trap' points in the more complex lower-case letters), could not withstand the new stereotyping and machining techniques imposed by the increasing speed of newspaper production. The use of 'dry' flong cut moulding time, but required a punishing

[1] '*Readability* is that quality of type which involves maximum ease and eye comfort over a period of sustained reading. *Legibility* or *visibility* involves quickness of perception of a single line or a compact group of lines. Thus readability is the test to which body type must be subjected. Legibility is the yardstick for headlines. The two need not—in fact do not—coincide' (Arnold, op. cit., p. 24).

'The legibility of a type face has an exact parallel in the audibility of a human voice. A lecturer must make every word audible and distinct; yet within the limits of audibility lie the whole range of speaking tones from a metallic monotonous drawl to the infinitely flexible and persuasive tones of the good speaker. . . . What the book-lover calls readability is not a synonym for what the optician calls legibility' (Beatrice Warde, *The Crystal Goblet*, p. 137).

pressure; the type of rollers and the thin inks essential to the high-speed rotary exaggerated the defects of the now broken-down Modern. The only alternative was Century, the improved and somewhat stronger Modern introduced by T. L. De Vinne in America in 1896, and adopted by a number of the larger American newspapers after it was made available on the Linotype in 1904; but Century was still too weak, in the smaller sizes needed for news text, to be effective under the new mechanical conditions (Fig. 13). Since these were developing to their fullest extent in America it was natural that the first major innovation in newspaper text type should come from the Americans.

A well-designed paper explains itself at a glance. The typographical treatment distinguishes different kinds of news stories, and separates the news from features. Further, it maintains the interest throughout. **There should be a dynamic quality**

A well-designed paper explains itself at a glance. The typographical treatment distinguishes different kinds of news stories, and separates the news from features. Further, it maintains the interest **throughout. There should be a**

FIG. 13. A typical Modern Roman with Doric (Linotype No. 41) and Century with Bold.

This was the Mergenthaler Linotype Company's introduction, in the autumn of 1925, of Ionic (its formal designation is Ionic No. 5). Here was a strong-coloured letter, of open cut—no 'ink traps'—and large-bodied, which revolutionized newspaper text-setting not only in America but later in Britain and indeed in every country using the roman alphabet; within eighteen months it was adopted by 3,000 papers. It initiated a whole series of similar specially designed newspaper text types now known as the Legibility Group, a remarkable typographic achievement.

Extraordinary changes have bee:
1794 to 1835, when Halley's co
has so improved the system of c
are confident that a comet woulc

Extraordinary changes have been observable in astronomy during the interval from 1794 to 1835, when Halley's comet was

FIG. 14. Ionic and its background: left is a reproduction of the typefounders' Ionic No. 2, a jobbing letter of the 1860's, and right the 'news-text' Linotype Ionic No. 5 of the 1920's.

The peculiar thing about this American innovation was that it was neither an innovation nor American. It was an adaptation of an early nineteenth-century type face of British origin. This original Ionic, stemming from the early slab-seriffed, monotone 'Egyptians', was never intended to serve for continuous text but as a bold face (somewhat lighter than the then fashionable Clarendons and Antiques) for word emphasis. The point was specifically made by Miller and Richard, the Edinburgh founders, in their 1863 specimen of Ionic; and even that Ionic, the No. 1, had more of a text flavour than the Ionic No. 2, shown by the same founders about 1865. This square, over-big, monotone letter, more particularly in the slightly modified form later current among other British founders, and copied by their transatlantic brethren, was the true prototype of the Mergenthaler Ionic of 1925. Caslon's Ionic No. 2 shows this most clearly; and the exceptional range of sizes exhibited in that foundry's specimen books (up to the unusual 96 pt. and 120 pt.) confirmed its status as a jobbing and display, not a text, type (Fig. 14).

The Americans had underestimated a vital fact in text readability: namely, the relationship of the x-height of the letter and its set-width to the narrow measure of the newspaper column. By abnormally increasing both the x-height and the set-width, Ionic was made a face exceptionally big on its body and proportionately square. It was this bigness and squareness of Ionic which constituted its radical departure from the traditional Moderns, but the relative slenderness and medium x-height of the Moderns was an important factor in legibility, in respect of which Ionic did not therefore represent an advance.

There are sound ocular reasons for this. The eye in reading does not in fact examine the whole body of the letters in the lines it perceives; it takes them in at a glance, registering the characteristic features of the most commonly recurring letters almost instinctively. The salient portions of lower-case text lie in the upper half of the letter, along which the eye may be said to run. Thus, especially in the smaller sizes of text, the eye travels more quickly and easily if the upper part is reasonably proportioned; if, as in Ionic, the proportions of the body of the letter are abnormally increased both vertically and horizontally, the heavy reduction of the upper part —the ascender—produces a certain effect of confusion, or lack of distinctiveness, which tends to check the eye.[1]

News text readability is inevitably connected with, and conditioned by, the need to economize on space. This is a problem both of depth and width. A face like Ionic, so abnormally big on its body, was from the start too strong to be served neat; it had to be diluted with inter-linear white space; that is, instead of being set solid, it had to be set on a body at least 1 pt. or 1½ pts. larger. It will at once be seen that the 1 pt. leading of 7 pt. text, for example, involves a space loss in depth of one-seventh,

[1] A remarkable demonstration of the optical importance of the ascender (and lack of importance of the descender) was the decision of *The Times* in the spring of 1956 to substitute 8 pt. on 7½ pt. slug for its previous 7½ pt. The 8 pt. descenders were reduced half a point, involving the redesign of entire letters like 'y'; but even expert readers noticed no difference until they were told what had been done. The present writer, for instance, only remarked an improvement in the colour of the smaller type; this, in fact, was the reason for the change, since with the introduction of highly calendered mechanical printing instead of newsprint the 7½ pt. printed a little too grey.

practically 15 per cent.—or to express it concretely, over 3 in. of a standard 22-in. column. The excessive squareness, or fatness, of Ionic likewise loses space in width, in the word-count of a given number of lines; for instance, identical copy set to make a dozen lines in 9 pt., 13-em measure will yield only 55 words in Ionic as against 72 words in Times Roman and 68 words in a typical Modern.

These deficiencies in Ionic No. 5 led to the production, in 1931, of a modified successor. This 'Ionic Mark II', designated Excelsior, was fractionally lighter in weight and less extreme in its proportions; though improved by leading, it was tolerable when set solid in column measures below 12 ems. It was this improved Ionic which completed the conversion of the overwhelming majority of British newspapers to the new text style. Of similar character was Intertype Ideal.

Excelsior's advent was not the end of the Ionic story. New designs were created to meet new conditions, and between 1935 and 1940 three more faces were added to the Legibility Group to solve certain specific machining and newsprint problems of different American newspapers. Excelsior was first made fractionally heavier (Opticon) to maintain colour when running on a harder-surfaced and less absorbent newsprint, then lighter (Paragon) for papers which carried a good deal of heavy display and half-tones and thus tended to carry more ink. Intertype likewise con-

Ionic

A well-designed paper explains itself at a glance. The typographical treatment distinguishes different kinds of news stories, and separates news from *features. Further, it maintains* **interest throughout. There is a**

Ideal

A well-designed paper explains itself at a glance. The typographical treatment distinguishes different kinds of news stories, and separates news from features. **Further, it maintains interest** *throughout. There should be a*

Excelsior

A well-designed paper explains itself at a glance. The typographical treatment distinguishes different kinds of news stories, and separates news from features. *There should be a dynamic quality* **right through the issue and**

Opticon

A well-designed paper explains itself at a glance. The typographical treatment distinguishes different kinds of news stories, and separate news from *features. Further, it maintains* **interest throughout. There shou**

Paragon

A well-designed paper explains itself at a glance. The typographical treatment distinguishes different kinds of news stories, and separates news from *features. Further, it maintains* **interest throughout. There is a**

Corona

A well-designed paper explains itself at a glance. The typographical treatment distinguishes different kinds of news stories, and separate news from features. Further, *it maintains interest throughout.* **There should be a dynamic quality**

FIG. 15. The 'Legibility Group' of Linotype newspaper text faces (Opticon and Corona are American only) with the similar Intertype Ideal; all are set in 8 pt. and show their bold and italic.

tributed Regal as a modified Ideal. Last came Corona, described as a 'composite of the entire Legibility Group', designed to meet the distortions of abnormal mat shrinkage in stereotyping and, as its Mergenthaler creator said, 'with special emphasis on the factor of space economy'.[1] Size for size Corona averaged between 80 and 90 words more than Ionic in a standard 22-in. column. It is in many ways the best of the Linotype Ionic group but, like Opticon, it has not so far been available in this country (Fig. 15). Royal, the Intertype version of Corona, has now (January 1960) been introduced, with certain alternative characters, by *The Scotsman*.

From the newspaper printer's viewpoint Ionic and its successors had, and have, a particular virtue: namely, an exceptionally full range of sizes, each alternatively combined with the appropriate Italic, Doric, or Bold. The Modern Romans had been cut haphazard for machine-setting (a few sizes here, a few sizes there, distinguished by numbers only) and a complete repertory of a uniform news-text was virtually impossible. The Legibility Group brought both standardization and a hitherto unavailable size variety. To the usual sizes from 5 pt. to 10 pt. (or 12 pt.) there were added fractional between-sizes of notable practical utility; for instance, 6½ pt. and 6¾ pt. (the Americans cut the equally useful 7½ pt. and 8½ pt.).

When everything has been said about the Ionic group, its virtues as well as its vices, it is useful to return to the fundamental criticism already indicated. This was authoritatively summed up more than twenty years ago in these words:

> *Ionic* was originated as a heavy face. At no time, until the present, was it deemed sound typographical practice to use the face for texts of any considerable length such as the nature of books and newspapers requires. The American innovation, therefore, consists in reviving the *Ionic* for newspaper text use. This innovation seems to require a fuller justification than has so far been forthcoming, for, while it cannot be doubted that the average reader is glad to be provided with a full-coloured text type, it does not follow that this is the only important factor in readability. Certainly *Ionic* is materially better, technically, than most of the 'modern' founts made available during the past forty years to line-composed newspapers. It is open and clear in design; it is well drawn and perfect in cut. But a similarly high degree of technical ability given to the old-fashioned 'modern' would have transformed it into a very desirable face. It is more than probable that such a revised 'modern' would be more readable than the admittedly readable American *Ionic*.[2]

The Americans, however, were not the only innovators; and the British innovation, the evolving in 1930–2 of Times Roman (Times New

[1] C. H. Griffith, quoted by John E. Allen, *Newspaper Designing* (New York, 1947), pp. 83, 92.

[2] *The Monotype Recorder*, vol. xxxv, no. 1 (Spring 1936), pp. 3–6. The entire article, 'The Editorial Text', is worth study; unsigned, it was in fact by Stanley Morison.

Roman as it was first called), was characterized precisely by the prescribed transformation of the old-fashioned Modern Roman. This was the crucial stage in the design of what has since become a universal letter (adapted even for Greek and Cyrillic), enriching the entire field of display with its variety of weights and styles and extensively used for the setting of every conceivable text—book, periodical, advertising, catalogue, time-table—in addition to newspaper text. The problem as it was initially seen in Printing House Square had nothing of these immense implications; it was a problem of improving newspaper text, the text, moreover, of a particular newspaper, *The Times*. Before the crucial stage mentioned was reached there was elaborate experimentation and the most thoroughgoing expert and collective consideration of the principles involved. The experiments began in the summer of 1929. A number of existing founts were tried, including Ionic, together with a short ascender-descender adaptation of Eric Gill's Perpetua; dummy pages were set in selected founts, plated and run on newsprint under normal press conditions. Preliminary experiments were followed, in 1930, by the circulation to the technical committee appointed by *The Times* management of a *Memorandum on a Proposal to Revise the Typography of The Times.*

Prepared by Stanley Morison, this 38 pp. Royal 4to—of which twenty-five copies only were privately printed in *The Times* office—has been rightly called 'one of the most significant documents of XX century typography'.[1] Morison's historical and technical survey led directly to the decision to retain the slender proportions of Modern Roman, to counter its weak colour by relating its weight to that of Ionic, to avoid the Ionic monotone by approximating more closely to the traditional thick and thin structure. The *Memorandum* examined in some detail the problem of legibility and its relation to possible modifications in letter-form, with particular reference to serif-structure. The 1926 *Report on the Legibility of Print*, drawn up by R. L. Pyke for the Medical Research Council, gave Morison and his Printing House Square colleagues some scientific basis which the Americans lacked (their Ionic having appeared in 1925). To all this had to be added the consideration of quality, for the new face, as the *Memorandum* put it, had to be 'worthy of *The Times*—masculine, English, direct, simple, not more novel than it behoveth to be novel, or more novel than logic is novel in newspaper typography, and absolutely free from faddishness and frivolity'. To be 'worthy of *The Times*' also connoted a certain elegance, an 'urbanity' as it has been aptly said.

The face that finally emerged met all these technical and aesthetic

[1] Peggy Lang, 'Times Roman: a Revaluation' (*Alphabet and Image*, no. 2, Sept. 1946, pp. 5–17)—the best technical summary of the design of Times Roman, with further references. See also the *Monotype Recorder* article already cited.

requirements in a highly satisfactory manner. It combined legibility, strong colour, and space-economy. It did so by adapting to the proportions of the Modern the diagonal stress and sloped serifs of the Old Face. Since the stress in a Modern face is vertical, colour can only be increased by thickening the curved strokes of the key lower-case letters horizontally, i.e. by increasing the set-width and wasting space, or alternatively by encroaching on the counter, the interior white, and thus reducing the clarity of the letter. In the Old Face stress the thickening of the curved strokes is at an angle and avoids both difficulties. As for the serifs, they were firmly bracketed and strong in appearance and yet highly stylish in their sharpness of cut.

A well-designed paper explains itself at a glance. The typographical treatment distinguishes different kinds of news stories, and separates news from features. Further, it maintains interest throughout. There should *be a dynamic quality right through the issue* **and covering every page. Even if a story has**

A well-designed paper explains itself at a glance. The typographical treatment distinguishes different kinds of news stories, and separates news *interest throughout. There should be* **a dynamic quality right through the**

A well-designed paper explains itself at a glance. The typographical treatment distinguishes different kinds of news stories, and separates news from features. Further, it maintains interest throughout. There should be a dynamic *quality right through the issue and*

A well-designed paper explains itself at a glance. The typographical treatment distinguishes different kinds of news stories, and separates news from features. Further, it *maintains interest throughout.*

A well-designed paper explains itself at a glance. The typographical treatment distinguishes different kinds of **news stories, and separates news from features. Further, it maintains interest throughout. There should be a**

FIG. 16. Times Roman in four text sizes, 6, 7½, 8, 9 pt. with its italic and bold; the large size in wide measure (14 pt.) exemplifies the special features of the bold's design.

The drawings for the new face were prepared in *The Times* office by the end of 1930; between then and the paper's appearance in its new text and headline dress (on 3 October 1932) a vast task had to be accomplished. The first trial fount, the 9 pt., was first subjected to letter-by-letter criticism, set in columns to determine word-count, made up into dummy pages, plated, printed rotary, and submitted to an oculist, whose recommendations led to further revisions.[1] Some indication of the magnitude of the work can be deduced from the statement that for the 38 founts needed initially for text and headings some 7,048 punches were cut, of which 1,075 were rejected. More is said in Chapter 7 on the headline types in the Times range; here it will be suitable to refer to the notable Bold

[1] Stanley Morison, *Monotype Recorder*, vol. xxi, no. 246 (Sept.–Oct. 1932), pp. 12–15.

designed to sort with the Times Roman. Times Bold is not the normal bold variant of a roman letter, but rather a companion bold, of the same set-width, ingeniously thickened inside the letter without sacrificing the sharpness of the roman; it is bolder *vis-à-vis* its roman than are most bolds. While the caps. of the Bold relate closely to those of the Roman, the lower-case has a modern rather than an old-face flavour, with horizontal instead of sloped top serifs (Fig. 16).

At first Times Roman was cut only in the three text sizes ($5\frac{1}{2}$ pt., 7 pt., 9 pt.) then needed in Printing House Square. Now it exists in a text range more extensive even than the Ionic group; from the remarkable $4\frac{3}{4}$ pt. (Claritas) to 14 pt. for line-composition with either italic or bold, and on the Monotype likewise, with the addition of a display range up to 72 pt. in the Roman and Italic (Series 327) and the Bold and Bold Italic (Series 334).

The versatility of Times Roman as a book, periodical, and general text face tended to conceal the essential fact of its origin: namely, that it was designed for the text of a newspaper in a class of its own. The impeccable presswork and high-grade paper of *The Times* is necessary to exhibit Times Roman in its proper brilliance. Among nationals it was significant that only two 'class' journals, the *Observer* and the *Financial Times*, with high production standards, installed it. In the provinces the picture was different. Proprietors were attracted by the space-economy of Times Roman, as before they had been by the strong colour of Ionic, and quite a number of local papers, both dailies and weeklies, went over to Times. Rough presswork and common newsprint gave the superb face little chance, however, and it began also to be appreciated that the stylishness of the close-set Times had to be paid for by excessive matrix replacement, due to the speedier breakdown of the ultra-thin sidewalls. It became clear that a plainer, general duty news-text was required, a redesigning of the slender, space-saving Modern without the Old Face elegance and the sidewall-weakening close-set of Times Roman. At last, in 1954, two new text faces were independently launched, one British (Linotype Jubilee), the other American (Intertype Imperial); they are shown in Fig. 17.

The virtue of Jubilee is that it stands, in a sense, midway between Times and Excelsior. It meets modern stereotyping and rotary machining requirements, being as open and sturdy as Excelsior and as big on its body.[1] But in set-width it approximates to the economy of Times; in the normal body sizes in a narrow newspaper column its character count per

[1] Despite this equal x-height, Jubilee does not appear quite as large as Excelsior, because it is less wide and slightly lighter in weight. In 9 pt., Jubilee's ideal size, this does not matter; but in 6 pt. and 7 pt. care needs to be taken that a reasonably strong colour is maintained during machining. A grey page of 7 pt. Jubilee is not easy on the eye.

Jubilee, 7, 8, 9 pt.

A well-designed paper explains itself at a glance. The typographical treatment distinguishes different kinds of news stories, and separates news from features. Further, it maintains interest throughout. There should be a dynamic **quality right through the issue and**

A well-designed paper explains itself at a glance. The typographical treatment distinguishes different kinds of news stories, and separates news from features. Further, it maintains interest throughout. There **should be a dynamic quality right**

A well-designed paper explains itself at a glance. The typographical treatment distinguishes different kinds of news stories, and separate news from features. Further, it maintains interest **throughout. There should be a**

A well-designed paper explains itself at a glance. The typographical treatment distinguishes different kinds of news stories, and separates news from features. Further, it maintains interest throughout. There should be a

Imperial 7, 8, 9 pt.

A well-designed paper shows itself at a glance. The typographical treatment distinguishes different kinds of news stories, and separates news from features. Further, it maintains interest throughout. There should be **a dynamic quality right through the**

A well-designed paper shows itself at a glance. The typographical treatment distinguishes different kinds of news stories, and separates news from features. Further, it maintains interest throughout. **There should be a dynamic quality**

A well-designed paper shows itself at a glance. The typographical treatment distinguishes different kinds of news stories, and separates news from features. Further, it maintains interest **throughout. There should**

A well-designed paper shows itself at a glance. The typographical treatment distinguishes different kinds of news stories, and separates news from features. Further, it maintains interest throughout. There should

FIG. 17. The two principal contemporary news texts, Linotype Jubilee and Intertype Imperial, showing roman with bold in three sizes and the striking italic separately.

line is only one or two less than Times and at least three more than Excelsior. Its serifs are blunt, as in Excelsior, but not left square; the simple device of chamfering the ends gives finish and sharpness. Of particular importance is the shading; this has been contrived with special care so as to strike a balance between the old-face contrast of thicks and thins in Times and the even monotone of Ionic-Excelsior, while increasing the white in the counters and providing for markedly more side-space (i.e. space between the letters) than would normally be expected in a face so economical in set. One example will show the delicacy of the design calculation here. Taking an old-face thick-thin contrast in 10 pt., Jubilee transfers approximately 0·001 in. of shading from the thick stroke to the thin; this transfer of shading is the means of achieving the open counters and the side-spacing. That extra side space provides the needed thickening of the matrix walls.

In general character Jubilee is an original design, combining ease-on-the-eye with a note of style that was always lacking in the Ionic-Excelsior group. It can be set solid, though it takes kindly to a 1 pt. lead; more than 1 pt., in sizes below 9 pt., weakens it too much. It is available in the full normal range of news text sizes from 6 pt. to 12 pt., duplexed either with italic or bold; the italic is particularly good—its weight the same as the roman, its curvature handled to get a close, smooth fit—the bold vigorous and well differentiated from the roman.

Jubilee has the additional advantage that, as tests have shown, it is well suited for photogravure reproduction. Beatrice Warde's examination, by photomicrographs, of the performance of a number of text faces in different processes of reproduction suggests that no existing face is equally satisfactory for rotary letterpress and photogravure,[1] so Jubilee may achieve a significant versatility.

Nevertheless, Jubilee is not the final answer to the problem of that 'plainer, general duty news-text'. The description of it as standing mid-way between Times and Excelsior is not absolutely accurate; its top serifs have the old-face slope, the cut of several lower-case letters is near-Times in character and elegance (the 'k' and 's' for instance), while some of the caps. are perhaps even more stylish (the 'C', the slightly splayed 'M' and the 'R', to cite only three). Thus it leans more towards Times than Excelsior; when the present writer introduced it into his own paper, an astute compositor qualified a general approval of the face with the remark that it was 'a bit bookish'. A run-of-the-mill text type for news-papers should not really be one suitable for book setting; and it is true that Jubilee would not be out of place in book work (Fig. 18).

While Jubilee has already been adopted by a substantial number of papers, ranging from the Outram group in Glasgow and the Westminster Press papers in Birmingham to the *Morning Advertiser*, the *Daily Worker*, and an assortment of local weeklies, it scores best in the 'class' or 'quality' journal (e.g. the *Glasgow Herald*). Jubilee meets the case when neither Ionic-Excelsior nor Times are really satisfactory. It has effectively taken the place of Times in the award-winning Beckett weekly group (the *Worthing Herald* and its companions). Nationals like the *Daily Telegraph* and *Sunday Times* benefited greatly when they went over from Ionic to Jubilee for their text early in 1959; following the example of *The Times*, mentioned above (p. 53 n.), they are using an 8 pt. face, with shortened descenders, cast on a 7½ pt. body.

Intertype Imperial, though quite independent in design, has something of the smartness of cut of Jubilee (most noticeable in the caps.) but is fractionally bigger on its body and wider. It saves space as compared, say, with Excelsior, though not quite so much as Jubilee; and above 8 pt. the relative space-saving of Imperial declines. Its designer, Edwin W. Shaar,

[1] *The Bowater Papers*, no. 3 (1954), pp. 42–46.

has told how he sought to meet the 'real challenge' of news-text design—the conflicting demands of larger body and narrower measure, the need for good general page colour and strong matrix walls, the harmonizing of the italic and bold with the roman: in the first trial 8 pt. it was found that the minute increase in weight of 0·0005 in. 'made all the difference in the world to the production of a vigorous page'.[1] He notes that he introduced some Transitional characteristics to avoid monotony.

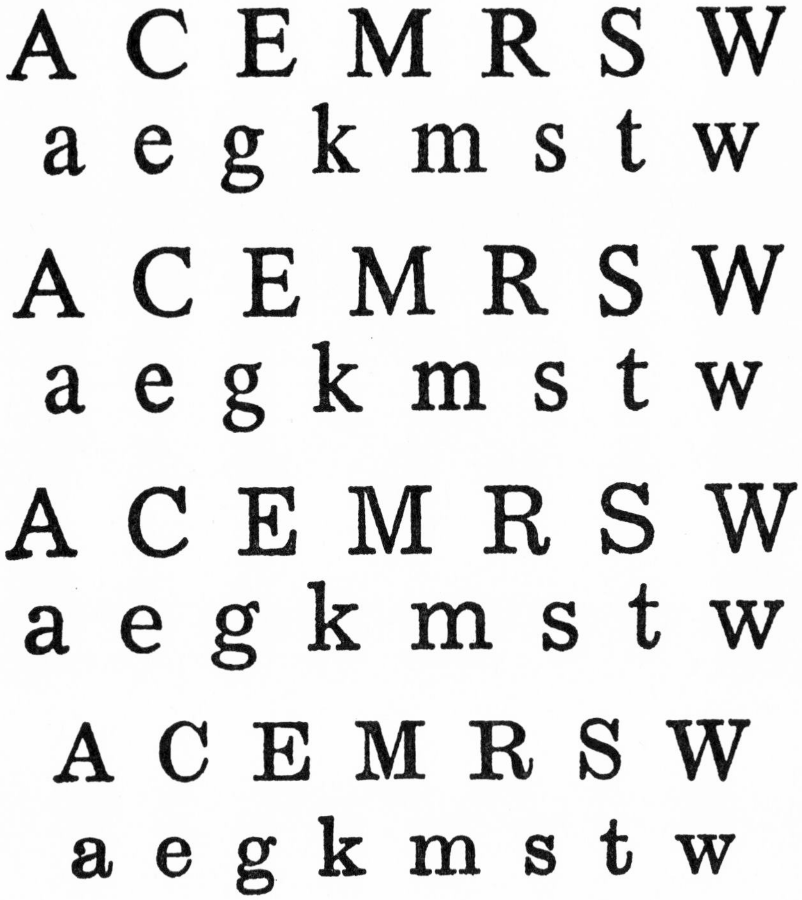

FIG. 18. These photographic enlargements of selected letters in Times, Jubilee, Excelsior, and a Modern Roman (No. 41) illustrate the differences in letter-structure.

Imperial may perhaps be regarded as a much-smartened, 'contemporary' (as they say) descendant of the Ionic-Excelsior group, towards whose heavy weight and even colour it tends to lean; the official Intertype

[1] Edwin W. Shaar, 'A New Look for News' (*Penrose Annual*, 1958).

descriptions say 'weight of face was paramount' and stress that it is 'first and foremost a near-monotone type face'. It has a good bold and an italic as remarkable in its way as Jubilee's, though with slightly less slope ('a happy medium between the cursive and purely sloped roman effect' says Shaar). Sizes available—5½ pt. to 10 pt., and in the United States up to 14 pt.—cover all normal text needs.

SIZE, MEASURE, AND STYLE OF TEXT SETTING

First consideration in determining a newspaper's necessary range of text sizes must be the size of the main run of the text—the 'body of the paper'. Traditionally this ranges around 7 pt. or 8 pt.; the pre-war trend to 8 pt., reversed under the stress of wartime and post-war paper restrictions, is now (1960) again marked. Even where the run of the paper adheres to the smaller size—down to the 6 pt. range in the case of some local weeklies—the front page uses 8 pt. as its body face; the main news page of *The Times*, the 'bill' page, is now set throughout in 9 pt. A careful balance has to be struck between the reader's eye comfort and editorial space requirements. This affects not only the body size but whether the type chosen should be set solid or leaded. It has already been noted that big-faced types, like the Ionic group, require at least 1 pt. leading to maximize their legibility (the Americans frequently leaded them 1½ pts.). Less overpowering faces respond well to the opening-up of half-point leading, e.g. 7 on 7½ pt. or 7½ on 8 pt. But leading requires very careful management; too much is worse than too little; as leading increases, the colour of the type in mass is lightened and its impact weakened. The degree of permissible leading is determined by the size of type and the measure. A 9 pt. or 10 pt. set wide measure will take a 2 pt. lead; but the same leading of 7 pt. in narrow measure will dilute the face far too much. One London suburban weekly group sets 6½ on 8 pt., in 10-em measure, for the body of its papers; the dilution is to the detriment of legibility (Fig. 19).

In practice few papers, in this country at any rate, feel able to afford what is thought to be the space luxury of leading. The general desire is to select a text face which appears well set solid. It can always be argued, of course, that 8 pt. set solid is not as easy on the reader's eye as 7 pt. opened up by being set on an 8 pt. slug; but in fact this can only be determined by experiment in terms of the type face, measure, and presswork of the given paper. In any event, with the short paragraphing now practised, the leading of paragraphs (say 2 pts.) as normal make-up procedure, goes far towards making the page as airy as half-point or 1 pt. line-leading.

The essential relationship of size and measure has to be borne in mind throughout. Before the war the most usual newspaper column measure was 13½ ems (seven to the page), which well suited an 8 pt. body; the wartime economy change to the 11½-em column (eight to the page) was accompanied by a general adoption of 7 pt. for the body; newspapers which went farther still, to the 10 or 10½-em column (nine to the page), found 7 pt. a maximum size for continuous matter; by the same token, so did the half-size 'tabloids', standardizing on the abnormally narrow 9-em column. The general point may be simply illustrated: in a 9-em column a fractional 6 pt.—say, a 6½ pt. set on 7 pt. slug—will be perfectly readable while in a double-column intro. setting (23½ ems for example), a 7 pt. will be far too small, or a 10 pt., set in a 10½-em column, far too large, for comfortable reading. The 11½-em column has come to stay, though rising newsprint prices have driven those huge consumers, the nationals, to drop to 11¼ ems and thus economize in newsprint by slightly reducing the width of their broadsheet. In either case 7 pt. continues to be a suitable body size, though 8 pt. has its advantages, depending on the face. An 8 pt. Times or Jubilee is narrower than a 7 pt. Ionic or Excelsior (Fig. 20).

The minimum practical range of sizes is three—the body plus one larger size for introductions, leaders, and so forth, and one smaller size for classified advertisements and other minimum-size matter. Given a 7 pt. or 8 pt. for the body of the paper this requires a 9 pt. or 10 pt., a 6 pt. or 5½ pt. (or even 5 pt.) respectively. This is the relationship of the three text sizes used by *The Times* (now actually 9 pt., 8/7½ pt., 4¾ pt.). A glance at that newspaper shows the considerable variety that can be obtained by the manipulation of this minimum three-size range. Main stories and articles can be set entirely in the largest size, while the smallest size enables lengthy subsidiary matter to be got in economically. By leading the 9 pt. it can be

A well-designed paper explains itself at a glance. The typographical treatment distinguishes different kinds of news stories, and separates the news from features. Further, it

A well-designed paper explains itself at a glance. The typographical treatment distinguishes different kinds of news stories, and separates the news from features. Further, it

A well-designed paper explains itself at a glance. The typographical treatment distinguishes different kinds of news stories, and separates the news from features. Further, it

A well-designed paper explains itself at a glance. The typographical treatment distinguishes different kinds of news stories, and separates the news from features. Further, it

A well-designed paper explains itself at a glance. The typographical treatment distinguishes different kinds of news stories, and separates the news from features. Further, it

FIG. 19. What leading does: these paragraphs in 7 pt. Excelsior are leaded respectively from 1, 1½ ('thin'), 2, 3 ('thick'), to 6 pts. (nonpareil). The diluting effect is noticeable.

given the necessary air of extra size and importance for the leading articles.

A well-selected three-size range leaves one problem unsolved, however: that of the short introduction, set over more than one column, for the paper's main story. This is discussed in detail below. Here it has to be noted that when we turn to the more elaborate text treatments normal in the popular nationals and their provincial companions, the various styles of intro. setting may easily require four additional sizes above the body size—say 8 pt., 10 pt., 12 pt. and 14 pt. It is also usual to find that an intermediate size (e.g. 6 pt.) will be carried between the body size and the minimum 5 or 5½ pt. Thus the three-size range rapidly swells to an eight-size range, with corresponding demands for additional composing machine capacity.

A well-designed paper explains itself at a glance. The typographical treatment distinguishes different kinds of news stories, and separates news from features. Further, it maintains interest throughout. There should be a dynamic quality right through the issue and covering every

A well-designed paper explains itself at a glance. The typographical treatment distinguishes different kinds of news stories, and separates news from features.

A well-designed paper explains itself at a glance. The typographical treatment distinguishes different kinds of news stories, and separates news from features. Further, it maintains interest throughout. There should be a dynamic quality right through the issue and covering every page. Even if a story has been pushed in at the last moment to fill a

FIG. 20. Relating size and measure: the small 6½ on 7 pt. Ionic is effective in the narrow 9-em measure while the 10 pt. Ionic is too large for 10½ ems, and the 7 pt. Excelsior set double-column (23½ ems) carries too much in the line for ease of reading.

Given the technical resources of a large newspaper organization it is no doubt highly agreeable for the editorial department to be able to draw upon as extended a range of text sizes as possible. But where the organization is unable to provide what after all amounts to a complete range of available sizes between 5 pt. and 12 pt. inclusive, it may prove a blessing in disguise. It cannot be emphasized too often that the mastery of minimum resources, so long as they are adequate for the basic requirements, produces better typography than the unimaginative handling of resources that are unlimited.

Consideration of the range of text sizes introduces the question of the secondary alphabet with which the normal roman is duplexed in those sizes. This duplexing provides a parallel range of either 'black' or italic, essential for emphasis, variant text settings and the like. The traditional newspaper 'black' in this country has always been the squat and chubby

Sanserif known in the trade as Doric; and this is still very largely used. But Ionic and its successors brought a seriffed Bold Face as the alternative and many newspapers have come to prefer this.

In general the Bold Face makes a more suitable 'black' than the Doric; it harmonizes with its associated Roman, while providing the necessary bold contrast (Fig. 15). The Doric does not relate at all and its contrast is a jarring and violent one; it has the added disadvantage that as an over-weighted and ill-proportioned Sanserif letter, it is not easily legible in mass in its small sizes, while in its larger sizes (10 pt. or 12 pt.) it is extremely ugly. For setting boxes, panels, or those special stories for which a contrasting text is desired the Bold Face solves the problem in far more readable a fashion than the Doric. At the same time it should be observed that, in the Ionic-Excelsior group, the lower one drops down the scale of sizes the less differentiated are the Roman and the Bold Face. In 5 pt. and 5½ pt. there is so little effective difference in colour that the Bold Face practically ceases to have any value for emphasis.

The contrast of Bold with Roman is much more satisfactory in Times, even in the minimum 4¾ pt. and 5½ pt. sizes; the same is true of Jubilee and Imperial, which thus set an important pattern for any future news-text design (Figs. 16, 17). These three faces, particularly Jubilee, contribute something new in respect of italic, conventionally held in this country to be unreadable as text; the French and Italian custom of using italic for editorials, or for a lengthy special news-dispatch, has not yet crossed the Channel. Jubilee's stout and close-fitting italic, as strongly coloured as the Roman, may well cause the ancient convention to be questioned (Fig. 17). On slug machines the italic duplexing goes with SMALL CAPITALS, whose use in modern newspaper practice is restricted to the caps.-and-smalls style for personal names and titles in some leader columns (e.g. *The Times*), and occasionally for date-lines.

THE SETTING OF INTRODUCTIONS

In its simplest form, taking the minimum three-size range outlined above, the *introduction* (the opening paragraph, or paragraphs, of a news story, generally abbreviated to 'intro.') will be set in the size above the body, leading directly into the body for the main portion of the story; a paragraph of 9 pt. will be followed by the rest of the story in 7 pt. There are two reasons why stories of any prominence should always open with a paragraph in a larger size of type. First, the reader's attention is caught and held; if the introduction is in the same size as the body the effect is flat, the smallness of the body-size seeming to be emphasized. Second is the normal journalistic practice of making the opening paragraph—the lead—convey the principal item of news in the story; setting in a larger size suitably signalizes the lead and its interest for the reader.

In single-column setting to use one larger size for the intro. and then go straight into the body solves most problems. But a refinement practised by many nationals on the longer single-column stories, especially main single-column tops, is to insert a paragraph in an intermediate size between the intro. and the body. Such a story might run in 9 pt., then 8 pt. into 7 pt.; or this triple arrangement may be employed to cover a larger intro. size—say 10 pt., running into 8 pt. and 7 pt.; on front-page single-column tops of special prominence it may be found expanded into a quadruple arrangement—12 pt., 10 pt., 8 pt., 7 pt. (Fig. 21).

The main principle here is what may be called shading down. The larger the type size of the intro. the more intermediate sizes will need to be inserted to shade easily down to the body size. In this way the entire opening portion of the story is given a sense of importance and the reader's eye is not suddenly jerked from a large-size intro. to a text whose smallness would thereby be irritatingly emphasized. Whether the elaboration of shading down is not sometimes overdone is another matter; it relates to the whole question of economy versus luxuriance in typographical resources to which reference has already been made. If the intro. is in 9 pt. it is certainly only a refinement to insert a paragraph in 8 pt. before descending to the 7 pt. body; if the intro. is in 10 pt. it is a necessity, for it may be taken as a general rule that the drop in size in shading down should not exceed 2 points, certainly in single column.

THESE are one or two of the main points in the physical development of English journalism.

By "journalism" I mean the printing of news; by "physical development" I mean the aspect of the paper.

It is an essential condition of the journal that it should be issued with a certain frequency; and that frequency greater than once a year, or once a quarter, or once a month.

Fortnightly appearance seems not to have become, for any time, a workable term; the conventional measure of frequency within the month has always been the week. English journalism started with weekly publication.

THESE are one or two of the main points in the physical development of English journalism. By "journalism" I mean the printing of news.

Fortnightly appearance seems not to have become, for any time, a workable term; the conventional measure of frequency within the month has always been the week.

THESE are one or two of the main points in the physical development of English journalism. By "journalism" I mean the printing of news.

Fortnightly appearance seems not to have become, for any time a workable term; the conventional measure of frequency within the month has always been the week.

FIG. 21. Varying styles of single-column intros. for 7 pt. text, all set in Excelsior: left, the full treatment—12, 10, and 8 pt.; right, top, opening in 10 pt.; below, opening in 9 pt.

So much for intro. setting in single-column tops. Down-column stories of some weight should also be given a larger size intro., though less in weight than the tops. For example, if a 9 pt., 8 pt., 7 pt. run were the practice on tops, 8 pt. to 7 pt. would be sound on the down-column stories; if the style for tops opened in 10 pt. the down-column stories could open in 9 pt. In the latter case it is important to see that the intros. are kept short—not more than half a dozen lines in standard 11½-em measure.

THESE are one or two of the main points which will stand out in considering the physical development of English journalism. By "journalism" I mean the printing of news.

By "physical development" I mean the size and folding of the paper, the size and display of the type, and all the features which contribute to the aspect of the paper.

It is an essential condition of the journal that it should be issued with a certain frequency; and that greater than once a month.

Fortnightly appearance seems not to have become, for any time, a workable term; the conventional measure of frequency within the month has always been the week. English journalism started with weekly publication.

FIG. 22. Double-column intro. styles: above are 12 pt. Metroblack and Metrolite leading into 9 pt. and 7 pt. Jubilee single-column; below are double-column alternatives, each in 12 pt., respectively Bodoni Bold, Century Bold, Caslon Heavy, Metromedium, Vogue Extra Bold (note the concluding comment).

These are one or two of the main points which will stand out in considering the *physical development of*

These are one or two of the main points which will stand out in considering the physical develop-

These are one or two of the *main* points which will stand out in considering the *physical* development of

These are one or two of the main points which will stand out in considering the physical *development of English*

These are one or two of the *main* points which stand out in considering the *physical* development

[Retain Vogue standard characters A M N V W e g v w but use alternates C G J Q i j t. Avoid the standard C G J Q i j t, alternate A M N V W e g v w]

Generally the length of intros. is of primary importance for the appearance of the paper. Nothing looks more clumsy or unbalanced than an over-lengthy intro., particularly in single column (where the problem for obvious reasons most obtrudes itself), and the well-conducted newspaper will always prescribe maximum wordages for intros. Such maximums will, of course, vary according to the column measure and the letter-count of the text face; and differentiation between intros. on tops and on down-column stories is necessary. An intro. that looks over-long and killing on a down-column story with, say, a three-line 18 pt. heading will appear normal on a top with a four-line 30 pt. heading; vice versa, the short intro. suitable down column looks insignificant on a full top.

Now for double-column, three-column, and special-measure intros. for splash and other lead stories. For the shorter down-page 'doubles' the largest normal size of text, say 9 pt., provides a perfectly adequate double-column intro. But for tops or page leads with double-column or three-column intros., 12 pt. or even 14 pt. is needed for the opening one or two paragraphs, dropping through at least one intermediate size to the text. It is partly convention, partly necessity (since most text faces do not run to 14 pt.), that for the largest intro. size a different type face is employed. Necessary or not, the convention is acceptable, since it contributes a useful note of variety, though the type needs care in its selection. A suitable face needs to be bold, roman, and either Sanserif or else in general accordance with the typography of the paper. For a Sans the choice is easy —since the face has to be machine-set—and is the one made by many newspapers, the sturdy but sharp Linotype Metro series, presenting an

A

THESE are one or two of the main points which stand out in considering the physical development of English journalism. By "journalism" I

B

THESE are one or two of the main points which will stand out in considering the physical development of English journalism. By "journalism" I

C

These are one or two of the main points which will stand out in considering the physical development of English journalism. By "journalism" I

D

THESE ARE ONE OR TWO OF THE MAIN POINTS which will stand out in considering the physical devopment of English journal-

E

THESE are one or two of the main points which will stand out in considering the physical development of Eng-

F

THESE are one or two of the main points which will stand out in considering the physical development of Eng-

FIG. 23. Drop letters, good and bad: (A) too small, and set with the ugly hanging indention; (B) correct size, set flush, first word in caps.; (C) correct and flush also, but first word kept lower-case; (D) set with hanging indention, adding to the ugliness by setting the opening words in caps. with turnover to the second line; (E) and (F) contrast dissonance and consonance—the Cheltenham Bold drop clashes with the Metrolite intro., which calls for a Metroblack drop.

admirable black and a convenient contrasting light, or an agreeable medium, with italic; of the other modern Sanserifs available on the slug machine Intertype Vogue is too mannered and fancy unless some of the alternative characters are used. Under the second head the bold versions of Bodoni, Century, Caslon may all be counted suitable (Fig. 22).

Indention of intros. is practised on many papers as a means of giving extra emphasis. The usual style is to indent 1 en of the body each end in single column, 1 em in double column. In narrow measures this style of intro. indention presents obvious difficulties in single column; but where it is practicable it has value in lightening the appearance of the page. Particularly when the intro. is in a contrasting bold face with a drop letter, indention—notably the reverse (hanging) style explained below—helps to set it off.

DROP (INITIAL) LETTERS

The use of two- or three-line drop (initial) letters for intros. is common practice in this country, though it is still eschewed by 'class' journals like *The Times* or the *Manchester Guardian*; and it has never taken root in America. The drop letter imports into the news columns a typographical feature traditionally reserved for the small advertisements and for the main lines in the old-fashioned semi-displayed advertisements not now often seen; or, to regard it from another aspect, retains in the news columns a style which the earliest news-pamphlets and sheets naturally took over from traditional book practice.

It can be argued that drop letters are superfluous, and impart a bookish or magazine-like air to news stories; let the headline provide the display, it may be said, and let the text be text. An added technical consideration is that the use of drop letters fractionally increases setting time, though only if allowance has to be made for the cutting-in of a movable drop, and presents certain problems of sub-editorial style. On the other hand, it has to be conceded that the drop letter does impart an extra element of display to an intro. and thus contributes to the variety and colour of the typography of a page as a whole. In any event the practice is now firmly established and the important thing is to see that it is agreeably carried out (Fig. 23). This involves the following:

(1) *Typographical consonance*: drop letters should agree with the general typographical display of the paper. If the headline dress is Century, then Century should be used for the drops; if Bodoni, that should be used, and so on. Too often the drop letters are ignored, even in elaborately restyled journals, and are left to the whim or convenience of the printer. With an elegant Bodoni dress incongruous Cheltenham Bold

drops can be seen; or at the best the drop letters will be the conventional and usually weak news titlings surviving, via the advertisement columns, from antique days.

The correct specification is simple: use suitably sized Bold Roman Caps. of the paper's main display face. This will make a fitting drop for either a roman or a bold-face intro., though not for a contrasting Sanserif intro., where a bold Sans drop needs to be used; a bold seriffed drop with a Sans intro. jars badly. The technical point may be noted here that the normal procedure is to set drops on the machine, by running in a display matrix at the beginning of the first line; this is cast as an overhanging letter, its bottom portion being accommodated on the appropriate blank left at the beginning of the succeeding line. The wide range of Linotype and Intertype display faces means that suitable machine-set drops can be provided to match any normal headline display.

(2) *Size and fit*: in general drop letters should not be more than two-line, i.e. should not exceed in depth two lines of the text. Three-line (or even larger) drop letters are only suitable for large-scale feature treatments (see Chapter 11). But a technical refinement is worth noting at this point. It is misleading to conclude that to provide a two-line drop for a given text size any capital twice the size is suitable, for there are very few series of full-face 'titling' caps. available. Especially when working with machine drops it is necessary, if it is desired to have the drops registering the full two-line depth, to measure precisely the face depth of the caps in the series to be employed. It will then be found, for example, that if Bodoni Bold is the choice it will be necessary to use the 24 pt. caps. to cover two lines of 9 pt. text (the actual face depth of 24 pt. Bodoni Bold caps. being just under 18 pt.), and so on. True two-line initials are available for slug machines, but they are the conventional news titlings already mentioned and in any case offer nothing weighty enough to sort with 9 pt. or above. The only two-line initials made for specific faces are in the Times range (two sizes, 9½ pt. and 11 pt., intended as small advertisement drops for the 4¾ pt. and 5½ pt. text) and Jubilee (two-line 8 pt. and 10 pt.).

The sound tradition that drop letters should be set flush with the text they cover is almost universally ignored in newspaper composing rooms, the last stronghold of the debased Victorian practice of setting drops with a hanging indention. A superfluous blob of white thus appears, with the indenting of the second and any subsequent lines covering the drop. The point may not appear one of major importance; but if drops are to be used at all they should be used properly.

(3) *Style*: it is usual for the first drop-initialed word to be in caps., with the corollary that the succeeding words, if completing a rank, title or proper name, shall also be in caps. In newspaper single column this may

easily result in a turning line of caps., a very ugly effect. For this reason some newspapers (e.g. the London *Evening Standard*) have abolished initial capping entirely, and follow the drop letter with lower-case. This unconventionality is undoubtedly helpful to sub-editors and avoids the unpleasantness indicated. But the caps. style seems preferable, always provided that care is taken to avoid opening on long titles or names, abbreviations (a fertile source of the most jarring effects) and the like.

POINTS ON PARAGRAPHING

After the introduction (and its drop letter) comes the *solid text* itself; the too, too solid text as it was in the classical newspaper days of the last century, when even paragraphing was virtually unknown and any subheading in text utterly unheard of. Suitable paragraphing[1] is indeed the primary way of breaking solid text, the first aid to ease in reading. This may sound a very obvious commonplace; but the important word is 'suitable' and to secure that, it is necessary to grasp certain technical principles which are not at all commonplace. They are, however, entirely common sense.

The main principle is the relation of type size (and letter-count: i.e. whether the letter is wide or narrow) to measure. The larger and wider the type and the narrower the measure the more paragraphing there needs to be; and conversely. Thus a 9 pt. Ionic in the $11\frac{1}{4}$-em column of the *Daily Express* calls for more frequent paragraphing than an $8/7\frac{1}{2}$ pt. Times Roman in the $13\frac{1}{2}$-em column of *The Times*. It is necessary to grasp that the paragraph is here being considered not in its literary or presentational, but solely in its typographical aspect; interest is limited to the varying slice of horizontal white space provided by the paragraph's concluding breakline.

The 'clarity and ease of reading' of any printed text depends as much on the disposition of white between and around its lines of matter as on the style and setting of the lines themselves. Newspapers are emphatically not exempt from this fundamental rule; hence the importance of well-balanced paragraphing—not too much, not too little, achieving a suitable variety of short, medium, and larger paragraphs to secure a varied breaking of the page. Here, too, differences in essential style between 'class' and 'popular' papers have to be borne in mind. If *The Times* were as heavily paragraphed as the *Daily Express* the effect, given its content and

[1] The customary paragraph indention is 1 em of the body, in single column; for paragraphs over more than single column the custom—another Victorian relic—is to multiply the indention by the number of columns; thus, 2 ems for double column, 3 ems for three columns, and so on. The effect in these wide measures becomes progressively more ungainly; and there is every reason why the 1-em indention should be made standard for all measures.

readership, would be insufferably jerky. If, on the other hand, the *Express* ran to paragraphs of *The Times*' length the comparable effect would be intolerably stodgy (Fig. 24).

The typographical importance of judicious paragraphing extends to paragraph-leading, to which reference has been made above. Paragraph-leading is another contributor to horizontal white, and relieves the solidity of text in a column. It should not be exaggerated; in double-column matter 3 pt. ('thick') leads are adequate, in single-column matter 2 pt. Even if consistent paragraph-leading is confined to lead stories and main tops, it is well worth while.

This morning the three western Ambassadors were handed Notes in which the Soviet Government states that it still prefers a summit meeting to discuss Berlin and a peace treaty with the two Germanys, but adds that it would be ready to take part in a Foreign Ministers' meeting in Vienna or Geneva during April, provided Poland and Czechoslovakia, as well as the two Germanys, are also represented.
This afternoon Mr. Macmillan and Mr. Khrushchev, with Mr. Selwyn Lloyd, Mr. Mikoyan, and Mr. Gromyko, with their advisers, had a two-hour business meeting which was said to be back on the free-and-easy manner of the first days of the visit.
Finally, later in the evening, Mr. Macmillan appeared on Moscow television and gave a statement, confident in substance and manner, which was probably seen by several million Russians in the Moscow region.

The Prime Minister's dignity and elegance made a hit with Russian families listening around more than a million TV sets. It is estimated that nearly 5,000,000 people saw him.
There was elegance—more, grandeur and magnificence—at the Kremlin banquet for Mr. Macmillan and his mission.
We crowded, a thousand or so, into the vast white St. George's Hall.
Long tables laden with champagne and wine, ice cream and sweetmeats stretched the length of the hall.
A band played in a minstrels' gallery and a Red Army choir sang Tipperary.
Mr. Macmillan came down to greet us all in the Hall of Vladimir, with its domed roof and huge golden chandelier.
Off to one side there were two other rooms covered with filigreed gilt and lacquered frescoes with the theme of The Last Supper.
He seemed relaxed, at ease, chatting happily with Krushchev and then taking on virtually all 15 members of the Communist Party Presidium in an animated discussion.

FIG. 24. Paragraphing style illustrated contrariwise: left is a portion of printed text from *The Times* reset in the type (7 pt. Ionic) and measure of the *Daily Express*, right is a portion of actual *Express* text reset in the type (8 on 7½ pt. Times) and measure of *The Times*.

Emphasis on the value of white space properly leads to the reiteration that there is one place where extra white is not wanted, namely between words and sentences in the line. The rush of newspaper setting in narrow measures gives little opportunity for finesse in spacing, as Chapter 1 remarked: but the general points there made about 'keeping in', not fearing word division quite so much, need to be constantly in mind; and it should be added that such technical aids to closer setting as extra-thin spacebands ought to be standard on newspaper slug machines. There can, after all, be no dispute that 'driven-out' setting is at once extremely ugly in a narrow newspaper column and a serious waste of space (Fig. 25).

A well-designed paper explains itself at a glance. The typographical treatment distinguishes different kinds of news stories, and separates news from features. Further, it maintains interest throughout. There should be a dynamic quality right

A well-designed paper explains itself at a glance. The typographical treatment distinguishes different kinds of news stories, and separates news from features. Further, it maintains interest throughout. There should be a

FIG. 25. Text setting, good and bad; these paragraphs are shown with normal, correct spacing (left) and 'driven out', which wastes space and is less readable.

INDENTION: ITS FORMS AND PURPOSES

The white on a page can be increased vertically as well as horizontally; this is one of the functions of the various styles of indention in text. Indention is also important for emphasizing a paragraph, or for giving variety and contrast to a whole story, short or long. Its usual styles (Fig. 26) are these:

(*a*) *Roman indent*: this is the primary form of indention. A paragraph in roman text is simply indented an extra em quad on the left; thus its first line has 2 ems on the front, the remainder 1 em (hence the style is technically called '2 and 1').[1] Providing a useful break in the column, and thus conveying a reasonable emphasis to the paragraph indented, it has developed as a more acceptable substitute for the traditional—

(*b*) *Black* (*Bold*) *indent*: the same '2 and 1' indent, but setting the paragraph in 'black' (the text fount's duplexed Bold or Doric). It requires much more discreet use than roman indent if it is not to defeat its own object—which was initially as much textual emphasis as the breaking of the column—and incidentally give the page an irritatingly spotty appearance. The comparable use of italic indent is rare but there is no reason why it should not be used as an occasional variant in special stories.

Here it should be stressed that in both the roman and bold indentions in text it is essential first to ensure that the paragraph indented is of medium length (above all not too long) and second, that a lead—not less than 2 pt. and preferably 3 pt.—is always inserted top and bottom. An indented paragraph run solid, especially if in black, is both ugly and ineffective.

(*c*) *Reverse* (*or hanging*) *indent*: here the normal style of paragraph indention is reversed, the first line being set full out to the measure and the remainder of the paragraph indented 1 em; thus the first line hangs over the white of the following indention. The technical specification is

[1] The composing room Victorian convention, already noted, that paragraph indention is multiplied by the number of columns is applied also to these indented settings. In double-column 2 and 1 becomes 4 and 2; the 'full out and 1' of hanging indent becomes 'full out and 2' in double column, and so on. The effect, of excessive white, is thoroughly bad.

'full out and 1'; on some papers '0 and 1'. This indention (in roman) is valuable when it is desired to throw up a group of allied or summarized points in the course of a news story; and, as such a series of points frequently lends itself to '1, 2, 3, 4' enumeration, reverse indent is the most suitable style for employing two-line drop figures, which gain emphasis when hanging in the white. Reverse indent can also be usefully employed for the setting of an entire story which it is editorially required to differentiate from the general run of the page; if of any length such a story will, in the ordinary way, have a larger-size intro. Roman or bold throughout, according to the emphasis needed, can be employed in such 'all reverse' stories; or, if they are short and of a light character, italic. Bold Reverse indent has already been noted as a useful intro. style.

(*d*) *Centred indent*: here the paragraph is indented an even amount each side, usually 1 en (a *nut* or half an em) for single column, 1 em (*mutton*) for double column. The specification may thus be 'indent ½ and ½' or '1 and 1'; more properly 'indent nut (or mutton) each end'. Some papers employ centred indent for paragraphs, either roman or black, in text instead of the normal 2 and 1; but this gives a squared-off effect which is not desirable. The true value of centred indent is for intros., for captions to blocks, for panels and special short stories, either in bold or italic. It can be employed in roman, as a variant on reverse indent, for an entire story, and it has become common practice on papers which adopted the ultra-thin and cramping 3 pt. column rule as a newsprint-saver. As a contrasting and emphatic style for a long single-column top in the centre of the page it is effective.

The general point needs to be made here that both reverse and centred indent settings must at all times be paragraph-leaded 2 pts., even if paragraph-leading is not the general style of the paper. The vertical white of the indention loses much of its value if the paragraphs are solid.

MISCELLANEA: BY-LINES AND DATE-LINES

Among subsidiary points in text-setting, largely questions of style and tending to vary from paper to paper, comes the question of word-emphasis —or, better perhaps, differentiation.[1] This arises, for instance, with proper names (or titles or institutions) in a leading article, with names of speakers in reports of Parliament, conferences, public meetings, and the like. In both cases the old custom, now only adhered to by the 'class' newspapers,

[1] The device of underscoring portions of text for emphasis is not to be commended. Rule has to be inserted by hand, it usually opens the lines too much, and most often draws more attention to itself than to the words supposedly emphasized. Typographically it is an admission of defeat.

2 and 1 roman

A well-designed paper explains itself at a glance. The typographical treatment distinguishes different kinds of news stories, and separates features.

Further, it maintains interest throughout. There should be a dynamic quality right through the issue and covering every page.

Even if a story has been pushed in at the last moment to fill a column it ought to look well.

2 and 1 black (solid)

A well-designed paper explains itself at a glance. The typographical treatment distinguishes different kinds of news stories, and separates features.
Further, it maintains interest throughout. There should be a dynamic quality right through the issue and covering every page.
Even if a story has been pushed in at the last moment to fill a column it ought to look well.

The same thick-leaded

A well-designed paper explains itself at a glance. The typographical treatment distinguishes different kinds of news stories, and separates features.

Further, it maintains interest throughout. There should be a dynamic quality right through the issue and covering every page.

Even if a story has been pushed in at the last moment to fill a column it ought to look well.

Nut each end roman

A well-designed paper explains itself at a glance. The typographical treatment distinguishes different kinds of news stories, and separates news from features.

Nut each end black

A well-designed paper explains itself at a glance. The typographical treatment distinguishes different kinds of news stories, and separates news from features.

Reverse (hanging) indent roman

A well-designed paper explains itself at a glance. The typographical treatment distinguishes different kinds of news stories, and separates the news from features.

Further, it maintains interest throughout. There should be a dynamic quality right through the issue and covering every page.

The same with drop figures

1 A well-designed paper explains itself at a glance. The typographical treatment distinguishes different kinds of news stories, and separates the news from features.

2 Further, it maintains interest throughout. There should be a dynamic quality right through the issue and covering every page.

Reverse indent black: drop letter

A WELL-DESIGNED paper explains itself at a glance. The typographical treatment distinguishes different kinds of news stories, and separates the news from features.

Further, it maintains interest throughout. There should be a dynamic quality right through the issue and covering every page.

A well-designed paper explains itself at a glance. The typographical treatment distinguishes different kinds of news stories, and separates the news from features. Further, it maintains interest throughout.

There should be a dynamic quality right through the issue and covering every page, even if a story has been pushed in at at the last moment.

Filling a column in such haste a news story still ought to look as though it was something that had to be written and wanted to be read.

Of those papers which showed evidence of real interest in good design, many spoiled their effort by individual failures such as set-off in printing, bad half-tones, grimly solid pages of small ads, and ugly title headings.

FIG. 26. Indention styles illustrated. The double-column setting shows the ugly effect of the conventional multiplication of the indention by the number of columns; the final paragraph retains the 2 and 1 em indention, the second paragraph has doubled it (as a newspaper compositor would usually do) to 4 and 2.

was to set the names in capitals and small capitals. It is a dignified old custom, usually abandoned in leaders by the popular papers which, for names of speakers in Parliamentary and similar reports, now usually use bold (upper- and lower-case). This latter style is not inconvenient for its purpose, but it needs to be limited to the initial citation of a speaker's name; if used in a summarized version, e.g. of a brisk Commons exchange, when several names occur within a paragraph, it can be distracting.

Bold caps. are useful for what may be called single-reference emphasis, e.g. in a series of short interviews for the name of each person interviewed, or in a foreign round-up for the names of capital cities or countries.

For the names of newspapers, periodicals, plays, films, books (when referred to in text) it was the old custom to use italic—sometimes with the added refinement of caps. and smalls for one's own paper. This again has been generally shelved, other than by the 'class' papers (there is an obvious technical inconvenience in styling italic for frequent references in text when most of a paper's composing machines are equipped with bold). The question simply is whether the names indicated should be set in roman quoted or unquoted; provided they are strictly 'kept up'—i.e. with an initial cap. to each word—the quotation marks are superfluous, certainly for names of papers.

By-lines and date-lines deserve more care and thought than they usually get. The style of wording of the former, an interesting and quite complex matter in itself, is an editorial affair; but typographically it is important that, especially with the impersonal by-lines, they should be distinctive but unobtrusive. Some papers seem to suffer from the delusion that the reader is impressed to see the words '. . . Correspondent' in glaring extra-heavy Sans a couple of sizes larger than the intro. of the story it covers. Actually the bold face of the text (or an allied bold italic; but it must be bold) is perfectly suitable for by-lines. It should normally be run in upper- and lower-case, though caps. are permissible in double column if the line is very short, and always a size or two sizes smaller than the intro.

With personal by-lines the name of the writer will be set in caps.; and, if desired, the name may be given emphasis by setting it in a contrasting type face, say Sans. Sometimes a by-line and date-line will be combined in one line (in condensed Sans for example) for lead stories in double or treble column. This style, while perhaps giving an exaggerated display effect to a by- and date-line, has the merit of combining boldness with space-saving (Figs. 27 and 28).

For daily papers the problem of the mode and style of agency acknowledgement relates both to the by-line and the date-line. In the old days the agency was acknowledged in what we would call by-line style; that is to

By MONTAGUE LACEY

TWO super-liners are to be built with Government help to replace the Queen Mary and Queen Elizabeth.

Express Staff Reporter

THREE well-dressed young men boarded the Caledonian Glasgow express at Euston station just before 4 p.m. yesterday

By ALEXANDER KENWORTHY

THE struggling British bacon industry receives a body blow this morning.

From
JAMES CAMERON
News Chronicle man
on the spot

Express Staff Reporter

DISASTER loomed seconds away last night as the horrified drivers of two electric trains — one crowded

By Gilbert Carter

BRITAIN'S crowded skies are to be made safer for everyone who flies.

HERALD REPORTER

A YOUNG doctor and his pretty wife have vanished — leaving a surgery full of patients

FIG. 27. A selection of by-line styles, actual-size, from newspaper stereos.

say, the words (REUTER'S TELEGRAM), for example, set in even small caps in parentheses over the story. It was a logical and practical method and, with characteristic traditionalism, still survives in the more sober American journals. It had the particular advantage that, in cutting on the stone, the agency acknowledgement line always remained above the battle and untouched; not to mention the value to the careful reader of instant indication of the source of the message.

These latter benefits also obtain with the other traditional American style of combining the agency acknowledgement with the date-line, e.g. CHICAGO, Feb. 23 (AP). But the practicality of this method largely depends on the convention of the specially supplied initial monograms for the Associated Press, United Press, and so forth; a spelt-out agency name would tend to make the date-line altogether too elongated and clumsy in

From GEORGE VINE: Bonn, Sunday

WEST GERMANY'S rigid opposition to the British plan for a thinned-out military area in Europe was reported today to be softening.

FROM OUR SPECIAL CORRESPONDENT

BELMONT, SURREY, APRIL 2

Three small boys from Lanarkshire were on their way home by the night train from London to-night with a story that will be the envy of their Wishaw

From Phillip Hunt

TORONTO, Sunday.

CANADA'S sagging aviation industry may get a shot in the arm from the American army with a

NICOSIA Sunday. — Sir Hugh Foot revealed today that half the major British Army units stationed in Cyprus in February will have left by the end of this month.

ACCRA, Wednesday. — Lord Listowel, Governor General of Ghana, is in hospital with gastritis. All his engagements have been cancelled.

From IRIS RUSSELL: Beirut, Sunday

FIERCE fighting has broken out again in Iraq—this time in the oil city

The trouble began last Tuesday as the Iraqis were celebrating the first anniversary of

From HENRY KHAN: Paris, Wednesday

THE Aga Khan's No. 1 girl-friend, 19-year-old blonde Sylvia Casablancas, was caught by her millionaire father in a chase on the French Riviera today.

FIG. 28. Some date-line variations including combined by- and date-lines.

narrow column measures. This is to say nothing of the insuperable difficulty presented by the use—a common thing—of two messages from different agencies with a special correspondent's message to make a single story. Hence the normal British style of slugging a single or multiple agency acknowledgement at the end of the story, run on with a metal rule to the last paragraph, perhaps differentiated in italic if italic is readily available, as on a 'class' paper.

Apart from the run-on Sans style already mentioned, there is little room, or need, for experimentation in date-lines. They can be seen set in lower-case, sometimes in black; but the traditional roman caps. for the town or place, lower-case for the date, is the most effective. And in general date-lines are better for being kept in the paper's text face, irrespective of the style of the intro. which follows them. Nor should they be run, say, in 12 pt. because the intro. happens to be in that size. Except when run on in the body size, date-lines are best kept (as by-lines) a size or two smaller than the following intro.; they need to be unmistakably present, but not to be obtruded on the reader's attention (Fig. 28).

Whether a date-line employs the style of day-of-the-week or date-in-the-month (abbreviated and with figures) is a matter of taste; but abbreviation of the day-of-the-week is ugly and should be avoided. If the name of the place is abnormally long it is better to turn the date-line, with the name in caps. indented not more than 1 em from the right, and the date as a separate line set full out right. In smaller stories the date-line can be run on with text, it being convenient in narrow measures to run that date-line opening full out.

5 · Special Text Settings The 'Smalls'

THE trend to a larger body-size does not apply in one specialized department of newspaper text setting. That is the customarily small-type field of the classified advertisements (the 'smalls') and those service-to-reader items the radio and television programmes, the Stock Market prices, and the sports forecasts and results. More extended reference is made to sports-page settings in Chapter 10; the general point to note here is that all such close-packed, strictly informational portions of text require the paper's smallest possible type for their accommodation. That type will normally be the one used for the 'smalls'. These, because of their great economic importance, determine what the minimum-size type is to be. Obviously the primary consideration will be the maximum space-economy, both in depth and set-width, consistent with legibility.

Thus there has been a steady downward evolution in the standard body-size for small advertisements: from 6 pt. to 5½ pt. to 5 pt.; finally to the 4¾ pt. Claritas (Times Roman) and the 4¾ pt. Linotype Adsans. In addition to Times and Adsans most modern newspaper text ranges have at least a 5½ pt., Ionic a 5 pt. The wide-set that has been noted as a characteristic of the Ionic group persists in these small sizes, where the economical set of Times shows up to corresponding advantage; the 5½ pt. Times, for example, gets in around 10 per cent. more than the 5½ pt. Ionic. This economy in set-width, plus the saving of ¼ pt. or ¾ pt. a line (according to whether they dropped from 5 pt. or 5½ pt.), made a number of Ionic-Excelsior text newspapers go over to Claritas for their 'smalls'. Financially gratifying though the change must have been, typographically it only served to show once more that Times Roman, especially in its smaller sizes, needs the presswork and paper of Printing House Square to appear as it should. The production rush of the mass-sale evening newspaper, for instance, is scarcely kind to Claritas (Fig. 29). Adsans, as the London *Evening News* shows, stands up to these conditions much better.[1]

[1] A 4¾ pt. advertisement Sans has since been produced by Intertype. First used by the London *Evening Standard*, it is named Standard Gothic. Its lower-case alphabet width is 80 pts., against Adsans' 84 pts.

MOURILYAN.—On July 14th, 1959, at Canterbury, MAUDE SARAH, youngest daughter of the late Staff Commander EDWARD MOURILYAN, R.N., of Deal.
MULLENS.—On July 14th, 1959, at Renscombe, Cooden, RITA, widow of MAJOR W. H. MULLENS. Funeral, to-morrow (Friday), at St. Mark's, Little Common, at 3 p.m. Flowers to Messrs. Mummery, Bexhill.
PICKWORTH.—On July 14th, 1959, suddenly, at Darlington, SIR FREDERICK PICKWORTH, aged 69 years, of 7, Endcliffe Hall Avenue, Sheffield, 10, dearly loved husband of Alice, and dear father of Margaret, Stanley and Barbara. Funeral service, St. Johns Church, Ranmoor, Sheffield, to-morrow (Friday), July 17, at 2.15 p.m., followed by interment at City Road Cemetery, 3.15 p.m. Flowers may be sent to Messrs. John Heath and Sons, Funeral Directors, Sheffield.
RICHARDSON.—On July 15th, 1959, ELIZABETH MAUD, aged 88, beloved wife of the late DR. MARTIN RICHARDSON, and mother of Norman, Dorothy Nichols and Joan Rose. Funeral at Putney Vale Crematorium, 2.30 p.m., Monday, July 20th. Flowers to E. B. Ashton and Co., 96, Fulham Road, London, S.W.3.
SIMON.—On July 14th, 1959, EDGAR CHARLES SIMON, beloved husband of Norah and father of Burich Umfreville. Cremation Putney Vale Crematorium, Friday, 17th July, at 2.30 p.m. No flowers, please.
VENNING.—On July 15, 1959, at Plymouth, GEORGE LOTAN VENNING, dear husband of Kathleen, and father of Russell. Funeral, Emmanuel Church, Plymouth,

BOOKSHOP ASSISTANT (female) wanted for Department Store. Canteen & shopping discount available. Age preferred 20/35. Apply Staff Manager, Civil Service Stores, 425 Strand, W.C.2.
CASHIER reqd. for West End cafe. Hours 8.30 a.m.-6 p.m. Sat. half-day, no Sundays. Pleasant conditions, meals provided. £6 5s. weekly. Apply Kardomah Cafe. 27 Brompton-rd. (nr. Knightsbridge Stn.).
EXPERIENCED first class poulterer & butcher, required immediately for Kosher trade. Wages £13 10s. Apply Simons, 15-16, Monkville-parade, N.W.11. MEA 3355.
EXPERIENCED SALESWOMAN required for gown shop, good wages. Apply ELIZABETH MARCH, 47/49 Brompton-rd., S.W.3. Tel. KENsington 9021.
FASHIONS SHOWROOM. Vacancy for experienced Saleslady. Remunerative position with excellent prospects for a lady possessing keen selling ability. Staff cafeteria. Social club. Spring and summer holidays. Apply Staff Controller Arding & Hobbs Ltd., Clapham Junction, S.W.11.
FLORIST for Mayfair shop. MAY 1911.
IRONMONGERY SALESMEN required. Also girl to learn in Electrical & Lampshade Dept. Apply Staff Manager, Civil Service Stores, 425 Strand, W.C.2.

FIG. 29. Times $4\frac{3}{4}$ pt. (Claritas) as printed: line-reproductions from the classified advertisement columns of *The Times* and of the London *Evening Standard*.

This is not to say that the use of a different face for the 'smalls' is in itself wrong; though if it is to be used, in accord with normal practice, for the setting of subsidiary small-size matter in text (e.g. on the sports pages) some general typographical consonance between it and the body of the paper is desirable. The point is that more attention requires to be paid to the special problem of the ultra-small text face. Setting problems of this sort occur in many other common forms of printed matter, such as time-tables and directories; and experience in those spheres has an obvious application to newspapers (Fig. 30).

Bell Gothic, the directory Sans specially designed for the Bell Telephone System of America in 1938, is a case in point. This remarkable space-saver offers a 6 pt. which is narrower than Ionic 5 pt. and almost as narrow as Times Claritas ($4\frac{3}{4}$ pt.). Originally cut by the Mergenthaler Linotype Company, it is available here from Intertype and has been adopted as the new standard British telephone directory type. American newspapers

6 pt. Directory with Doric

A well-designed paper explains itself at a glance. The typographical treatment distinguishes different kinds of news stories, and separates news from features. Further, it maintains **interest throughout. There should be a dynamic quality right** 1234567890 **1234567890**

6 pt. Bell Gothic with Bold

A well-designed paper explains itself at a glance. The typographical treatment distinguishes different kinds of news stories, and separates news **from features. Further, it maintains interest throughout. There should be a dynamic quality right through the issue and covering 1234567890**

6 pt. Gothic No. 17 with No. 19

A well-designed paper explains itself at a glance. The typographical treatment distinguishes different kinds of news stories, and separates **news from features. Further, it maintains interest throughout. There should be a dynamic quality right through the issue and covering 1234567890**

6/$5\frac{1}{2}$ pt. Bell Gothic Bold/Gothic No. 6

A well-designed paper explains itself at glance. The typographical treatment distinguishes different kinds of news stories, and separates news from features. Further, it maintains interest throughout. There should be a dynamic quality **right through the issue and covering 1234567890**

FIG. 30. Space-saving 6 pt. faces: note the semi-bold news figures duplexed with the Doric of the Linotype Directory and the marked contrast of light and bold in the Linotype 17/19 Gothic. The Intertype Bell Gothic secures this contrast by substituting the heavier Gothic No. 6 for the normal Bell Bold.

frequently use Bell Gothic for narrow-measure small-size settings, notably the market prices, and in this country it is gaining popularity for the various programme and similar settings on sports pages (see Chapter 10). It will be noticed that the variation between the normal weight and the bold is slight, and a heavier Gothic is needed for contrast.

In this connexion also a narrow and strongly coloured 6 pt. Modern Roman, cut many years ago by the Linotype organization and called Directory, is suggestive. Of the same set-width as 5½ pt. Times or 5 pt. Ionic, Linotype Directory was duplexed with a sound contrasting Doric and semi-bold Sans figures of exceptional clarity (of similar cut to those currently seen in the London Telephone Directory). Design and experiment along these lines, opening-up the drawing of the 'ink trap' letters and strengthening the serifs, might lead to a more satisfactory general duty 'smalls' face than the Ionic which is at present the only practical minimum-size seriffed alternative to Claritas. With the secondary fount an adapted modern Sans rather than a Doric (see below), the value of the innovation might be still greater.

THE PROBLEM OF THE 'BLACK'

Meantime the practical considerations remain of how to handle the faces available. Below 6 pt., the normal choice is limited to Times (4¾, 5½ pt.), Ionic (5, 5½ pt.), Paragon (5½ pt.), Ideal (5½ pt.), Imperial (5½ pt.). At once the question arises—what is to be the secondary 'black' duplexed with the Roman? It has been noted in Chapter 4 that in the smallest sizes of Ionic the differentiation between Roman and Bold Face is insufficient for the bold to exercise satisfactorily its function of emphasis. The user of 5 pt. Ionic will thus be well advised to have it duplexed with Doric, even if his larger text sizes carry the Bold Face. The blackness and distinctiveness of the Doric, alike in caps. and lower-case, survives indifferent presswork and poor inking. With Times the position is different; the Bold–Roman differentiation is somewhat better, and in any event that combination is the only one (other than italic) available. Nevertheless, Times does provide one significant alternative, in 4¾ pt. Claritas: that is in respect of the figures (Fig. 31).

Figures are of major importance in 'smalls', as well as in the other minimum-size settings (radio programmes, market prices, sports matter). In 5½ pt. and below the normal figures of the fount tend to be too narrow, and to set too close, for easy legibility. Wider and more open figures, of even colour and a modified Sans cut—traditionally known in the trade as 'news figures'—make a valuable alternative. Figures of this sort are available for 5 pt. and 5½ pt. Ionic and as a standard alternative in Claritas,

$4\frac{3}{4}$ pt. Claritas with Bold

A well-designed paper explains itself **at a glance.** The typographical treatment distinguishes different kinds of news stories, and separates **news** from **features.** Further, it maintains interest throughout. There should be a **dynamic quality** right through the issue and covering every page.

$5\frac{1}{2}$ pt. Times with Bold

A well-designed paper explains itself **at a glance.** The typographical treatment distinguishes different kinds of news stories, and separates **news** from **features.** Further, it maintains interest throughout. There should be a **dynamic quality** right through the issue and

5 pt. Ionic with Doric

A well-designed paper explains itself **at a glance.** The typographical treatment distinguishes different kinds of news stories, and separates **news** from **features.** Further, it maintains interest throughout. There should
1234567890 1234567890
1234567890 1234567890

$5\frac{1}{2}$ pt. Ionic with Bold

A well-designed paper explains itself at **a glance.** The typographical treatment distinguishes different kinds of news stories, and separates **news from features.** Further, it maintains interest throughout.
1234567890 1234567890
1234567890 1234567890

$4\frac{3}{4}$ pt. Adsans with Bold

A well-designed paper explains itself **at a glance.** The typographical treatment distinguishes different kinds of news stories, and separates **news** from **features.** Further, it maintains interest throughout. There should be a **dynamic quality** right through the issue and

$5\frac{1}{2}$ pt. Paragon with Bold

A well-designed paper explains itself **at a glance.** The typographical treatment distinguishes different kinds of news stories, and separates **news** from **features.** Further, it maintains interest throughout. There should be a **dynamic**

$5\frac{1}{2}$ pt. Ideal with Doric

A well-designed paper explains itself at **a glance.** The typographical treatment distinguishes different kinds of **news stories,** and separates **news** from **features.** Further, it maintains **interest** throughout. There should be a dynamic quality right

$5\frac{1}{2}$ pt. Imperial with Bold

A well-designed paper explains itself **at a** glance. The typographical treatment distinguishes different kinds of **news stories,** and separates **news** from **features.** Further, it maintains **interest** throughout. There should be a dynamic quality right through

FIG. 31. The range of available text faces below 6 pt. The superior contrast of Doric (as compared with Bold) in these sizes is to be noted, as are the alternate figures shown here in the 5 pt. and $5\frac{1}{2}$ pt. Ionic.

duplexed with Doric figures in place of the Bold; they are 0·054 in. wide, as against the 0·043 in. of the normal figures. If fractions are needed it is wise to specify the diagonal, or 'compound', style (normal usage in market price columns) since the conventional vertical fraction is virtually unreadable in these minute sizes (Fig. 32).

CRESTA, regd Oct '58, rdo pink/white, 7,300 mls, gd cond, £895, BAT **8108.**
VELOX Grosvenor Estate car '57, duo colour, exc, htr, £865. PRO **7648.**
$\frac{1}{4}\frac{1}{2}\frac{3}{4}\frac{1}{8}\frac{3}{8}\frac{5}{8}\frac{7}{8}\frac{1}{6}\frac{1}{3}\frac{2}{3}$ $^1/_4\,^1/_2\,^3/_4\,^1/_8\,^3/_8\,^5/_8\,^7/_8\,^1/_6\,^1/_3\,^2/_3$
$\frac{1}{4}\frac{1}{2}\frac{3}{4}\frac{1}{8}\frac{3}{8}\frac{5}{8}\frac{7}{8}\frac{1}{6}\frac{1}{3}\frac{2}{3}$ $^1/_4\,^1/_2\,^3/_4\,^1/_8\,^3/_8\,^5/_8\,^7/_8\,^1/_6\,^1/_3\,^2/_3$

CRESTA, regd Oct '58, rdo pink/white, 7,300 mls, gd cond. £895. BAT **8108.**
VELOX Grosvenor Estate car '57, duo colour, exc, htr. £895. PRO **7648.**
$^1/_4\,^1/_2\,^3/_4\,^1/_8\,^3/_8\,^5/_8\,^7/_8$
$^1/_4\,^1/_2\,^3/_4\,^1/_8\,^3/_8\,^5/_8\,^7/_8$

FIG. 32. Alternate figures and fractions for Claritas: the wider 'news' figures (with Doric) are more legible, as are the diagonal fractions. Compare with Adsans (right).

'DROPS' ARE NOT ESSENTIAL

The convention that each small advertisement opens with a drop letter has long since ceased to have universal application. It slows down setting, takes space, and in solid 'smalls' pages of eight, nine, or even sometimes ten narrow columns would have the effect of a black rash, dazzling the eye and defeating its original aim of distinguishing each individual advertisement without the need for leads or cut-off rules. Where the technical circumstances are favourable, as in a 'class' paper like *The Times*, drop letters can still be effective and agreeable; but it is essential that their weight and size be correct. That is to say they must be sufficiently strong in colour, but not too strong—a common fault with small advertisement drops—and they must provide precise two-line cover for their text. In the Times range special two-line initials are provided, sized $9\frac{1}{2}$ pt. and 11 pt. to cover the Claritas and $5\frac{1}{2}$ pt. texts respectively. For the Ionic 5 and $5\frac{1}{2}$ pt. Linotype 10 and 11 pt. Two-line No. 3, a medium weight news titling, would be suitable; or the experimentally minded might try normal fount 12 pt. or 14 pt. caps. which do not show more than 10 or 11 pts., e.g. Times Heading Bold, Times Heading, Bodoni Bold, Century Bold, Bold Face No. 2 (Fig. 33).

WELL-DESIGNED papers explain themselves at a glance. Their typography distinguishes different news stories and stories. They have a dynamic quality in every page. Last-minute stories do not lack the element of design and purpose. Every line demands to be read.

WELL-DESIGNED papers explain themselves at a glance. Their typography distinguishes different news stories and stories. They have a dynamic quality in every page. Last-minute stories do not lack the element of design and purpose.

WELL-DESIGNED papers explain themselves at a glance. Their typography distinguishes different news stories and stories. They have a dynamic quality in every page. Last-minute stories do not lack the element of design and purpose. Every line demands to be read.

WELL-DESIGNED papers explain themselves at a glance. Their typography distinguishes different news stories and stories. They have a dynamic quality in every page. Last-minute stories do not lack the element of design and purpose.

FIG. 33. Light and bold drop letters in small advertisements: respectively $9\frac{1}{2}$ pt. Times Two-line (Claritas), 11 pt. Times Two-line ($5\frac{1}{2}$ pt. Times), 12 pt. Bold Face No. 2 (5 pt. Ionic), 11 pt. Two-line No. 3 ($5\frac{1}{2}$ pt. Paragon).

Vacancy for keen car salesman with good prospects. Box 345.
Director of textile firm seeks new sales outlets in Brazil. Inquiries warmly welcomed. Box 3455.
Capital can double in a year. Investors please contact Box 666.

Vacancy for keen car salesman with good prospects: Box 138.
Director of textile firm seeks new sales outlets in Brazil. Inquiries warmly welcomed: Box 345.
Capital can be double in a year. Investors please contact Box 666.

FIG. 34. A small advertisement style favoured by some continental (particularly German) newspapers: the first word of a normal roman setting is emphasized in a medium condensed Sans—thus (left) 6 pt. Metromedium and Jubilee, (right) 6 pt. Gothic No. 6 and Imperial.

If drops are not to be used the opening of each advertisement has to be signalized by setting the first word or two in Bold or Doric; and it is accepted that this bold setting should be in caps. which, given the 'blacks' available, is sound practice. Continental examples suggest, however, that a modern Sans (say of the weight of Metromedium or Bell Gothic Bold) enables the opening words to be set lower-case, increasing their legibility without reducing their distinctiveness; such a style, however, requires the duplexing of the modern Sans with the roman used for the body of the advertisement or the use of a 'mixer' machine (Fig. 34).

With its opening word or words in 'black' caps., the small advertisement can either be set full out (no paragraph indention) or with a hanging indention; ordinary 1-em paragraph indention would be ineffective and is not normally practised. The full-out style needs adequate leading, or a cut-off rule, between each advertisement. The hanging indention style requires minimum or no leading, and the loss of space on the indented lines can be minimized by reducing the usual 'full out and 1' setting to 'full out and ½' (Fig. 35).

Important space-saving follows the general removal of cut-off rules, possible with good drop-letter setting or hanging indention. Where cut-offs are used they need to be of the minimum body. One American newspaper gave this example: an average column of its classified advertisements carried 74 cut-offs; using 1 pt. rule this approximated 1 inch per column for cut-offs; if ordinary 6 pt. rule were used the loss in advertising space would be 5 inches a column or around two full columns per page.[1]

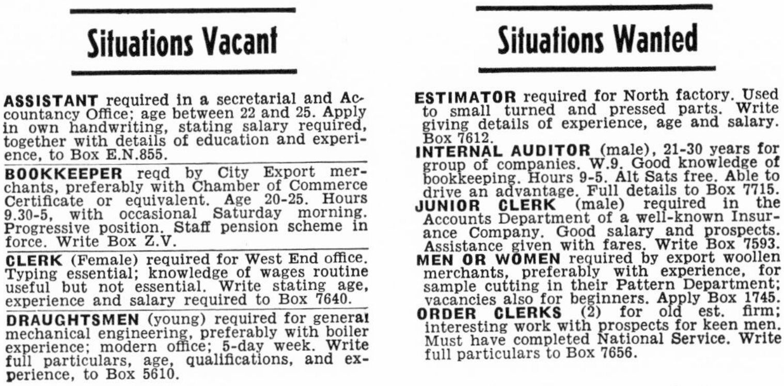

Situations Vacant

ASSISTANT required in a secretarial and Accountancy Office; age between 22 and 25. Apply in own handwriting, stating salary required, together with details of education and experience, to Box E.N.855.

BOOKKEEPER reqd by City Export merchants, preferably with Chamber of Commerce Certificate or equivalent. Age 20-25. Hours 9.30-5, with occasional Saturday morning. Progressive position. Staff pension scheme in force. Write Box Z.V.

CLERK (Female) required for West End office. Typing essential; knowledge of wages routine useful but not essential. Write stating age, experience and salary required to Box 7640.

DRAUGHTSMEN (young) required for general mechanical engineering, preferably with boiler experience; modern office; 5-day week. Write full particulars, age, qualifications, and experience, to Box 5610.

Situations Wanted

ESTIMATOR required for North factory. Used to small turned and pressed parts. Write giving details of experience, age and salary. Box 7612.

INTERNAL AUDITOR (male), 21-30 years for group of companies. W.9. Good knowledge of bookkeeping. Hours 9-5. Alt Sats free. Able to drive an advantage. Full details to Box 7715.

JUNIOR CLERK (male) required in the Accounts Department of a well-known Insurance Company. Good salary and prospects. Assistance given with fares. Write Box 7593.

MEN OR WOMEN required by export woollen merchants, preferably with experience, for sample cutting in their Pattern Department; vacancies also for beginners. Apply Box 1745.

ORDER CLERKS (2) for old est. firm; interesting work with prospects for keen men. Must have completed National Service. Write full particulars to Box 7656.

FIG. 35. Small advertisements without drop letters, but with the first word or words in Doric caps. (the settings here are in 5 pt. Ionic). The full-out style (left) is shown with 2 pt. cut-off rules, the hanging indent style is solid, saving space by making the indention 'full out and half' instead of the usual full out and one (em). The headings are in Erbar Bold Condensed.

COLOUR BREAKS AND SEMI-DISPLAY

The immense reader-interest in small advertisements should never be taken for granted to the point of making no effort to add some elements of attraction and variety to the damnable iteration of solid 5 pt. (or 4¾ pt.). The classification headings—'Personal', 'Situations Vacant', and so on—should be distinctive and bold; a bold, somewhat condensed Sans between medium-heavy rules, for instance, or processed as a reverse block on solid, dark tint, or lined ground (Fig. 35). The colour break of any illustration, whether a half-tone or a strip cartoon, is most helpful. The development of semi-display advertisements among the 'smalls' is perhaps the most effective method of all in lightening the solidity of these pages. Here there are two basic styles: to use the larger sizes of the paper's text

[1] Arnold, op. cit., p. 259.

WOKING MOTORS LTD.
The
MERCEDES-BENZ
DISTRIBUTORS OFFER
A number of new 220S Saloons in a selection of colours; also, the largest selection of secondhand Mercedes-Benz in the U.K. All covered by our unique 12 months' guarantee.
We are also County Distributors for the astonishing
VOLVO 122S,
a 4-5-seater saloon of the right size with sports car performance; 0-60=14 secs., 95 m.p.h. top speed, with roadholding to match. Price, including underseal, radiator blind, heater, &c., and purchase tax, £1,399.
We also have a unique secondhand car,
1959 FERRARI G.T. Saloon by Farina; right-hand-drive; 4,000 miles only. The owner has been forced to dispose of this car for personal reasons, and it is offered at a very attractive reduction on its original list price of £6,600.
WOKING MOTORS LTD.,
MAYBURY HILL, WOKING, SURREY.
Tel., WOKING 4277.

MERCEDES-BENZ
THE CARS FOR TO-DAY AND THE FUTURE.
LITERATURE ON REQUEST.
Our demonstration cars are here for YOU to drive—and JUDGE. Many superb second-hand examples, from £895 0s.0d. Mostly supplied new, and serviced exclusively by us, and taken in exchange for latest models from entirely satisfied owners. Full details of current stock gladly submitted.
JOHN S. TRUSCOTT, Ltd.,
MERCEDES-BENZ DISTRIBUTORS.

Spring Cruising
By the "DUKE OF LANCASTER" (5,075 tons), fitted with stabilisers. In May and June to Rouen, Ostend and Amsterdam. Duration, 6 to 9 days. From £27 10s. or September to Scottish Lochs and Western Isles, 9 days from £40. For detailed guidance apply:
THOS. COOK & SON
Dept. D/G/A, Berkeley Street, London, W.1, and branches or from DEAN & DAWSON Ltd.

SHAW SAVILL LINE
to
SOUTH AFRICA, AUSTRALIA, NEW ZEALAND
Southern Cross (Tourist class) .. Mar. 4
Ceramic (1st class only) .. .. Mar. 26
Dominion Monarch (1st class only) Apr. 25
Gothic (1st class only) .. .. May 21
11A, LOWER REGENT STREET, S.W.1
(WHItehall 1485)
or Local Travel Agents.

NEW COLLEGE, OXFORD
Fellowship & Chaplaincy
The Warden and Fellows of New College propose to elect a Chaplain who shall be a Fellow and will be expected to lecture for a Faculty of the University. Experience in choral service will be an advantage. Salary will be according to age and qualifications with pension under F.S.S.U.
Candidates should apply to the Warden by 4th April, 1959.

FIG. 36. Semi-display in 'smalls': a portion of an advertisement column from *The Times* (left) showing the use of Times Roman caps., with (right) specimen settings using respectively Memphis Light, Metrolite, and Memphis Medium.

face for the simple display lines in these advertisements (as *The Times* does) or to use a light Sans like Metrolite (as the London *Evening Standard* does). The main thing is that the type for these lines should be light as well as distinctive; hence the value of Linotype Metrolite or its contemporaries Ludlow Tempo Light, Intertype Vogue Light, Monotype Gill Light (Series 362), and the thinnest Egyptians, like Linotype Memphis Light, Ludlow Karnak Light, Intertype Cairo Light, Monotype Rockwell Light (Series 390) (Fig. 36). To meet the requirements of charging per line, or multiples of lines, for semi-display in 5½ pt. 'smalls' the Americans have designed a special, slightly condensed light Sans face, cut in odd sizes; this is Mergenthaler Linotype's Classified Display,

TEXTILES

Amal. Cotton	10/6	+1½d	H'rocksesCrew	29/0	..
Bleachers Assn.	13/0	..	Hoyle, Joshua	1/9	..
Bradford Dyers	17/0	..	Ilg'wth Morris	4/4½	..
Brit. Ctn. Dyers	3/9	..	Lancs. Cotton	41/9	+6d
Calico Printers	40/6	+6d	Linen Thread	23/6	−3d
Coats (J. & P.)	24/0	+4½d	Lister & Co. ..	12/9	+3d
Com.Eng.Mills	8/6	..	Morley, I. & R.	11/9	−3d
Corah, N. ..	17/4½	+3d	Moygashel ..	7/1½	..
Courtaulds ..	33/7½	+4½d	Patons Baldwin	36/10½	+3d
Crosses, Heat'n	9/1½	..	Salts (Saltaire)	5/6	..
Eng. Sew. Ctn.	27/9	..	Tootal ..	27/9	+10½d
Fielding & John	5/6	..	Wardle & Dav.	24/0	..
Fine Spinners	19/9	+1½d	West Rdg. Wl.	52/9	+3d
Henry, A. & S.	47/3	+2/0	Woolcombers	54/3	+3d
Hollins (Wm.)	21/9	+3d			

AMUSEMENTS

A B Pic	..45/3	+ 0/3
G.R.A.	....4/-	+0/1½
Mss Em	12/10½	−0/1½
Olymp	....6/3	+ 0/9
Stoll	......8/1½	−0/1½
Wimbldn	2/11¼	−0/0¾

BANKS AND INSURANCE

B Montrl	.22⅜	+..⅜
Can Com	23¾	+ ⅛
Com Un	..49/3	− 0/3
Dist	......62/9	− 0/3

Vickers	....32/-	+0/1½
Ward T.W.	94/-	+ 0/6
Whessoe	..33/6	− 0/3

FOOD

Bibby J	..26/3	+ 0/3
Brk Bond	10/4½	−0/0¾
Cerebos	..33/-	+ 0/6
Cros & B	48/9	+ 0/9
Home Col	21/4½	−0/1½
Horlicks	..30/-	+ 1/3
Hovis	....22/9	− 0/3
Int Tea	..12/1½	+0/1½
Liebigs	..52/9	− 0/9
Lyons A	..71/9	+ 0/6

FIG. 37. Narrow measure City prices: from *The Times* (Claritas) and *Daily Express* (5/5½ pt. Doric).

available in 11, 22, 27½, 38½ pt., to make 2, 4, 5, 7-line multiples of 5½ pt., that size (under its old name Agate) being the American basis for charging.

Of the remaining ultra-small settings to be considered here, there is not too much to be said. The Stock Market prices are usually set half-measure, so that they can be evened up with the normal make-up of the paper. Monotype or even hand-setting is sometimes used. Fractions and special signs are used, with bold caps. of the text for each of the company classification lines; possible substitution of a small-size lower-case Sans (e.g. 6 pt. or 8 pt. Metroblack or Metromedium; 8 pt. or 10 pt. Erbar Condensed—bold or light) for the bold caps. is about the only display variation that can be suggested here (Fig. 37).

RADIO AND TELEVISION PROGRAMMES

The radio and television programmes offer somewhat more scope for initiative, with the need to distinguish the different programmes and the importance of making the times instantly perceptible, even to the extent of using drop figures. Most papers, however, have understandably settled down to a routine presentation, labelling each programme with a suitable

V AND RADIO FOR TODAY

1.45-4.30 Steeplechasing : Stratford-upon-Avon.
5 Animal Parade.
5.25 Fury.
5.55 News. 6.10 Ivanhoe.
6.40 Shopping For You.
7 Close-up on Yul Brynner.
7.30 Song Parade.
8 Double Your Money.

8 As ITV London.
8.30 Letter from an Unknown Woman : film.
10-10.45 As ITV London.
10.45 Montage.
11 Sea Hunt ; Epilogue.

ITV—S.W. & W.

1.45-4 Racing : Stratford.
4.20 Newyddion Y Dydd

6.5 Southern News.
6.10 Sea Hunt.
7-8.30 As ITV London.
8.30 Scarlet Thread : film.
10-11 As ITV London.
11 Three's Company.
11.25 Nightlight.

ITV—Northern

2 Racing : Stratford.

RADIO—HOME

6.45 — Market Report. **6.50** — A Thought For The Week. **6.55**—Weather. **7**—News. **7.10**—Programmes. **7.15**—Today. **7.35 app.**—From Today's Papers. **7.40**—Records. **7.50**—Lift Up Your Hearts. **7.55**—Weather. **8** —News. **8.10** —Programmes. **8.15**—Today. **8.35**—From Today's Papers. **8.40**—Monday Date. **9**—News **9.10**—Letter From America. **9.25**—Italian Songs. **9.45**—Purcell **10.15**—Service. **10.30**—News. Music While You Work **11**—Sing Us The Old Songs. **11.30**—Birds in Britain. **12**—Concert Hour. **12.55**—Weather. **1**—News. **1.10**—Desert Island Discs **1.40**—The Autobiography of Margot Asquith. **1.55**—Cricket Scores. **2**—Marching and Waltzing. **2.45**—Worthington and the Teddy Boys **3**—Rod Steiger : Abe Lincoln in Illinois. **4.40**—They Came to London. **5**—Children's Hour. **5.55**—Weather. **6**—News. **6.15**—In The South-East. **7**—The Story of the Proms. **8**—Monday Night At Home. **9**—News. **9.15**—Play : The New Morality. **10.30**—British Medical Association. **10.45**—Today in Parliament. **11**—News, weather. **11.6 app.**—Music At Night.

B.B.C.—TV

11.50 Mass. 1.0 O Sul I Sul. 1.10 Asbri. 2.0 Farming. 2.35 News Review. 3.0 Rescue Dig. 3.30 Royal Philharmonic Orchestra. 4.15 BRAINS TRUST. 5.0 Hans and Lotte Hass. 5.30 "The Tchaikovsky Story." 6.5 Sunday Special. 7.0 Meeting Point. 7.25 News Summary. 7.30 Charlie Drake. 8.0 JIMMY EDWARDS. 8.30 "WHISTLING IN THE DARK" (Play). 9.45 News. 9.50 Canadian Panorama. 10.20 "Two Brothers" (ballet). 10.50 Epilogue.

Midlands ITV

11.15 Church Service. 2.30 Preview—"Marriage Bureau." 3.0 The Other Man's Farm. 3.30 The Film Show. 5.25 Sunday's Child. 5.50 What's In Store. 6.5 News. 6.15

FIG. 38. Radio and television programmes: stereos from the *Daily Express* (Ionic), *Daily Mail* (Claritas), *Daily Mirror* (Bell Gothic).

display line or small reverse block, and saving space by running-on the items. The importance of clear figures for programme times, if minimum-size text is being used, is thus enhanced (hence the value of the alternative Doric figures in Claritas). Sometimes the programmes are set narrow measure, perhaps an odd measure that can double up, say, three columns to the paper's normal two, allowing for reasonable white between the columns and perhaps boxing the whole in heavy rule or a fancy border. Alternatively the radio programmes may be set narrow measure with the television programmes wide measure, the whole squaring up across, say, four columns at the foot of a page (Fig. 38).

6 · The Sub-Heading

THE sub-heading in text is the connecting link between solid matter and headline display. Its consideration therefore falls naturally between the discussion of text and headline typography. The function of the sub-heading is simple: it is the reader's main optical aid to the easy perusal of solid text. To secure its full value it thus has to be heavier in colour than the text, and is always set in a bolder face. Apart from the more elaborate sub-headings in lengthy stories or reports, which begin to develop into headlines in their own right and have thematic importance—summing-up the essential news in the section of text they cover—the simple sub-heading does not so much aim at adding to the reader's information as at the convenient breaking-up of the text. Like all other collections of words in a newspaper even the simplest sub-heading needs writing with care; but provided its wording is reasonably relevant and fits the measure well, what the sub-heading does, i.e. break the text, is of more moment than what it says. The point is exemplified in those papers which sometimes abandon the sub-heading entirely for the purely conventionalized break of a star or comparable ornamental symbol; there are prize-winning American papers which use starlines only to break up their main news stories.

First foreshadowing of the sub-heading (though also the headline in embryo) was the run-on heading, usually in roman caps. and small caps. of the text, for the smaller news items. When the sub-heading came to occupy a line of its own it was usually set in the even small caps. of the text; frequently it was run on in the different sense that it consisted of three or four words picked out of text and centred, but reading on from the preceding breakline to the following unparagraphed text.

Nowadays set in bold, the run-on heading still has a certain utility. When a series of itemized paragraphs—say, a programme or manifesto, or some sort of descriptive list—forms part of a story, the run-on heading, in black caps. or lower-case according to circumstances, can be of value for labelling each paragraph. The heading should not exceed one or two short words and turnovers should be avoided. The paragraph runs on after a colon or a full point and a metal rule. Such a series of paragraphs is often set reverse indent, which emphasizes the run-on headings.

The run-on heading, usually in lower-case, is also useful for the News in Brief column; it is becoming common in such columns to construct the paragraphs in such a way that the first two or three words can be blacked up, thus giving the effect of a run-on heading. This style can be elaborated to the point of setting the first word or words of each brief in a bold display face to cover two lines of text, which runs on from it; this gives heavy, not to say dazzling, impact to a usually somewhat retiring column, but is obviously not commendable for speed in setting (Fig. 39).

BOMB CATCH.—An unexploded German bomb, estimated to weigh about 500lb., was landed on the beach at Hastings yesterday.

RETURN FROM CYPRUS.—The 1st Battalion The Suffolk Regiment, who have been in Cyprus since 1956, are coming home on or about May 22.

£500 RAID.—Three masked men attacked the wages cashier at a British Road Services depôt in Centaur Street, S.E., yesterday and stole £500 from the safe.

SWIMMING BATHS DEATH.—Colin Yeoll, aged 12, of Ravenscroft Road, Beckenham, Kent, was found yesterday dead in the deep end of Beckenham Public Baths.

TWINS' CONDITION.—The Thackeray Siamese twins, Timothy and Jeremy, who were separated on March 23 at St. Bartholomew's Hospital, London, are both continuing to progress satisfactorily.

Tests begin next month with East Anglia's TV station mast at Mendleshaw, near Ipswich.

Cheque for nearly £1,500 from the diocese was presented to the Bishop of Norwich, Dr. P. W. Herbert, on eve of his retirement.

Widow Mrs. Rebecca Lambert saw her son Kenneth, 18, drown in trying to recover a child's 2s. 11d. toy rubber lifebelt off beach at Blyth, Northumberland.

Captain Edward Lawrey, 61, of Plymouth, who went to sea from an orphanage, is new Commodore of the Port Line, London.

FIG. 39. Run-on sub-heading styles in newsbriefs: the traditional caps. and small caps. of *The Times* and the more elaborate treatment of the *Daily Mail.*

CROSSHEADS AND SIDEHEADS

Sub-headings, in the basic single-line style, are either centred (the crosshead) or flush left (the sidehead). They may be set in caps. or upper- and lower-case, either in the Bold or Doric duplexed with the text—which has the advantage that they can be written in copy and set on the same machine —or in a larger size of a bold or other contrasting face set on another machine or by hand. It is usual for the text-size sub-heading, particularly when it is a crosshead, to be set in caps., which makes the most of its breaking-up effect; but the upper- and lower-case style, more usual in America than here, is quite agreeable, provided that black upper- and lower-case is not otherwise used in text at all. Which is to be preferred for general use—the crosshead or the sidehead? It is a matter of taste; but general practice leans to the crosshead, written to retain reasonable white each end (not less than an em and a half of the body, or three letter-units) and never turning into a second line. That last is a not uncommon, and always slovenly, fault; if a sub-heading is to be a two-liner it should not be by accident (Fig. 40).

A well-designed paper explains itself at a glance. The typographical treatment distinguishes different kinds of news stories, and separates news from features. Further, it maintains interest throughout.

SENSATION IN TOWN'S COUNCIL

A well-designed paper explains itself at a glance. The typographical treatment distinguishes different kinds of news stories, and separates news from features. Further, it maintains interest throughout.

COURT SENSATION

A well-designed paper explains itself at a glance. The typographical treatment distinguishes different kinds ot news stories, and separates news from features. Further, it maintains interest throughout.

SENSATION

A well-designed paper explains itself at a glance. The typographical treatment distinguishes different kinds of news stories, and separates news from features. Further, it maintains interest throughout.

SENSATION IN COUNCIL CHAMBER

A well-designed paper explains itself at a glance. The typographical treatment distinguishes different kinds of news stories, and separates news from features. Further, it maintains interest throughout.

FIG. 40. These four crossheads in the bold (black) caps. of 7 pt. text exemplify (i) the line too wide and run solid, (ii) the line of reasonable width and correctly leaded, (iii) the line too short and excessively leaded, (iv) the clumsy turnover to a second line.

For indented settings, as described in Chapter 4, sub-headings must agree with the mode of the indention. Thus a centred indent requires a crosshead (a flush-left sidehead projecting beyond the matter would clearly look ungainly), and a reverse indent a sidehead: a centred crosshead over the full-out opening line of a reverse indented paragraph is out of harmony with the stress of the text setting; again it is a not uncommon fault.

LARGER-THAN-TEXT STYLES

Where technical resources permit, it is always better to have larger-than-text sub-headings for the main stories; and for these sub-headings the superior legibility of upper- and lower-case makes it, broadly speaking, preferable. Determination of the style and size of these larger sub-headings requires some care (Fig. 41). There are three possible style categories:

(i) *Display of the paper*: a newspaper headlined in Times, Bodoni, Caslon, Century, Cheltenham (for example) can employ the appropriate sizes of those series in bold (and bold italic) for sub-headings. A word of warning may be uttered against the use of the Bold Extended letter which exists in the Century and Cheltenham families; it gives a cramped and squat look to sub-headings, accentuated by narrow column measures.

(ii) *Sans contrast*: a contrasting bold Sans of the modern character is extremely effective, using either roman or italic. Linotype Metroblack is one of the best (with the slightly lighter and more condensed Metromedium as an alternative), while Ludlow Tempo Heavy and Intertype Vogue Extra Bold are of comparable genre.[1] Tempo Heavy has a

[1] Intertype Vogue has already been described as 'too mannered' and fanciful in its standard form. The alternative characters provided for C, G, J, Q and i, j, t greatly improve it for news use: see p. 67.

Sound headline

Sound headline

Sound headline

Sound headline

Sound headline

Sound headline

Sound headline

Sound headline

Sound headline

Sound headline

Sound headline

Sound headline

FIG. 41. Suitable types for larger-than-text crossheads or sideheads, all shown in 12 pt.: respectively Times Bold, Bodoni Bold, Century Bold, Metroblack, Metromedium, Poster (Ultra) Bodoni, Pabst.

Condensed Italic partner notably useful for combining strong colour with economical set in extra-narrow measures like those of the tabloids.

(iii) *Extra-heavy contrast*: the extra-heavy faces like Ludlow Black, Linotype Pabst, Ultra-Bodoni (the slab-serif Egyptians are perhaps a trifle too clumsy in sub-heading sizes) give maximum weight for size, are normally duplexed with an italic, and provide the strongest colour break for main stories. Discretion in their use is recommended for obvious reasons.

As to size, this has to be related to the general make-up of the paper, size of page, length of stories, and column measure. For the average paper with a column measure around $11\frac{1}{2}$ ems a sound crosshead size is 12 pt. in any of the ordinary bold faces (including Sans), with 14 pt. optional for splashes or major page leads. Regard must, of course, be had to the size of the particular type on its body: to get the equivalent effect in a small-faced type like Bodoni of a 12 pt. Century (for example) the 14 pt. size would be needed. For medium stories, in which it is still desired to use a larger-than-text crosshead, an intermediate size—conveniently, 10 pt.—in the same bold face series can be specified. It should be noted that as the small-faced types need a slight scaling-up (as against a 12 pt. norm) so the extra-

A well-designed paper explains itself at a glance. The typographical treatment distinguishes different kinds of news stories, and separates news from features.

Cross Head

A well-designed paper explains itself at a glance. The typographical treatment distinguishes different kinds of news stories, and separates news from features.

FIG. 42. Too big and too heavy: a 14-pt. Pabst italic crosshead in a 7 pt. $10\frac{1}{2}$-em column.

heavy faces need a slight scaling-down, say to 10 pt., unless they are being used in a very heavy splash. With the extra-heavy types the relationship of a crosshead's weight to the column measure becomes very important. A too large extra-heavy crosshead in a narrow column merely serves to distract and irritate the reader (Fig. 42).

UNDERSCORING AND OTHER ELABORATIONS

The underscoring of the larger sub-headings, especially crossheads, is commonly practised, often rather indiscriminately. Unless it is restricted to occasional use in special stories, underscoring amounts to an admission that there is something wrong with the display value of the sub-heading type. When underscoring in plain rule is specified, the weight of rule should not be left to the whim of the compositor; there should be an understanding with the composing room that the weight of the underscore should approximate to the weight of the face, e.g. if the thick strokes of the sub-heading type are 3 pts. wide the underscore should be in not less than 2 pt.-face rule; nothing looks more unbalanced than a heavy face underscored in light column rule. For 'fancy' underscoring choice should be confined to the simplest of the Monotype or other strip borders; the square dot for preference, or the wavy as a very occasional variant (Fig. 43).

Cross Heading ***Cross Heading***

Cross Heading

FIG. 43. Underscoring large crossheads with rule (the first is too light, the second the correct weight) or simple border.

For exceptionally long stories or reports of whatever kind, two-line crossheads or sideheads are invaluable. They can be constructed from a suitable bold or Sans face (and its italic or light) selected as described above. The first line is set in caps., the second in lower-case; they are independent lines and should not read on. For the crosshead style both lines are centred, the best effect being secured if the cap. line is slightly within the measure of the lower-case line. For sideheads the accepted style is the hanging indention ('full out and 1'). In either style a roman and italic fount, whether bold or Sans, offers three effective variations:[1] (*a*) roman caps., roman lower-case; (*b*) roman caps., italic lower-case; (*c*) italic caps.,

[1] The fourth variant—italic caps., roman lower-case—is excluded since roman as a subsidiary to italic is not normally acceptable.

italic lower-case. Of these (*b*) and (*c*) may be regarded as the best. The same variations in a bold and light Sans, e.g. Metroblack and Metrolite, would be: (*a*) bold caps., bold lower-case; (*b*) bold caps., light lower-case (the most suitable combination in this style); (*c*) light caps., light lower-case (too light for most purposes) (Fig. 44). An additional variation can be employed if the suggested intermediate size is available; this can be used for the lower-case lines in the three styles indicated. A smaller size for the second line is essential if one of the extra-heavy faces is used for a two-line sub-heading, the combined weight being otherwise too massive. Normally a 14 pt. extra-heavy cap. line will not require more than its own 10 pt. italic for the second line.

Century Bold/Italic

GRAND STYLE
A winning paper

GRAND STYLE
A winning paper

GRAND STYLE
A winning paper

Metroblack/Metrolite

GRAND STYLE
A winning paper

GRAND STYLE
A winning paper

Pabst 14 pt./10 pt. italic

FINE STYLE
A winning paper

FIG. 44. Two-line caps. and lower-case sideheads (hanging indent) or centred crossheads showing roman/italic or bold/light variations in the same size (12 pt.), and the roman/italic variation with a drop in size for the lower-case second line.

It has become fashionable in the more lavish 'populars' to box two-line sub-headings, usually in one or other of the elementary 'fancy' borders already mentioned. The box is frequently 'broken' at the bottom, often at the top as well; and if the sub-heading is of the elaborate kind that turns its subsidiary line, making a three-line heading, the break-line or even the whole heading is cut into the box. These decorative treatments take

He said: "I believe that I will fill the office in a way corresponding to its importance.

Warning

"I would like to say with the utmost emphasis: the position, task and work of the Federal President are much greater than you think."

FIG. 45. An example of a boxed sub-heading; a simple dotted border may be substituted for the rule.

time and (especially if composition is on piece-rates) money; nor are they sparing of space in make-up (Fig. 45).

PLACING AND SPACING

The last point to consider is in many ways the most important: namely, the placing and spacing of sub-headings (for the convenience of the remaining exposition—crossheads). For placing there are no hard-and-fast rules. To have too many crossheads is as bad as to have too few. To say that normally there should be a crosshead not less often than every fifth paragraph is to leave out of account the length of the paragraphs, the total length of the story in relation to the size and weight of the cross-heads, the column measure, and the general make-up of the page. Thus the proper placing of crossheads depends on the skill and judgement of the sub-editor and the make-up man, particularly the latter. A crosshead appearing well placed in galley proof may fall very badly, either too low (the commonest fault) or too high, when the story is turned across two or more columns in make-up, or has to be cut to fit. The man on the stone can obviate this error by a quick transposition, which will only rarely necessitate rewriting the crosshead. The lifting or dropping of an offending crosshead by one or two paragraphs is usually enough to correct the defect and make a substantial difference to the overall appearance of the page. A newspaper with badly placed crossheads proclaims itself a badly made-up newspaper.

On the spacing of crossheads it is possible (and necessary) to be quite precise. A crosshead must be leaded top and bottom and under no circumstances of space-pressure must those leads be removed; a crosshead run solid with text is worse than useless. Nor is the case much better if the leading is insufficient: for example, if a crosshead in caps. has only one thin ($1\frac{1}{2}$ pt.) lead inserted over it. Reasonable leading for a 12 pt. crosshead would be 7 pts. or 8 pts. over and 4 pts. under; for smaller sizes 5 pts. or 6 pts. over, 3 pts. under. Some papers have been known to require the

A well-designed paper explains itself at a glance. The typographical treatment distinguishes different kinds of news stories, and separates news from features. Further, it maintains interest throughout.

Sound headline

A well-designed paper explains itself at a glance. The typographical treatment distinguishes different kinds of news stories, and separates news from features. Further, it maintains interest throughout.

Sound headline

A well-designed paper explains itself at a glance. The typographical treatment distinguishes different kinds of news stories, and separates news from features. Further, it maintains interest throughout.

FIG. 46. Leading adjustment with a short breakline over a crosshead. The first example shows normal leading (6 pts. over), the second a reduction to 2 pts. over; in each case there is a 3-pt. lead under the crosshead.

automatic insertion of 5 or $5\frac{1}{2}$ pt. blank slugs over and under all crossheads, categorically forbidding their removal or reduction by the stonehand whatever the make-up exigencies; but identical heavy white under a crosshead is superfluous and the proportion indicated is superior. An important refinement has to be noted here. The suggested proportions for crosshead-leading assume that the breakline of the preceding paragraph is full, or nearly so. If the breakline is short, especially if it is not more than a quarter of the column measure—a frequent occurrence—its white has to be taken into account in relation to the crosshead (Fig. 46). That is to say, the top-leading requires discreet reduction if the white appearing over the crosshead is not to look excessive. The discretion must be left to the skill of the stonehand; but, as a rough indication, it can be said that the reduction may be to as little as 2 pts., if both the breakline and the crosshead are short enough.

This chapter has traced the sub-heading through developments of some complexity. For very many papers, however, particularly the local weeklies, this complexity is not necessary. Adequately leaded and well-placed ordinary crossheads, set in the bold face of the body of the paper (7 pt. or 8 pt.), plus one contrasting larger size for lead stories (say 12 pt.), will satisfactorily solve their sub-heading problems. Too much emphasis can never be laid on those two vital factors in sound crossheading—*spacing* and *placing*.

7 · Headline Types and Styles

THE typography of the newspaper headline is sharply conditioned by its function and its technical circumstances. For it has to serve at once as a *signal* and as a *summary*; and this it has to do within a fixed and inflexible measure, to which its set-width, or letter-count, and consequent reasonable ease of writing, have perforce to be related. Even with the modern newspaper's use of many multi-column headlines the determining factor of measure, from the standpoint of headline typography, remains the width of the single column. Given the narrow measures of today it is idle to select a basic headline type which is too wide for easy and lucid use in single column, however conveniently it may display in three- or four-column heads.

But if the importance of this mechanical factor of measure is recognized, it has to be conceded that the effective determination of headline types fit to perform their dual function, as defined above, depends upon a whole series of complex secondary considerations. Reasonable regard must be had for tradition, though this does not mean blind obeisance to the styles of half a century ago: the persistence of the weak mid-Victorian News Titlings here and there, even in a first-rank national newspaper like the *Daily Telegraph*, is not to be commended. Newspaper typographical tradition, in any event, is a changing thing, steadily modified by fashion; the fashion which wins general adoption becomes itself the tradition.

In general it may be asserted that during the past quarter of a century the trend of headline typography has been to stronger colour. Headlines have not only become freer and more flexible; they have become blacker. The day of the light, spindle-shanked headline, swimming almost indistinguishably in the grey ocean of the text, is long since done.

Colour, then, is a primary point to which attention has to be directed in selecting headline type. Allied to colour are *crispness* and *contrast*, two qualities which require a word of explanation. Crispness implies a clear-cut, sharp design of letter; one which tends to angularity rather than elegance, which is harsh rather than handsome; one, in short, which could never be classed as delicate, florid, or soft in its outline or serif-structure. This is certainly not an exhaustive definition. It might be read as including such angular and harsh letter as that of the prolific Egyptian family

(Rockwell, Memphis, Karnak), affected in the United States for news headlines. But here *contrast* would operate as a specific exclusion: for the monotoned, even-stroked Egyptians do not meet the requirement of clearly contrasting thin up-strokes and thick down-strokes; and a satisfactory headline type is one that embodies that traditional stroke differentiation. This proviso does not, however, apply to Sanserif letter, which can be of considerable use in the headline sphere, and which normally has even strokes.[1] In this last case contrast of a different, but also important, nature is present—the sheer contrast of black and white which results from sharp cut and strong colour accentuated by the absence of serifs.

With these general considerations in mind we can proceed to discuss in some detail the principal headline types upon which the newspaper man can call. They can be broken down by their serif-structure into these four specific groupings for the present exposition:

(*a*) *Blunt serifs*: as in the Edwardian *Cheltenham* family (Fig. 47), whose longevity and ubiquity are alike proverbial. An even-toned letter without sharp serifs, Cheltenham essentially contravenes the crispness and contrast requirements already outlined; but it is nevertheless admissible on the important qualifying grounds of tradition and association. A newspaper is ill-advised to break radically with tradition, to make itself provocatively unfashionable. Whatever subtle improvements and fine differentiations may be introduced, the newspaper must look like a newspaper. That is to say, the reader must subconsciously recognize and accept the headline style as being in line with normal newspaper patterns.

Cheltenham certainly has that outmoded period quality which so often stamps Edwardian design and makes it of less permanent value than some of its Victorian predecessors; by the same token it has nowadays a marked air of provincialism. Yet it has the considerable technical advantage of an enormous range of variations in weight and style. These include the weights most needed for news headlines—a Bold and a Bold Condensed, each with its corresponding italic (the Bold Extended is a squat and rather flabby letter not to be recommended though it may be necessary for a cap. streamer in an all-Cheltenham make-up). A clean and workmanlike newspage can be made by the sound use of its Bold and Bold Condensed, with the normal weight Wide and Condensed for light contrast where needed. A word of warning—the italic of the original Cheltenham Old Style is a feeble and fussy letter to be avoided under all circumstances.

The prime condition of success is the availability of the full range of sizes needed, both in roman and italic, for Cheltenham must be used

[1] The late Victorians produced some modified Sans faces with stroke differentiation. The style survives, e.g. in Ludlow Radiant Bold and Heavy. It is to be eschewed in news headings.

NEWSPAPER HEADLINES
Newspaper headlines are a sig

NEWSPAPER HEADLINES
Newspaper headlines are a s

NEWSPAPER HEADLINES ARE A
Newspaper headlines are a signal and

NEWSPAPER HEADLINES ARE I
Newspaper headlines are a signal a

NEWSPAPER HEADLINES ARE A
Newspaper headlines are a signal and a

NEWSPAPER HEADL
Newspaper headliners

FIG. 47. The main variants of Cheltenham (Ludlow) suitable for headlines—Bold and italic, Bold Condensed and italic, Condensed, and Bold Extended.

unmixed, never as one ingredient among other type faces. The only tolerable combination is Cheltenham and Sans (used occasionally for contrast); but even that depends on the Sans and how discreetly it is used. The only safe rule with Cheltenham is to have nothing but Cheltenham, which in view of the many variants mentioned is not difficult.

The extent of an all-Cheltenham range will depend on the character of the paper. The two roman and two italic founts specified, each in a full run from 12 pt. to 48 pt. inclusive with a 60 pt. roman cap. for streamers, would cope with the requirements of a daily paper with headlines freely displayed in the modern style. Indeed, even for this purpose the range could be modified without loss of effect, as follows: Bold roman 12 pt. to

48 pt. (60 pt.), Bold italic 12 pt. to 48 pt., Bold Condensed roman 14 pt. to 36 pt., Bold Condensed italic 14 pt. to 36 pt. Further modifications in the range can easily be determined in relation to the number and style of headlines designed. Thus a local weekly which does not run to more than double-column headlines may find 24 pt. or 30 pt. the largest size it requires; one which adheres to classical all single-column style may find its ceiling at 18 pt. or 24 pt. In these cases, too, the range can be reduced to two variants only: either the Bold Condensed roman and the Bold italic or the Bold roman and the Bold Condensed italic. A country weekly's

NEWSPAPER HEADLINES A
Newspaper headlines are a sign

NEWSPAPER HEADLINE
Newspaper Headlines are a
Newspaper headlines are a

FIG. 48. Clearface Bold—an Edwardian shocker of American extraction that has had far too long a news-heading life—with its Extra Bold, in which the unpleasant idiosyncrasies of the design are less obtrusive.

admirably simple Cheltenham headline scheme is illustrated in Chapter 8 (Fig. 77); and reference may be made to the sound employment of Cheltenham in the *Daily Herald* when it was first taken over and remodelled by Odhams in 1930. Few of the many subsequent typographical transformations of the *Herald* have proved as fully satisfactory as that initial Cheltenham style (Figs. 8, 10).

Cheltenham is incidentally one of the few news headline faces equally and fully available from the typefounders (though the unwary are cautioned against an early and highly unsatisfactory imitation called Winchester), Linotype, Intertype (Cheltonian series), Monotype (Gloucester series) and Ludlow.[1]

[1] Availability of this convenient kind can sometimes be a snare; a warning example is that other, and far worse, Edwardian American type-face, Clearface Bold (*c.* 1907). It is still the basic heading type of a number of local papers. Few faces, the monstrosities apart, have more departures from normal letter-design—strokes curved where they should be straight, blobs substituted for serifs, Modern and Old Face stress and serif-structure mixed, counters misshapen, horizontal strokes made diagonal. The Extra Bold version (typefounders only) is less offensive, since the thickening-up does something to conceal the basic defects (Fig. 48).

(*b*) *Fine* (*bracketed*) *serifs*: the largest group which fully satisfies the colour, crispness, and contrast requirements. Attention concentrates on three series:[1]

(i) *Caslon Old Face Heavy* is, like Cheltenham, of Edwardian vintage, but with a difference. It was not an original design, being essentially a thickening-up of the so-called 'Lining' Caslon Old Face, which was introduced by the Americans around the turn of the century as a cropped-descender, big-on-the-body version of the historic eighteenth-century letter. Stemming from such a source it has a clarity, sharpness and contrast not to be found in Cheltenham. As a large-faced letter (its 14 pt. has the weight of an 18 pt. in a long-descender face like Bodoni) with full, rich colour, it attained early popularity for news headlines (Fig. 50).[2]

NEWSPAPER HEADLINES A
Newspaper headlines are a signal

NEWSPAPER HEADLINES A
Newspaper headlines are a signal

FIG. 49. Caledonia Bold with its italic—a distinguished headline type.

The drawback to Caslon O.F. Heavy is that it is essentially a letter of a single range, its roman (except in its Ludlow version, as described below). At a late stage in its career it was provided with an unsatisfactory italic, a stiff and angular letter singularly lacking the qualities of the roman with which it was intended to sort, and recalling the italic of the long obsolete late Victorian jobbing letter, De Vinne. This italic, whose defects increase in direct ratio to its size (it is tolerable up to 14 pt.), is in any event only available in a full range of sizes from the typefounders; for keyboarding it may be had, up to 14 pt. only, on the Intertype. The totally different and highly agreeable Caslon Heavy italic designed for the Ludlow is a rounded and colourful letter, sorting admirably with the roman and a first-rate

[1] Among machine-set types in this group not further specified, though it may become fully available in this country soon, is the handsome American Caledonia Bold (Fig. 49). Both the roman and italic of this bold display extension of Linotype Caledonia make an admirable basic heading style for the more distinguished paper—an alternative in colour to Bodoni Bold, but with more warmth.

[2] See the facsimile of a *Daily News* front page of 1914, showing Caslon Old Face Heavy in decker style headlines, contrasting with Cheltenham Bold headlines in a *Daily Express* of the same date, reproduced in Morison, op. cit., pp. 308–9.

Ludlow Caslon Heavy/Italic: Typefounders' Heavy italic

NEWSPAPER HEADLIN

Newspaper headlines are a

NEWSPAPER HEADLI

Newspaper headlines are

Newspaper headlines are sign

Intertype, Linotype Caslon Heavy, Monotype 159

NEWSPAPER HEADLIN

Newspaper headlines are a sig

Newspaper headlines are a s

Newspaper headlines are a

Ludlow Caslon Bold and Bold Condensed

NEWSPAPER HEADLIN

Newspaper headlines are a

NEWSPAPER HEADLINES A

Newspaper headlines are a sign

Linotype Caslon Bold Condensed: Typefounders' Heavy Compressed

NEWSPAPER HEADLINES ARE A

Newspaper headlines are a signal and

NEWSPAPER headlines are a sign

Ludlow Caslon Light/Italic

NEWSPAPER HEADLIN

Newspaper headlines are a

NEWSPAPER HEADLIN

Newspaper headlines are all

FIG. 50. Headline variants of the modernized Caslon family. Note the significant differences in width of the various versions of the Heavy.

headline italic. As an exclusive Ludlow face it can, of course, only be specified when that machine is used.

A Condensed variant (formally named Compressed) is too emaciated, particularly in its lower-case, to have the strength for sound headlining; it does not retain the colour of its parent Bold as does its Cheltenham parallel. It is likewise a version restricted to the typefounders. Modified Condenseds, of somewhat greater strength, are available in Linotype and Ludlow matrices. Other weights of this Caslon range can be had on the Ludlow, the light italic and the Bold roman being specially worth remark for news headings.

Caslon O.F. Heavy roman can be used with equal effect in caps. or upper- and lower-case; though, because it is so big on its body, an all-cap. headline must always be judiciously leaded. It sorts well with either Century or Bodoni italic. And while the italic and Condensed are not fully available, as noted, the roman can be had equally from the typefounders or on the Linotype, Intertype, Monotype, and Ludlow.[1]

(ii) *The Times Bold and Titlings*: in the twenty-five years since Printing House Square devised these bold accompaniments to its typographical revolution, they have enormously extended their range (Fig. 51). Colour–crispness–contrast are found in full measure, and in appropriate balance, in these types. Perhaps no other designs of this century so well combine smartness with strength; these letters are handsome, but they hit. Times Bold is both big on its body and has (unlike Caslon O.F. Heavy, for example) a relatively condensed lower-case; the x-height and narrow set, the upright oblong rather than square aspect, which specially mark the

[1] Slight variations in set-width between these versions contribute to subtle differences in appearance and are of some practical significance. The Monotype version (series 159, designated Old Style Bold No. 2 by its makers, though commonly sold as Caslon Heavy) is wider than the keyboard versions, for instance; in their turn these vary, Intertype's being narrower than Linotype's.

NEWSPAPER HEADLINES
Newspaper headlines are a sign

NEWSPAPER HEADLINES
Newspaper headlines are a sign

NEWSPAPER HEADLINES ARE

NEWSPAPER HEADLINES ARE

NEWSPAPER HEADLIN

NEWSPAPER HEADLINES ARE

FIG. 51. The headline range of Times Roman: in the original Monotype versions respectively Bold with italic (334), Bold Titling (332), Bold Titling No. 2 (328), Extended Titling (339), Titling (329).

Times Roman, have been retained in the Bold, colour and weight being gained by an internal thickening of the strokes; its italic is not so satisfactory. Of the Bold Titlings, the Extended is a square, full-face letter, of considerable weight for its size; the Heavy (Bold Titling No. 2) is a letter of outstanding quality, strongly coloured, and with remarkable brilliance and bite; the thicker Bold Titling has its value as a variant.

There is an important mechanical restriction, from a newspaper point of view, on these fine faces. The full range of Times Bold and Italic, Extended Titling, Heavy Titling, Bold Titling up to and including 72 pt. is available only on Monotype (Series 334, 339, 328, 332 respectively). Newspapers which machine-set all their headings are cut off from the full Times repertory.

For keyboard setting (Linotype matrices) Times Bold, roman only, exists up to 24 pt., Times Extended Titling (designated Times Heading Bold) up to 18 pt., Times Heavy Titling (designated Times Heading Bold Condensed) up to 24 pt. The less generally useful medium-weight Times Titling (series 329) is available on the Linotype also up to 24 pt. (designated Times Heading).

(iii) *Century*: this extensive family (Fig. 52) has long shared with Bodoni the widest popularity for headline purposes. Among national

NEWSPAPER HEADLINES
Newspaper headlines are a si

NEWSPAPER HEADLINES
Newspaper headlines are a si

NEWSPAPER HEADLINES
Newspaper headlines are a si

NEWSPAPER HEADL
Newspaper headlines t

FIG. 52. Century—Britain's most popular headline type; these are the Ludlow versions, respectively Century (often designated Century Expanded), Bold with italic, Bold Extended.

newspapers it provides the basic headline type for the *Daily Express*, *Mail*, *News-Chronicle*, and *Manchester Guardian*. Of American origin (the two faces described above, the reader may be reminded, are English in design or provenance), it began life sixty years ago as an improved Modern Roman text letter commissioned by that famous printer Theodore L. De Vinne for his production of the *Century Magazine*. A stronger and more even tone, falling short of the complete monotone of Cheltenham or Ionic, gave it a certain plain, prim clarity which made it also popular for school textbooks and, to a certain extent in pre-Ionic days, for newspaper text.

This original roman subsequently proliferated into a near-Cheltenham medley of variations—Bold, Extended, Condensed, with corresponding italics. The Bold and Bold italic are the most useful, and most used, variant for newspaper headlining. No one can contend that Century Bold is a handsome letter: it possesses neither the richness of Caslon O.F. Heavy nor the distinction of Times Bold; but it has one important practical affinity with the last named—a relatively condensed lower-case, which is not the least of its virtues in the modern narrow column. The essential proportions of Century Bold, that is to say, are the 'upright oblong' of the Moderns; it is big on its body; its unassuming, but sturdy, appearance admirably fits it for its newspaper purpose. It has a complete range of a fully satisfactory italic, sorting most faithfully and acceptably with its roman: again an important practical point in its favour.

The Bold Condensed need only be mentioned to be dismissed. It is an abnormally compressed letter of the order of Cheltenham Bold Extra Condensed; and it is not available in an effective range of sizes. The Bold Extended has a certain utility, though not in the small and medium sizes and certainly not in single column; like most similar over-wide faces it is too overblown, except in its large sizes (from 48 pt. upwards) for cap. streamers or multi-column upper- and lower-case page lead heads. The original roman of Century can be used for light contrast with its bold brethren.

As regards availability the Century family is in precisely the opposite position from Times. It is exclusively machine-set, either keyboard (Linotype and Intertype) or Ludlow (the only means of obtaining it in the larger sizes, i.e. above the slug machine's upper- and lower-case limit of 36 pt.). In America it could be had from the typefounders, but never in this country; nor has it ever been cut for the Monotype.

(*c*) *Hairline* (*unbracketed*) *serifs*: only one type falls for consideration in this category—the brilliant *Bodoni*. The modern type family which bears the name of the illustrious Parmesan printer and type-cutter of the turn of the eighteenth-nineteenth centuries is not a reproduction of any one of his faces but, as has often been pointed out, a synthesis of the main features of all of them (Fig. 53). Thus it emphasizes, more than its individual prototypes, the characteristics of the so-called 'mechanically perfect' letter, the great divide between Old Face and Modern. Extreme sharpness and straightness of cut, absence of curvature, the greatest possible contrast in up- and down-strokes, straight hairline serifs, give Bodoni its specially acute and arresting quality.

Like Century, our modern Bodoni was devised in the United States; the standard weight was first cut in 1911, for movable type, by Morris Benton, chief designer of the American Type Founders Company, and was shortly afterwards made available on the Linotype. Versions of Bodoni, closely approximating to this first cutting, followed on all other composing machines. But for news headline purposes, except as a light contrasting letter, this primary Bodoni lacked boldness, especially in its larger display sizes. Its virtues for news display were not fully apparent until it was provided with a Bold and Bold italic. By thickening the down-strokes, while leaving the hairlines untouched, this Bold variant exaggerated the inherent extremism of Bodoni but at the same time added the colour which was needed. Nowadays this is the version which, to the average newspaper composing room or editorial department, is Bodoni *tout court*; the normal Bodoni is likely to be designated Bodoni Light.

Unlike all the other types so far described, Bodoni is small on its body, retaining the long descenders of its prototype. This has to be constantly borne in mind. There is, of course, the countervailing advantage that Bodoni can at a pinch be set solid whereas the bigger-faced types require leading if they are not to look cramped and crushed.

The special virtue of Bodoni for editorial display lies in its Bold italic, outstanding as an italic headline face. It is both colourful and crisp; its cursive effect contrasts admirably with its own, or almost any other, roman; it provides perfectly that visual and colour differentiation which makes a sound italic an essential ingredient of vigorous newspage make-up. Not least among its qualities is what may be called its universality: that is to say, it makes up well as a contrasting italic with the roman of any of the three rounded-serif faces analysed above, or with any of the San-serifs discussed below.

As for availability, the position is in one sense plain and straightforward. There is no version of the standard modern recutting of Bodoni or Bodoni Bold to be had from the typefounders in this country; the Caslons produced, in the 'light' weight only, a distorted Bodoni with short descenders whose roman was badly proportioned though the italic was not unpractical, since its slope was so contrived that kerns were avoided, even with the lower-case 'f'. But complications arise between the comparable Bodoni versions provided by the Monotype, the keyboard slug machines, and the Ludlow. Compare, for example, Monotype Bodoni Bold (Series 260) with Linotype or Intertype Bodoni Bold. The differences in the roman are not great; but in the italic they are marked. The Monotype italic, with a more pronounced slope, is appreciably wider than the keyboard versions; it is also fully kerned, even to the hairline serifs on many of its caps. The closer-set, slightly condensed, slug italic may be conceded neater and more practical for narrow-column headline display, despite inelegancies like the mutilated lower-case 'f'. The angle matrices of the Ludlow italic enable some kerning effect to be retained even in the solid slug line; it will be noticed, however, that the Ludlow Bodoni Bold is somewhat heavier, and this is most evident in the larger sizes.

The normal weight Bodoni, useful for light contrast, can be had in both roman and italic on the slug machines, Ludlow, and Monotype (Series 135); variants are Ludlow Bodoni Modern, a more elegant rendering favoured by some papers, and the semi-bold Monotype Bodoni Bold No. 2 (Series 195). Of the normal weight there is a condensed version, again of value for light contrast, on the Linotype only; while two substantially different Bold Condenseds, most practical for narrow column measures, come from Linotype, Intertype, and Monotype (Series 529). The Linotype

Linotype and Monotype (135) Bodoni/Italic

NEWSPAPER HEADLINES ARE
Newspaper headlines are a signal
NEWSPAPER HEADLINES ARE
Newspaper headlines are a signal

NEWSPAPER HEADLINES ARE
Newspaper headlines are a signal a
NEWSPAPER HEADLINES A
Newspaper headlines are a signal

Ludlow Bodoni True-cut (Modern) with italic

NEWSPAPER HEADLINES AR
Newspaper headlines are a signal
NEWSPAPER HEADLINES ARE
Newspaper headlines are a signal and

Ludlow Bodoni Campanile/Italic

NEWSPAPER HEADLINES ARE A SIGNAL AND
Newspaper headlines are a signal and a summ
NEWSPAPER HEADLINES ARE A SIGNAL AN
Newspaper headlines are a signal and a sum

FIG. 53. Varying versions of the great Bodoni range, illustrating the differences in design and set-width, e.g. in the Bold Italic and Bold Condensed; continued on next page.

Linotype, Ludlow, Monotype (260) Bodoni Bold/Italic

NEWSPAPER HEADLINES ARE

Newspaper headlines are a signal

NEWSPAPER HEADLINES AR

Newspaper headlines are a signal

NEWSPAPER HEADLINES A

Newspaper headlines are a sign

NEWSPAPER HEADLINES A

Newspaper headlines are a si

NEWSPAPER HEADLINES A

Newspaper headlines are a sign

NEWSPAPER HEADLINES

Newspaper headlines are a sig

Linotype Bodoni Condensed

NEWSPAPER HEADLINES ARE A SIGN

Newspaper headlines are a signal and a s

Linotype and Monotype (529) Bodoni Bold Condensed

NEWSPAPER HEADLINES ARE A SIGN

Newspaper headlines are a signal and a su

NEWSPAPER HEADLINES ARE A SIGNAL

Newspaper headlines are a signal and

Monotype (595) Headline Bold/Italic (Typefounders' Grot No. 9)

NEWSPAPER HEADLINES ARE A
Newspaper headlines are a sig

NEWSPAPER HEADLINES ARE
Newspaper headlines are a sign

Ludlow Gothic Medium Condensed, Linotype Gothic Condensed No. 25

NEWSPAPER HEADLINES ARE A SIG
Newspaper headlines are a signal a

NEWSPAPER HEADLINES ARE A SUM
Newspaper headlines are a signal and

Ludlow Square Gothic and Square Gothic Heavy

NEWSPAPER HEADLIN
Newspaper headlines as

NEWSPAPER HEADLINE
Newspaper headlines are

Monotype Grot Bold Extended 150, Grot Condensed 33

NEWSPAPER HEADLI
Newspaper headlines

NEWSPAPER HEADLINES ARE A SI
Newspaper headlines are a signal a

Monotype Grot Bold 216

NEWSPAPER headlines

Ludlow Gothic Condensed and Intertype Alternate Gothic No. 1

NEWSPAPER HEADLINES ARE A SIGNAL AND A
Newspaper headlines are a signal and a summa

NEWSPAPER HEADLINES ARE A SIGNAL AND A SU
Newspaper headlines are a signal and a summary

Linotype Gothics, 19/17, 20/18

NEWSPAPER HEADLINES ARE A SIGNAL AND A S
Newspaper headlines are a signal and a summ

NEWSPAPER HEADLINES ARE A SIGNAL AND A S
Newspaper headlines are a signal and a summ

NEWSPAPER HEADLINES ARE A SIGNAL
Newspaper headlines are a signal and a

NEWSPAPER HEADLINES ARE A SIGNAL
Newspaper headlines are a signal and a

Ludlow Record Gothic Extra Condensed

NEWSPAPER HEADLINES ARE A SIGNAL AND A SUMMARY
Newspaper headlines are a signal and a summary of what

FIG. 54. The Victorian Sanserifs (Gothics and Grotesques), with their modern adaptations and different versions.

and Intertype face has wider caps. than the Monotype, but more condensed and less strongly coloured lower-case.

Associated with Bodoni in trade parlance are ranges of extra-heavy and extra-condensed letter which have nothing to do with the great typographer but share the thick–thin contrast and hairline serifs. The 'ultras' —Monotype Ultra Bodoni (Series 120) or Falstaff (Series 323), Ludlow Bodoni Black, Linotype Poster Bodoni, Intertype Bodoni Modern—are all versions of the English Regency 'fat face', later called Elephant by the typefounders; with their italics, they are powerful auxiliaries (for strap-lines, block headings, crossheads) but are not suitable for main news headings. The principal extra-condensed available is Ludlow Bodoni Campanile, derived from an early Victorian elongated and compressed roman; modern narrow measures have brought it into some favour. It needs care in handling, though, and its italic, actually a sloped roman, is a most uneasy letter. Of similar character, but more refined in cut, is Monotype Onyx (Series 591). The general comment may be made that both the extra-heavy and extra-condensed 'Bodonis' have wider utility in feature-page and magazine typography than on news pages.

(*d*) *Sanserifs*: this is a field of great variety and complexity. But here it can be dealt with summarily under two main heads:

(i) *The Victorians*: the extensively revived old-world Grotesques and Gothics (eccentric misnomer) break down into three main weights—a Bold (the Square Gothic or Grot), a Bold Condensed (Medium Sans), and a lighter Extra Condensed (usually called Condensed). Fig. 54 will make the characteristics of these clear, in their varying versions, without further description. Ludlow Square Gothic is outstanding in its class and has a Heavy partner; the typefounders' and Monotype versions (bar Series 216) rank below it. Ludlow also provides a sound Medium and Condensed Sans, as do the typefounders; the last named, in fact, originated the best of all Medium Sans, the famous Grotesque No. 9, also available in a full Monotype range, italic as well as roman, designated Headline Bold (Series 595). The Ludlow condensed Gothics now have keyboard parallels—Linotype Gothic Condensed No. 25, from 12 pt. to 36 pt. (Medium), and Intertype Alternate Gothic No. 1 (Condensed).

The Medium and Condensed series form the accepted basic ingredients of the 'tabloid' style (*Daily Mirror* and *Daily Sketch*) but are too heavy and bludgeoning for fullsheet display (e.g. the *Daily Herald*). Square Grot serves as a strong streamer and lead headline variant for a lighter, seriffed—Caslon, Century, or Bodoni—make-up; and in the same way Medium Sans, especially in lower-case, makes the ideal occasional contrast, particularly for single-column tops.

(ii) *The Moderns*: let it be said at once that the great Gill Sans family,

Spartan (with Italic)—Medium, Bold, Black, Black Condensed

Newspaper headlines are a sig
Newspaper headlines are a sig

Newspaper headlines are a s
Newspaper headlines are a s

Newspaper headlines are a
Newspaper headlines are a

Newspaper headlines are a signal and
Newspaper headlines are a signal and

Erbar Bold Condensed with Light Condensed

NEWSPAPER HEADLI NEWSPAPER HEADLI
Newspaper headline Newspaper headline

FIG. 55. Modern headline Sanserifs, of American design. Spartan has been a U.S. Linotype speciality but Erbar Condensed is available on the Linotype in Britain.

equipped though it is with all the necessary variants (Bold, Bold Condensed, and the rest), is not really suitable for news headlines. Just that superiority of design, those individual letter points of finesse, which give it its note of urbanity in good job or advertising display, irritate in a headline, where there cannot be the delicacies of composition needed to give Gill its full effect. The same applies to the less elegant but still mannered Granby, the main Sans family fathered by the British typefounders. The curious may refer to the Granby typography of the *News-Chronicle* in the thirties, and may note the far less satisfactory use of Granby in some local papers (Fig. 9). Either Gill or Granby can certainly be used to provide an harmonious and balanced make-up; but it will lack the sharpness and urgency that a good newspaper make-up should have.

Of the modern German Sanserifs Erbar, in its condensed version, has won wide popularity as a news headline type in America; a range is now

METRO: Black No. 1/Italic, Medium No. 2/Italic, Lite No. 2

NEWSPAPER HEADLINES AR
Newspaper headlines are a sign

NEWSPAPER HEADLINES AR
Newspaper headlines are a sign

NEWSPAPER HEADLINES ARE A
Newspaper headlines are a signal

NEWSPAPER HEADLINES ARE A
Newspaper headlines are a signal

NEWSPAPER HEADLINES A
Newspaper headlines are a su

FIG. 56. These modern Sanserifs, Linotype, Ludlow, and Intertype (last two on facing page), are also all of American origin, but have long been available, and popular, in Britain.

being provided on the Linotype here. Ranking with Erbar is the American-designed Linotype Metro series, long available in this country, and one of the best modern Sanserifs for news headlines.[1] Metroblack and Metromedium, with their italics, provide a fine Bold and Semi-Condensed range; the Metrolite is available for light contrast. The angularity and sharpness of Metro give it precisely that punch and urgency that make a first-rate news heading (Fig. 56). As a keyboarded type, its ceiling (with lower-case) is 36 pt.; but the Ludlow offers a suitable companion letter in Tempo Bold and Heavy, especially the Bold Condensed, the Heavy italic, and the Heavy Condensed italic. With Tempo Heavy roman it is

[1] The American newspapers themselves prefer Linotype Spartan (Fig. 55), a Sans approximating more to the Ludlow Tempo family, and comprising a comparable range of graded weights, each with italic (Medium, Bold, Black, Black Condensed). Spartan has not yet been available in this country; its popularity in the States was enhanced by the arrangement between Mergenthaler Linotype and the American Type Founders Company whereby the large display sizes (up to 120 pt.) were cut for hand-setting in movable type.

TEMPO: Heavy/Italic, Heavy Condensed Italic, Bold Condensed/Italic, Extra Heavy Cond.

NEWSPAPER HEADLINES!
Newspaper headlines are a

NEWSPAPER HEADLINES
Newspaper headlines are a

NEWSPAPER HEADLINES ARE A SIG
Newspaper headlines are a signal and

NEWSPAPER HEADLINES ARE A SIG
Newspaper headlines are a signal and

NEWSPAPER HEADLINES ARE A SIG
Newspaper headlines are a signal and

NEWSPAPER HEADLINES ARE A
Newspaper headlines are a sig

VOGUE: Extra Bold/Oblique, Bold, Extra Bold Condensed

NEWSPAPER HEADLINES AR
Newspaper headlines are a si

NEWSPAPER HEADLINES ARE
Newspaper headlines are a sign

NEWSPAPER HEADLINES ARE A SIGNAL AND
Newspaper headlines are a signal and a su

necessary to specify the alternative 'squared' characters for A, M, N, W; with these caps. in their normal pointed form the type has the look of one that has strayed from advertising display into news. Similarly with the Intertype Vogue series, if used for headings; the alternative characters already mentioned (Fig. 22) are essential.

The foregoing survey of type faces suitable for news headlines does not of itself answer the question: *What is the best heading dress for our newspaper?* But it provides the material for the answer, which has to be given in terms of quantitative, qualitative, and mechanical availability, i.e. the size-range and variants of a given type face, and on what machines it can be had (a paper keyboarding the great bulk of its headings cannot choose an exclusively Ludlow or Monotype heading type, and vice versa). Within these constantly operating objective terms, however, there remains the subjective element of choice; yet even so, that choice is far from purely subjective, for it does not—or should not—express an individual preference in isolation from the whole personality of the paper. Every paper has such a personality, or character, determined by its policy and its readership. The type dress of its headlines should express that character, should fit the purpose of the particular paper. Thus a 'class' journal might choose from the Times or Bodoni range (or Caledonia Bold, when available), though a suitable manipulation of the Caslon range could be effective. A 'popular' sheet could get a colourful and strong result by a bolder and more varied handling of Caslon, or could find the answer to all its problems in Century (with a Bold Sans 'kicker'). For a solid country weekly a simple arrangement of Cheltenham might well fill the bill. A weekly in a more urban or suburban area could score with a modern Sans like Metro (Black and Medium) or Tempo, with or without Bodoni Bold as a contrast. For a militant, aggressive sheet the brusque heaviness of square and condensed Gothics is attractive (provided the lighter contrast, e.g. Bodoni Bold italic, is not forgotten).

BASIC HEADLINE STYLE

There are three basic typographical styles of headlining: (i) all caps., as in *The Times* or the *Telegraph*; (ii) all upper- and lower-case, as in the *Observer* (a style first made famous, and still adhered to, by the *New York Herald-Tribune*); (iii) caps. and upper- and lower-case mixed, as in the great majority of newspapers.

The all-cap. style has the weight of classic tradition behind it, and little else. Its utility is severely limited to the austere columns of the 'class' newspaper. And here it requires, to be acceptable, a handsome and strong titling letter (as in *The Times* range); while, since the headlines are set in traditional decker fashion, the most liberal whiting-out is essential. Within these limitations the all-cap. style can be effectively employed, though its field cannot but remain restricted. One of its important elements is colour contrast, i.e. good management of light and bold in the headlines.

The all upper- and lower-case style has one powerful recommendation—that lower-case lines are always more legible than cap. lines. Further, the squared-off and static effect of caps. is banished by the dynamic impression of upper- and lower-case's irregular white arising from the ascending and descending letters. Essentially this style is equally suitable for 'class' or popular newspapers; but in the latter case there is at least one important limiting factor. If multi-column streamer or lead headings are employed, the liberal letter-count of lower-case, together with the need for emphasis, will compel the use of very large sizes (e.g. 72 pt.); and even so it will often be found that the brief wording required is too short for a

Yard Talk Will
Hear Much Of
The Dispute

Yard talks will
hear plenty of
the dispute

FIG. 57. The 'all up' and 'all down' styles in upper- and lower-case headlining.

lower-case line or lines of the size desired; the sub-editors will therefore be driven to the ungainly device of padding-out main headings with superfluous wordage, or constructing them in a circumlocutory fashion that defeats the primary aim of good headline writing. On the other hand, if headlines do not normally exceed double column the all upper- and lower-case style can be made entirely effective.

For practical purposes style (iii), the mixture of cap. and lower-case headings, makes the best of both worlds and will be found the most flexible. That it is by far the most general style is sufficient justification for its utility without further argument. It can be applied to the traditional decker (with cap. and lower-case decks alternating) or to the modern free style, with some headlines in caps., some in lower-case, and varying combinations discussed in more detail below.

At this point an important question of style may be broached. Should lower-case headlines be in upper- and lower-case throughout (the first letter of each word capitalized or 'kept up') or should they be in even lower-case, apart, naturally, from the first word and any proper names? To 'keep up' uniformly is both space-wasting and ugly, with a cap. letter introducing every short prepositional and similar word; the top-heavy

'Of' is particularly offensive (Fig. 57). Thus the upper- and lower-case style in any event requires that articles, prepositions, conjunctions should be 'kept down' for the sake of decent appearance. It appears only logical, therefore, to keep everything down; and the adoption of the even lower-case style by many newspapers is a natural consequence of this and of the not inconsiderable contribution that even lower-case makes to 'keeping in' in narrow column measures.[1]

Related to the three basic headline styles are the four methods of securing headline variation. These are:

(i) By *Size*: this primary variation, while obviously applying in general to any scheme of graded headlines, is rarely employed as an exclusive method. Even *The Times*, which dresses its away news pages in graded sizes of its Extended Titling, changes to graded sizes of Heavy Titling for the top of the Bill Page (and normally sets at least one top heading on that page in the lighter Titling for contrast). Nevertheless, large areas of *The Times* are admirable examples of pure size variation in headlines—variation solely by graded sizes of a uniform style (in this case, all caps.) of one type face. It is essential to note how the satisfactory effect of so simple a mode depends first on the superlative design of the face itself and second on the ample whiting.

(ii) By *Weight*: this is a further stage, which employs the differentiation between Bold and Light, Bold and Condensed, &c., in one type family. As in variation by size only, variation by weight implies uniformity of style, either all caps. or all lower-case. It is thus highly restricted but achieves the aim of varied colour on the page.

(iii) By *Style*: in its simplest form this uses the caps. and lower-case of one type face, either all roman or all italic. With two alphabets, the cap. and the lower-case, it thus greatly increases the possible variety in appearance of headlines but retains a uniformity of structure and colour which may make for monotony in the page as a whole unless whiting is generous, as in the *Manchester Guardian*'s original Century Bold roman style of 1952 (Fig. 58). But this monotony can be overcome, even within the confines of the same series, by using both the roman and the italic. Not only is a variety in appearance thus secured; it is enhanced by the subtle differences in colour between any Bold roman and its italic.

This use of four alphabets—roman caps., italic caps., roman lower-case, italic lower-case—in a suitable range of sizes, provides the backbone for any sound scheme of headline display in the modern style.

(iv) By *Contrast*: this method of securing variation, by the use of con-

[1] Some American authorities, like the late John E. Allen (*Newspaper Designing*, pp. 407–8), have argued that lower-case headings look 'ragged' unless the opening word of every line is kept up; this seems to sacrifice consistent and agreeable style to a very incidental aspect of form.

trasting types, operates within the wide limits of possible type contrast. There is an obvious difference between, say, contrasting Caslon Old Face Heavy and 'light' Bodoni roman, Times Heavy Titling and Bodoni Bold italic, Square Grot and Bodoni Bold roman, to mention some combinations current since the war. The reader may recall earlier observations on the suitability of Bodoni Bold italic for combination and contrast with any of the rounded-serif faces or with Sans; and, equally, on the unsuitability of Cheltenham to combine with anything but itself. One general point should be added. In any variation by contrast the heavier type (e.g. a Bold Sans) should never follow the lighter (e.g. Bodoni Bold italic), but always the other way about. If in a particular heading the heavier type is to be subsidiary to the lighter, it should always be as a strap- or over-line, never a second deck (Fig. 59).

SINGLE FAMILY OR MIXTURE?

Should news-headline style be based on a single type family (with its own variants) or on a mixture of types? For a 'class' paper, with decker headings, the single family amply suffices (and in at most two variants, say roman and italic, or Bold and Light, or Bold and Condensed); the conservative majority of local weekly newspapers are in like case. For the freer make-up of the popular daily the single family, in its Bold roman and

FIG. 58. Simple style variation in headlines; a portion of a *Manchester Guardian* news page after the 1952 change to an all-Century Bold heading style.

italic can also, as already suggested, provide the basis; but here it is necessary to make certain qualifications.

First, the single family must be available in the fullest possible range of sizes in both roman and italic. Second, the uniformity of single-family treatment requires the addition of one contrasting typographical ingredient to avoid flatness, to give savour to the page. This commonly, and aptly, means the use of Sans (No. 9 style) for an occasional upper- and lower-case multi-line single-column top heading, best placed in the centre of the page. The reader's eye is immediately caught (a valuable point for the prominent 'talking-point' story which does not rate lead or second lead position) and any tendency to a dull over-even appearance is avoided. The Sans top, in short, gives a kick to the whole make-up; which was why it was first devised by the Century-based *Daily Express* (Fig. 8). The general adoption of the device of the Sans 'kicker' is sufficient proof of its utility.[1]

It will be appreciated that this case for discreet, controlled, and specific sharp contrast is not a case against the single-family basis. If the Sans, that is to say, were allowed to spread until the page were half Sans and half the basic family the style would have departed fully from the single-family approach in favour of the mixture, and a muddled, self-defeating mixture. That is not the kind of mixture visualized, which is the use of a contrasting italic (e.g. Bodoni) with the basic roman. Does such a mixture present any advantages over the single family basis? Certainly a slight extra differentiation in cut, colour, and weight, which can add to the variety of the make-up but at the same time requires more careful handling to avoid over-balancing (e.g. too much Bodoni or too much basic roman). It does not obviate the need for the Sans 'kicker'.

The virtue of the single-family approach, as of any reasonable limitation of typographic resources, is the discipline and economy of means it helps to enforce. To extract maximum variation from minimum resources is the most salutary of all exercises in typography, whether in a newspaper or in any other medium. Let the newspaperman note how the changes can be rung on the four alphabets of any fount of roman with italic. For normal keyboard-setting this requires only one double-letter fount of matrices (one magazine) up to 14 pt. and with a special adjustment up to 24 pt. On this basis a three-size scheme, providing twelve alphabets, would need only four matrix founts on the slug machine: e.g. 14 pt. roman/italic, 24 pt. roman/italic, 36 pt. roman, 36 pt. italic. Such a simple scheme would meet the headline needs of a substantial local weekly, for example,

[1] In a Sans make-up, the Sans 'kicker' would be a contradiction in terms, obviously. Given the marked weight variation that is possible in Sans the contrasting-type heading is perhaps less necessary; where required, any Bold italic, the coarser the better (e.g. Cheltenham), can suitably be employed. The term 'kicker', it may be noted here, is used differently in America where it means a species of strap-line.

with as much variety as could possibly be desired (Fig. 60). Only a large-size front-page streamer is not catered for, and that can always be hand-set, either from type or on the Ludlow.

THE SIZE AND STYLE OF HEADLINES

The size range for headlines needs to run from a lower limit of 10 pt. (or 12 pt.) to an upper limit of 30 pt. (or at the most 36 pt.) for 'class' make-up with decker headings; for popular make-up the ceiling has to be raised to not less than 60 pt. (with a small-faced letter like Bodoni it may be 72 pt.). Within these limits the range of sizes carried, in both roman and italic,

GOOD TYPE IN WIDE HEADS

Design tells in long run

GOOD TYPE IN WIDE HEADS

Design tells in long run

TYPE CALLS FOR GOOD TASTE

Design a problem for typographer

FIG. 59. Type contrast in headlines—good and bad. In No. 1 the 36 pt. Metroblack caps. go well with the 24 pt. Bodoni Bold italic lower-case second deck, though No. 2 shows that to reverse the style is most disagreeable. The third shows that a strap-line in Sans caps. of a suitable size (14 pt. Metroblack here) suits a main deck in 36 pt. Bodoni Bold italic upper- and lower-case.

1
Good headline offers

2
Good headline offers
bigger appeal

3
Good headline offers

4
Good headline offers
bigger appeal

5
GOOD HEADLINE

6
GOOD HEADLINE
MAKES NEWS

7
GOOD HEADLINE

8
GOOD HEADLINE
MAKES NEWS

9
GOOD HEADLINE
MAKES NEWS
Helps to win sales

10
GOOD HEADLINE
Helps to win sales,
please readers

11
Good heading
makes news

12
Good heading
scores with
good news

13
Good heading
makes news

14
Good heading
scores with
good news

15
HEADLINES
THAT HIT
They please reader

16
HEADLINES
THAT HIT

FIG. 60. Some headline variations, in single and double column, possible with three sizes of roman and italic, from four founts of Linotype matrices (Bodoni Bold)—14 pt. with italic, 24 pt. with italic, 36 pt. roman, 36 pt. italic (with a number-code). The larger double-column styles can be set three column; and numerous other variations can be devised; continued on following pages.

17
HEADLINES
THAT HIT
ARE GOOD

18
HEADLINES
THAT HIT
ARE GOOD

19
Headline
style is
dynamic

20
Headline
style is
dynamic

21
Headline style makes the
biggest reader-impact

22
Headline style makes the
biggest reader-impact

23
HEADLINE STYLE HITS
A READER HARDEST

24
HEADLINE STYLE HITS
A READER HARDEST

25

Headline styles are dynamic in effect

26

Headline styles are dynamic in effect

27

HEADLINES ARE VITAL ITEMS

Biggest impact on reader

28

HEADLINES ARE VITAL ITEMS

Biggest impact on reader

29

HEADLINES ARE VITAL ITEMS

Biggest impact on reader

30

HEADLINES ARE VITAL ITEMS IN YOUR PAPER

should be complete, i.e. 12, 14, 18, 24, 30, 36, 42, 48, 60 pts. Where a contrasting Sans is used for single-column 'kickers' as described above, its size range can be limited to 24–36 pts. inclusive; in modern 11–11½ em measures the most useful size is the 30 pt.

The largest sizes are needed for setting the front-page lead heading or streamer, normally in caps., and usually not a full-page 'banner': a column within page width, or even less with a turn line (five columns to three, for instance), is preferred. Stepping down from the streamer to the splash heading calls variously on the 48–36 pt. range, also needed for the main lines of lead headlines throughout the paper. Double-column headlines take 42–24 pt., according to position and prominence. Single-column tops scale down to the 36–24 pt. range. Medium weight middle-page headlines call for 24–18 pt. Shorts run down to 18–12 pt. It is worth noting that headlines for shorts gain emphasis, and save space, if their linage is reduced and they are put up a size (in lower-case): e.g. if two lines of 18 pt. upper- and lower-case are run instead of three lines 14 pt. caps. Single line filler heads are often put up to 18 pt. lower-case.

With classical decker headings the size scaling is somewhat different. The strict convention, exemplified in *The Times*, is to drop a size with each deck, e.g. 24, 18, 14 pt. for a main top three-decker, 18, 14, 12 pt. for a secondary top. This is for *The Times* all-cap. uniform style; but if alternate decks are contrasting, either in Light caps. or italic upper- and lower-case a scaling of 24, 18, 18 pt. and *pro rata* may be suitable. It is necessary to note the rule that decker headings are always centred, with the first two decks normally turning, the third deck single line. In two-decker headings a turning first deck usually carries a single-line second deck, and vice versa. Reference has already been made to the absolute necessity of retaining full white in decker headings. A refinement to be observed here is that the decks can either be separated by unbroken white space (as in the *Manchester Guardian*), by narrow-measure rules, or by a swelled dash after the first deck and thereafter rules (as in *The Times*).

The rules can be run even measure through the heading; say, 3 ems for single column, 6 ems for double column; but for the initial rule, following the first deck, it is better to approximate to *The Times* style with its opening dashes and increase the measure by one-half to two-thirds.

Once a suitable type has been selected and the mode of variation agreed upon, the determination of a decker headline scheme is a tolerably simple affair. The number of headings required is not great and once these are drawn out, and exhibited on a headline specimen card, there is an end of the matter. The material for editorial news display is docketed and ready; it does not call for any substantial treatment.

With the free make-up of the 'populars' things are by no means so simple. Especially is this the case with the large-size lead headlines. The editorial executives have at their disposal the size ranges, indicated in a preceding paragraph, of their paper's chosen basic roman and italic; from these, appropriately varying and balancing the caps. and upper- and lower-case, they build the lead and second lead display, arranging subsidiary headlines to suit. The art of page-making, in short (discussed in detail in the next Chapter), becomes the principal factor in determining main headline styles, on the general basis of the substitution of the multi-line single-deck headline for the multi-decker.

These modern 'free' headlines are capable, without departing from their basic style, of numerous variations. They can, if tops, be three or four line; if down column two or three line. Further, there are these five immediate variations in setting:

(i) *Flush left*, with the lines ending uneven at the right (but not too uneven, an obvious temptation with this style). This 'streamlining' was the most popular mode when modern headline style was first introduced; indeed it was regarded as an essential part of that style. It has the considerable advantage of ease in writing. The most common fault, very noticeable in American practice, is to set the lines full out left, so that the headline jams tight on to the column rule. Flush-left headlines should always be indented an even 4 pts. to 6 pts., and the compositors so instructed.

(ii) *Stepped*, with the first and last lines respectively full out left and right and the middle line (if a three-liner) centred. The step is a classical American style and calls for great precision in writing, so that each line gauges exactly the same measure. Nothing is worse than an uneven step, or a step whose lines are too short. A fair average for step indention is to write each line 1 em of the body (i.e. two normal en units) short of the measure.

(iii) *Centred*; a compromise style which is the most usual in multi-line headline display in this country. It is practically as easy to write as

A National Body
for Newsmen
Well Backed

Impertinence
of Institute's
Circularising

This Evidence
Should Not
be Published

LEEDS AS
EXECUTIVE'S
BACKER

Reporters
Quit Council
in Body

Reporters Quit
Council as
Protest

FIG. 61. The basic styles of headline setting—flush left, stepped, and the different forms of centring (long-short-long, short-long-short, inverted pyramid).

flush left (most headlines in the latter style can be centred), with the advantage that it distributes its surrounding white more evenly. For a typical three-liner it has three variants: (*a*) *Long-Short-Long*, in which the first line should nearly approach the column measure, the second be $1\frac{1}{2}$ to 2 units shorter each end, and the third be slightly (half a unit to a unit each end) within the measure of the first; a fault to avoid is making the third line the longest. (*b*) *Short-Long-Short* is generally less satisfactory than (*a*). The two short lines should be approximately the same length and should not exceed $1\frac{1}{2}$ units each end within the measure of a nearly full long centre line. This style is best limited to occasional single-column tops in caps. (*c*) *Long-Shorter-Shortest*, i.e. the inverted pyramid, is a self-explanatory style. It requires some skill in writing, but less than the step. The first line should be full, or very nearly full, and the succeeding lines indented each end up to 2 and 3 units respectively.

Fig. 61 illustrates these variations, adding some warning examples. Four-line tops are best centred, adding final short or long line respectively to styles (*a*) or (*b*) above. For down-column two-line headings the straight full out and centred turn style is the best, though a fairly close step is permissible as an occasional variation (in cap. styles). The ugly effect of lines too short and ranging, or reversing the proper order to centred and full-out turn, is to be marked and rigorously avoided; it is a key sign of slovenly work on the part of the sub-editor (Fig. 62).

The starkness of early 'streamlining' has been modified in two respects.

There has been a certain, qualified, return of the *deck*. And the use of subsidiary lines—*strap-lines* over headings, *tag-lines* following them—has become a feature of headline practice (Fig. 63). The modern decker adds one or two lines (usually italic) centred to a main three- or four-line heading; if the main heading is in caps. the following deck is in upper- and lower-case, and vice versa, though in the latter case the size is usually dropped one (e.g. if the deck to a main 24 pt. cap. heading is 14 pt. italic upper- and lower-case, it may drop to 12 pt. caps if the main heading is in upper- and lower-case). The general tendency is for the second deck to be not one but two sizes below the main heading; though this does not

Student Editors **Hold Conference**	**Student Editors** **Meet at Conference**

FIG. 62. These headline shapes should always be avoided; ranging lines or first line shorter than the turn.

always apply in double column. There is considerable scope for variety in the treatment of decks in the modern style, but where a paper uses a bold roman with a contrasting italic (like Caslon and Bodoni) it is a mistake to use the roman, in any size or style, for a following deck to a main italic headline; in general a roman second deck looks ungainly after a main italic, even if they are both of the same type family. One word about whiting: the second deck in the modern style does not require the heavy whiting of the classical decker head; in single column 6 pts., in double column 8 pts., will be found ample.

Tag-lines (required for '—Court Story' and the like) should be unobtrusive but not neglected. Set full out right and preceded by a metal rule, they should be three sizes less than the heading they follow: a 10 pt. tag for an 18 pt. headline, a 12 pt. tag for a 24 pt. headline; it is sound practice for them exactly to reverse the style of their main heading—e.g. an italic cap. tag to a roman upper- and lower-case main, and so on.

Strap-lines are most suitable over double-column headlines and upwards though they have their uses in single column. They may be regarded as a sort of deck in reverse, presenting a subsidiary thought or angle which is more appropriate as a precursor to the main heading than as a following deck. The general rule of reversal of style (italic to roman, caps. to lower-case) outlined above for decks and tags applies to straps. Essentially the strap is a single-line affair; it should never run to full measure but be reasonably kept in each end (at least 2 units, or 1 em of

JET PLANES COLLIDE
News disturbs Ministry

NEWSPAPER LED ME TO CRIME
—Court story

Marsh Torso Worries Yard Experts
LONE WATCHER REVEALS CLOSE-KEPT SECRETS

FIG. 63. Simple forms of the deck, the tag (both in Century Bold and italic) and the strap-line (Ludlow Black upper- and lower-case over Century Bold italic caps.).

Agreed

Agreed

a plan

a plan

A man who tries to keep faith

A man who can work miracles

Three more Boeings run into trouble

FIG. 64. Underscoring headlines is only effective if the correct weight rule or border is used and if (as with Ludlow lines) the underscore can be 'profiled' close to the face, breaking at the descenders. The hooded and boxed headlines show the difference between a rule that is too heavy and one of correct weight for the face. The modern fashion of a light-boxed headline within the column rules is also shown.

the body, in double column, and 3 units in treble column). In size a strap should not be more than one-third to one-half its following main heading, e.g. a 12 pt. or 14 pt. caps. strap over a 36 pt. upper- and lower-case main. While strap-lines can be fittingly set in the sizes and styles indicated of a paper's basic roman and italic it is common and suitable to use a contrasting type, for instance Sans caps. (No. 9, Metroblack, Metroblack italic) or the extra-heavies—Ultra-Bodoni, Ludlow Black, Linotype Pabst.

The variation and emphasis obtainable by adding rule or simple border to a heading have been touched on in Chapter 6. To the points there made about agreement in weight between type and underscore rule should be added an emphatic warning against attempting to underscore long-descender faces, unless they are Ludlow-set, when the supporting blank can be removed and the rule or border closed up (Fig. 64). The more

"Rugger Sign-up Alarms Men" **'Rugger Sign-up Alarms Men'**

'Rugger Sign-up Alarms Branch' **'Rugger Sign-up Alarms Branch'**

FIG. 65. Quotes, good and bad. The fussy double quotes (top left) and the ungainly line-up with quote (bottom left) are contrasted with the correct settings on the right.

complicated rule treatments, the three-sided hood or curtain and the full box, can look too heavy if the rule is approximated to a fairly heavy type; sound practice is to use 'medium' (1½ pt. face) rule or a medium-weight border like square-dot. A boxed heading should never be cut off from the story, the bottom rule being 'broken' or the last line of the heading cut in. Any rule treatment adds to both time and cost, it must be remembered; in curtains and boxes the rule-joining must be perfect or the effect is spoiled.

Two final style points deserve attention, since they have a direct relation to headline appearance. (i) *Quotes* in headings should always be single. Double quotes waste space and are irritating. In hand-set headings, for example from Monotype display faces, the proper opening quotes should be insisted on; this is specially important in long-descender letter like Bodoni, where the slovenly device of the turned comma for an opening quote produces a most ill-fitting effect. Quotes should be ignored in the centring of lines and with flush-left headings should 'hang in the white', thus ranging the initial letters of the lines; keyboard operators using an automatic quadder must make a special allowance for this (Fig. 65). (ii) *Full points in initials*: it is common to omit these, e.g. T U C, R A F, but it is helpful to have a thin letter-space, particularly in cap. headings, where the effect is anyhow not very agreeable; to avoid certain obvious confusions—'U.S.' and 'U S', for instance—the points have sometimes to be retained.

THE HEADINGS CARD

With a traditional decker scheme, as already suggested, the editorial headings card or sheet is a straightforward affair, exhibiting each heading complete (specified by letter or number) in the style to which it will always be written. A card for the modern free style may exhibit the simpler and smaller single-column headings in the two- or three-line style in which they will normally be specified; but all that is really necessary is to have one-line showings of the full headline range, in roman and italic, caps. and lower-case; say, in single column up to 24 pt. or 30 pt., in double column

19

NOW THAT THE

19A

Animals go down a

38

BLACKMAIL STORY

38A

Publications day news

39

WE ARE NOW ON

39A

Members are now in

FIG. 66. Portion of a headings card with a number code.

from 24 pt. to 36 pt., and treble column thence upwards; a portion of rule, or a figure, should be inserted to mark the single-column measure in the multi-column lines (Fig. 66).

The sub-editor only needs clear indications of measure and count to enable him from (for example) a marked-off three-column line in 30 pt. roman lower-case—assume it is numbered '12'—to follow instructions like these: '4-line (12) s/c', '2-line (12) X–2'. A simple numbering code saves much time in specification by the chief sub-editor or copytaster and in the marking of headline copy by the sub-editor, since it only needs one figure instead of type size, name, and style: thus (1) instead of, for example, '14 pt. Century Bd Rom u/lc'.

Any numbering jointly agreed on between editorial and composing departments will serve; but it is convenient to number the smallest roman lower-case heading (1), its italic (2), its roman caps. (3), its italic caps. (4), and so continue up the size range. It may be thought useful to differentiate italic by adding a letter rather than increasing its number; thus the code indicated above would read (1), (1A), (2), (2A) and so on.

It is usual to indicate the average number of letters and spaces in each line and each measure. The en is taken as the unit, calculating the wide letters 'w' and 'm' as two units, the narrow letters 'i', 'j', 'l', 't' as half units; this is for lower-case—in caps., only the 'I' and 'J' count as half units, while the 'W' and 'M' in most founts pass at 1½ units. The value of working only to unit specification, a common practice, may be doubted; if the card itself is carefully displayed, with the specimen lines avoiding the narrow letters, and at the same time not filling out with the wide letters, the skilful sub-editor will work as accurately, and usually faster, by counting out on the card. In this way, too, he keeps the feel of the type, for he is always visualizing the appearance of his headline, and does not limit himself to a mere calculation.

8 · News Page Make-up

NEWS page make-up—the assembling of news headlines, text, pictures, into whatever space the advertisements have left—may be thought of as the production of a pattern; but it is, or should be, a pattern with a purpose. A good make-up is one which brings shape and order, with a suitably varied emphasis, to what would otherwise be a confusing mass, not to say mess, of news. By balancing and contrasting its different typographical elements with a thought for the reader's eye-comfort, by appropriately positioning its half-tone 'colour', by avoiding clashes between editorial and advertising display, the well-made news page produces an agreeable overall pattern which makes the text easier to read.

The purposeful pattern of the page transcends the actual typography, which naturally varies, and should vary, according to the character of the paper. In addition it embodies certain constant factors whose importance it is the more necessary to grasp because they may appear subsidiary or incidental. These factors are: white space (and its correct manipulation); the vertical and horizontal separation of matter (by white or rules; and the weight, width, cornering of the latter); and the page folios or running heads (ruled off or 'open'). They are examined in detail below.

Chapter 3 has discussed the evolution of make-up from the *vertical* to the *horizontal*, the most characteristic feature of its twentieth-century development. Even the 'class' papers, once the strongholds of the long-column, up-and-down style, have now succumbed. When *The Times* first ran a three-column heading down page it was perhaps even more of a revolution than when it first led the 'bill' page with a heading across two columns. The essence of modern make-up is the understanding that the bottom of a page is as important as the top, and is not just the place where top stories and leads tail off into shorts and fillers. 'Strength below the fold' might indeed be considered the primary slogan of the make-up man today. The use of suitable multi-column headlines down page makes for an attractive page pattern, maintains interest, avoids top-heaviness, prevents the reader's attention trailing away into a morass of minor items. Extra positions are created whose attention-value equals that of top-of-the-column positions, so that the possibilities of arresting news display on a given page are considerably increased.

In the past there were attempts to reduce news page make-up to a formula; and even today the Americans postulate half a dozen 'basic styles' in make-up, of which more in Chapter 14. It is not hard to see, however, that in a sphere where flexibility is the first requirement a rigid and mechanical formula is a menace. The point is well exemplified in the so-called 'diagonal' principle, according to which a page was visualized as divided by two crossing diagonal lines, and main headlines were placed up and down these imaginary lines. Here the formula itself embodied the cardinal error that lies ever in wait for the enthusiastic make-up man—making the news fit the make-up, instead of handling the make-up to give the most effective display and weight to the news.

Certainly no news page make-up can be left blank until every major news story has been finally weighed and given its appropriate position. But, within the inescapable technical limits, no make-up should be regarded as sacrosanct; it should always be fully flexible, so constructed that last-minute changes are facilitated. The problem is a delicate and difficult one, and its proper day-to-day and edition-to-edition solution calls for much experience; nevertheless it is a problem whose nature—once more, it will be seen, the effecting of the correct relationship between form and content—has to be appreciated from the beginning. Newspaper typography, here as in all its aspects, has no existence other than as the instrument of journalism.

THE LIMITATIONS OF FORMAT

In applying these general principles the make-up man operates within predetermined physical limits: (i) the *format* of the paper—the shape and size of the page, expressed in the depth, number and measure of its columns; (ii) the space, position, and character of the *advertising*.

Within the mechanical limitations of a given newspaper, format is fixed by practical, technical, and economic considerations; the possible variations are slight, and in any case are not usually regarded as an editorial concern. On a rotary-printed full-sheet (broadsheet or text) paper the machine's 'cut-off' fixes the page depth, though its width can be varied within certain limits by varying the width of the newsprint reel. On a half-sheet (folio or tabloid) paper the position is reversed: the width of the page is fixed, the depth may be varied (and, since there are two pages to a forme, the width of the type area, that is to say the column measure, can in fact be slightly varied by manipulating the centre margin or 'gutter').

Rotary cut-offs vary considerably, producing broadsheet pages ranging from 21 to 26¼ in. in depth; the deeper cut-offs, producing a formidable blanket sheet, are found here and there among local papers. There is, however, a long-standing general trend to the so-called 'standard' (or *Daily Mail*) cut-off of $23\frac{9}{16}$ in. The presses of most national and major provincial newspapers are nowadays of this dimension. The column depth of this cut-off is 22 in. and on normal reel widths the page accommodates seven $13\frac{1}{2}$-em columns, eight $11\frac{1}{2}$-em columns (now usually cut to 11 or $11\frac{1}{4}$ ems, with a narrower reel, in order to economize on newsprint) or nine 10–$10\frac{1}{2}$-em columns. The half-sheet of this cut-off can yield six $10\frac{1}{2}$-em or seven 9-em columns from $15\frac{1}{2}$ to 16 in. deep; but many folio newspapers are products of slightly deeper cut-offs and can thus carry six 11- or $11\frac{1}{2}$-em columns. The abnormally narrow 9-em column is the accompaniment of the seven-column make-up adopted by the tabloid nationals.

Format itself has always to be reckoned with in scheming make-ups. This is especially the case when the emphasis of the page's shape is extreme either vertically or horizontally. A deep cut-off and a narrow reel, yielding a broadsheet, say, of nine 10-em columns produces the first effect; a shallower cut-off and a normal reel, yielding eight $11\frac{1}{2}$-em columns, produces the second. The folio in each case will, of course, reverse this result. The conclusion is simple: a page with extreme vertical emphasis requires the correction of additional horizontal display, by way of two- and three-column headings, particularly below the fold; a page with extreme horizontal emphasis requires the correction of its squareness by the playing-up of deep (e.g. four-line) single-column headings.

ADVERTISING—AND ASYMMETRY

Format fixes the framework of the page; but the make-up man has to handle the space left within that framework after the placing of the advertisements. The amount and shape of that space are of some importance; if it is strictly symmetrical, say by the placing of an 11-in. treble at the foot of each side, the news make-up will need special asymmetrical emphasis in order to avoid any static or rigid effect. More important still, though, is the relationship of the news make-up to the character, or more precisely the colour, of the advertising; whether solid smalls, semi-display, or display (and, in the last category, whether all type or illustrated—in line, line and tint, or half-tone). The central point here is that editorial and advertising matter cannot merely coexist on the same page (even if by sheer luck they avoid the more violent clashes). They have to be visualized together, though they are entirely separate; for advertising, particularly modern display advertising—usually illustrated—links with the news display to form the overall pattern of the page (Fig. 67).

It may be regretted that the logical American pyramidal style of 'stepping' display advertisements from bottom left to top right has never been adopted in Britain. The relatively haphazard disposition of advertisements on a given page seems too deeply rooted in our newspaper tradition, and perhaps also in the economics of our space-selling. It presents the make-up man here with more problems than those of his American colleagues.

The news–advertising relationship in page make-up varies according to the variation in the colour of advertising style and should be considered in terms of that variation, as follows:

(i) *Smalls*: a solid squared-off mass of $4\frac{3}{4}$–$5\frac{1}{2}$ pt. classified advertisements (even if partially lightened by some semi-display of the kind detailed in Chapter 5) requires the juxtaposition of the strongest-coloured headings and/or half-tone blocks, or the page will tail weakly off into a grey morass. The lighter headings—italic lower-case, for example—should be avoided for such positions. It is useful to rule off the smalls from the rest of the page with a slightly heavier face ($1\frac{1}{2}$ pt. or 'medium') rule than the conventional column rule.

(ii) *Display* (*all type*): generally speaking the principle of contrast

THE PEOPLE, SUNDAY, OCTOBER 13, 1957. PAGE 13

'Get out!' orders for the landlords

—WHO LIVE IN COUNCIL HOUSES

SOME private landlords are taking advantage of the Rent Act to get more from their tenants while they themselves continue to live in rent-subsidised council houses.

Now a drive is being started to get such council tenants evicted. The situation has been spotlighted by the case of Mr. Thomas Jones, of Hill Road, Rowley Regis, Staffs.

Mr. Jones, a 63-year-old engineer, lives in a 18s. 9d.-a-week council house. He is also the owner of two private houses. And he has told his tenants that the £1-a-week rent each pays is to be increased under the Rent Act by two stages to 35s.—the maximum allowed.

Now Mr. Jones is to be evicted from his council house and the house offered to one of his tenants, Mr. William Bagnall.

Said Councillor Vic Wakeman, chairman of Rowley council estates management committee: "We consider the rent Mr. Jones is levying is excessive.

"We don't think anyone should be allowed to live in a subsidised council house while making a profit on his own property. We are going to ferret such landlords out."

'No chance'

Mr. Jones said: "This is outrageous. I have lived in the same house for 20 years and I've spent a lot of money improving it.

"My own houses were left me by my father and I've never had a chance to live in them or make very much out of them.

"I was hoping the money from the rents would help me along in a few years when I retire."

Council spokesmen at Nottingham, Brighton, Cardiff, Plymouth, Derby and Salford all supported Rowley Regis Council and said that in similar circumstances they took, or would take, similar action.

At Brighton, housing manager Arthur Holt said: "We had such a case once. . . . now we ask every council house applicant whether he is a property owner."

MOON-shine

Stranger than fiction are some of the stories that poured into "The People" yesterday—inspired by the 'Red moon's' meanderings round the earth . . .

LITTLE RICHARD, the 6-ft. Negro rock 'n' roll singer who was in the Jayne Mansfield film "The Gal Can't Help It," is convinced that the end of the world is coming.

"The Russian satellite proves it," he said in Sydney last night. Then, pausing only to fling £3,000 worth of diamond rings into the harbour to prove his sincerity, he left by air for Los Angeles "to put his affairs in order."

That done, and "the last show of my life given," he will be baptised into the Seventh Day Adventist Church, "to prepare for the end of the world."

Says Little Richard: "If you want to live for the Lord, you cannot rock 'n' roll, too. God doesn't like it."

Recordings by Little Richard—who has a large teenage following for his singing, at least—have been in Britain's "top twenty" for most of the year. Earlier, he announced that he would tour Britain.

● Japanese are queueing to buy plots of land on Mars. Even though the price has gone up from four bob to £1 an acre.

The Japanese Astronautical Society is selling the plots at its Tokyo office.

● Barmen in Paris started shaking a new cocktail called "Satellite." Mostly vodka.

MOON-sense

A 42-YEAR-OLD Russian woman scientist, Mme. Lydia Kursenova, said yesterday: "We are now preparing pilots for flights into space."

She was speaking in Barcelona, where the international astronautical congress ended with most of the 400 delegates convinced that man will be on the moon sooner than they had imagined.

● Dr. Olin Eggen, chief assistant to Britain's Astronomer Royal, said yesterday that, theoretically, a moon flight was possible now—money was the only snag.

"Every penny of our national resources would have to go in one gigantic effort," he said at the Royal Observatory, Herstmonceux, Sussex.

● The Russian satellite had travelled three million miles in a week, when it passed over Britain at dawn, on its 110th world circuit.

● The world's biggest radio telescope, at Jodrell Bank, Cheshire, got an "extremely good" picture of two objects—either the rocket and satellite or the rocket and the "cone" that protected the satellite.

● A Cambridge radio astronomer said the rocket was now *in front* of the satellite and also nearer to the earth.

BURSTING POINT—BY MAC

MR. HAROLD MACMILLAN, the Prime Minister, gave another grave warning on the dangers of inflation when he spoke at the Conservative Party Conference at Brighton yesterday.

Speaking of wages chasing prices, he said:

"The spiral won't keep going up—sooner or later it will blow up.

"Then all will lose in a common disaster in which the trade by which we live, our savings of the past and our hopes for the future would all be involved.

"That is where the real threat of unemployment lies—not in the Government's measures to deal with the problem."

Self-inflicted

Mr. Macmillan said the Tories did not seek unemployment.

"If it ever comes to the people in this country it can only come in one way—it will be a self-inflicted wound," he said.

Attacking Labour's plan for public ownership of certain industries, Mr. Macmillan commented:

"There is to be a short list which are to have their throats cut, and a longer list which are to be bled slowly to death."

On foreign affairs, Mr. Macmillan said: It had been the West's possession of the H-bomb which had deterred Russia from open aggression.

For 'Old Ben'

Famous stage, screen and television stars will be appearing next Sunday (7.15 p.m.) at the London Coliseum to raise funds for "Old Ben," the newsvendors' benevolent fund.

Tickets, price 3s. 6d. to two guineas can be had from the Secretary, Newsvendors' Institution Memorial Hall Buildings, London, E.C.4. Telephone Central 9569.

'Be slower to condemn'

PEOPLE are too ready to blame mental patients whenever there is a brutal murder, said Mr. Frederick Ellis, chairman of the National Society for Mentally Handicapped Children, at Bristol yesterday.

He spoke of four recent child murders which "shocked and angered the nation."

Police, he said, had made it known that their inquiries centred round mental hospitals. Yet, in no case was the murderer from such a hospital.

Miss Ellen is 100

Miss Ellen Lymsbury, a patient at West Hill hospital, Dartford, Kent, was 100 yesterday.

BOFFIN HEROES SAVED A-PILE

ALL danger from radio-active dust and fumes which escaped from an overheated atomic pile at Windscale, Cumberland, is over, it was stated officially yesterday.

Workers at Windscale have been given "Don't talk" orders but, last night, several ignored it to tell of the heroism of 20

93, he weds again

A NINETY-THREE-YEAR-OLD retired clergyman, the Rev. Horace Edgar Yorke Brefitt, of Whitton-terrace, Rothbury, Northumberland, married his 54-year-old housekeeper yesterday.

After the ceremony, at Rothbury, the couple cut a wedding cake and left for a honeymoon.

The bride, Mrs. Constance Mary Coburn, formerly of North Shields, has kept house for Mr. Brefitt for five years. He has been a widower for 30 years.

He said: "I was rather worried about what would happen to Constance when I die."

Gosh, Mum's a pin-up!

NO doubt about it—singer Rosalie Dawn (right) is a mother any lad would be proud to boast about.

In fact, Rosalie's two sons, Larry, aged seven, and Gregory, five, did more than boast about Mum.

They decided to cash in on a figure which makes a shapely registration of 43-23-37.

So one day, while Mum was away on tour and Dad was out at work, the boys got their heads together and did some ready reckoning.

Some good, glamorous pin-ups of Mum should go down well at school, they reasoned.

So the boys looked through the cupboards at their Staines, Middlesex, home and tracked some nifty pictures of Mum.

Then they took them off to school. Soon Rosalie Dawn's boys were doing a brisk barter in toy lorries and cars.

But their ruse was discovered when Rosalie wondered where the spate of new toys came from.

Then one day she overheard some neighbouring lads talking. Says Rosalie: "It seems Larry and Gregory had been driving some pretty hard bargains with my pictures aboard the school bus."

But although the glamour trade has now ceased, Mum's not really cross.

Secretly, in fact, Rosalie Dawn is rather flattered.

And the boys? Says Larry defiantly: "All our chums agree that Mum's a smasher!"

FINLAND FREES BRITONS

TWO British students gaoled in Finland after a "trophy-hunting" adventure, were freed yesterday—a month early.

Percy Hitchcock and Michael Creek, both 24, were arrested at the end of August after taking away a frontier sign to prove to friends at London University that they really had crossed the Russian border.

They were accused of illegally crossing the frontier and sentenced to two and a half months' gaol.

Before they left by air for London from Helsinki yesterday, the Ministry of Justice said they were freed early because of good behaviour.

Percy and Michael, both veterinary students, who live in Weymouth, were arrested while driving through Finland in their motor-cycle combination.

They told the court that they wanted to see the Iron Curtain—and to convince their pals that they had done it.

Ike's birthday

President Eisenhower, 67 on Monday, will celebrate his birthday in the White House, Washington.

FIG. 67. A not uncommon sort of editorial/advertising clash: similar pictures juxtaposed.

applies to the news make-up of a page with all-type display advertising. If the advertising display is heavy, keep the news display light (though not too light); if it is large-scale and well-whited, try to juxtapose an appropriately packed column of shorts; if it runs to a mass of small-space separate ads.—the line-illustrated 'Bargains by Mail' 2-inch singles fall into this category—try to keep to longer stories in the adjacent columns. Beware of the lining-up of a headline with an advertisement display line in identical size and style of type; the read-on may be ludicrous.

(iii) *Display* (*illustrated*): the illustration, frequently half-tone, which dominates so much display advertising, provides good colour below the fold and is often of such a character that the page has an agreeably 'pictured' effect even if editorial half-tone display is minimal. It is important not to multiply editorial half-tone colour on a page heavily pictured in its advertisements; in particular it is necessary to avoid the solecism of juxtaposing a half-tone news block and a half-tone advertisement, or of running a prominent editorial block of the same size and subject (e.g. a 'pretty') as an advertisement block on the same page. In the case of line-illustrations in advertisements editorial half-tones may be handled more freely; though here, obviously, any prominent editorial line-work, like a cartoon, would need watching.

Clearly, the co-ordination of news and advertising make-up prescribed here cannot be achieved without proper co-ordination between the advertising and editorial departments. Too often this is not merely lacking; it is thought unnecessary or impossible. The advertising department limit themselves to the preparation of a dummy make-up showing the position and size of the spaces they are taking. Yet it is essential that they should indicate whether display advertising is all-type or illustrated, and in the latter case whether half-tone or not; such an indication of half-tones is standard American practice, always marked on the ad. dummy as it goes to the editorial department. To get the best results a proof of main all-type display, and of all illustrated display, should be provided for editorial information. Arguments that lateness of advertisement copy prevents this can be dismissed; since proofs go to the advertiser one extra can be pulled for editorial. The truth is that the importance of the practice is not accepted. Directly it is, and editorial and managerial executives insist on it being followed, it will be found as easy as any other routine procedure; and it will greatly improve page make-up.[1]

Because there is a certain complexity in the general approach to news

[1] Reference may be made here to the still somewhat controversial question of front-page advertising versus news; the steady trend to front-page news has already been mentioned in Chapter 3. Few papers, other than *The Times*, really benefit nowadays from the classic front page of 'smalls'; and those local weeklies which make up their front page with display advertisements only succeed in producing a jumble which must be of little real benefit to the advertisers.

page make-up, which is indeed a many-sided affair, there is no reason to conclude that the initial emphasis on 'strength below the fold' is an over-simplification. That primary slogan of the make-up man, it should now be clear, has to be supplemented, even conditioned, by the slogan 'be dynamic'; or, perhaps better, 'never square'. The avoidance of even squared-off effects is essential to that calculated asymmetry of the page pattern without which it lacks a sense of movement, lacks life. This applies both to the build-up of the headlines and the placing of the half-tone or other illustrations.

The simplest example of what to avoid is the placing of two double-column headed stories one under the other in the same pair of columns (unless they are tie-ups being built into a related news display). The lower one should be run off a column. Treat blocks in the same way, running them off even farther if possible; if there is a double-column block at the top of columns six and seven and a down-page double-column block scheduled, place the latter down columns two and three.

Here a danger point should be signalled. The dynamic effect of a page made up as described can be rendered sluggish by the spread of grey patches of text, i.e. of long stories with no more than normal cross-heads running side by side over several columns. A long story should have adjoining columns well broken with medium and short stories. Alternatively, a necessarily many-columned story needs the break of heavier sub-headings, as indicated in Chapter 6, as well as its own illustrations and such other colour breaks as may be devised. Grey patches can also appear when the single-column text of a story with a double-column intro. is turned into the second column immediately under the intro. This common practice, not always avoidable, is to be avoided whenever possible. The shoulder position should be used for a single-column story or for a box or panel; these last make useful eye-catchers and the main story can, if need be, turn under them.

TEXT—OR TABLOID

The two formats, text or tabloid (broadsheet or folio), can be found nowadays in all parts of the newspaper field, the general run of morning papers excepted. The tabloid mornings—the *Daily Mirror* and the papers modelled on it, like the *Daily Sketch* and the Glasgow *Daily Record*—are a special case; so special indeed that the term tabloid is currently used among British newspapermen in a loose and confusing sense, meaning either (*a*) a *Mirror*-type sheet with extra-large Sans headings, dominating pictures, and minimum text, or (*b*) any folio paper, whatever its typography and general presentation. The second, broader meaning is the one now current among American newspapermen, the original inventors of the term in its narrower sense to describe the New York prototypes of our *Mirror*; this contemporary American usage is the one generally followed in these pages.

Tabloid, or folio, format has spread markedly among evening and weekly papers, more especially weeklies in suburban areas (including under this head the New Towns). Readers appreciate the convenience of the easy-to-handle half-sheet, to which in any event they have been progressively conditioned by the immense circulation coverage of the *Mirror–Pictorial* group and their imitators. This last factor undoubtedly accounts for the tendency, most noticeable in the tabloid local weeklies, to use heavy Sans as an important ingredient in their make-up. It is significant, though, that these locals eschew the extreme Sans treatments developed by the *Mirror*. The sizing is usually not so overpowering; in place of the heavy Victorian Grotesques and Gothics there is considerable play on the more mannered Sans families like Tempo Metro and even Gill (the reader may be reminded of the strictures on the last-named in Chapter 7); contrast is sought by the use of lighter Sans italics or a bold roman like Century.

The comment may be interpolated here that whatever is thought of the *Mirror*'s full tabloid treatment one fundamental point must be conceded: the folio page is the limit for such typographical club-swinging, which defeats its own end if expanded from the half-sheet to the broadsheet. That no broadsheet paper of consequence has fallen into this error, with the single exception of the *Daily Herald*, requires no comment (Fig. 10). The point is really the elementary one that the reader's eye must have points of rest, requiring contrasts in colour and, if possible, in style. A heavy black half-sheet is tolerable; double the blackness, i.e. fill a broadsheet with it, and it is intolerable.

Two general points now remain to be made about tabloid make-up. First comes the *front page* (Figs. 68, 69). As compared with the eight full-depth columns of a broadsheet, the much-reduced type area of the tabloid page obviously implies a more exacting selection of main news stories, to say nothing of tighter writing and subbing; selection can indeed be carried to the point of one heavily presented story, with picture or pictures, in which case some prominent pointer or pointers to inside news highlights is well worth considering. Where stories must inescapably run to length they should be turned, preferably to the back page. A corollary of this is that the back page becomes the second main news page of the paper—or, as the *Mirror* has ingeniously made it, and calls it, the second front page. Turns should be restricted to occasions of absolute necessity; as far as possible there should not be more than one. The turn to the back page is not only the most convenient for the reader; it has the considerable technical advantage that, as the front and the back are in the same forme, last-minute news affecting the turn can be handled without any hold up.

These particular advantages are lost if the turn is made, as in some tabloid evenings, to the *centre-spread* (the second of the two points). As the term suggests, the two centre facing pages in tabloid make-up can be turned into a double page going the full width of the spread, by taking the gutter into the type area. This gives the tabloid make-up man his

DAILY SKETCH

No. 10,442 : (Exxx) : THURSDAY, OCTOBER 29, 1942 : ONE PENNY : A KEMSLEY NEWSPAPER

RUSSIA THIS PAGE

Nazis make new thrust in Caucasus

FAR EAST THIS PAGE AND PAGE 2

Japs repulsed in Guadalcanar battle

EUROPE PAGE 2

Nazis demand French merchant fleet

Stalingrad holds; Nazis strike south in Caucasus

THE GERMAN Army in the Caucasus, stopped in their drive towards the Grozny oilfields, have struck south.

Moscow's communique this morning tells of a new offensive towards Nalchik, a small town in the Caucasus footholls, 70 miles south-west of Mozdok. It is separated from the important Transcaucasian town of Ordzhonokidze by difficult mountains.

It seems that the Germans' object may be to secure their right flank before starting a new push farther east.

Moscow also announces that inside Stalingrad's factory area von Hoth has made slight gains at tremendous cost.

The communique says: "On one sector in the area of Nalchik the Germans, with tanks and infantry, succeeded in slightly pressing back our units.

"North-east of Taupse the Germans, after receiving reinforcements, launched attacks on Soviet positions. Throughout the day Societ troops withstood the onslaught of the enemy and then passed to the counter-attack.

"More than 200 Germans were killed. Two German planes were shot down by Soviet machine-guns.

"The attacks were repulsed.

"In one sector alone hte enemy succeeded in advancing 100-200 yards.

"A group of German mechanised infantry broke through to the south-western fringe of one of the factories, and was here wiped out to a man.

"North-west of Stalingrad the Germans renewed their attacks against an inhabited locality. These attacks were repelled. The enemy lost about 500 officers and men killed."

Here are Berlin's latest claims:

Stalingrad.—Broken Russian resistance in the area of the bread factory north of the Red October works. Volga bank reached at this point.

South of Stalingrad.—German counter-attack for Kuporossnoye gaining groun dslowly. Russians held their own only in southern parts.

Berlin radio said last night that the Russians had filled tanks with dynamite and sent them hurtling against the German defences inside Stalingrad.

The tanks are started up, abandoned by their crews and sent forward at full speed against German pillboxes and barricades, it was claimed.

Solomons: land, sea, air battles for Guadalcanar

WASHINGTON, WEDNESDAY.—American troops on Guadalcanar key island of the Solomons, repulsed several small-scale enemy thrusts against U.S. positions covering the airfied on Monday night, says to-night's Nvay Department communique.

Enemy losses in men and equipment in troop actions on the island since last Friday, when the new Japanese offensiev began, have been very heavy as compared with American losses, the announcement adds.

It concludes: "No report of any other actiton in the Solomons Islands area has been received since the issue of the previous communique."

The Navy Department scpkoesman said to-night that American losses in the land fighting on Guadalcanar had been light.

The naval action is believed to be still going on.

While awaiting the climax of ington to-night is neither optimistic nor pessimistic. "Tensely anxious" would sum up the mood of the American nation.

It is recognised that the Japanese Navy is gathering recklessly

8th Army win big tank battle, again advance

HEAVY ATTACKS are still being launched by the British in Egypt, and latest messages fro mCairo say that the Eighth Army have won the biggest tank action so for fought, in which the Axis have suffered what is described as a "substantial blow."

General Montgomery's infantry have again deepened the area of their penetration.

Berlin and Rome admit that the Eighth Army gained "slight local advantages on a front of two and a half miles," but claim that an important ridge occupied by the British was retaken in a counter-attack.

The British communique makes the significant revelatiotn that when the enem yattempted dive-bombing, our fighters destroyed 13 aircraft, making a total of 18 for the day and as many again damaged.

Our air superioty has shaken the Germans. One of their front-line reporters said on the Berlin radio yesterday: "We have never seen such a picture. For days the enemy bomber squadrons have come over in parade formation, without deviating an inch, surrounded by swarms of fighters which hover in the air like bees."

The Ameircan "Fighting Cocks" and "Black Scorpion" squadrons are taking part in the attacks.

During October 24 Axis supply ships were sunk or damaged by British submarines—14 of them definitely sunk.

Phenomenal barrage

Men who have been out here since Wavell's day say they never believed the desert would see such a concentration of gunfire as that which has shaken the desert for days. It certainly rivals anything I have seen in this war so far.

I spent some hours to-day in a position a thousand yards or so from the enemy's outposts. A fighter plane which made a forced landing quite safely on an enemy minefield before our attack still lay there, and two of our Bren gun carriers which came to grief while we were going through on Friday night were near it, awaiting recovery.

They brought home one advantage owned by the Eighth Army. It has been advancing and has therefore overtaken its own damaged vehicles. These are now being brought back to be repaired until we attacked came in useful. and use dagain.

Dotted around were men more or less cosily installed in one-man trenches. One I saw was munching fruit from a tin and reading a newspaper which had somehow got through to the battlefield. This man even had beside him an expensive-looking briefcase. He gave me a broad grin after we had both ducked to shield ourselves from an enormous dust-cloud raised by a passing tank.

Through uprooted minefields

Men marching by in single file looked even more like made-up film actors than others in the neighbourhood, for they had a two-day coating of sand over their faces against other people's one. Some wore bloodstained bandages.

Leading them was a major, who told me something of the men's adventures since they went through uprooted minefields to

Arrows indicate our land, sea and air attacks on the Axis concentrations

capture and hold a strongpoint whose nucleus was an 88 mm. gun protected by snipers.

He said: "We attacked in mid afternoon and had a pretty hot reception. The 88 mm. opened up on us as well as a bunch of machine-guns and other weapons and its muzzle was pointed so low at us that its shells actually recochetted off the sand in front of us.

"The Germans fought very hard had made in the sand with our entrenching tools we went at them after dark. They made lots of noise as we got near, apparently barking many orders at each other. After a tough struggle we beat them and got the strongpoint.. We found the 88 mm. gun crew lying dead beside it.

"The enemy later counter-attacked, but not very determinedly, and we beat them off, and for a good part of the next day we were able to sleep in our little holes. We were cut off, and a British motor cycle which the Germans had evidently captured some time ago and had been using I rode it back to H.Q., and was able to take the welcome news back to my men that another company was coming forward to push through us and assault another strongpoint deeper in the enemy's lines.

TIMELY WORDS OF FAITH

He shall blow upon them, and they shall wither, and the whirlwind shall take them away as stubble.—Isaiah, 40, 24.

FIG. 68. An experimental dummy front page for a tabloid, suggesting a novel form of high-lighting inside news.

FIG. 69. The packed front page of a tabloid during the close-rationing days (1947) with, above, the tabloid ultimate—a single theme, a single reverse block, to make the front page.

biggest space for news or picture display and thus calls for careful exploitation. The space of the gutter can be taken up in various ways, either by odd-measure setting or block-sizing or a mixture of both. Thus if the gutter measures half a column in width, the simplest plan is to reduce the overall number of columns by one (from twelve to eleven, if it is a six-column tabloid), setting $1\frac{1}{2}$-column matter to make up the necessary depth with whatever $1\frac{1}{2}$, $2\frac{1}{2}$, $3\frac{1}{2}$-column blocks are schemed (Fig. 70).

THE FRONT PAGE—RIGHT THROUGH

Whether a newspaper is text or tabloid the importance of its front page is obvious. The common description of the front page as a paper's 'shop window' is an apt metaphor, underlining the need for inviting (typographical) window-dressing. But there is a danger here; after commendable efforts have been concentrated on the 'shop window' too little may be done to make the display of the wares inside equally attractive. Since the Annual Award for Newspaper Design was instituted in 1954 the judges have repeatedly commented on the tendency for papers with good front pages to fall away thereafter. It seems that the metaphor should be somewhat modified: a newspaper is like a store with many windows, each one of which should be dressed to the same high standard. Or, as the 1957 Design Award judges said of the *Observer*, naming that newspaper winner of the Bronze Plaque for the second year running, it 'had a sense of unity; it appeared to have been produced according to a plan, a plan that embraced not only the front page but went right through to the back and so created a unified structure of good typographical detail'.

Given this approach to the make-up problems of the daily newspaper, it has to be noted that the solving of these problems varies according to the newspaper—morning or evening, 'class' or popular. Additionally there is the difference between the average daily paper's front page and its inside pages: the first has only a solid double-column advertisement at the foot of the last two columns, while the others present that complex of varied advertising, the importance of which in relation to news make-up has already been outlined.

The simplest front-page proposition is that of the 'class' morning paper (Fig. 71). Once the headline typography is settled, and a suitable variety of decker headings specified, the building of the front pages of newspapers like the *Manchester Guardian* or the *Scotsman*, of the 'bill' page of *The Times*, is a straightforward affair. The lead is fixed at double-column (on important occasions the first deck may be made three-column), a strong news picture decorates the top centre of the page (not invariably with *The Times*), while appropriately size-graded and contrasting double- and

SATURDAY PICTURE SPOT
LONDONERS HEAD FOR THE LIDO
THE COOLEST SPOT IN TOWN
Airline chief aged 50 gets 2-way race record
ASTOR GEM FOUND IN GUTTER
CHANNEL BOAT MAN KILLED
Second man on £49,500 charge
'Think of this as a moment of temptation'
'We want him' say dog lovers
Arnhem pennant goes back
3-death charge man remanded
FREE TRIPS FOR MPs
New dropping zone
MAN TELLS OF THE VANISHED SIX
Missing ketch crew named
SUN SHINES ON 10-MILE ROAD JAM
A TRAIN FAILS—SO THEY WALK
Small man with a big heart
Sharon Lee seeks divorce
'We were first'
NYE BEVAN TALKS ABOUT H-BOMBS AND—
Mac, the iridescent aspidistra
AND ON THE RIVIERA
NOT TOO HOT FOR A BITE?
U.S. ROYAL TYRES

FIG. 70. A tabloid centre-spread; the London *Evening Standard*.

A CARPET for every room — carpeting for every need—now at WYLIE & LOCHHEAD LTD. SHANDWICK PLACE, EDINBURGH

THE SCOTSMAN

THE WORLD'S MOST EXPENSIVE TWIST SUITING CLOTHS Reid & Taylor SCOTLAND

No. 35,947 EDINBURGH, WEDNESDAY, AUGUST 13, 1958 PRICE 3d.

COMET SETS NEW RECORD

6¼-hour flight from New York

AVERAGE SPEED 558 M.P.H.

CAPTAIN REJOINS U.S. SUBMARINE BY HELICOPTER

Commander W. R. Anderson, captain of the U.S. submarine Nautilus, being lowered from a helicopter on to the deck of the submarine near the Shambles Lightship prior to the Nautilus docking at Portland.

"BRITAIN AND U.S. HAVE GIRDED THE EARTH"

Ambassador welcomes Nautilus

U.S. SUBMARINE DOES IT AGAIN

Skate surfaces 40 miles from Pole

OPPOSITE ROUTE

A large crowd of cheering spectators welcoming the Nautilus as she docks at Portland.

Mr John Cunningham

The Comet IV jet airliner

EISENHOWER TO ADDRESS U.N.

1800 U.S. Marines withdrawing from Lebanon to-day

LLOYD HOPES FOR END TO "RADIO WAR"

AN ANTI-MISSILE MISSILE

U.S. nuclear blast over Pacific

SEEN 700 MILES AWAY

SUPERSONIC TARGET MISSILE INTERCEPTED

LATEST NEWS

EISENHOWER VETOES U.S. NUCLEAR ICE-BREAKER

ROYAL FAMILY PICNIC ON SANDS OF JURA

Informal cruise begins

QATAR RULER'S VISIT

CHILDREN SEE MOTHER KILLED BY LIGHTNING

Three die in storms

BUILDINGS BURNED BY INDIAN RIOTERS

Police fire on mobs

STORM BREAKS OVER STROMA AS TV PRIZE

New York's Scottish community are up in arms

The island of Stroma from Gill's Bay, near Castle of Mey, the Queen Mother's home on the Caithness coast.

IN TO-DAY'S ISSUE

FESTIVAL CRISIS

OFF THE RAILS

BOOM IN BEEF

Page of Pictures—Page 5.

Regular items

CLASSIFIED INDEX

ICFC provides finance in the form of

Industrial & long-term loans on fixed terms, or Commercial share capital, to industrial or Finance commercial enterprises established Corporation in Great Britain Limited

Subscribers: The Scottish and English Banks

ICFC

Our booklet, H2, 'Capital for Business and Where to Find it', will be sent on request.

SCOTTISH OFFICE: 33 Charlotte Square, Edinburgh. Tel. Edinburgh 30212

FIG. 71. A 'class' newspaper front page, using two weights only of Bodoni (Bold and Condensed).

single-column headings can be easily disposed, according to the weight and variation of the news, to make a simple, well-balanced page pattern. It is usual for papers in this category to have cap. headings, either throughout —as with *The Times* and the *Daily Telegraph*—or with only second decks in lower-case. On the other hand, there is the brilliant all lower-case style of the *Observer* and some distinguished provincial mornings combine lower-case and cap. styles (e.g. the Norwich *Eastern Daily Press* and the Darlington *Northern Echo*). 'Class' journals should beware of the temptation to borrow the streamer style of front-page lead presentation from the populars. It strikes the wrong note and, since it tends to be done rather half-heartedly (say with a 42 pt. line in place of the populars' loud 60 pt.) does little in any event to strengthen the lead's display; the *Yorkshire Post* is an example of this.

A 'class' paper's inside pages likewise present few special problems. The standard decker headings are used, as on the front page, though they may have their first decks extended to three or sometimes even four columns to cover lengthy reports. With such heading styles, and no great play of pictures, the relating of the news make-up to the advertising is not so exacting a task. The careful departmentalizing of news common in these papers—Foreign, Parliamentary, City, and so on—can call for special attention in make-up; but it is mainly the breaking-up of many-columned matter like the Parliamentary report or the full text of some official statement (calling for suitable dropped-in headings), or the disposition of special setting like the Market Prices. Style and make-up of leader pages and the like are discussed in Chapter 11.

THE HANDLING OF THE STREAMER

Turning now to the broadsheet popular morning's front page, the first obvious item is the dominating multi-column streamer, the main line on what the particular paper presents as the main news of the day (Figs. 72, 90). The running of this streamer as a banner (i.e. the full width of the page) is much less common than it used to be; the banner is kept in reserve for the heaviest news. The streamer today is set one or two columns less than the full page; on an eight-column page a favourite streamer measure is seven columns (for a one-liner); or the streamer may turn over the lead intro. (6–3, 5–4, 5–3 columns are all possible arrangements). The shortened streamer has several advantages over the full banner. It functions immediately as the corner-stone of an asymmetrical, dynamic make-up; and it gives more prominence to the top display of the outside column or columns. The assumption here, it will be noted, is that the streamer always starts on column 1—as it should—reading in

DAILY PRESS

No. 12105 WEDNESDAY JANUARY 5 1955 PRICE 1½d.

Chancellor quits as Churchill proclaims new theory of economics

BUTLER GOES ON EVE OF BUDGET

Money crisis rocks City

REPORTER REPORTER

THE Government is looking for a "strong man"—a man outside its own ranks—to speed the supply of fighting aircraft to the Services.

They claimed, and the Lord Chief Justice agreed, that Ministry orders—for dispossession in one case, and supervision in the other—were illegal because "some independent person" had not been appointed to hear their representations against the Ministry's action.

In these cases and others, said Lord Goddard, the person who heard the representations was a member of a husbandry sub-committee which had already made up its mind about the orders. It had probably been done all over England.

Done all over country

They claimed, and the Lord Chief Justice agreed, that Ministry orders—for dispossession in one case, and supervision in the other—were illegal because "some independent person" had not been appointed to hear their representations against the Ministry's action.

In these cases and others, said Lord Goddard, the person who heard the representations was a member of a husbandry sub-committee which had already made up its mind about the orders. It had probably been done all over England.

Lightship wreck is drifting

ALARM SIGNALS ON GOODWINS

Reporter Reporter

A JEALOUS suitor, who had held his girl friend at gun point in a textile mill here for more than 24 hours, released her this afternoon, then surrendered to the police.

Police cars

Drugged food

Train delay

Union poll reported

JOAN CONQUERS HER TRAGEDY

WHAT'S Barbara's line? A wire, firmly hooked in her back as she makes her first "flight" at the Scala Theatre, W., rehearsing for her part of Peter Pan.

COMMONS DEBATE DEATH

THE House of Commons is to discuss the death penalty early in the New Year. This promise was made yesterday on behalf of the Government by Mr. Harry Crookshank, Leader of the House.

Jack Peters to get back job

REPORTER REPORTER

WITHIN a few hours of its publication, all 5,000 copies of the students' own Glasgow University Magazine were sold out yesterday. Reason? It contained a kind of junior Kinsey Report about the students called "Survey on Sin."

Only students

Article's tone

GOOD NEWS FOR YORK

One-job township now saved

REPORTER REPORTER

TWO farmers from opposite ends of Britain yesterday won a legal victory over the Ministry of Agriculture which gives them back their farms.

READER TELLS A STORY

TWO hooded bandits held up an all-night garage man at gunpoint yesterday and robbed the till.

All wrong

Police cars

Train delay

Bomb news good

Printers keen for unity

Scot sees own still explode

INTO London Airport last night flew 65-year-old Mr. Gregory Sawyer, looking for an old-fashioned Christmas:

Bomb news good claims Nehru

His girl grabbed a gun

A JEALOUS suitor, who had held his girl friend at gun point in a textile mill here for more than 24 hours, released her this afternoon, then surrendered to the police.

Article's tone

Bomb news good claims Nehru

COURT GETS HEADACHE

Newspaper make-up must always take note of advertisements

Many holidays were ruined

Many holidays were ruined

Union poll reported

Bomb news good claims Nehru

Union poll reported

FIG. 72. A trial dummy front page for a 'popular' morning paper, based on the Ludlow Caslon range (Bold, Bold Condensed, Heavy, Heavy italic, Light italic) with Tempo Heavy for streamers. For actual front pages, *Daily Mail* and *Daily Express*, see Figs. 88, 90.

to a lead also opening on column 1; the only admissible qualification is that the lead intro., though not the streamer or heading, may open on column 2 if there is a front-page leader or extra-special item of some kind on column 1; this throwing-in of the lead intro. should not exceed one column.

So much for the measure of the streamer. Three other main points have to be considered: (i) *size*—normally 60 pt., rising to 72 pt. (or photographed up even larger)[1] on sensational occasions; (ii) *style*—in roman caps., as square as may be. Excessive letter-count leads to padding and a flabby effect; condensed letter should therefore be avoided. Most Century-styled papers, for instance, rightly use the Century Bold Extended caps. for their streamers; (iii) *treatment*—the use of a lower-case strap-line, strongly contrasting in weight or style (e.g. light roman, light Sans italic, Ludlow Black or Pabst italic, Ultra-Bodoni) helps to throw up the cap. streamer, and is essential if the paper's title-piece is in caps. The strap-line can be used for devices like the news highlighting first introduced by the *Daily Express*, though whether a device of this kind is more than a gimmick may be doubted.

The streamer should read in to a contrasting head on the lead; italic if in caps., lower-case if in roman; and if the second lead is, as it normally will be, under the streamer cut-off, its heading also needs careful specification to maintain the necessary contrast. The general point is to have sufficient strength in these headings, but nothing to detract from the full impact of the streamer, nothing approximating to the streamer in style or colour. Hence, to take the point farther, the value of a second line—preferably in a large lower-case italic—following a full-page banner; a strong roman cap. heading can then be carried on the lead or second lead without any conflict with the streamer.

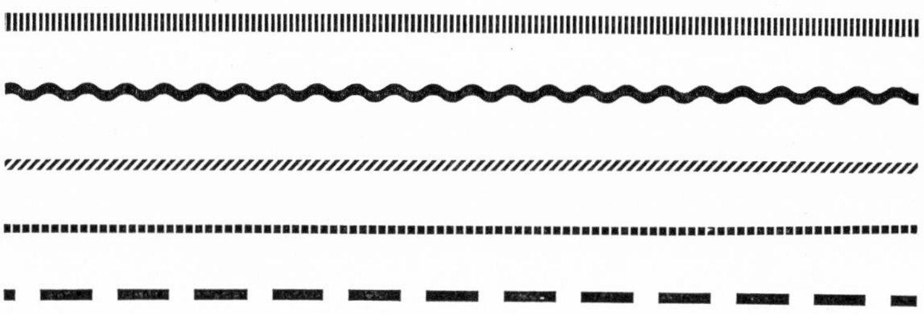

FIG. 73. Specimens of borders suitable for panels or boxes. For rules see Fig. 84.

A valuable by-product of the streamer run one column short of page width is the creation—if there are no advertising ears—of an end-column position of exceptional strength, since the story can start right at the top of the page. This might be thought an ideal position for a four-line single-column Sans 'kicker' heading of the kind described in Chapter 7; and such a heading often serves well in this special outside top position. But,

[1] There is no excuse for the badly spaced and badly aligned blown-up streamers sometimes seen in well-equipped national newspapers. This can always be obviated by setting the required line accurately in the largest available size of the desired type and to the appropriate proportionate measure to secure the body-depth needed on the final blow-up.

as already explained, the Sans 'kicker' has its maximum impact when placed towards the centre of the page; this is a point to be borne in mind when scheming the make-up. Sans can also be used for an occasional heavy contrast heading in double column; two lines will be found sufficient, in most cases, with or without strap or deck; and when such a heading is used it is advisable to avoid any other Sans on the page.

FRONT-PAGE MISCELLANEA

With the lead and top heading dispositions thus broadly treated, remaining details of front-page make-up must be left to the comprehension and application of the general principles expounded earlier in this chapter, and in its predecessors on text, headline, and sub-heading styles. No two front pages are alike, and the scope for variation from edition to edition is enormous. The nature of the front-page picture treatment, discussed in more detail in the next chapter, should be noted here as having an obvious bearing on the general make-up. So, in varying degrees, have the following:

(i) *Front-page leaders*: while few British papers follow what Stanley Morison called the logical French principle of putting their leading article on column 1 of page 1, there is a great deal to be said for the practice, and it has shown signs of spreading. The outstanding national example is the *Daily Mail* (the *Daily Worker* varies between column 1 and across four at the foot, according to news display needs). The *Daily Herald* has compromised with a boxed leader from the top of the end column to the solus advertisement, giving markedly less space for the leader but leaving the opening columns of the page free for news display. A full leader on column 1 needs the sort of dress it gets in the *Mail*—set in 9 pt. and 8/9 pt., all reverse indent, with a reverse block label, a distinctive two-line Sans heading and carefully placed side-heads (the *Mail* uses 18 pt. Metroblack, reserved for this purpose, with drop letters).

(ii) *Typographic colour*: boxes and panels, normally set in black (the bold of the text or a text size of a Sans like Metro), make useful spots of colour to break the page and emphasize some striking but not lengthy news item. The fully ruled box takes more time, since the measure is changed, the box rules have to be mitred and the box carefully made up. For most purposes the panel, set ordinary measure with an indention each end, and with rule or border top and bottom, saves time and is quite sufficient; with a panel the column rules box it off at the side, while a full box should have the column rules cut and be whited at the sides, an operation taking the little extra time that can ill be spared on edition. Boxes and panels should be deeper than square to look their best. The rules or borders used for them should be simple, as the specimens (Fig. 73) suggest. Avoid the fussy and flamboyant, or a rule or border cast on a body larger than that of the column rule; multiple rule on, say, a 12 pt. body looks overpowering. Though not seen as much as it might be, the plain swelled rule or dash is an attractive panel rule. Generally panels should be placed in shoulder positions or at the top of columns rather than dropped into stories just to break up the text.

(iii) *Special text display*: there are various methods of special text display which are useful for unusual stories and which can form a novel element in make-up. Stories can be set all double column, say in 9 pt. indented each end, with or without bold or italic paragraphs for emphasis. They can be set in similar style across $1\frac{1}{2}$ columns and made up across three. Either of these styles can be fully boxed; the matter, if short, can be set all in bold. Ingenuity will suggest numerous variations; the important thing is that such special settings should be kept as novelties and not made banal—as well as over-complicating the normal make-up—by constant use.

BACK PAGE ☆☆ ☆☆ **PAGE ONE**

★ ***continued on p. 4*** ★ ***continued from p. 1***

FIG. 74. 'Continued' lines, or turn indicators.

(iv) *Turn indicators*: when stories regrettably have to be turned (that is, continued on another page, or 'jumped' as the Americans say) the turn lines must be bold and distinctive, indicating both the page and the column of the turn. Sans lines at least two sizes larger than text, reverse blocks, or specially continued lines with some form of distinctive signal, are called for (Fig. 74). Since turns should be confined to one page, or at most two, lines or blocks with the page-and-column indications can be kept standing ready for use. It is sound practice to make the heading on the turn, even if it is only one line, recall a key word in the main front-page heading, rather than form a separate news heading on the matter in the turn. Everything must be done to help readers find a turn instantly.

What has now been said about the front page should be applied in principle to the inside pages, bearing in mind always the reiterated point about the complications of the display advertising. Otherwise the main make-up difference is that the inside page is not tied to the necessity of a cap. streamer for its lead story. Large lower-case, in italic as well as roman, can be used for the lead heading; for example, a 48 pt. three-column line 'banking' into two 48 pt. double-column lines, or two three-column lines turning into one double column. Large italic caps. turning (say 5–3, 4–2 columns) with a lower-case italic deck of either one or two lines make an effective variation (Fig. 75).

THE EVENING NEWSPAPER

In a broad general sense the principles of news page make-up apply to the broadsheet evening newspaper as they do to the broadsheet morning. But many evenings are tabloids and need to adapt the broadsheet style in any event. Further, the evening paper works to a tighter schedule and has to make more changes quicker than the morning usually does; thus it is important for evening newspaper make-up to be kept somewhat simpler, with as many prominent single-column positions as possible, since single-column setting is the fastest. This last point is of special importance where competition puts a premium on being 'first on the street'; it may be cited as one of the reasons for the dominant position of the London *Evening News*.

The evening paper is always a local paper. Small advertisements are a vital part of its economy and of its make-up. Sport also makes big calls on space and time; forecasts and features in the early editions, the latest results in the stop press of the Late Night Finals; an evening paper front page has to allow up to a column of 'fudge' space if broadsheet and the equivalent across the foot, continuing on to the back, if a tabloid (see Chapter 13).

Metropolitan and big-city evenings, having to meet the direct competition of a contemporary and the indirect competition of television—blamed for recent substantial falls in evening-paper circulation—tend to more and more strident front-page make-up. Papers with bold roman typography, using Sans only for contrast and emphasis, are smothering their front pages with bigger and heavier Sans headings; one day a two-line banner in 72 or 84 pt. Heavy Gothic across a tabloid page, the next a banked three-line three-column in the same 72 pt., flanked by a three-line three-column 60 pt. Heavy Sans italic, and so on. Make-ups like this frustrate themselves by shouting too much in too many places (Fig. 76).

It is curious that some of the very solid provincial evenings, enjoying monopoly or near-monopoly positions and with satisfactorily stable circulations, should have shown signs of succumbing to this species of typographical hysteria. Such papers have usually no sort of reason for bludgeoning the reader with screaming Sans headings; and for size the half-sheet can often be adequately served with a 48 pt. cap. for the lead heading (sometimes even down to 42 pt.).

FIG. 75. Continuing the typographical theme of Fig. 72: two top halves of trial dummy inside pages for a 'popular' paper, the second being designed to accompany a heavily illustrated half-page advertisement.

NEW WAYS WITH WEEKLIES

Local weeklies vary from the truly rural—'the county newspaper' is the usual label—to the suburban, with numerous nuances in character and readership in between, and their make-up problems vary accordingly. This is insufficiently appreciated by many local weeklies, which seem to think that it is enough to graft one or two make-up notions imitated from the nationals on to their primeval dullness. There are distinguished

SPORTS FINAL

Evening Standard

42,019 SATURDAY, JULY 18, 1959 2½d.

SPORTS FINAL

Sir Humphrey de Trafford wins the £23,642 race

IT'S ALCIDE AT 2-1

And then the decision: 'He will not run again'

Alcide wins the big race at Ascot this afternoon.

Evening Standard Reporter

Sir Humphrey de Trafford's great-hearted horse Alcide came up from nearly last to race away by two lengths with the £23,642 prize in the King George VI and Queen Elizabeth Stakes at Ascot this afternoon.

Alcide, 2-1 favourite, was ridden by Harry Carr and trained by Boyd-Rochfort.

The same owner, trainer and jockey won the richest-

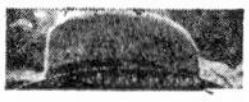

Moss breaks lap record twice

From ROBERT WALLING: Aintree, Saturday

Stirling Moss in a BRM clung grimly on the tail of Jack Brabham (Cooper Climax) in the British Grand Prix at Aintree today. He broke the lap record twice and reduced Brabham's lead from 16 seconds in the early

Schoolboy Mike gets two Indian wickets

Mike Smith, 17-year-old Enfield Grammar School boy playing his first game for Middlesex, took the wicket of Indian Test opener Pankaj Roy at Lord's. Later he dismissed Abbas Ali Baig, 20-year-old Oxford University freshman, who scored 102 in his first game for the Indians.

The Enfield boy's namesake, Warwickshire captain Mike Smith, who tops the scoring in first-class cricket this season with a total of 2163 runs, was out for a duck against Derbyshire at Burton.—Page FIFTEEN.

Radford clocks 9·5 for 100 yards

Peter Radford equalled the British and native records for 100 yards with 9.5sec. at the Waddilove Trophy meeting at Perry Barr, Birmingham, today. —Page TWO.

Australian soccer

Complete Australian soccer results and pools check.— Page FOURTEEN.

Crash kills girl, 17

Podola —more hospital tests

Evening Standard Reporter

Doctors at St. Stephen's Hospital, Fulham, expect to be able to decide tomorrow whether Guenther Fritz Podola, lying silent in Ward 5b, is suffering from schizophrenia.

The doctors have told the police that the results of some tests will establish Podola's mental state within the next 24 hours.

Podola, 30-year-old German-born Canadian, arrested in a raid on a Queen's Gate hotel on Thursday, is in a bed screened off at the end ward on the second floor of the hospital.

Not a word

He has not spoken a word. Four men—two detectives and two constables in plain-clothes—have orders not to leave his bedside, even when the doctors examine him.

Express and Star

LAST EDITION

AND BIRMINGHAM EVENING EXPRESS

Established 1874
Telephone 22233
No. 25988

WOLVERHAMPTON, FRIDAY, AUGUST 1, 1958

PRICE 2D.

'BEAT THE JAMS' PLAN READY FOR WEEKEND

Weather prophets fairly hopeful, too

ALTHOUGH Britain's weather may still be in a naughty mood for the August Bank Holiday weekend, the road clubs have prepared their biggest-ever joint "beat-the-jams" plan, on the assumption that 6,000,000 holiday vehicles may load the roads.

All leave has been cancelled for patrols of the Automobile Association and the Royal Automobile Club, and the country's highways will develop a forest of temporary signposts indicating diversions.

This move follows an appeal to the clubs by the Ministry of Transport to help cut out bottleneck hold-ups. Secondary routes to coast and inland beauty spots and holiday events have become so popular that traffic on them often reaches main-road proportions.

Apart from their patrols and normal services, the clubs will stage aerial sweeps by spotter aircraft to detect jams and help clear them.

The A.A. sums up the plan's object thus: "To keep traffic on the move by using all resources in men and equipment."

The clubs have good indications that this could be a record holiday-traffic bank holiday.

An instance is the number of requests for routes made to the R.A.C.'s Midland office. "We have

Used car as taxi, said to have got £34 for trip

The Premier emphasises a point

The Prime Minister, Mr. Harold Macmillan, wags a finger in emphasis as he talks with the Italian Premier, Signor Amintore Fanfani, at 10, Downing-street today. The Italian Prime Minister is visiting London for talks with British Ministers, on his way home from

Doctor drowned as family jump in yachting mishap

A BRITISH doctor was drowned at Brest, France, early today, when the yacht in which he and his family were sleeping was holed by a French tug and sank.

He was Dr. William Henry Casswell Spooner, of Old Bank House, Blandford, Dorset. His wife, Ailie, and three children—Anthony (17), Timothy (11) and Carol (14) were saved.

Dr. Spooner, a general practitioner at Blandford and a keen yachsman, had brought his 30ft. motor yacht, Remarie, to Brest to watch sailing races starting tomorrow.

The Remarie, was anchored alongside two other British yachts in the harbour when at about 2.30 a.m. a French tug, named by police as the Pontallac, became involved in collision with the three yachts.

Mrs. Spooner roused the others, and, when they discovered the yacht was sinking, they jumped overboard.

All were picked up except Dr. Spooner, who was the last on board. His body was found later by a frogman.

The two other British yachts, Freedom and Maia II., were damaged. Police and harbour authorities have opened an inquiry.

Mrs. Spooner and her children were taken to the local sub-prefecture where the sub-prefect's wife, Madam de Solminihac, has taken charge of them.

Four holidaymakers, a Briton, a German and two Austrians, are missing, believed drowned, following fierce storms last night in the province of Carinthia, south-west Austria.

The name of the British tourist missing was given by police at Millstatt as Edward Barton (43), of Edmunds-drive, Stanmore (Middlesex).

Mr. Barton was last seen when the storm began. He was sitting in his car before the Post Hotel in Millstatt.

All the cars which were standing in the street before the hotel were washed into the lake. It was believed that he might have been washed with his car into the water.

ON OTHER PAGES

FIG. 76. Evening paper contrasts: the London Square Gothic sledge-hammer and the more restrained Wolverhampton all-Cheltenham style.

exceptions, and a couple may be taken at random from each end of the scale (Figs. 77–80): the *North Devon Journal-Herald*, Barnstaple—a triumph of simplicity in an all-Cheltenham Bold make-up (four sizes only, 10–24 pt.), with double-column leads, decker headings, admirably close subbing and multiplication of stories, good whiting, and a notable eye

North Devon Journal-Herald

Vol. CXXVII No. 7,205 BARNSTAPLE, THURSDAY, MAY 28, 1959 THREE PENCE.

DRY SPELLS DANGER TO HAY CROPS

Harvest begins—but many cuts are light

FARMERS STILL HOPING FOR STEADY DOWNPOUR

REBUKE CALLED AN INSULT

Ratepayers upset at 'anti-council' tag

NO WISH TO BE MAGISTRATE

HONOUR REFUSED

THOUGHT FIRE SIREN WAS LIGHT SWITCH

Boy starts great commotion

BRAUNTON DUTCH BARN ON FIRE

Petrol tanker derailed

WAGON HOLDING 4,000 GALLONS OVERTURNS

FINE STRAWBERRIES

HELICOPTER RACES 90 MILES TO CARRIER

Man seriously injured

SHE SERVED DRINKS AT NINETY-ONE

Oldest licensee dies

CHAUFFEUR LEFT £100 IN CHULMLEIGH WILL

ON OTHER PAGES

MORE BUSINESS IN PUBLIC

ILFRACOMBE MOVE

TANKER DE-RAILED. This petrol tanker, holding 4,000 gallons of fuel, remained intact when it overturned, on Saturday, in a siding during shunting operations at Barnstaple's Victoria Road Station goods yard. The tanker became de-railed at the points, and the brake van behind it was de-railed, but stayed upright. A mobile crane returned the vehicle to the line.

EX-R.S.M. PULLED BUTTONS OFF CONSTABLE'S COAT

Former Chindit on drink charge pleads 'driving ban may cost me job'

Girl saved by motor boat

SWEPT AWAY AFTER SWIM FOR BALL

COUNCILLOR WANTS AN APOLOGY

Official's letter quoted

CONTROVERSY OVER WOMAN PASTOR

Bideford invitation

BARNSTAPLE DOCTOR FLIES TO HOLLAND

CRICKETER ON FIRE AT THE WICKET

Death of Ald. Tom Dunn

LEADER IN POLITICS AND PUBLIC SERVICE

ALD. DUNN

MECHANICAL DIGGER STUCK IN SAND

Covered by tide

NEW HEAD MASTER APPOINTED

BUILDING SOCIETY LOANS DOWN HALF PER CENT

Interest paid to investors will stay at present level

YOUTH CENTRE REFUSE HELP

Offer from YMCA not accepted

UNWANTED PETS LEFT TO DROWN IN RIVER

Cat found in sack

BIDEFORDIAN DEVON GOLF CHAMPION

TV STAR TO VISIT CHULMLEIGH

New telephone exchange

JOURNALIST MARRIES NURSE

FIG. 77. An ideal and economical handling of Cheltenham Bold to make an attractive weekly paper front page.

AN INDEPENDENT NEWSPAPER (Reg. at G.P.O.)

ESTABLISHED IN 1906. THREEPENCE.

BRIDGWATER MERCURY
and County Press

TUESDAY, JUNE 17th, 1958

FALSE PRETENCES CHARGES

Petrol, cigarettes and office supplies

LOCAL MAN FOUND GUILTY

Index

APPELLANT'S PROTEST

"Dirty end of stick"

On short time

Soldier for trial

The Somerset scene

The River Barle at Withypool.

NEW BATHS SCHEME

Family "lido" envisaged

Public house to close

Staggered into police station

This is what the proposed swimming baths will look like. A close-up view of a model prepared in the Borough Architect's department.

One-way traffic at the Docks

Industry's great need

Died in hospital

PARKING OF CARS WITHOUT LIGHTS

Trades Council resolution to Town Council

Rosier for Mr. Rosier

How to give 'the very thing'

—when you don't know what they want

Anyone can give—and cash—

MIDLAND BANK GIFT CHEQUES

FIG. 78. Basically Bodoni, with omission of column rules in doubled-up stories.

to the correlation of news make-up and advertising;[1] the *Bridgwater Mercury*, Somerset—a freer and more horizontal style in Century and

[1] Noteworthy is the *Journal-Herald*'s handling of its village news: a simple open-box heading and the various items subbed short, each with a 10 pt. Cheltenham Bold italic lower-case side-head for the name of the village or township. Thus the 'District News'—a most important feature for a country weekly—is kept to the general typography of the paper, and kept together. Papers which throw in these items in solid slabs, with the village names in some battered standing type bearing no relation to their general style, or else divide them up as a species of filler here and there throughout the issue, are adopting a dangerously cavalier attitude to one of their main pieces of reader-interest.

THE SURREY COMET

and SOUTH MIDDLESEX NEWS

No. 8425 104th YEAR SATURDAY, AUGUST 2, 1958

UNSKILLED JOBS ARE FEWER

BUT ENGINEERS HAVE PLENTY OF WORK

PROBLEMS AHEAD FOR SCHOOL LEAVERS

M.W.B. OPENS NEW £5M. PLANT

BIGGEST EVER BUILT IN EUROPE

LOOKING AHEAD

MOLESEY LOCK BEST ON THAMES

CUP FOR KEEPER

Crinoline in flowers

Bravery saves child

Quick action helps old man

MAN HANGED AT SURBITON

SCHOOL GARDENER'S DISCOVERY

TWELVE PATIENT JURORS

SEVEN DAYS IN COURT WITHOUT A CASE

MYSTERY OF 100 GAS CYLINDERS

FOUND IN BASEMENT

MISSING SAFE AT WORLD'S END

£200 STOLEN FROM IT

WOMAN (84) DIES AFTER ACCIDENT

PRAM STOLEN

FIVE-YEAR BAN ON DRIVER AGED 72

DRINK CHARGE CONVICTION

Grass skirts were fair fashion

YOU MUST READ MONTGOMERY'S MEMOIRS

HURLEYS Book Dept.

Clapham Observer

One of SOUTH LONDON'S SUBURBAN GROUP of NINE PAPERS

WEDDING RECEPTIONS ANNIVERSARY PARTIES, Etc. A. J. CARPENTER (London) LTD. RECEPTION ROOMS and RESTAURANT

No. 4709 Telephone: Macaulay 1092 (Two Lines) FRIDAY, NOVEMBER 14, 1958 Registered at the G.P.O. as a newspaper Price: FOURPENCE

This has gone on too long. It's time to act quickly—MP

VICE: PROTEST TO HOME OFFICE

Residents say: Stop this vicious trade

MR. CHARLES GIBSON, M.P. for Clapham, acting on complaints from residents of North Side, Clapham Common, has written a strong letter of protest to the Home Secretary about the spread of vice in the district. Chief complaint of the residents is that prostitution is being carried on quite openly from dusk on seven nights of the week now.

£20 a night: That's what prostitutes earn on Clapham Common

Find jobs MPs are told

SCHOOLBOY FOOTBALLERS

They found the shop's weak spot

£157 snatch at Clapham Junction

'Baby snatch might have ended disastrously'

Stole to give his children a holiday

FIG. 79. Suburban contrasts: the Kingston *Comet*'s sober Bodoni-Times roman cap. headings (decker style) or Clapham's big play with Tempo Heavy and Bodoni Bold upper- and lower-case multi-liners.

Bodoni Bold, white in place of some column rules, and an elegant title-piece in Times Heavy Titling; the *Surrey Comet*, Kingston-on-Thames—a double-and-single make-up in Bodoni, Century, and Times, with a Times Semi-Bold title; the *Bournemouth Times* in Sans, Century, and Bodoni, with frequent use of colour.

BOURNEMOUTH TIMES

No. 2420 3d. FOUNDED 1858 FRIDAY, 27th JUNE, 1958

TOWN EDITION

'SHAME ON YOU . . . WE DON'T DESERVE THIS STIGMA'

YOUTH HITS BACK AT THE MORAL MONGERS

CHOIR GIRL

ATOM MIRACLE GIVES TOWN GOLDEN CHANCE

TIME FACTOR

QUESTIONED

'JAG' OF THE JUNGLE

MISSING

Veteran's Le Mans triumph

Take my advice

Buy your used car at IMPERIAL MOTORS – they have the best in town

BLASTS ALERT WINS PRAISE

10s steak cost him £5

Now is your Opportunity

DO NOT HESITATE!

SIX MONTH WARRANTY

Cox calls for legal advice

Storm strands 500 on steamer trip

Mrs. Hession

Royal visit

Speedier stamps

SALES RISE!

with the SELMORE

PALACE COURT THEATRE

WESTOVER ROAD - BOURNEMOUTH

THE BARRY O'BRIEN COMPANY WILL PRESENT DURING JULY

July 7 Week BETH

July 14 Week The LOVE BIRDS

July 21 Week SAILOR, BEWARE!

July 28 Week SPIDER'S WEB

HE COULDN'T KEEP HIS EYES OFF THE MAYOR

FIG. 80. A highly sophisticated weekly front page. Note the low placing of the lead heading in tabloid Sans caps. The page area is larger than standard and colour is used, often more extensively than in the top right reverse block here.

The papers cited are all broadsheet; but the tabloid format is gaining ground in what may be called the outlying suburban areas, including under this head the New Towns like Crawley and Harlow and Home Counties residential resorts. The new approach made by two half-sheet papers in this category, the *Worthing Herald* (one of a South Coast group of four weeklies: Figs. 81, 82) and the *Harlow Citizen*, rated awards and

WORTHING HERALD

No. 2039 FRIDAY, MAY 29, 1959 PRICE 4d.

WIND AND TIDE RIGHT, BUT

Hitch in the trawl for seaweed

WIND and tide were just right yesterday (Thursday) morning for the first trawl of the seaweed beds off Worthing, in an effort to release the weed before summer gales tear it up and dump it on the beach.

So the trawler *Girl Pat*, of Shoreham, under her skipper, Mr J. Howell, of Brighton, hired by the Corporation which has ben voted £1,000 for exploratory work in clearing the weed, began her first sweep of the marked 1,000 yards by 300 yards plot.

But the *Girl Pat* was soon in trouble. By 11 o'clock on one of her earliest runs from just off the end of the Pier to the other end of the plot off Heene-road, her speed dropped to less than one knot. Then she stopped dead and despite full power from her 25 hp engine she failed to overcome the obstruction her trawling chains had fouled on the sea bed.

So round she swung, retraced her course, and then hove to while her crew manhandled the trawl wires and eventually released the chains. Afterwards, trawling continued steadily.

Holidaymakers watching from the Promenades saw occasional pieces of seaweed fluttering from the trawl wires as they were hauled aboard.

THE PLAN

Watching, too, from the Promenade was Mr D. G. Sutton, chief assistant engineer of the Borough Engineer's department, who described the Corporation's plan for the preliminary sweep.

"After today's trawling, expected to take about three hours, we shall make another survey of the beds and see how effective it has been," Mr Sutton told the HERALD.

"The Brighton, Hove and Worthing Sub Aqua Club made eight dives for us at Whitsun weekend, taking photographs of the beds, and will be making another dive for more photographs after this sweep so that we can compare the two sets of prints.

"We hope they will be able to

Continued page 9, column 2.

Findon fears loss of identity

AN outline application for building 61 bungalows at The Vale, Findon-road, Findon, was refused by Worthing Rural Council on Tuesday because "further residential development in this area between Findon and Worthing would be likely to lead to the coalescence of the two communities."

The Planning Committee, recommending refusal, said that development would lead to the loss of the separate identity and village character of Findon and would be detrimental to the character and visual amenities of the locality.

Other reasons given were that the site was in an area of great landscape value and was contrary to development plan provisions; and that further development beside this unrestricted part of the Worthing-London road would be a source of danger and inconvenience.

SUNNIEST SINCE JUNE, 1957

WORTHING is having its sunniest month since June, 1957. Up to Wednesday, May had recorded 237·2 hours, compared with the average for 1st-27th of 192 hours, and Sunday, with 14·8 hours, was the sunniest day since June last year.

Two years ago May recorded 270 sun hours.

With 22 rainless days and a fall of only ·79in., the month has been the driest May for three years. Worthing's average May rainfall is 1·65in. No rain has fallen since the 20th.

Since the weekend temperatures have dropped 12 deg. Sunday recorded 70 deg., but Tuesday's reading of 58 deg. was 4 deg. below average.

Hurt in collision

After a collision with a car while walking in Brighton-road, near the junction with York-road on Wednesday, Mrs Ethel Ruff, of 7 Sussex-road, was taken to Southlands Hospital, Shoreham, with a broken thigh. Yesterday (Thursday) she was stated to be quite comfortable.

IN THE UNIFORM of Ottway's Regiment, as the Royal Sussex Regiment was known in 1759, Pte. V. Dunne (right), of Worthing, and Pte. E. Harrington wait to play their part in the regiment's Royal Tournament display.

MOTHER OF THREE DISAPPEARS

A SOMPTING husband is waiting anxiously for news of his wife whom he has not seen for a week.

Mrs Jessie Bertha Booth, aged 33, of 32 Halewick-lane, disappeared last Friday after sending

MRS BOOTH

her three children, Iris, aged 13½, Maureen, aged 12, and Eric, aged eight, off to the pictures.

The children were waiting for him alone when their father, Mr Roy Booth, aged 40, returned from his job as a builder's labourer at about 6 p.m. on Friday.

She had taken a small suitcase and an open work plastic bag with her, and Mr Booth thought she would return by the weekend.

Sunday night came and she had not returned. Then Mr Booth began making inquiries. He found that she had not gone to relatives.

He also checked with her employers, the Southern Services Laundry in Lancing, and found that she had left her job there the previous Wednesday.

Mr Booth has informed the police. He thinks that she may have gone to Wallasey, Cheshire, where she had been evacuated as a child. Many times she had spoken of returning there, but he knows of no address there to which she could go.

Two lunch hour raids

MORE than £60 in cash was stolen from an office and a shop within a few hundred yards of each other in the Rowlands-road area during the lunch hour yesterday (Thursday).

The sum of £12 8s. in a green cash box was stolen from Messrs Potter Bailey's ironmongery shop in Crescent-road, and £49 14s. 4d. in cash and a cheque was stolen from the office of John Barclay, estate agents, at 33 Rowlands-road.

The raids took place between 1 p.m. and 2.15 p.m. while the premises were closed for lunch.

A duplicate key is believed to have been used to gain entry in each case.

£119 CLOTHES RAID

Pour suits and a jacket, together worth £119, were stolen from Hector Powe Ltd., Chapel-road, on Tuesday night, some time between the closing and opening hours of the shop.

Entry was obtained by forcing a rear window open. Nothing else was taken.

ON THE SPOT

A passing ambulance pulled up seconds after Mrs Doris Gathern, aged 45, of 26 Orme-road, had been involved in a collision with a car while riding her moped in West-parade on Wednesday.

Mrs Gathern was taken to Worthing Hospital with a knee inury, but was allowed home after treatment.

FEWER OUT OF WORK

UNEMPLOYMENT in Worthing is lower than at any time since last September. On Monday, the local employment exchange recorded 476 people out of work, 380 men and 96 women, compared with 539 on the corresponding day in April.

There is still a problem in trying to find work for older people, commented a Ministry of Labour and National Insurance official. It was difficult to persuade some local employers to take on people over 50.

The unemployment in Worthing has been largely seasonal, and there are increasing numbers of vacancies in hotels and catering.

The scope for clerical work is still limited.

Assault on councillor

HAROLD WILLIAM VENIS, aged 34, an asphalt worker living in Maybridge-crescent, Goring, was at the adjourned Quarter Sessions at Chichester on Tuesday sent to prison for six months for assault.

He pleaded not guilty and conducted his own defence.

Mr Geoffrey Lawrence, Q.C., the chairman, told Venis, "It was a disgraceful and lawless piece of conduct. You deliberately assaulted a man at least 20 years older than yourself in a particularly brutal way, generally behaving in an arrogant and bullying fashion."

Mr A. McCowan, prosecuting, said that Mr Richard Paton Purchase (57), a Chichester rural councillor, was assaulted by Venis in the car park of the Regnum Club at Chichester on December 17.

Venis, he said, twisted Mr Purchase's arm behind him and pushed him against a car.

Venis, in evidence, denied that he ever touched Mr Purchase, apart from snatching some papers from him after Mr Purchase refused to give him his name.

Venis admitted two previous findings of guilt at Worthing for larceny; and one previous conviction for taking and driving away a car without the owner's consent.

Why weeds surround new church

THE striking modern building which is Findon Valley Free Church stands on a prominent main road site. The surrounds, untended, are overgrown with weeds—and the subject of adverse comment.

Church members want to lay out the land, but are concerned at the delay in the making-up of the service road which is to be continued south from the Findon-road parade of shops.

The Borough Engineer, Mr G. H. Kempton, told the HERALD that no provision for the construction of the continuation was made in this year's estimates, and the matter was likely to remain as it is for some time.

But, he added, there was nothing to stop the church from laying out its grounds.

The minister, the Rev. H. Bonser, told the HERALD that it was hoped the road would be put in before the land was laid out.

The church architect said that they planned to raise the level of the ground so that the laid-out part of the site would be higher than the road.

The absence of any road would make it difficult, as they did not want to go to the expense of walls if this could be avoided; and there would be nuisance from weeds.

"But we are getting out costs and schemes for doing our corner," he added.

BUBBLE CAR OVERTURNED

Mrs Elizabeth Doig, of 6 Malvern-close, was treated at Worthing Hospital yesterday (Thursday) morning after the three-wheel "bubble" car in which she was travelling overturned at the junction of Ham-road and Chesswood-road.

She was taken to hospital by ambulance and allowed to go home after treatment.

Her daughter, who was in the car with her, was shaken but unhurt.

Good in parts

A 1937 Ford 8 — like "the curate's egg" — is one of the scores of bargains offered in the classified advertisements on pages 32 to 39 of this issue.

PRISON CAMP SOUVENIRS

AN idea of conditions that prevailed in Malayan prisoner-of-war camps during the 1939-45 war is given in a display in one of Jones and Tomlin's windows in Chapel-road.

Arranged by two members of Worthing District and West Sussex Far Eastern Prisoner of War Social Club, Mr C. J. Banham, chairman, and Mr. J. Garnham, welfare officer, it heralds the National Federation of Far Eastern Prisoner of War Clubs' 1959 National Conference which will be opened by the Mayor, Coun. H. W. Bradley, at the Richmond Room tomorrow.

It will be the first time that the conference has been held in Worthing.

Mr Banham told the HERALD that the two Japanese swords and a Japanese soldier's full uniform used in the display were lent by ex-prisoners who brought them back as souvenirs.

Photographs taken at one of the camps are included in the display.

About 130 delegates from 45 clubs throughout the country are expected to attend the conference.

Mr Garnham dressing a model

FIG. 81. Front page of the first weekly paper to win the top Newspaper Design Award—the bronze plaque for 'best designed newspaper of the year' (1958).

26 The Herald, Friday, May 29, 1959

POND TO BE 'A THING OF BEAUTY'

THE clerk of Storrington Parish Council, Mr E. Davies, told members on Monday that the West Sussex River Board was preparing plans and specifications for restoring Storrington Pond to "a thing of beauty."

Mr Davies explained that ownership of the surrounding land had been partly determined. "Part still remains in the ownership of the Zouche family," he said, "and the other part appears to belong to Mrs Kerr-Davies or whoever succeeded her in title."

Mr Davies said that acquisition of land was not necessary, the Open Spaces Act of 1906 could be applied. This permitted "a local authority to undertake entire or partial care, management and control of any such open space or burial ground whether any interest in the soil is transferred to the local authority or not."

"We must now wait for the specifications and plans to arrive from the River Board," said Mr Eddolls, "and we hope it's soon."

Firemen from Lancing were called to Lancing Carriage Works on Saturday afternoon to deal with a small fire.

More damage by hooligans at East Preston

CONSTANTLY faced with repair bills for damage caused to the Rifle Range and other council property, East Preston Parish Council is wondering what can be done about the hooligans causing the damage.

At Tuesday's meeting of the council, members agreed that the clerk should ask police advice.

The clerk, Mr R. J. Stanford, reported that the roof and guttering of the Rifle Range had been damaged, and it was estimated that repairs would cost about £30.

"Where is it going to stop?" asked Mr Wright. "No sooner do we repair something than it is damaged again." He pointed out that, together with an estimate already received for repairing broken windows at the Rifle Range, the council was now facing a bill of over £50 for wilful damage.

The meeting re-elected Mr Allen as chairman, and Mr J. A. C. Wright as vice-chairman.

Rats complaint

Worthing Rural Council on Tuesday asked its Chief Public Health Inspector to look into complaints from nearby residents that the use of land beside Angmering Recreation Ground for poultry-keeping had led to infestation by rats.

FERRING—VILLAGE OF RELUCTANT MALES

FERRING is the village of the reluctant male. At least, it is when the dramatic society is arranging a cast for production.

The society's chairman, Mr Kenneth Lavington, told members at the annual meeting in Greystoke Manor Hotel on Friday that the shortage of men was providing the FADS with a real problem.

"I have never belonged to a society before where the men have been so reluctant to take part in the plays," said Mr Lavington, who hoped that in future casting would be made easier by the availability of more male performers.

Mrs Constance Clarke, hon. teasurer, reported a credit balance of £71 6s. 9d. compared with £62 11s. last year. Twenty-five new members had joined during the year.

"The balance sheet would look very different indeed," said Mr Lavington, "if we had had to pay for our rehearsal rooms. There's no doubt about that and we have to thank Mrs D. M. Blundell (proprietress of the Greystoke Manor Hotel) for allowing us to rehearse here."

Mr Lavington also paid tribute to Miss Doreen Dawson for arranging catering facilities at the annual party and various socials throughout the year, and to Miss Ellen Ewen, hon. secretary, and Mrs Clarke, hon. treasurer, who were both re-elected.

Play reading had been a great success, he said, between 15 and 18 people attending each session. The three plays, *Without The Prince*, *The Man From Toronto* and *Present Laughter*, presented during the season had proved happy selections. It was hoped to produce a pantomime during the Christmas season.

Mrs Sybil Barber was re-elected president, but Mr Trevor Best, the "matinee idol" in Noel Coward's *Present Laughter*, succeeded Mr Lavington as chairman. Mrs E. H. Madley, vice-chairman, and Mr A. B. H. ("Bob") Crowder, stage manager, were re-elected. The new committee is, Mr P. Leach, Mr H. Redman, Mr J. Cooper, Mrs M. Scott, Mrs U. Allen and Miss D. Dawson.

His last year as chairman

Mr T. J. Tilston was re-elected chairman of Rustington Parish Council on Monday. It will be his third year in office, but he told councillors, "It will be my last year as chairman and my last on the council." This is his 11th year on the council.

Mrs N. E. Magnus-Osborn was appointed vice-chairman.

WHY NOT TALK IT OVER WITH THE DOGS?

Storrington is still being worried by dogs that foul footpaths.

At Monday's annual meeting of the Parish Council, the chairman, Mr F. W. Eddolls, said that it was easy to appeal to people but what could be done with animals.

"Perhaps we could discuss the matter with the dogs who give offence," he said.

Mrs B. Langton, M.B.E., and Mr S. Marsh were elected to meet representatives of Storrington Chamber of Trades and Professions, who complained to the council of the nuisance, to discuss this and the question of litter in local streets.

Water pipe cut by hooligans: cattle suffer

NEARLY 50 head of young cattle, a mixed herd belonging to Mr B. L. A. Cornford, of Clapham Farm, Clapham, suffered acute thirst recently as a result of damage to a supply pipe carrying water to a cattle tank at Cote-street.

Mr Cornford told the HERALD that approximately 140.000 gallons of water were lost. The pipe had been smashed and water flooded a barn.

"It took me some time to get the water flowing again and the cattle, by this time suffering severely from the lack of water, had to be taken to Clapham village, about a mile away, where they were given attention."

Mr Cornford said that he thought the damage was the work of youths, and a recurrence of earlier outbreaks of hooliganism in the area. A few days ago tiles on a barn were smashed.

"It couldn't have happened at a worse time. Everything's so dry and we have plenty of other jobs to get on with on the farm," said Mr Cornford.

Balance in hand up by £143

Mr S. C. Ridge, chairman of the finance committee, told the annual meeting of Storrington Parish Council on Monday that the council had a balance in hand of £361 compared with £218 the previous year.

"This is a very satisfactory position indeed," said Mr F. W. Eddolls, chairman, "especially when you remember this council was 'in the red' when it started."

"We only took £600 in precepts," said Mr Ridge, "which is equivalent to a 4d. rate. General expenses were very close to the figure we proposed at the beginning of the year."

'Cheeky' to the rent man

Rustington Parish Council on Monday agreed to get tenders for cutting down the weeds which have grown to two or three feet high on about 30 unused allotments.

Mr T. J. Tilston, chairman, reported that their clerk had had great difficulty in collecting rents from some allotment holders. One man had been very "cheeky" to him and another had paid nothing for two years. The clerk, Mr E. Wheeler, said that he had, however, got the arrears down to just over £2.

Is it advisable?

Is it advisable to put sodium lamps down the beautiful Old Manor-road, Rustington?

The question was raised at a Rustington Parish Council meeting on Monday by Mr F. Campbell. He said that the appearance of Old Manor-road had been greatly improved by recent road and paving works there.

He did not press the point when Mr H. E. Hiscocks, chairman of the Lighting Committee, said that it had been fully considered by the committee.

Mr Hiscocks said that sodium gave light to a bigger area and caused fewer shadows than ordinary lighting. Also their fuel bills had gone down since sodium lamps had been introduced.

The council approved recommendations for the installation of 15 sodium lamps in Old Manor-road.

Speeding costs £8

Bruce William Gurney, of Broadmark-lane, Rustington, was fined £8 by Worthing magistrates on Friday for exceeding the speed limit in West-parade, Worthing. He admitted the offence in a letter.

10-day cycling and camping trip to Paris

"IT was a wonderful way to end one's last term at school." 16-year-old Richard Lucas, son of Major and Mrs H. Lucas, of Rosanne, Lansdowne-road, Angmering, told a HERALD reporter this week, "and I now feel better equipped for tackling my GCE examination."

Richard was referring to a recent tip to France on which he and 15 other boys of the senior class of the new Andrew Cairns Secondary Modern School, Littlehampton, were accompanied by the headmaster and his wife, Mr and Mrs K. A. Hodges, and their daughter.

Richard and his companions returned home on Sunday after a 10-day cycling, camping and youth hostelling trip which took them to Paris by way of Rouen and the valley of the Seine.

The boys contributed towards the cost of the trip and received a "dole" of 1,000 francs a day with which to buy their own food which they cooked themselves.

Now that the excitement of the trip is over Richard is concentrating on making a success of his exams. He wants to become a cadet in the Criminal Investigation Department of the Metropolitan Police.

WOMEN'S INSTITUTES

Angmering

Another new member, Mrs Sexton, was welcomed by the president, Mrs Ells, at the May meeting of Angmering Women's Institute. Sympathy was expressed with Miss K. Collyer who broke her leg, after being involved in an accident with a lorry.

The outing to Leonard's Lee was most successful, it was reported. Names of members wishing to go to the Isle of Wight outing were taken. There is to be a group meeting evening outing to Trundle Hill, Goodwood, on June 29.

At the Chichester Handicraft Exhibition Mrs Hatcher gained 90 per cent. marks, Mrs Bowker and Mrs Peskett gained 80 marks each and Mrs Humphreys 75 per cent. The institute will entertain the old folk from Hurstpierpoint on August 10.

The hand-painted picture competition was judged by Miss G. Watkins. Results: 1 Mrs Bowker, 2 Mrs Darlington, 3 Mrs Jeffries.

The delegate to the annual meeting at the Albert Hall will be Mrs Ron Smith, who will also represent East Preston. Mrs Tait, VCO, gave a talk on the annual meeting.

The competition for next month will be a Vase of Flowers in One Tone, and for the social half-hour a limerick on WI members.

Cootham

The well-attended May meeting of Cootham Women's Institute made final arrangements for the garden meeting for June. A sub-committee was formed to make plans for a jumble fete to be held on June 27.

Miss Asher, of Amberley, came to speak on resolutions for the annual meeting. She was accompanied by Mrs Penny who is to be delegate.

A bring-and-buy stall in aid of WI funds made an attractive display. Miss F. Macdonald and Mrs Breach were in charge and £5 13s. 6d. was raised.

Competitions for "My prettiest cup and saucer" and for the "Bloom of the month" brought many entries. Mrs Dean was awarded three stars for the first and Mrs Greenfield three stars for her blossom.

Mrs Hodgson and Mrs Bennett were in charge of refreshments.

Pulborough

Mrs Fowler presided over the monthly meeting of the Pulborough WI when 51 members attended.

Members stood in silence in memory of three members who had died since the last meeting—Mrs Brockis, Mrs Thirkettle and Mrs Chatfield.

Articles entered for the recent handicraft exhibition in Chichester were on view, and all the entries had received good marks.

The spring fair raised £72 for the WI.

"Our wonderful feet and how to help them" was the title of the talk given by Mrs Tait. The competition, "Miniature garden in a soup plate," was won by Mrs Pavey, 2 Mrs Skeggs and 3 Mrs Jackson. Tea hostess: Mrs Hatfield.

Margaret Ann Peplon, of Brighton-road, Lancing, was fined 15s. at Steyning on Monday for riding a bicycle without lights, and 5s. for having no rear reflector.

Fill your glass with 'Sunshine'...

and enjoy all the goodness of a summer's day

Pour yourself a 'Sunshine'. See its dancing brilliance—bright as the sun. Taste its fine flavour. Centuries of brewing experience have put the sun in 'Sunshine'. Only natural, wholesome ingredients are used. That's why it does you good. Drink 'Sunshine' where you see the Brickwoods sign and enjoy all the goodness of a summer's day.

BRICKWOODS

SUNSHINE

PRIZE ALE

Best Beer under the Sun

FIG. 82. An inside page of the plaque-winning *Worthing Herald*; note the careful correlation of news make-up and display advertising.

commendations in the first three contests for the Newspaper Design Award, whose 1955 judges said this of the *Herald* and *Citizen*:

These papers are worthy of close study by every publisher of a weekly. They may fairly be regarded as having broken with traditional weekly newspaper design and as having achieved a readability much greater than that of any other weekly entered. . . . Their typographical good manners are equally noticeable on every page, and the style is consistent from beginning to end. Yet there is plenty of life in these papers; and the varying importance of their news items is skilfully marked by typographical treatment.

Fortunately, a detailed analysis of the make-up policy of the *Worthing Herald*—first local weekly to win (1958) the Design Award bronze plaque—has been provided by Frank Cave, editor and creator of its make-up. Given as a paper to the Young Newspapermen's Association in 1955, it is of exceptional importance as a fundamental statement on make-up by a working newspaper executive and is summarized[1] here:

The Approach: to meet the demands of an urban middle-class readership 'conditioned to the bright, sometimes flashy make-up' of the London mornings and evenings, it was decided to aim at content of the quality of *The Times*, but to adapt the make-up of the similar-sheet *Star* and *Evening Standard*, without imitating their 'more flamboyant essays'.

Advertising: 'the good editorial executive works with the advertising executive who plans the advertisements in the pages; as the good advertising executive has understanding of the editorial viewpoint. . . . Positioning of half-tones, size and placing of headings and general balance of the page all demand the closest co-operation between editorial and advertising. . . . It is folly to try and shout down, or even to compete with the advertiser, in the size of type for headings. The editorial just can't beat the advertiser. . . . The answer lies in contrast. Accept the artist's precept who, to make the white appear whiter, does not apply more white paint but paints darker the colour adjacent to the white.'

Typography: 'there is as great danger in having too wide a variety of faces from which to choose as of having so few that it is impossible to achieve variety'. Text of the *Herald* is in 8, 7, 5½ pt. Times [*since January* 1958 *changed to* 8, 7, 6 *pt. Jubilee*] with 9 pt. for intros. News is headed in Century Bold roman and italic—36 pt. maximum size—with Bodoni roman and italic for decks; the front-page lead only is headed in 42 or 48 pt. Tempo Heavy lower-case. Other pages are typographically differentiated: features with Century Bold Extended (36 or 48 pt.), Caslon Heavy roman and italic (Ludlow), Bodoni; entertainments substitute 48 pt. Chisel for the Century Bold Extended; sports combine Tempo Bold with Century; the leader page is set to five 13-em columns instead of six 11-em columns.

[1] The full text appeared in *World's Press News*, 28 Oct. 1955. A further most valuable exposition of the author's views appeared in the Newspaper Society's *Production Journal*, nos. 4, 5 (April, September 1959).

Half-tones: 'we restrict them to the better printing pages', aiming all the time at 'quality of reproduction'.

Make-up: the available news area does not call for many large headings. Only a limited number of 30 pt. cap. headings are used and very seldom 36 pt. caps. 'We believe in the down-page double-column story . . . not for design motives alone but because the story is important and the editor wants it quite unmistakably to be apprehended as important.'

The real aim: 'the fundamental aim which temptation, however great, must not be allowed to obstruct, is clarity and ease of reading for the reader. We are not engaged in the creation of patterns solely for our own satisfaction or enjoyment. . . . The make-up man's job, as I see it, is to create a page which is as easy as can be for the reader to follow. That is the first task.'

The style that has been worked out for the *Worthing Herald* is, of course, no more to be imitated than is the style of any other well-made and successful paper. The principles guiding the creation of this style are the important thing; this is why Frank Cave's exposition of these principles is so apposite, being based on twenty years' study and application of them (he began to remould the *Herald* series in 1936). Whatever its format or character, any weekly newspaper needs to understand and apply these principles if it is to increase its reader-appeal to the utmost by an appropriate make-up. At the same time Cave's closing words should never be forgotten:

Good design, good make-up, depends, of course, on what one wants to achieve. If one wants to scream, if one has a low assessment of the intelligence of one's readers (if, even worse, one doubts the literacy of one's readers) then, presumably, one does shout and hector. . . .

The content of a newspaper is what is paramount. Make-up is important, for it is much more than a veneer. It is something to be *used* and not just a job to be done. Used to help express the paper's individuality or character; used to make even more interesting the facts and opinions contained in the body matter, make-up (if one is very good at it) can be exciting—to the creator and the reader. But always it must be fundamentally simple and conducted to arouse and retain the interest of the reader and facilitate his journey through the pages. The achievement of good make-up depends on co-operation between the person planning the advertisements and the editorial man who charts the news and blocks. . . .

A newspaper benefits from establishing a style and, essentially, sticking to it, so that the paper is recognisable at a glance. This is not to say that one conceives a style or general appearance, executes it and then, metaphorically, goes on perpetual holiday. There must always be room for experiment and change within the style. Once having settled on a style, however, I think that, basically, it should be adhered to.

CONSTANT FACTORS: 1. SPACE

Whatever the typography and make-up of a news page there are three factors which may be called the constant factors, since they have always to be taken into account. The first is spacing, the 'white'. That the proper allocation of white space is of the first importance has been repeatedly stressed throughout this book; here the point has to be stressed again in respect of the due whiting over headings, over and under cut-offs, that is to say between stories. The word 'due' deserves some thought, for white can be either too little or too much, and either extreme is disagreeable. Pressure on space may be a temptation to skimp the white, leaving what the 1956 Design Award judges picturesquely called 'almost breathlessly small space' over main headings, just as shortage of matter during make-up may lead to grotesque over-whiting (18 pts. where 6 pts. suffice).

No rigid prescription can be given for the correct whiting for a particular paper; one or two simple trials will soon show the most agreeable effect, which has to be judged on proof, since it is an optical effect. Then the white as thus determined should be specified and made firm style. Approximately it may be said that a minimum white under the front-page folio rule is a pica, and with large-type streamer make-up even 18 pts., suitable white being allowed for between the strap-line (if any) and the streamer, and between the streamer and any cut-off rule beneath it. On the same basis a minimum 6–8 pts. is required over double-column headings and single-column tops, 4 pts. over down-column singles and 3 pts. over fillers. These approximations are offered on the basis of 6 pt. column rule and cut-off rule, itself carrying 3 pts. of white either side, and they refer only to the space over a heading, i.e. under a cut-off. The view is sometimes held that no white is needed over a story cut-off, on the grounds that the indication of the story's end should be as tightly tied to the story as possible, but it is preferable to insert a minimum white, say 2 pts., over such cut-offs.

The meticulous approach to even whiting of a good news page is illustrated in a story of the *Birmingham Post*'s handling of the tremendous news night in 1930 when the R 101 crashed. It happened to be a young deputy chief sub-editor's first night in charge and he felt that he had acquitted himself well. The next night he was summoned to the editorial presence and George W. Hubbard, most famous of the occupants of the Midland daily's chair, made the single comment that on the main news page there was a 7 pts. white after one cut-off, 8 pts. after another. 'That will not do for the *Birmingham Post*,' said he. 'You must keep the spacing uniform throughout.'[1]

[1] H. R. G. Whates, *The Birmingham Post 1857–1957*, p. 201.

A well-designed paper explains itself at a glance. The typographical treatment distinguishes different kinds of news stories, and separates news from features. Further, it maintains interest throughout. There should be a dynamic quality right through the issue and

A well-designed paper explains itself at a glance. The typographical treatment distinguishes different kinds of news stories, and separates news from features. Further, it maintains interest throughout. There should be a dynamic quality right through the issue and

A well-designed paper explains itself at a glance. The typographical treatment distinguishes different kinds of news stories, and separates news from features. Further, it maintains interest throughout. There should be a dynamic quality right through the issue and

A well-designed paper explains itself at a glance. The typographical treatment distinguishes different kinds of news stories, and separates news from features. Further, it maintains interest throughout. There should be a dynamic quality right through the issue and

A well-designed paper explains itself at a glance. The typographical treatment distinguishes different kinds of news stories, and separates news from features. Further, it maintains interest throughout. There should be a dynamic quality right through the issue and

A well-designed paper explains itself at a glance. The typographical treatment distinguishes different kinds of news stories, and separates news from features. Further, it maintains interest throughout. There should be a dynamic quality right through the issue and

He spoke for only an hour. The House, he said, was stunned into a painful silence until he came to the end, when he roused cheers by quoting Swinburne:—

All our past proclaims our future: Shakespeare's voice and Nelson's hand,
Milton's faith and Wordsworth's trust in this our chosen and chainless land,

who first proclaimed this principle. All that Britain wants to do is to see whether or not better arrangements can be negotiated to preserve the rights of West Berliners. It has been explained on many occasions to Dr. Adenauer that Mr. Macmillan is not an apostle of disengagement. His proposals for an arms limitation is not such that it will discriminate against

FIG. 83. Specimens of 6 pt., 4 pt., 3 pt. column rule; below is an example of 10 pt. rule (from the *Yorkshire Post*; the same wide rule can be seen in *The Times*).

2. COLUMN RULES AND CUT-OFFS

The effective vertical separation of columns is vital to a news page. It may be done by the conventional column rule—fine rule centred on its body, usually 6 pt.—or by white space. For the normal newspaper, particularly the daily newspaper, it is better to use column rule on the news pages, restricting the white separation of columns to the feature pages and to occasional indented and doubled-up or otherwise specially displayed news stories. News pages made up entirely without rules, though favoured by some American experts, inevitably produce too much of a general tie-up effect; it is not difficult to imagine circumstances in which such apparent, though not intentional, tie-ups could be unfortunate, not to say disastrous. In any event the white separation is more extravagant of space, since it needs to be a full pica (or on a tabloid page at least 9 pts.), while 6 pt. column rule is adequate.

Column rule on bodies either larger or smaller than 6 pt. is not uncommon. Larger-bodied rule (8 pt. and upwards) will be found excessive in the mass of newspapers using 11-ems-plus column measure; but it can help to increase the openness and ease of the wider columns of a 'class' paper (thus *The Times*, with 13½-em columns, employs 10 pt. rule). Of the narrower rules 4 pt. and 3 pt. are the most frequent; the second in particular is too narrow to provide adequate visual separation of the columns, and lacks solidity in locking-up the forme; papers with 3 pt. column rule are driven to much indented setting if they wish to maintain a reasonable appearance of column separation (Fig. 83).

Clean, straight rule work, with all corners snugly mitred, is absolutely essential for a good-looking page. 'Rules in anything less than perfect condition make a page as untidy as a woman with her slip showing' says a contemporary American authority.[1] Local weekly papers are persistent offenders in this respect; all corners are gaps, the face is battered and if the rule is pieced it is allowed to gape there too; the special problems of Cossar-printed papers have been indicated in Chapter 2. Rule freshly cast in type metal on Monotype or Elrod machines has taken the place of brass rule in the larger newspapers; and it is the only complete solution of the rule problem, namely, fresh rule each time. It can be cut to any length required and mitred easily and accurately to join the pre-mitred corner cut-offs of varying measures that every stonehand should have by him, with his spacing-out material. Brass rule, if kept in good condition, can be used if it is carried in a sufficient assortment of lengths; even so, metal rule is the only practical way of providing the mitred corners. In passing, it may perhaps be said that the common American device of using a border unit (a disk, star, or lozenge) cast at the end of the cut-off to avoid mitring it and the column rule may fractionally save time but has nothing else in its favour.

Cut-offs between stories fulfil the same separating function horizontally that column rules do vertically; and, as with column rules, it has been argued that they are unnecessary, that white space between the end of one story and the heading of its successor is separation enough. In America at any rate several variations on this theme are practised, if not preached. There are papers with neither column rule nor cut-offs; others keep the column rule but drop all cut-offs; others again keep the cut-offs though dropping the column rule. The simple point surely is that to drop all cut-offs is to confuse the reader; he needs to know when a story has finished or when an associated story is being tied up with it.

The traditional separation of news stories was by the *half-double* (a thick-and-thin rule approximately half the width of the column and centred: Fig. 84A). In this case the column-rule face *half-single* (B) was

[1] Arnold, op. cit., p. 46.

used to indicate the tie-up of connected stories; this is still the style of *The Times*. But the general trend has been to abandon the half-double for the half-single, using white only for tie-ups;[1] this can be regarded as standard practice nowadays, an occasional variant being the use of medium rule (D) instead of column rule. Whichever style of cut-off is employed it is important to see that its width is well proportioned to the column measure, neither too wide nor too narrow. This is particularly necessary if the half-double is retained, because of its heavier colour; in this case, too, care should be taken to avoid any over-heavy version (E) or the feeble double-fine (C). Dashes of any kind are quite inappropriate for story cut-offs.

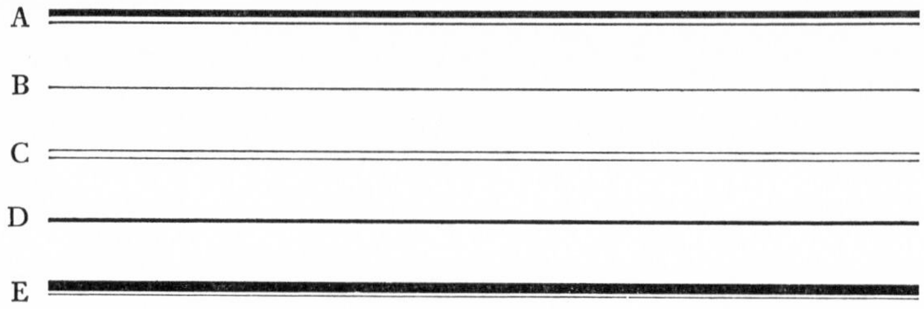

FIG. 84. Common styles of rule for newspaper work, including cut-offs.

The cut-offs so far discussed are those in single column. For double column and over the style should agree with that for single column; this includes full cut-offs over advertisements, where some papers tend unnecessarily to use thick-and-thin or double-fine rules when they have adopted column rule for their news cut-offs. One further style point arises here: should news cut-offs for double column and over be full (still the most common style) or be shortened a few ems each end? The short rule seems only a logical continuation of the single-column style and by providing some extra white—it additionally demands somewhat more white over and under than a full cut-off—helps to open up the page.

3. PAGE FOLIOS

The traditional style for the page folio—the newspaper equivalent of the book's running head—is to have the name of the paper, the day, and the date centred in roman caps. with the number of the page full out to left or

[1] When a single-column story is tied up under the shoulder of a double-column intro. the heading can either be fully whited, top and side, or the mitred cut-off rule be halved in width. The first seems the most logical arrangement, in terms of the general tie-up style indicated above. It suggests the danger in the not uncommon practice of omitting any cut-off over a shouldered-in single-column story, merely letting the column rule ride up into the white. This looks unfinished and prevents any proper typographical indication of a tie-up when that is needed.

right, and a full cut-off rule across the page. 'Class' newspapers still follow this style, and for them it is certainly the best; the size, style, and spacing of the folio line offers an opportunity for some finesse. The page cut-off should be column rule only. Use of double-fine or thick-and-thin is not commendable; over-heavy versions of the last named give a quite superfluous emphasis to the folio.

THE TIMES FRIDAY APRIL 3 1959

PAGE 16 **DAILY MIRROR, Saturday, August 15, 1959**

DAILY 11
HERALD
Thursday
April 23 1959

DAILY EXPRESS TUESDAY JULY 7 1959

DAILY MAIL, Monday, July 20, 1959

FIG. 85. Some examples of page folio lines.

For most papers the open top first adopted by the popular nationals, with its abandonment of the page cut-off, is preferable. There are two main styles here (Fig. 85): the usual folio details, set in a small size—e.g. the 6 pt. roman caps of the body type, and perhaps underscored—are run at the inside top of each page, with the page number in a larger bold figure in the usual outside position; or the folio details, set in a small-size contrasting type—e.g. a 6 pt. or 8 pt. light Sans, roman or italic—with the larger page figure cast at the end of the line, are disposed at the top of the two outside columns of each page. Either style saves space, the second the most, and gives the main headlines the full advantage of the white of the head margin. Ingenuity, and the length or otherwise of the name of the paper, can suggest varying styles, even a reduction to single column or less; but the ingenuity of the New York tabloids, running the folios up or down the outside margins (in one case set to read vertically), seems quite misplaced.

THE PLAN AND THE PAGE

The achievement of what has been outlined in this chapter requires precise page-planning. The practice of using miniature ruled make-up sheets is of long standing; but these sheets need to be scaled if they are to be reasonably accurate blueprints of the final page. The inch-scaling of make-up blanks, first introduced by the Americans, became general among national newspapers here when the wartime four-pagers compelled virtually line-by-line planning. Yet even today there are papers which do not realize that an inch-scaled make-up is essential under any circumstances if visualizing, planning, and sub-editing instructions are to be accurate, over-setting to be avoided, and time saved on the stone.

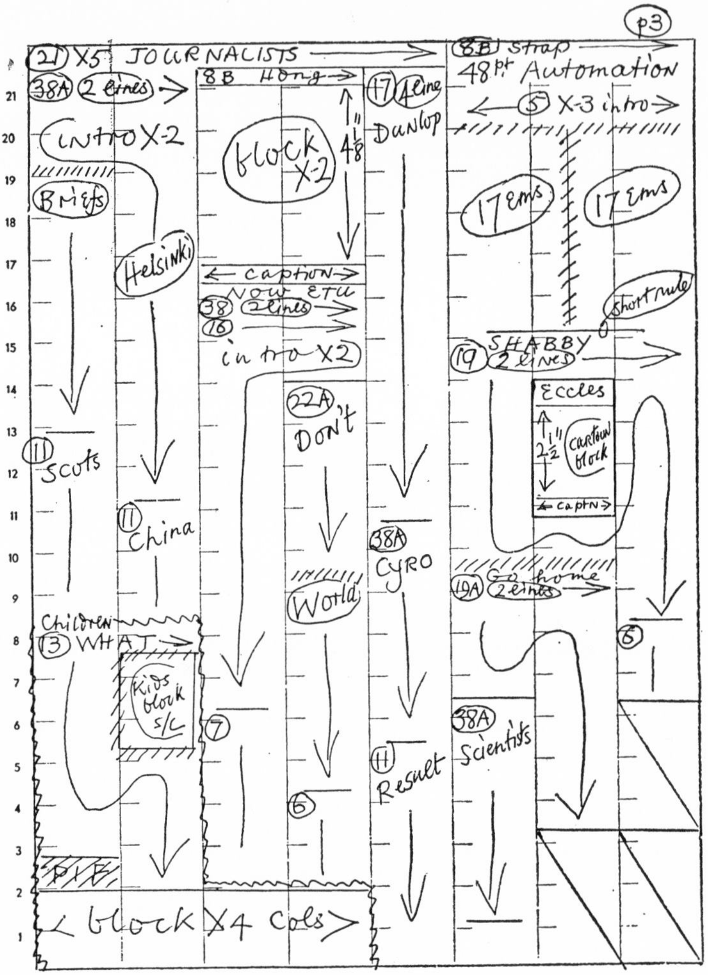

FIG. 86. A reduced facsimile of a scaled miniature page make-up.

Exact allowance can be made on a scaled make-up sheet for depths of headings, intros., text, blocks. If a late story is scheduled for a position which might delay make-up (e.g. a double-column story at the foot of the page), an exact depth can be schemed and the story subbed to length, dropping in at the last moment without trouble into its space in a completely made-up page.

JOURNALISTS' NEW DEAL

Let reporting barriers be broken down

NEWS IN BRIEF

Housewife argued with a record

Scots unions seek time on BBC

China wants independent thinkers

CHILDREN'S CORNER

WHAT 'O' MEANS

Adventures of PIF

THE BABIES LIKE JENNY

NOW E T U CHIEFS ACCUSE PRESS

'Defenders of capitalism'

Gross distortion

More branches

FRENCH RAIL CRASH KILLS 9

Last rites for Tony Murphy

DUNLOPS ANNOUNCE BOUNCING PROFITS

Don't let us down

£138 6 8

THE WIDER WORLD

Singapore danger

Result soon of Sobell trial appeal

Malaya wants tin ban lifted

TV exchange

Cyro men give notice to strike

TECHNICIANS' LEADER DISCUSSES . . .

Automation and you

It's economic suicide

Redundancy inevitable

SHABBY, SHABBY GOVT TO TREAT THE AGED SO

ECCLES AT WORK

TUC pressed

Depressed areas

Go home, Yankees, say vehicle men

'Let's withdraw'

Car output falls, commercials up

Scientists welcome Assembly

Japanese unite

ROYAL FESTIVAL HALL

BORIS GODUNOV

Are your NERVES on EDGE!

FIG. 87. The page as made up—from the 1956 award-winning *Daily Worker*.

A completed page-plan is shown in reduced facsimile here, together with the resultant page (Figs. 86, 87). In this example the conventional numbering of the headings card is used to guide the stonehand as to the depth of the headings and (together with a tag-word) for quick identification of stories. Larger types, not numbered on the card, are given their point sizes; some papers do this for all headings, but with a numbered headings card, well known to editorial and compositors alike, this is not necessary.

Make-up sheets should always be drawn up in pencil, not too light and not too heavy (a B is about right). It is sound practice to rule lightly for the depth of main headings. All tie-ups or breaks of rule should be clearly marked, as shown in the facsimile; to use a colour for this purpose—red, for example—is a help to the stonehand, as it is to use a contrasting colour (say blue) to indicate any rule other than ordinary column rule.

9 · The Handling of Pictures

AFTER type and white space, illustration is the third basic ingredient in the make-up of a newspaper page. Its management has equally to be mastered by the make-up man. Most important is the handling of pictures, i.e. half-tone blocks from photographs. Half-tone 'colour' makes a vital contribution to the attractiveness of a news page, and some points on its general disposition on the page have already been made in the preceding chapter. But just as the typographic pattern of a made-up page must have a journalistic purpose, and not be merely pleasant to look at, so must the picture; though it should be decorative its function is not decoration; it either illustrates the news, with which it is tied up, or it is a piece of pictorial news in its own right. Every picture, indeed, *should* tell a story.

Pictorial journalism, the assessment of news value in pictures, is not within the scope of this chapter. It does bear closely, however, on the central problem of picture-handling for news make-up, namely the sizing of the print. The expression 'sizing' is used here to cover the related operations of removing superfluous or static background, the gauging of the most dynamic presentation that can be got from the print, the co-operative determination by the picture and news executives concerned of the measure best combining the desirable and the possible (in terms of actual make-up exigencies), and the scaling of the depth that the block will occupy in the measure agreed upon.

Good sizing is the essence of the picture editor's skill; it is itself an art, difficult to reduce to any set formula, and acquired by experience added to aptitude. Perhaps the best single piece of advice is—add a column to the measure you first thought of. Naturally this is not always practical, but the approach is sound; if a picture is a good news picture it is worth playing big, as big as is necessary for full effect and as the make-up can be adjusted to take. The impact of one big picture is far greater than that of two pictures each half its size; if it is a dynamic, well-sized, and well-positioned picture, it will have both a unifying and livening effect on the entire page make-up (Figs. 88, 91).

Both in selecting news pictures and in their sizing it is necessary to remember that the coarse newspaper screen for half-tones (average 65 for rotary printing compared with 85 for flat printing on newsprint and 100

DAILY EXPRESS

No. 18,310 THURSDAY APRIL 9 1959 3 a.m. forecast: Sunny spells; showers; hail Price 2½d.

Britain's new challenge in the Atlantic

SUPER-LINERS AHOY

Struggle for power goes on as . . .

Dr A lashes at Britain

From COLIN LAWSON

BONN, Wednesday.

THE fight for power in Western Germany's new political era began today—and Dr Adenauer crashed into it with a challenge.

He also spoke scathingly of Britain.

They will replace Cunard's Queens

By MONTAGUE LACEY

TWO super-liners are to be built with Government help to replace the Queen Mary and Queen Elizabeth. They will counter foreign competition now threatening the Cunard Company.

Talks are going on between the Government, Cunard, and John Brown, Clydeside builders of the Queens.

News that the Government is planning once again to uphold Britain's prestige on the Atlantic was disclosed in the Commons yesterday by Transport Minister Mr. Harold Watkinson.

Last night Cunard's chairman, Colonel Denis Bates, said that the "whole position" of the weekly service between Southampton, Cherbourg, and New York has been put before the Government.

THE QUEEN MARY

He said the company had been compelled to do this "owing particularly to the policy of heavy subsidies given to our North Atlantic competitors and on the score of national prestige."

Replacement of the Queen liners, which cost £5,000,000 each in the 1930's, would now total at least £60,000,000.

If the Government gives the go-ahead the first new Queen could be ready in six years—two years for planning and four for building. It will mean work for thousands of Clydeside builders.

The new Queens are expected to be about 60,000 tons—much smaller than the Queen Mary (81,000 tons) or the Queen Elizabeth (83,000 tons).

But they will still be able to carry the 2,000 passengers which the present Queens carry.

Will the ships be atom-powered? It is unlikely. The final decision may be affected by experiments being made by the Admiralty and Ministry of Supply.

The Queen Mary, which made her maiden voyage in 1936, and the Queen Elizabeth, whose keel was laid the same year, were built with the help of Government loans. Now the Government may consider a subsidy.

THE QUEEN ELIZABETH

THE AMERICAN Government is planning to subsidise a liner for the North Atlantic service. Estimated cost is £47,000,000. She will be sold to the United States Lines for around £17,000,000.

THE FRENCH Line's 60,000-ton liner, due to come on the Atlantic in 1961, will cost £32,000,000. The French Government is subsidising building to the extent of many million pounds.

Of the American subsidy Mr. Watkinson said in the Commons: "That adds to the difficulties of the Cunard Company but does not mean that it must leave the North Atlantic service in which it has such a wonderful record."

Two years ago Cunard spent £500,000 fitting stabilisers for the Queen Mary.

It was estimated this would give the liner another 10 years of life. It means she must be replaced by 1967. The old liners will be sold as scrap.

'RAB'S' COUSIN SWEPT FROM LEDGE

RAF hero saves ex-deb from waves

From RICHARD KILIAN

PORTOFINO, Wednesday.

WARTIME fighter ace Paul Richey told today how, for an hour, he kept ex-deb Sally Butler from drowning in a raging Mediterranean sea.

SALLY BUTLER She is recovering.

TROUBLE ALL THE WAY SAYS CRANKO

Express Staff Reporter

THIRTY-ONE-YEAR-OLD John Cranko, brilliant ballet designer, and author of the successful revue "Cranks," was fined £10 at Marlborough-street court yesterday for importuning men.

HIS NEED

She disappeared

PAUL RICHEY He dived in

POCKET CARTOON by OSBERT LANCASTER

2 women die on line

Picture to cap it all!

THREE COOL MEN ROB TRAIN—AND LEAP OFF

Express Staff Reporter

THREE well-dressed young men boarded the Caledonian Glasgow express at Euston station just before 4 p.m. yesterday—and on the way North sauntered forward to the mail van and rifled it.

It was one of the best organised railway robberies for years. Last night the three men were still free, with a holdall filled with the "pickings" from 30 mailbags.

SPOTTED

Ideas . . . Speed . . . Power . . .

4.30 a.m. LATEST

TV BREAKDOWN

TREMOR

4,020,703

FLEet-street 8000

My New K Shoes

Up and coming dancer cossets her feet in light K Skips

FLEET-STREET, Midnight

SWEARING ROW HOLDS UP V-BOMBERS

WHO'S THIS?

GRANNY'S LETTER

MAGIC NAMES

SHARES SOAR

TWIN SITS UP

£600 TRIP

FIGHT IN HALL

LAMA LEAVES

Fiancé killed on new motor-cycle

Fig. 88. A *Daily Express* page showing the effectiveness of an extra-deep single-column block.

for magazine work printed flat on surfaced paper) is not kind to fine detail. If faces in a group, for instance, are to be recognizable likenesses, they need to be reduced as little as possible from the original print. For the same reason a quality of sharp contrast in the print (or the securing of as much as possible of that quality by skilful retouching) is important, as is the cutting out of background detail which may be of photographic value but which would be totally dissipated by the coarse screen, moulding, and high-speed printing from a rotary plate.

Three other aspects of sizing need mentioning: (i) *Cutting out* flat and wasteful background, allowing for block heading or caption, or for an accompanying story heading to drop in. Such cutting can on a suitable print produce an irregular-shaped block giving extra movement both to the subject and the page (e.g. a runner in full stride scaled for five columns

S WINS BUS BAT

otes t call

won the big-
fe last night.
n busmen to
in immediate
Government
ek pay claim

Before the final
egates voted 83
call a strike, or
overtime.
majority of two-
88 votes in favour
sion effective. So
tes from a verdict
d services.
m., after Mr. Cousins
wrestling with the
litants for more than
the policy of trying
ration was carried by
to 40.
t does not follow that
end the clash with the
nent.
decision to accept arbi-
on the express condi-
the award is not binding
tion.

ld say No

his reason Mr. Iain
the Minister of Labour,
sked to refer the claim
he Industrial Disputes
whose decision would
but to the Arbitration
hich can only make

Ice-cream drivers

The Princess and Mr. Bailey at a ball.

Princess robbed as Mr Bailey gets her coffee

By CLIFFORD LUTON

PRINCESS ALEXANDRA was robbed early yesterday while she was having coffee with a friend in London. Two of her suitcases, containing clothing and jewels, were stolen from a parked car belonging to Mr. David Bailey.

He and the 21-year-old

ANGI IN ON TRII

By V

ANGER and
Commons
on the report of t
bunal. The Dep
MacAndrew, thr
sitting.

It was one of the no
debates since the
crisis.

The climax was a ro
tween Mr. Peter Thorney
the ex-Chancellor, and
Aneurin Bevan, who he
and shouted from his
front bench.

Mr. R. A. Butler,
Prime Minister, who open
debate, announced tha
position of part-time dir
of the Bank of England is
examined.

It will be investigated t
committee headed by Lord
cliffe already inquiring in
banking and monetary syst

Jeers

Mr. Butler castigated
Socialists for pursuing
"leak" campaign when s
charges were groundless
everyone involved was blai
Tory backbenchers cheered.

When Mr. Harold
Shadow Chancellor and
sponsor of the campaign
his sentences were punc
with their jeers and laugh

It was the turn o
Socialists to heckle and
rupt when Mr. Thorne
who was cleared b

FIG. 89. Cutting out to add movement to a picture, taking in the caption heading; from the *Daily Mail.*

overall but with a deep double-column cut top right and another cut, bottom right, across three columns) (Fig. 89). When cuts of this kind are made it is most important to ensure that the actual-measure cut is made on the printing surface remaining, not on the cut space; thus, in the example in parentheses above, the top double-column cut would be made by cutting the top portion of the block to three columns; if the cut were exactly double column the block remaining would be slightly over three columns and thus prevent the insertion of a column rule. Take the simpler case of a double-column block with a single-column cut-out, 1 inch deep, top right; the block is made with its top left portion exact single column to a depth of 1 inch before extending to double column. Usually all such cut-outs should be even measure. (ii) *Proportion*: a strong vertical or horizontal stress is better than a square. Some subjects may naturally size to a squarish shape and in such cases big play (i.e. never less than three columns) will overcome the difficulty. But in general the deep single or double, or the shallower four- or five-column picture, is better for the make-up; the deep double, up to 8 inches or even more, perhaps best of all (Fig. 90). (iii) *Bastard measures*, meaning the addition of half a column to even measure, not infrequently solve a sizing problem without encroaching too ponderously on the general make-up. When 1½- or 2½-column blocks are scheduled the odd half-column of their depth should be taken up by setting a story at the side, including its headings if necessary, to the paper's 1½-column measure; this requires a little calculation of the exact number of lines to be so set, but it avoids the make-up snag of a deep half-column space and a half-column caption which only fills about a quarter of it, and after monstrous leading still leaves great gaps of white into which heavy stars have to be dropped. A half-column caption of any length is, in any event, slow to set and trying to read. Bastard measure blocks can always be captioned in their own measure or, more conveniently and flexibly, in single column (Fig. 95).

Marking a print for block size can be done in various ways: with process white on the front, easily removable afterwards, or by some form of masking if the print is unique and mounted; but for ordinary practical purposes marking on the back in pencil is the standard procedure. Marking should be done lightly with a soft pencil so as to avoid scoring the surface of the print; when the suitable sizing has been squarely ruled off, block depth is quickly determined by the well-known diagonal system. A diagonal is drawn from top left to bottom right of the marking, the proposed measure marked off along the base from bottom right, and a right angle taken from the measure mark to the diagonal, the rule reading at the point of intersection being the depth of the future block. Cut-out depths can be calculated in the same way and if a print is being blown up to more than its

Daily Mail MORNING SPECIAL

NO. 19,240 FOR QUEEN AND COMMONWEALTH FRIDAY, FEBRUARY 28, 1958 PRICE 2½d.

Heath, Hammersley, Bellson guilty—sentence today

RIDGE FREE ON BAIL

Comment

WEAKENING BRITAIN

Reinforcing

Recruiting

Conferring

Turn to Page 5, Col. 2

Kiss for warder after his 'agony'

By LOUIS KIRBY

CHARLES Feild Williams Ridge, the 59-year-old Chief Constable of Brighton, was last night acquitted of conspiring to obstruct the course of justice.

He was released on bail amid dramatic scenes at the Old Bailey after being on trial for 19 days.

As he ran down the steps from the dock he embraced one warder and kissed another, weeping and saying over and over again: "Thank God, thank God."

Two of his officers, Detective-Inspector John Richard Hammersley, 40, and Detective-Sergeant Trevor Heath, 36, were found guilty on the same charge. So was Samuel Bellson, 42-year-old bookmaker. They will be sentenced by Mr. Justice Donovan this morning.

Lyons is cleared

He was bewildered

THIS MAN LAWRENCE DOES IT AGAIN

Jubilant

Two-page Daily Mail fine focus on the Brighton Affair—Pages 4 and 5

35 die in day-trip plane disaster

£750,000,000—and all on HP

Kenneth Horne has stroke

The rebel inch

The vanished £15,000 bonds

MRS BUSBY BREAKS THE NEWS TO MATT

By MONTY COURT

MATT BUSBY has been told the news . . . the news that eight of his Babes died in the Manchester United air crash at Munich—and the doctors at Munich's Rechts der Isar Hospital are annoyed.

THE PRIEST

THE NAMES

THE TRUTH

TWO H-bombs fired by Russia

Congratulations, Sir Winston

MP to quit

TV backs Hallé

Cheaper tyres

This is the show of shows

Win your ideal home

DR. FUCHS: 130 MILES TO GO

DAILY MAIL: FLEET ST. 6000

Family Fitness

In March winds and April showers

Spread extra goodness

MARMITE

For goodness and flavour

FIG. 90. The dramatic effect of turning a normally single-column subject into a deep double column.

DAILY MAIL, Tuesday, August 5, 1958

Collins took bend too wide says Mike Hawthorn

TEARS RUN DOWN HIS FACE AS HE TALKS ABOUT CRASH

By Daily Mail Reporter

Mike Hawthorn brings Collins's widow, Louise, to London last night

JUAN FANGIO
My opinion . . .

PUTTING THE HUNT OFF THE SCENT

By Daily Mail Reporter

Rainproof

Your Daily Mail

Breakaways seek bail

Coal Board cut rent increases

Theft charge at 85 . . .

Maud has a baby

NUCLEAR SWITCH

TODAY'S WEATHER AT A GLANCE

LORD RAGLAN SNUBS THE EISTEDDFOD

By Daily Mail Reporter

Stupid

In English

The home-built sports car sets a record

Other results

Stunned

In black

A house

'I go on'

Tear-gas attacker injures taxi man

By Daily Mail Reporter

Blinded

Murder charge

OLDEST ADMIRAL

SUB-TITLE

TV 'judge' joins the Battle of the Bench

By Daily Mail Reporter

Afterthought

MR. DAVID ENSOR
As the TV judge

JULIE IN WAX

A bass in the boat

FIG. 91. A superb example of picture-sizing in one of the deepest three-column news blocks ever carried in a British newspaper.

own size the top marking only has to be extended to the block measure decided, and the diagonal continued—their rectangular link will give the block depth.

MEASURES AND MOUNTING

Before discussing the fixing of the various column measures for blocks it may be remarked that the once-popular half-measure or thumbnail portrait block is little used nowadays. It belongs to an age when there was comparatively little picturing of news pages; it takes time for the running-round of type; and if a portrait is not worth running single-column it is hardly worth running at all. If half-measure portraits are used they should be full or three-quarter face, not profile, and cut close to the head, leaving at the base the minimum necessary of neck, or collar and tie. The same applies to single-column portrait blocks, unless there is some special reason for including more clothing detail. Trick cutting of faces—producing, for instance, an elongated view of the front of the face and so on—is to be discouraged; it only gives an effect of distortion.

Fixing the various measures for blocks is not just a matter of translating the printer's pica ems and fractions of ems into inches for the process department. The amount of vertical margin desired, or needed, has to be allowed for. This depends in the first place on the width of the column rule and the requirements of the stereotyper. Column rule allows for a white of half its body on each side: a 6-pt. rule gives 3 pts. of white, a 4-pt. gives 2 pts., and so on. The white of the column rule forms part of the block margin and has to be taken into account in calculating the block measure. Some newspapers take their blocks to the full type measure of the column or its multiples, in which case the rule white is the only margin; many stereotypers object to this on the technical ground that, in moulding, the block may 'bear off' the rule, breaking its printing surface. As a general rule it may be suggested that, subject to this stereotyping requirement, block measures should be kept as wide as possible; with most column rules a block measure (or base-width) calculated on the basis of $\frac{1}{16}$ in. reduction each end from the type measure will provide a sufficient margin. A slight increase in the margin for the larger blocks is a matter of taste.

All block measures should be calculated, in inches and fractions, for every measure from single column to full page width, including the bastard measures ($1\frac{1}{2}$, $2\frac{1}{2}$, and so on). Any variant type measures in the paper should in addition have their appropriate block measures calculated and scheduled, e.g. boxed settings, narrower (or wider) measure on feature pages, and the like. It is all to the good, of course, if newspapers with their own process departments can induce them to work to ems and points instead of inches.

The foregoing applies to rotary-produced papers, with blocks cut flush and laid flush (or almost flush) on solid metal bases. Papers printing from the forme, either flat-bed or Cossar, have the problem of mounting the block to consider. Electronically engraved plastic foil blocks can be secured to a mount with adhesive, and present no problem; but conventionally engraved metal blocks have to be flanged on at least two opposite sides to allow of securing to a mount. Wide flanging on four sides not only produces an excessive margin; it stands any heading or caption too far away from the block. Flanging should be kept as narrow as possible and restricted to two sides. On multi-column blocks it may be advantageous to flange vertically (watching that the margin does not become excessive) so that the heading or caption can be made up as close to the block as required. The guiding principle should be the avoidance of the wide white bordering of the block which is too often seen in local papers.

The style of finishing half-tone blocks has varied from the various combinations of white and black ruling, once fashionable, via the plain black rule of medium weight, long the standard style, to the raw edge now gaining favour (largely, perhaps, because it is the normal finish of the electronic engraver). The raw edge is perfectly satisfactory, with the added advantage that a block can be cut at any moment without raising any awkward question of finish. Elaborate cut-outs, 'fancy' finishes, the 'masking' of faces, vignetting, or any other such fussy treatments are entirely outmoded for the news pages.

HEADINGS AND CAPTIONS

Unless a news picture has a heading as well as a caption (or cut-lines, as the Americans call them) it has a curiously naked appearance on the page. The most usual style is heading over picture and caption under; but heading and caption can run together, either over or under the picture; the last is the least common arrangement here, though much favoured in the United States (Fig. 92). Apart from these variations in position there are many possible variations in setting. Thus a double-column picture can have a double-column heading and a caption either double column or single column; or a single-column heading (probably two- or three-line) with captions varying as before. Over double column a picture will not normally have its caption set full measure (the lines are too long for the size of type), though a three-column picture may have its heading so set. Over three-column pictures need captions not less than double column, unless the type size is suitably increased. Wherever a single-column

News picture that won a prize

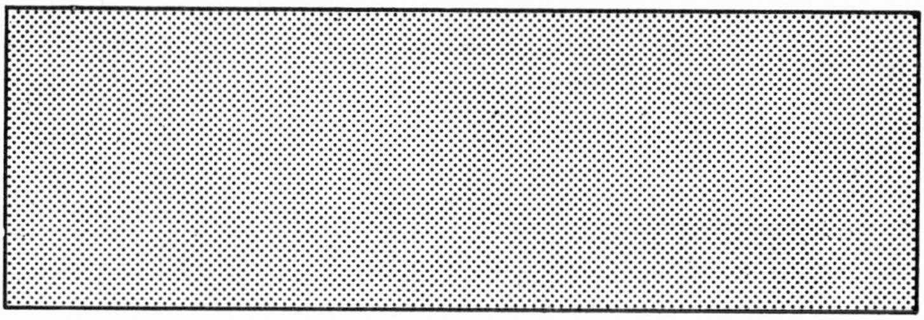

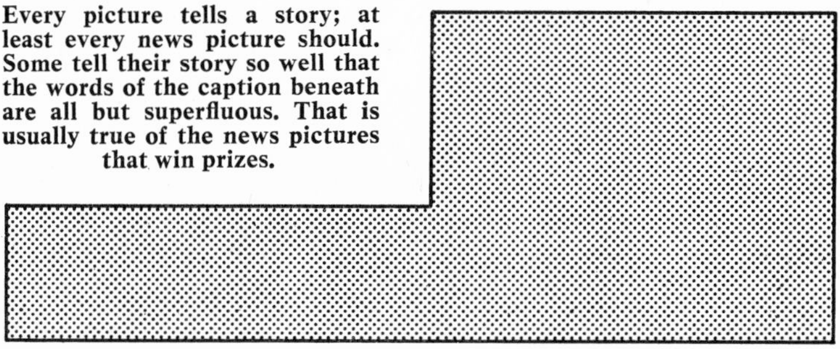
Every picture tells a story; at least every news picture should. Some tell their story so well that the words of the caption beneath are all but superfluous. That is usually true of the news pictures that win prizes.

News picture that won a prize

Every picture tells a story; at least every news picture should. Some tell their story so well that the words of the caption beneath are all but superfluous. That is usually true of the news prizes.

FIG. 92. Headings and captions for a double-column picture: heading over, single-column caption under, or heading and caption (both double-column) under. Headings in 14 pt. Poster (Ultra) Bodoni, captions in 8 pt. Jubilee Bold.

caption can be retained it will prove by far the most flexible for the general make-up. In special cases bastard measure, doubled-up to the measure of the picture, can be employed, e.g. 1½-column doubled up under a three-column picture.

Headings permit of considerable typographical variation. Pictures of exceptional news interest may have a news heading in the paper's standard style, selected to accord with the page make-up; the occasion may even be one when the Sans 'kicker' style is called upon. Here the size and measure of the heading will be determined by the size and importance of the picture. But for the general run of pictures through the news pages a heading type contrasting with the normal headline style should be selected and standardized. The best choice is one of the modern Sans faces, preferably somewhat condensed, e.g. Metromedium or Tempo Bold Condensed, or one of the extra-heavies, e.g. Ultra-Bodoni or Pabst (italic preferred). These can be used in caps. or lower-case as required. For most purposes one size will serve—the 18 pt. in the Sans and the 14 pt. in the extra-heavy; if extra weight is needed the 24 pt. and 18 pt. (Fig. 93).

The basic caption style is the bold face of the body size of the paper, indented each end (1 en for single column, 1 em for double). Italic, if used for variety, should be restricted to the occasions when a larger size, 9 pt. or 10 pt., is specified. Roman does not secure enough differentiation from the text, even if indented; though if the caption is developed into a caption-story, indented roman, suitably broken with a crosshead or a star, may be easier on the eye than the same number of paragraphs in bold. Except in caption-stories exceeding three or four paragraphs—which should be set ordinary paragraph style—captions should be set with the first line full out to the measure (as indented) and the final breakline centred; in captions above single column it is important to avoid an ultra-short breakline of only one or two words by suitable rewriting or cutting when possible.

METROMEDIUM HAS
A good italic also

TEMPO BOLD CONDENSED
Presents its own italic

ERBAR BOLD CONDENSED
Has its light version

VOGUE EXTRA BOLD COND.
Has a Bold Condensed also

MEMPHIS EXT.
Bold with Italic

PABST PACKS
A mighty punch

FIG. 93. Some types for block headings.

As an alternative to the paper's text bold for captions there is much to be said for a modern Sans (Metro particularly) used either in its bold weight alone, or varying captions between its bold and its light. If the paper has a 7 pt. text the Metro captions should be set in 8 pt. A condensed Sans of the order of Bell Gothic might suit very well in extra-narrow column measures (10 ems and under). Should a variant seriffed letter be preferred for captioning, Bodoni Bold with italic could be recommended; its 8 pt. and 10 pt. sizes should cope with all normal needs. In general it may be said that the use of such distinctive type faces for captions helps to give a certain sense of unity to the picture presentation and is therefore not without value as an element in the general make-up (Fig. 94).

So far nothing has been said about complete *picture pages*, since they no longer play the part they did. They call for a keen eye in the selection and sizing of pictures and should always be made up on an accurately ruled full-size sheet. Only so is it possible to size the pictures closely and precisely and to give an exact specification for odd-measure captions or cut-in headings. Provided the make-up sheet corresponds exactly to the dimensions of the forme the pictures can be sized to allow an even white between them (most important for the workmanlike appearance of a picture page). Alternatively, where some variation is required it can be prescribed and controlled from the start. The full-size make-up also enables the wordage of captions and the depth of headings to be accurately specified. In general the visualizing of the finished page becomes much easier. It can readily be seen how necessary it is for the lead picture to 'look in' to the page; that is to say, at least to have its visual stress—maybe the angle of some dominant object in the picture—leading the reader's eye into the page and not off it. Equally it is easy to perceive the importance of close captioning; letting every picture be captioned individually as far as possible, and in such a way that the reader sees picture and caption simultaneously, or all but simultaneously; nothing is more irritating than to have to peer for the explanatory matter to a picture.

Bold Face No 2 is a good type for news picture captions.

Jubilee Bold is a good type for news picture captions.

Times Bold is a good type for news picture captions.

Metrolite is a good type for captions.

Bodoni Bold Italic is a good type for captions.

Bell Gothic Bold is a good type for news picture captions.

Metroblack is a good type for captions.

Metromedium is a good type for captions.

FIG. 94. A selection of types (all 8 pt.) suitable for captions; for blocks of any size above single column 10 pt. is usually necessary.

As a final note on half-tone news pictures it may be recalled—the point has been made in Chapter 2—that in rotary printing, despite the improvements in modern presses, there are always some pages better than others for half-tone reproduction. The variation depends on the machine and its inking system, on whether the paper is full-sheet or tabloid, among other things. When the 'good' pages are known it is obvious common sense to try to concentrate the principal half-tones on them, though it may be impossible to do as some papers do and avoid using them entirely on the 'bad' pages.

THE USE OF LINE-DRAWINGS

Some reference has now to be made to the non-photographic newspaper illustration, the line-drawing. Cartoons, maps, diagrams, and the like may sometimes be half-toned; under certain circumstances the overall grey background, with its softening of the normal black-and-white contrast, can produce an agreeable effect; but the line-drawing is properly conveyed by a line-block, with or without mechanical tints or other shading devices. The line-block's black and white gives it obvious value in contrast to the half-tone photograph.

Cartoons, like good news pictures, need to be played up in size. The conventional oblong-horizontal or 'landscape' shape, run at least across four normal columns, sometimes across five, is well suited for most cartooning themes and techniques. On the other hand, experimentation in shape and finish—omitting the heavy black border drawn by the cartoonist—is well worth encouraging, provided always that the ultimate size allowed is adequate (Fig. 95). A reduction in width requires a suitable increase in depth. This freedom of treatment is only applicable to the single main cartoon. Strip and pocket cartoons are necessarily more formalized, their respective four-column and single-column presentation being of the essence

THAT, MR BUTLER TOLD THE COMMONS IS THE LESSON OF THE BANK RATE

WALTER TERRY reports the debate on the Leak That Never Was

MR. BUTLER, the acting Prime Minister, said yesterday during the Commons debate on the Bank Rate Tribunal report:

"Let us be thankful for this. The machinery of the Tribunal has broken the political weapon of smear."

The inquest on the findings of the "leak" tribunal—it ruled that all the charges were groundless and no one was to blame—was one of the noisiest and bitterest debates since Suez.

THE LAUGHTER
And thr retaliation

At first it was the Tories who made most of the row. They taunted and jeered at Mr. Harold Wilson, Shadow Chancellor, who led the campaign for a "leak" inquiry.

They roared with laughter every time he tried to explain he had been trying sincerely to establish the truth of rumours in the City and "gossip" in the newspapers.

The Socialists retaliated later by heckling Mr. Peter Thorneycroft, the ex-Chancellor. And, to the surprise of everyone, Mr. Bevan stormed into this row, became its leader—and was rebuked by the Deputy Speaker.

The excitement was so great that Mr. Thorneycroft could not be heard.

THE KNIGHT ERRANT

"We wanted to protect all concerned, especially the employee of the Conservative Central Office [Miss Susan Chataway] from possible victimisation."
—*Mr. Harold Wilson.*

Bevan joins the row...

could not be run from an ivory tower, nor entirely from behind a desk in the atmosphere of Whitehall.

"This is really part of a problem which exists in the whole of our public life today—the problem of dual loyalty."

In a sense, all M.P.s had an experience of it.

The present practice derived from the Act of 1946 passed by the Socialist Government.

The present Government was not prepared to take snap decisions on whether any change was desirable.

Speaking of why the Government had agreed to an inquiry, Mr. Butler said:

"Had the Opposition agreed with the Prime Minister that the preliminary examination by the Lord Chancellor disposed of the flimsy evidence they had put forward there would have been no need to set up this tribunal."

Mr. Poole's name was first mentioned on November 12 by Sir Leslie Plummer (Soc., Deptford). Later he claimed he had made no imputation against Mr. Poole's honour.

It was left to Mr. Wilson to enlarge on the imputation.

"He asked Mr. Thorneycroft to say clearly whether he had or had not seen Mr. Poole, 'who has vast City interests,' the day before Bank Rate went up.

STANDARDS
Must be higher

"These insinuations were made under the cover of privilege. The Prime Minister decided they could be cleared only through a judicial tribunal."

And, said Mr. Butler, the realisation that the machinery of the tribunal is the only existing path of justice after a defamatory statement is made in the House regarding an individual outside it "surely imposes on us infinitely higher standards of responsibility for our privileged utterances than has guided the Opposition."

The Opposition amendment, moved by Mr. Wilson, was:

Whilst not dissenting from the findings of the report of the tribunal, this House regrets the prior disclosure on September 18, 1957, by the then Chancellor of the Exchequer of secret information about the Government's financial policies to certain selected journalists and to officials of the Conservative Central Office.

The amendment also demanded that the Government should take steps "to obviate the present conflict between public duties and private responsibilities of part-time directors of the Bank of England"

MR. THORN
He was

the Financial
days later that t
made even the m
inquiries into th

Mr. Wilson t
letter of Septem
Governor of the
land in which l
"private infor
transactions by
tions in which
Bank of Englan
of the boards of
tions, might be
concerned."

It was the P
duty, Mr. Wilson
ing that letter
matter further.

Referring to t
cellor's inquiry,
Macmillan, Mr.

"Did the P
withhold the le
Lord Chancellor
Chancellor have
fail to follow it

"Or did the I
in fact see the C
Bank of Englan
led by the Gove

"I would not
be the case."

PRIVILEG
And its u

"I think it is
Governor that
told, but we do
cause the Gover
to publish the
lor's report."

It was then th
spoke of the Opp
"to protect a
especially the en
Central Office [M
from possible vict

Speaking of th
Mr. Poole, he s
that parliamen
should not be
people outside t

"But there is
mentary conven
constitutional im
that is the an
Ministers to this

FIG. 95. A deep bastard measure (approximately $1\frac{3}{4}$ columns) cartoon used to illustrate a news report. Note the bastard measure setting to cover the block.

of their style. The make-up of strip sections or pages presents no special features; individual strip or pocket cartoons are helpful in breaking up a news page, providing points of visual interest in contrast with text and headings. Pocket cartoons should be placed well over or well under the fold; simply boxed in medium rule, they should whenever possible have the column rules cut away each side. Strips should be placed right at the head or, more usually, right at the foot of the page.

Heading and captioning of cartoons follows the general principles indicated above. A main cartoon will sometimes have its caption incorporated by the cartoonist, and most strips have 'ballooned' captions lettered in. Type captions for large cartoons should be in 12 pt. or 14 pt. Metroblack or comparable bold Sans, set to the measure of the cartoon in caps. or lower-case according to the wordage; generally speaking, a cartoon caption should not be more than one line. Since a pocket or strip cartoon, a regular feature by a particular artist, has some sort of standing heading, this may be better rendered by a reverse block or other type-processing treatment. An obvious and effective device is a reverse block of the cartoonist's signature.

Of maps and diagrams—particularly those diagrams which endeavour to make visual, not to say pictographic, a main news story of some statistical complexity—there is not much to be said here. Like cartoons, they present the make-up man with 'colour'-contrast spots on his page. Their main purpose, however, is to assist the reader to follow the news. Thus maps should be conventionally cartographic, and incorporate as much detail as possible; the sketchy or pictorialized map is an abomination. The explanatory diagram needs to be comprehensible at the first glance; its design and execution call for skills beyond the sphere of typography.

The use of line-drawings, with special type treatments or hand-lettering, to make decorative headings, is more a matter for the feature than the news pages. It is therefore touched on in Chapter 11.

10 · Style for the Sports Pages

BRITISH newspapers in general eschew the strict sectionalizing so highly developed by their American contemporaries with one exception—the sports pages. This recognition of the special character and appeal of sporting news and comment is in itself enough to suggest that sports pages benefit by a measure of typographical differentiation from the rest of the paper. The nature of that differentiation arises directly from the nature of sports news and its readers. It is hardly necessary to labour the point; if the mass reader is alleged to need cunningly varied sugarings of his news pill, the sporting enthusiast requires no such adventitious attractions; all he asks is the plain and clear setting out of detailed information, the more detailed the better, and full-length reports by experts on the major events.

Accuracy and expertise in content appear to call for a bold and straightforward typographic form. And the sports reader is a down-to-earth, practical fellow who likes his newspaper diet plain and strong. Thus the indications seem clear enough: the overall appearance of a sports page should be black rather than comely—its most appropriate headline style, in short, some arrangement of Sans. If the headline typography of the body of the paper is seriffed, here also is the sports page differentiation already advised, and in most respects the best differentiation that can be had.

So complete a differentiation is not always possible. Indeed, many successful papers use the same basic heading types for sports as for news, making only subtle changes in style, e.g. playing down italic, playing up lower-case as against caps., using more underscoring, and so on. A further step is exemplified by the *Worthing Herald* group, whose news heading style is Century Bold, with Tempo for occasional Sans contrast, but whose sports headings play heavily on Tempo, with Century Bold for contrast. Or the suggestive example of the *Sunday Express*, an all-Sans paper, may be noted. Its sports pages are given a distinctive flavour simply by the multiplication of double-column headings in Square Gothic lower-case (24 pt. and 30 pt.) and the exclusive use of two sizes (18 pt. and 24 pt.) of the Linotype Gothic Condensed No. 13—caps. only—for down-page single-column headings. The heavier Medium Gothic is used only as an element of contrast (Fig. 96).

Arsenal shocked by Wednesday ★ Fulham get debut hiding ★ Blackpool's fighting come-back

SPURS (£182,000—and worth it!) SLAM NEWCASTLE

Broadbent injured—but 10-men Wolves triumph

BIG GAME specials page

by ALAN HOBY

THE SECOND THAT COUNTS

MIGHTY MEL LOOKS BETTER IN ATTACK

Highbury fans stunned

Fulham run into a lot of trouble

West Ham's magic name—John Smith

Maurice Norman is centre-half star

BRENTFORD ARE IN LUCK

Leary goal earns draw

DAZZLER GREAVES TORMENTS PRESTON

Q.P.R. CAN THANK MIKE PINNER

MISTAKE BY ROUSE COSTS A POINT

SOUTHEND'S RALLY FAILS

DENIS COMPTON reports the Test—all the cricket scores ON PAGE 23

SPORTING SAM by Reg. Wootton

MILLWALL FIND IT SO EASY

Schemer White plans the Orient goals

WATFORD HAD NO FORWARD ZIP

Higher Mileage at LOWER COST! BIG PRICE REDUCTION GIVES AVON USERS EVEN MORE MILES PER PENNY

singers like GRANT'S STAND FAST Scotch Whisky in the tall triangular bottle

FIG. 96. The main sports page of the *Sunday Express.*

SIMPLE SETTING AND STANDING HEADINGS

Simplicity is the main point in sports-page typography and make-up, which is why the *Sunday Express* can be taken as a sound model. No sports page should ever be allowed to succumb to the temptations of type trickery. All it needs is to be a reasonably flexible, uncomplicated medium for good sports writing; no one will dispute that sport is one newspaper sphere where good writing and objective judgement really matter. This in its turn indicates that sports-page text treatment will also be simple. While using variant settings, like roman or bold reverse indent, for an entire piece, the tendency is to avoid the usual text-decorating devices of blacking-up, indention, and the like. Since the principal by-lined stories run to length, the greater part of their text is often dropped to 6 pt.; it is apparently felt that the sports reader prefers to peer rather than lose an iota of his favourite football writer's informed account of a crucial match. Not all papers give their top sports writers such elbow room; the tabloids, for instance, in whose narrow columns the smaller text sizes would stand up better, ride their sports aces on as short a rein as their news colleagues.

FIG. 97. Sports section block headings.

The separation of the sports pages from the rest of the paper, especially if their typography is sharply differentiated, makes any specific sports labelling, or titling, unnecessary. There is, however, much to be said for the view that a bold label, incorporating the name of the paper, has its value for instant identification of the pages and for associating the paper's title with them. Some form of reverse block, with or without drawings or other decoration, is the most suitable. It is usual to take the key word of the paper's title for this block, e.g. MIRROR SPORT; often a further title block, in a varied style, will label the racing page, e.g. RACING MIRROR, EXPRESS RACING SECTION (Fig. 97). It would seem a sensible piece of association to reproduce the key word of the title, whether reversed or not, in the same style as the front-page title-line.

With a sports page's considerable number of standing, or at least standardized, headings—racing, greyhounds, score-cards, forecasts—there is evident scope for reverse or type-on-tint block treatments. A watchful eye has to be kept on the reverse blocks, since a surfeit of them is distracting to the eye. For reverse and type-on-tint blocks it is sound practice to use the caps. only of heavy square Sans—or one of the 'reversed' type faces may be employed, thus obviating the need to make blocks (Fig. 98). Further details on the style and finish of block headings will be found in Chapter 11 (pp. 212–14).

RUNNERS & RIDERS

RACING TODAY

FIG. 98. Sports reverse block headings in type—Monotype Gill Cameo (233) and Gill Cameo Ruled (299). See also Fig. 118.

The handling of sports-page pictures does not require any substantial difference in approach from that outlined in Chapter 9. There is the obvious point that a good sports picture, even more than a good news picture, needs to be an action picture, the more startling and dramatic the action the better. Whenever the dynamic quality of such a picture can be enhanced by cut-outs, these should be done; though bastard measures should be avoided, at least on evening and Sunday newspapers, with their tight schedules for sports setting and make-up.

Here it is necessary to appraise the impact of television on sports pictures. Television's brilliant newsreel coverage of major sports events is

WINNERS AND SP

GOOD GOING

Epsom

2.0 **BANSTEAD SELLING STAKES; 3-y-o; 1m abt 110yds.**
Checkmont (Mr T H Degg), 7-13* **T Stringer** 1
Trafalgar Square, 8-9 **A Breasley** 2
Dear Delinquent, 7-13 **D Keith** 3
Princess Wil ...S Clayton 4
Primo ....D Smith 5
Press Ticket J P Dolan 6
Starliner ....G Lewis 7
Grace Gladys ...J Berry 8
Pyrotic ....D Small 9
Ushant ....D L Jones 10
Tool Merchant G Harper 11
Dicky Bird ......R Court 12
Won: 3l.; 2l. 1m 52 4-5s.
S.P.: 100-30 Primo (op 5-2), 7-2 **Checkmont** (op

3.10 **CITY AND SUBURBAN HANDICAP; 1¼m.**
Guersillus (Mr Phil Bull), 4-9-3 ...**E Hide** 1
Pardonez-moi, 4-6-7* car 6-10 **R Court** 2
Hard as Nails, 4-7-0 **D Greening** 3
Chief Barker R P Elliott 4
Roxburgh ......M Hayes 5
Blackness ......D Smith 6
Fair Victor ......R Reader 7
Master Nicky ...J Lynch 8
Pall Mall ......W H Carr 9
Pandour ......S Clayton 10
Beau D'Argent E Smith 11
Prince Moon A Breasley 12
Dambuster ......T Carter 13
Illinois ....L Piggott 14
Masquerade P Boothman f
Won: Nk; 2l. 2m 12s.
S.P.: 9-4 **Guersillus** (op

place in the last furlong, but could make no impression on Farley Star.

4.15 **WARREN STAKES; 3-y-o; 1½m.**
Frasco (Miss M L Pinder), 9-5 **L Piggott** 1
Josephus, 9-8 **W Rickaby** 2
Dominate, 9-8 **D Smith** 3
Rousseau's Dream W H Carr 4
Ferragosto ...A Breasley 5
Pappas Way ...E Mercer 6
Nobly Born ...S Clayton 7
Won 4l; 4l. 2m 48 2-5s.
S.P.: 7-4 Frasco (op 9-4), 9-4 Ferragosto (op 11-4), 7-2 Josephus (op 9-2), 6 Dominate (once 7's), 100-8 Rosseau's Dream, 20 others. 11/10; 8/6, 8/2; Dual F: 18/4. (P Walwyn, Blewbury).

FIG. 99. Racing results set narrow measure (three columns for two); from the *Daily Herald*. The style can also be adapted for the simplest form of racing programme setting.

without doubt the outstanding actuality achievement of the new medium. No newspaper can compete pictorially with the television presentation of the Boat Race, a front-rank soccer match, or a turf classic. It has sometimes been argued that a series of good sequence shots of such an event is worth sports-page play as a sort of potted TV. The proposition seems doubtful. Occasionally a short sequence, of three or four pictures, capable of dramatic presentation in not too extravagant a space, may be well worth while in its own right, but not as a mode of supposed competition with television. It seems clear enough that sports pictures today must secure freshness by striving for the angle that television has missed, for example the striking close-up that the far-ranging Sportsview cameras normally do not get.

Sports pages include features as well as news; but there is little to say here about sports-feature treatment in advance of the general discussion of feature typography and make-up in Chapter 11. The note of extra simplicity and directness desirable in the presentation of sports news is just as desirable in the presentation of sports features; both, after all, are essentially written by experts for experts, even the highly popular sports gossip columns, and exotic typographic titivations are quite out of place.

2.0 —**POLAR JEST APPRENTICE HANDICAP.** 1m. Winner £405. **FORM IN A FLASH**

0-10034 **(1) Bedecked** (D H.-Hutchinson), Budgett. 4-8-7 **S. Francis** 43
1-12000 **(2) Doctor Tadgh** (Col. A. Renton), Vallance, 5-8-2 **(D)** **D. Deeping** 41
04-2400 **(3) Frederique II** (W. Nightingall), Nightingall, 4-8-0 **Saxby** 47
00040-0 **(4) Two Royals** (Mrs. A. Wallington), Wallington, 8-7-11 **(D)** .. —— 44
201†-102 **(5) Golden Thread** (Brig. H. Harris), Wightman, 5-7-8 **(D, F)** .. **Brownsea** 50
1-23122 **(6) Tarquinian** (T. Frost), Todd, 4-7-5 **(SF)** .... **Foster** 43
013343 **(7) Gay Trio** (Mrs. D. Moore), K. Cundell, 9-7-4 **(D, EW)** .. **K. Cox** 48
000000 **(8) Saint Cecilia** (Mrs. E. C.-Bailey), Nelson, 4-6-9 **J. Hill**—
00-0221 **(9) Galante Verte** (O. King), K. Cundell, 4-6-8 **Marston** 45
00-0442 **(10) Kaper** (Mrs. R. M.-Scott), Vallance, 4-6-5 .. **Fowler** 49
041003 **(11) Torphins** (Mrs. B. Watkins), Payne-Gallwey, 3-6-5 **(D)** **Walpole** 47

1† Dead-heated for first place.
Mirror Betting Forecast.—3 Golden Thread, 4 Tarquinian, 5 Bedecked, 11-2 Galante Verte, 7 Kaper, 10 Gay Trio, Frederique II 100-8 Torphins.
* Allowance: 4lb.
1958: CAUGHT OUT, 6 8-9 11-8 f. J. Friar (Todd).
Favourites: Two in five.

FIG. 100. The *Daily Mirror*'s double-column racing programme, using reverse blocks and giving full details.

PROGRAMMES, FORECASTS, AND RESULTS

The final aspect of sports-page make-up to be considered here is in some ways the most important. It is certainly the most complex. The reference is to the minimum-size (normally under 6 pt.) settings for those prime essentials of the sports pages, the various programmes, forecasts, and results, most of which involve some form of tabulation. Chapter 5 has already analysed the principal features of the 4¾, 5, and 5½ pt. faces currently available, including their duplexed 'black' or bold, their alternative skeleton or 'news' figures, and so on. The settings now to be discussed exemplify the practical significance of that analysis. Whether it is the racing programme and results, football forecasts or cricket scores, the distinctiveness of the 'blacking-up' for emphasis and the clarity of the

SELECTIONS

TEMPLEGATE	FORM	NEWMARKET
2.00 Starshine	2.00 Starshine	2.00 ——
2.35 Aalsund (nap)	2.35 Walter H	2.35 Golden Judge
3.10 Fiorentina	3.10 Minnie	3.10 Rose of Medina
3.40 Petticoat Rule	3.40 Gentiana	3.40 Petticoat Rule
4.15 Signal	4.15 Falstaff	4.15 Signal (nap)
4.45 Logarithm	4.45 Cintrist	4.45 ——

Places.—4.15 Falstaff; 4.45 Cintrist.

TEMPLEGATE'S DOUBLE.—Aalsund and Fiorentina.

TEMPLEGATE'S TRIO.—Aalsund, Fiorentina (Epsom) and Felway (Pontefract).

4.15—EPSOM HANDICAP STAKES; value to winner £506 8s; three-year-olds; about one mile and a half.

201- **COLLEGE QUEEN** (B Samuel), P Walwyn, 9-0 ...**L Piggott**
8-4 (S Clayton) won by 1l from Elf-Arrow (8-7) with Branston Miss (8-4) hd away 3rd of 17, Newmarket (7f) Oct 17. Good. 1m 30.49s.

0-02 **FALSTAFF** (Duke of Norfolk), W Smyth, 8-12 **A Breasley**
8-3 (S Smith) beaten sht hd by Josephus (9-0) with Music Master (7-4) same distance away 3rd of 18. H'urst (1¼m h'cap) April 11. **Frost Warning** (7-5, J Dolan) was out of first 8. Soft. 2m 19 1-5s.

0-01 **SUPERTICULAR** (Capt A Wills), Nelson, 8-7 ...**D Smith**
8-9 (A Breasley) won by 1½l from El Remo (7-13) with Kalydon (8-9) 2l away 3rd of 13, Birmingham (1¼m) March 30. **Barbary Pirate** (8-9, S Smith) was 5th Yielding. 1m 15.70s.

000- **PRIME MOVER—Btn fav—**(Col P Wright), Budgett, 8-6 ...**B Jago**
8-0 (E Cracknell) fav when not in first 9 of 14 to Decoy (8-4), Newmarket (6f h'cap) Sept 30. Soft.

21-3 **SIGNAL** (Maj G Lim), F Armstrong, 8-6 ....**P Tulk**
8-6 (P Tulk) 3rd of 9 beaten 1½l, same by Black Sumatra (8-7) and Elche (8-7), Nottingham (1¼m h'cap) March 24. Good. 2m 10 4-5s.

00-0 **FROST WARNING** (Lt-Col R Bushman), R Smyth, 8-0 ...**P Dolan (7)**
See **Falstaff.**

FIG. 101. A 1½-column (doubled-up across three columns) racing programme; from the *Daily Herald*. Note the boxing of the selections.

figures are obviously of great importance. The racing programmes shown in Figs. 99 to 102 indicate the superiority of Doric to Bold Face as a 'black' with 5–5½ pt. Ionic, and the greater legibility of the 'news' figures; when 4¾ pt. Times is used the value of these same figures, duplexed with Doric, is also apparent (Fig. 102).

From these examples the notable variety in 'race-card' measure and style can be appreciated. In its barest possible form the racing programme can be set bastard narrow measure, i.e. two-thirds of a column, to double up three columns to two (this style of setting is also useful for racing results), whence it steps up to single column, 1½ columns, and even two columns, according to the form, weights, prices, and other details given. In the wider measures it will be noticed that various styles of boxing-up the selections for the particular race are adopted. The use of drop figures for the times of the races is general, the value of a drop bold enough to catch the eye being evident; and the distinctive setting of the name of the race, preferably in a size larger than the body of the programme, is an advantage. Other refinements, like the *Daily Mirror*'s use of small reverse blocks for race times, and for indicating the column of mystic numbers

TOTE DOUBLE.—3.0, 4.0. R.-H. Course.

2.0—JULY HANDICAP. £250 added (value to winner £279 10s.). 1½m. **Formcast**

213 **Glenborne** (C. R. Beadell), H. Smyth, 5-8-2 **E. J. Cracknell** **74**
423 **Caernarvon** (Lt.-Col. B. P. Smyth-Piggott), H. Price, 5-8-0 —— **70**
000 **Astrid Slipper** (W. Stephenson), W. Stephenson, 6-7-13 **D. Cullen (5)** **75**
423 **Persian Cossack** (Mrs. D. Fletcher), Goodwill, 7-7-10 **K. Temple-Nidd** **74**
0-03 **Juvenile Court** (Mrs. M. G. Maslen), R. Moore, 7-7-6 **R. P. Elliott (5)** —
104 **Filbert** (J. U. Baillie), Kerr, 4-7-3 .... —— **73**

Probable S.P.: 9-4 Glenborne, 11-4 Persian Cossack, 4 Caernarvon, 10 Juvenile Court, Astrid Slipper.

2.30—JUVENILE SELLING PLATE. 2-Y.-O. £300 (£287). 6f.

0 **No Myth** (A. Bird), Gosden, 8-10 ....**S. Clayton**
120 **Cumalus Melody** (A. W. Goodwill), Goodwill, 8-10, or
033 **Monastic Code** (A. W. Goodwill), Goodwill, 8-10 **D. L. Jones**
Toga Virilis (Mrs. W. Gwillim), Gates, 8-10 .... ——
132 **Donnelly's Hollow** (R. Merrick), Kennedy, 8-10 .... ——
0 **Bold Pixie** (F. More O'Ferrall), Hanley, 8-7 ......**W. Rickaby**
020 **Monarch's Hope** (C. M. C. Royds), A. Taylor, 8-7 ...... ——
040 **Wychwood Shamrock** (A. Portman), Kennedy, 8-7 ...... ——

Probable S.P.: 6-4 Donnelly's Hollow, 3 No Myth, 4 Cumalus Melody (or Monastic Code).

FIG. 102. Another 1½-column setting, from the *Daily Mail*; text is in 4¾ pt. Claritas with alternate figures.

presented as the summation of form, are possible when desired. The full-scale double-column treatment, using both 5½ pt. and 5 pt. in the programme, is admirably broken up in the *Daily Herald* by using 18 pt. Metroblack figures as two-line drops to the name of the race set in 10 pt. Metroblack. A bold modern Sans, as in the Metro series, is preferable for race-card drop figures to a narrow Sans.

The complexities of racing-programme setting scarcely apply to the other major tabulations, like cricket scores or football League Tables and Pools Forecasts. These scores and tables naturally follow a conventional form; but some typographical novelty in treatment can be well worth while. Since heavy word or figure emphasis is not always necessary in these presentations there is much to be said for setting them in Bell Gothic. This is already done with dog-racing programmes and pools forecasts in the *Greyhound Express* and on the sports pages of the *Daily Mirror*, *Sunday Pictorial*, and London *Evening News* (Fig. 103).

DIVISION III

BARNSLEY ...... (1)...1	**BRENTFORD** ... (2)...2
Lunn	Francis 2 7,418
BRAD. C. ...... (1)...2	**YORK** .... (0)...0
McCole 2	12,333
BURY .... (1)...3	**COLCHESTER** ... (0)...1
Calder, Atherton, Turner	Langman 11,509
COVENTRY ...... (0)...2	**MANSFIELD** ... (0)...0
Ryan, Straw	19,769
GRIMSBY ...... (2)...5	**CHESTERFIELD** (0)...1
Hunt 2, Cullen, Rafferty 2	Frear 11,794
HALIFAX ...... (1)...2	**SOUTHEND** ...... (0)...1
Smith, Blackburn	Houghton 7,665
Q.P.R. .... (1)...2	**SWINDON** ...... (0)...0
Longbottom, Whitelaw	12,000
READING ...... (1)...2	**PORT VALE** ... (1)...3
Ayre, Lacey	Barnett 2, Poole 14, 833
SHR'W'BURY ... (0)...0	**B'NEMOUTH** ... (0)...0
	9,224
TRANMERE ...... (2)...5	**ACCRINGTON** ... (1)...3
Finney, Rowley, Eglington (1 pen.) 3	H. Anders 12,537
WREXHAM ...... (0)...0	**NEWPORT** ...... (0)...0
	13,301

SOUTHERN LEAGUE.—First Division—Bexleyheath and W. 1, Rugby 1; Burton 4, Dover 0; Folkestone 2, Trowbridge 1; Gloucester 3, Merthyr T. 1; Guildford 0, Romford 0; Hinckley Ath. 8, Ashford 1; Margate 3, Cambridge Utd. 2; Sittingbourne 2, Kidderminster 1; Tunbridge Wells 1, Clacton 2; Yiewsley 0, Corby 1.

FIG. 103. League results set in 6 pt. Bell Gothic Bold with Gothic No. 6; from the *Sunday Pictorial.*

MAKING UP THE RACE CARDS

Having now indicated the principal points arising from the setting of the minimum-size sports-page programmes and results a word should be said about the make-up of these items. Their positioning should always be logical, their heading bold and instantly identifiable; they should be tied up with the main story or stories of the sport to which they refer. It is essential to avoid shovelling them in below the fold haphazard as a sort of necessary evil which detracts from the appearance of the page; handled like that they certainly will. The race card, or cards, will of course often be the dominant matter on a page; they should be linked and made up as one, with identical or closely similar block or type headings (the main word the reader wants to see, after all, is the name of the race meeting). When the race cards begin to ramble about over the page, headed in sharply varying styles, the effect is ragged in the extreme. If, say, three cards are grouped together under a single block heading of the RUNNERS AND RIDERS AT THREE MEETINGS sort, the name of the meeting over each separate programme should be identically set; use of contrasting type faces and styles is here an irritant, not a useful variant.

A last word may be said about something which, though sporting, is not strictly sports page; namely, the tabulated and classified football results on the front pages of Saturday's final evening papers and of the Saturday sports specials familiar in the Midlands and the North. To tabulate the day's match results in a sufficiently large size—around 9–10 pt. is desired—requires, with our narrow columns, a type-face combining boldness with a considerable degree of condensation. Some papers have found the answer by departing from a text face to Metromedium; there are also effective examples in Times Bold. In either case team names are heavily abbreviated when necessary, since the team and its score can take no more than half-measure, and most papers use a heavier figure for the score than the normal figure of the fount (e.g. a Square Grotesque figure with Metromedium) (Fig. 104). These result tables are much easier to read with a modicum of leading; best of all when they are given the extra white of a short line, in a smaller size of type in roman, recording the half-time score immediately under each bold result.

RESULTS

(Half-time scores in parentheses)

DIVISION I

Bolton W ....(1)2	Everton ....(1)1
Burnley ....(1)1	WEST HAM ..(1)3
FULHAM .....(1)1	Blackpool ....(0)0
Leicester City (2)3	CHELSEA .....(0)1
Luton Town .(0)0	Leeds United (1)1
Manchester U (3)3	Newcastle ...(1)2
Nottingham F (1)2	Blackburn R .(2)2
Preston NE ...(1)1	West Brom A (1)1
Sheffield W ..(0)1	Manchester C (0)0
TOTTENH'M (0)0	Birmingham C (0)0
Wolves ......(1)3	ARSENAL ....(0)3

FIG. 104. Saturday night evening-paper classified football results.

11 · The Feature Pages

THE evolution of the feature pages to a position of importance equal to, and sometimes greater than, that of the news pages, is one of the most marked characteristics of the modern popular newspaper. It is beyond the scope of this book to discuss whether this is in practice good or bad. From the standpoint of newspaper typography the fact has to be reckoned with, and it presents a number of problems which differ substantially from those concerning news page typography and make-up, which we have already met.

Newspapers have always carried articles of one kind or another as distinct from news reports; the tradition of making the leader page—always boldly labelled 'Editorial Page' in America—the receptacle for comment and communications, not news, is of long standing. Feature pages as we know them have developed far beyond this both in extent and in character. Often they occupy most of the left-hand pages of a many-paged paper; and they are really best described by their earlier designation—'magazine pages'.[1] Both the content and the form of newspaper feature pages are simply an adaptation of the dual techniques of an easily digestible and personal style of writing, usually on lighter or 'human' themes, and of free, boldly illustrated display, first developed in the mass-circulation magazines of the United States.

Greater freedom of display, with its common corollary of greater variety in text setting, demands keener discipline in the precision of page-planning. This point must be stressed at the outset, for it is essential to the well-made feature page. What it means is that feature pages must be planned and laid out, not on the scaled miniature make-up sheets used for news pages, but on accurately ruled full-page make-up sheets. These need not have the inch side-numbering of the miniatures, since the features editor or sub-editor will work on them with a type-gauge (described in Chapter 2), measuring off his headings, blocks, and text in picas or inches as required. It is a useful refinement, however, and an aid to accurate planning, if these full-page feature blanks are made up with two

[1] This may be the place to remark on the much-applauded initiative of the *Sunday Times* in its 1958 introduction of a Magazine Section, including its principal features, and differentiated by reverse block folios and headline typography. *The Observer* followed (1960).

fine rules separating each column—showing the precise white between columns, usually a pica—instead of plain column rule (Fig. 105). The point arises from the practice, described in more detail below, of setting feature matter slightly narrower than news, normally not by changing measure but by indenting on the front of each line sufficiently to show, with white in place of column rule, an overall space between columns of approximately a pica. A full-page blank with column rules will thus show

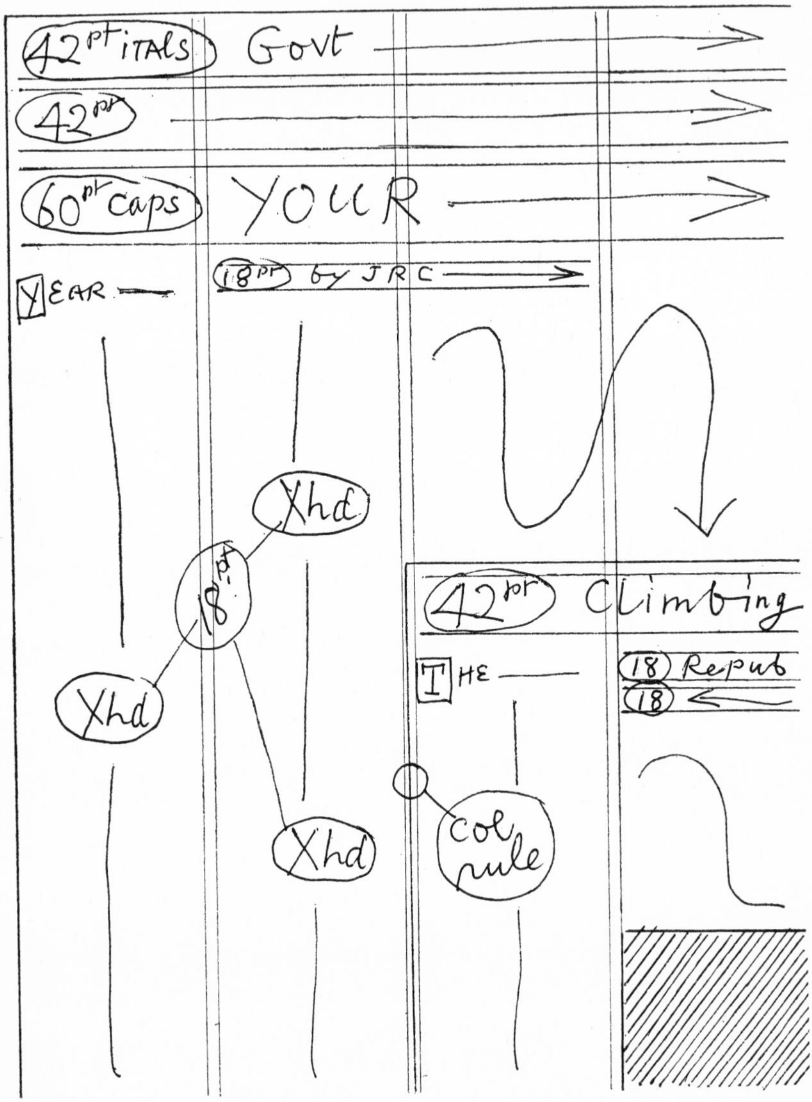

FIG. 105. Portion of an actual-size make-up sheet with simple layout indications for the page illustrated in Fig. 125; note the double rules.

news measure, not feature measure; and though an experienced hand can allow for this, it is not accurate and inevitably engenders a certain confusion.

In fairness it should be said that a simple feature treatment can be laid out on a miniature make-up sheet, given a high degree of skill in allowing correct depths and lengths in reduced size; but the emphasis is on the 'simple', and even the most knowledgeable practitioner would be ill advised to attempt a miniature make-up of any complexity. Any time saved in the planning and layout stage would be more than lost on the stone. On the other hand, it may be convenient in the composing room, if many feature pages are being made up at the same time, to work from miniatures rather than the full sheet. In this case, after the close planning of a page on the full-size blank, there is no reason why a quickly sketched miniature, giving exact positions of headings, blocks, cut-offs, and so on, but not elaborately ruled out, should not go to the stone hand as his working plan; the full sheet can always be available for checking.

THE VALUE OF VISUALIZING

Not the least important aspect of working on a full-size layout is that visualizing is much easier. From the start the picture of the page emerges in exact detail. Headings are ruled off in pencil, with a type-gauge, to their depth in pica ems or points (which is indicated), the required space being allowed for between lines; blocks are likewise ruled off to their depth in inches (also indicated), with captions allowed for. Once the estimated, or specified, length of the various features has been calculated on the basis of the wordage per column-inch of the types selected, the requisite text space can be schemed. This has to include any special items like intro. measure, by-line or other panels, decorative breaks or crossheads. When crossheads have not been sent with copy, but are indicated on the make-up sheet (to be written on page-proof), it is necessary to specify the size. Finally, the whites or cut-offs between features, any vertical rules and their style—column rule, medium rule, and so on—must be indicated. If two main rule styles are used, a simple colour code (red, blue) can be agreed with the composing room, and will prove a help to quick and accurate make-up.

Some feature departments like to finish their make-ups with some care, lettering in the headings, shading the blocks, even roughing out the text lines, so that the make-up sheet resembles an agency's advertisement layout. The real value of the extra labour involved is doubtful. It can certainly be claimed that, like an agency layout, a finished make-up sells itself better to the customer—in this case the higher editorial executive—but the

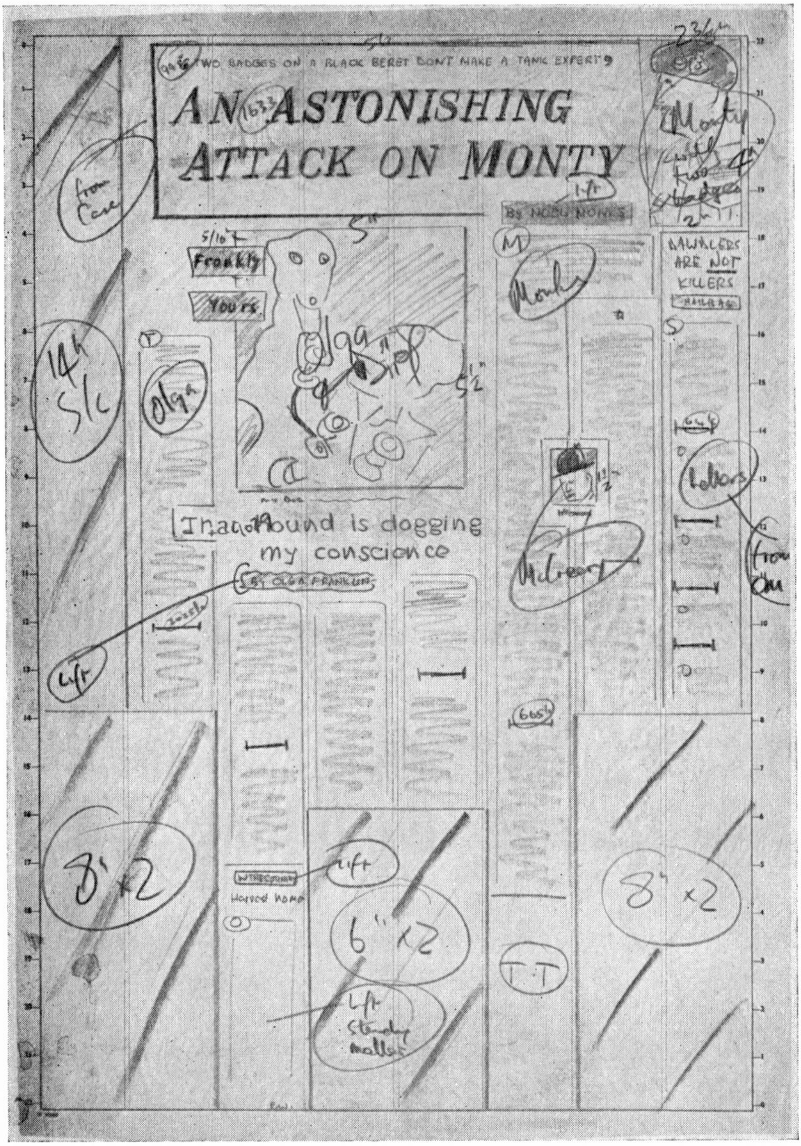

FIG. 106. A fully elaborated actual-size make-up for a *Daily Mail* feature page; the figures are type notations.

truth is that, to the expert eye, an accurately ruled off full-page sketch should do just as well. As for the compositors, accurate layout, not handsome lettering, is all that they need (Figs. 106, 107).

A point on cut-out blocks needs noting: the more complex the cut-out the more important it is. There should be a standing instruction to the process department to provide a tracing of any cut-out feature block at the

PAGE 4

DAILY MAIL, Tuesday, August 11, 1959

'TWO BADGES ON A BLACK BERET DON'T MAKE A TANK EXPERT'

AN ASTONISHING ATTACK ON MONTY

By NOEL MONKS

MONTY was wrong. He was wrong about infantry tactics and wrong about the employment of tanks. And because he was wrong about these things many lives were unnecessarily lost at Alamein in October 1942.

This is the charge made by General Sir Richard McCreery, who was Alexander's Chief of Staff, almost the only senior wartime commander who has not yet written his memoirs.

In a 4,000-word article in the monthly journal of his old regiment, the 12th Royal Lancers, General McCreery, who took command of the Eighth Army himself in 1944, begins slowly and gently:

"Recent war memoirs have prompted me to write these notes. ... What follows has been described by some senior officers who have read it as 'the first real account of that part of the desert campaign.'"

He goes on to say: "In my opinion Monty made a big tactical mistake over the conduct of Alamein. His 'crumbling' operations were expensive, and that caused great ill-feeling between the infantry and the armour.

"There is no doubt in my mind that the armour was not given a good directive for the early stages of the Great Alamein Battle.

"It is no reflection on General Montgomery to say that the wearing of a black beret, even with two badges on it, did not make a tank expert.

"Experience of armoured warfare was necessary. Where Monty failed in regard to armour was that he was not willing to listen to his experts' advice.

McCREERY

"He was determined that the new broom should know all the answers."

There are many other criticisms of Monty that, until now, no other British general has either dared, or seen fit, to utter.

The article has startled high-ranking officers of all three Services and is the talk of clubs all over Britain.

It is at Monty's plan—his Master Plan, the little field-marshal called it on television—that 61-year-old General McCreery tilts hardest.

He says: "When it was clear well before D-Day that Rommel would have too much depth to his defences for one infantry attack to reach beyond the minefields, it would have been far sounder to make two bites at the cherry.

"In other words, 30 Corps should have had a second set-piece attack either the following night, or, if it were difficult to move guns, the next night. This would have been a far simpler plan and less costly."

(Monty's plan was to force two corridors through the enemy's minefields and defences with the infantry of 30 Corps, to be followed by armour of 10 Corps.)

Great rivalry

AS anyone who was there knew there was great rivalry between General Anderson's First Army and Monty's Eighth when the two joined up south of Tunis. General McCreery blames Monty for this:

"Monty, in his build-up of the morale and reputation of the Eighth Army, had led everyone to adopt a very intolerant attitude to others including Allies. Certainly the inflated ideas of the Eighth Army made my task more difficult in the last few weeks of the African campaign."

He describes a talk in Monty's caravan between Alexander and Monty at Benghazi.

"Alex suggested it might be possible to send a mobile force across the desert to cut off Rommel at El Agelia which our forces had twice reached before and had been pushed back violently.

"Monty said: 'If anyone thinks I am going to be the fool to get a bloody nose for the third time they are very much mistaken.'"

Of another meeting in the famous caravan, General McCreery writes:

"Monty wanted Horrocks to command an armoured corps—called the Corps de Chasse—instead of General Herbert Lumsden. I rarely spoke at these discussions, but on this occasion I did venture to say that it would surely be very difficult for an officer straight out from home, no matter how capable, to command an armoured corps in the desert, whereas General Lumsden had controlled at least three armoured brigades and he was the one armoured commander in whom everyone had great confidence. Afterwards I was delighted to hear Monty say Lumsden had been appointed.

"Later, not far from Tunis, Monty fired Lumsden and replaced him by General Horrocks. They never got on together, Monty and Herbert, and Monty was determined to get rid of him. He was sacrificed at Gambut."

Of Field-Marshal Lord Alexander General McCreery has nothing but good to say.

"I shall never have a more splendid man to work for," he says. "He was the man for the great occasion. No man had more battle experience than he had, and wherever he went he was able to deal with the tactical problems facing the junior leader."

Left hook

IN a last left hook at the victor of Alamein General McCreery says:

"I have always argued that Monty's failure to prevent the withdrawal of the remnants of Rommel's forces to Tripoli and beyond, coupled with Hitler's refusal to accept any withdrawal from Africa, led to a great strategic success.

"If Hitler had been turned out of Africa by Christmas 1942 it would have been difficult for the Western Allies to remain inactive for some months owing to Russian pressure for a Second Front."

From Africa General McCreery returned to the U.K., became a corps commander, and in 1944 was in Italy—commanding Monty's old outfit the Eighth Army!

His last big job: Again in Monty's footsteps C.-in-C., Rhine Army.

Frankly Yours

MY DOG ... MY TROPHIES ... ME

That hound is dogging my conscience

BY OLGA FRANKLIN

THE man said he would be glad if I'd call and collect the prizes. It would be a great help. He didn't have an awful lot of room for big trophies.

"Big trophies?" Yes, said the man ... a silver-plated ice-bucket and one engraved candelabrum. The bucket really belonged in a cocktail cabinet and the candelabrum should stand on a piano. It would only get damaged lying about in his office.

It wasn't the weather for hoaxes. "Look," I said, "I'm awfully busy ..."

Oh, he was truly sorry to trouble me, but there was also the little matter of the prize money that was waiting for me—£93 it was.

And that's how I got the news that my dear, faithful dog, Frankly Yours, that I've neglected all these months, had been quietly and loyally working for me all this time.

How could I know that the black greyhound with the great, hungry eyes which was registered as my own dog could be a prize-winner after what happened last September?

I felt guilty. Perhaps it was a bit mean never to go and see her. I knew she was earning her own keep by getting 30s. each time she ran at Harringay. But to hear after all this time, of shining trophies, prizes and her name in the papers. (The man said she had won that trophy race on Bank Holiday Monday at four to one by 7½ lengths.)

I sat a bit stunned and thought back to that night of September 15, 1958, when it all began.

Confident

I HAD just taken possession of Frankly Yours. I had visited her in her own O.R.A. kennel-house at Northaw, Middlesex. I gave her chocolate, walked her twice round the duck-pond, patted her and discussed her diet—glucose, steak, and vegetables—with trainer Mr. Eric Hiscock. We were both confident. She was going to be a winner.

For her first race that night I gave a party. Mr. Laddie Lucas, M.P., president of the Greyhound Racing Association, solemnly shook my hand. All the G.R.A. officials were there to wish me luck. I was saving my breath to cheer when she raced home with the prize money, a mere £10 that night.

Well, she was a flop. When the hare was released, Frankly Yours just stood there looking round, bewildered.

She's new, they told me. Very young, hardly more than a puppy. No experience. It was poor consolation. She won third place with a hard finishing burst.

I gave her a second chance. We all went back the following week. I gave another party for her. I bought chocolate for her. She had experience now. She wouldn't fail again. Her parents had both been big prize-winners too. She was third.

First win

IT was weeks later that I heard she'd won her first race. And then people kept ringing me up and asking how much they should bet on my dog. Was she any good?

I got so angry with all the questioning. People said I was getting testy, always saying "Oh shut up about the dog." But who wants to be made a fool of by a bit of a little black dog, no more than 60lb. of streamlining?

I was glad when the fuss all died down. I forgot about her. A few weeks later I got a card from the G.R.A. She'd gone lame, they said. And I heard no more about her, except she went down for her rest on February 1, came back on April 24. In June she went lame again for two whole weeks.

Then came this news. I dashed out there to the Northaw kennels immediately.

Mr. Eric Hiscock met me at the gate. He seemed a bit cold, I thought. "Yes, Frankly Yours was doing rather well. She was 12 lengths faster than when she started, and won five races out of 24, finishing second three times."

"I've been a fool," I told him. "I never thought. ... Take me to her." We went into the kennel house where Frankly Yours was now rooming with Lord Savernake's dog, Rookery Copse.

She knew me at once. "You see," I said. "No more chocolate," said Mr. Hiscock, coming between us. She was running in a big race next week. Chocolate wouldn't help. (How mean, I thought, all *he* cares about is the trophies.)

We went through Mr. Hiscock's rose-garden and into his sitting-room, where he handed over my trophies. They were standing on Mr. Hiscock's own home-built bar. If I wished, he could swap the ice-bucket and have a pair of candelabra instead.

I sat down on the divan to think it over and Frankly Yours came and sat beside me, affectionately. I felt more guilty than ever. She sat there so proud, head erect, while I discussed what to do with the trophies.

The trainer's wife, Mrs. Barbara Hiscock, said she would go and wrap them up for me. Would I say what they should do with any others the dog might win? Many dog-owners preferred trophies to prize money. Oh, I was overwhelmed.

"Can't I take the dog home with me," I said to her trainer, "and you keep the trophies?"

Understood

FRANKLY YOURS seemed to understand. She started to tremble all over. "What about the treatment for her rheumatism ... and her exercise and diet?"

"No," he said, "she'd go soft, win no more prizes."

Who wants prizes? What a fool I've been.

I am told I shall have to wait another three years to have her home with me, when she's due to be pensioned off. That is, they said, if you think you'll have room for the dog and the trophies.

Really! How can people say things like that? Don't they know what it means to have a dog of your very own?

IN THE COUNTRY

Harvest home

ON one side of the valley the large, modern estate uses combine harvesters on the vast barley fields.

The red monsters work the fields in strips, leaving lines of straw that give the fields a candy-striped pattern.

On the other side of the valley we have a glimpse of the old days, even though the binder drawn by a team of three Suffolk Punches would have been considered very modern only 40 years ago.

The smallholder, who for the past two days has been working steadily round his barley field on the valley slopes, remembers the days before the horse-drawn binder came to his father's farm which he works now. The corn was cut by scythe.

After the harvest there would be a supper for all who had taken part, with barn-dancing and much fun.

But such days are over, said the old man. Happily, I was able to tell him that the owner of the large estate across the valley was, this year, going to revive the old custom of end-of-harvest celebrations and give all his men a "Harvest home" supper. S.W.

DAWDLERS ARE NOT KILLERS

MAILBAG

SIR. — Undoubtedly, many, if not most, of the casualties on the roads are caused by impatient drivers overtaking. But to say, as in Comment (August 5), that "dawdlers" are the cause of their impatience is to misrepresent the facts.

To accuse law-abiding, sensible motorists of causing accidents to "impatient motorists" is like exonerating Teddy Boys who push elderly people off the pavement because the elderly either do not wish to, or cannot, walk as fast as the Teddy Boys can.

F. RODGERS, Thames Ditton, Surrey.

Catching-up

Tax on drivers

Few listeners

He backs Mac

TEDDY TAIL

FIG. 107. The page, schemed in Fig. 106, as made up.

earliest possible moment. The tracing can be pasted on the make-up sheet in its exact position and any consequent odd measure setting of heads or text precisely specified without there being any need to wait for the block proof. If there is time to wait for the proof before planning the page, well and good; but this is rarely so. Most dangerous of all is to ignore the cut-out and plan the page as if the block were normally squared-off to the specified measure and depth; desert areas of waste white will inexorably appear on the page proof.

It will be easily understood that the prescribed method of feature make-up is adaptable to all stages of copy preparation: before any subbing has been done, while subbing is proceeding, or even when some text is already set and proofed. The existence of any matter in proof is an obvious aid to accurate make-up. Measurements can be checked, crossheads written, and so forth, without resort to the paste-up. In general the paste-up method is hardly relevant to the circumstances of modern newspaper production, though it is still normal in periodical work. The present writer frequently used paste-ups in making up Sunday newspaper feature pages; and the paste-up, when practicable, is naturally the most precise of all methods of make-up.

FEATURE TEXT SETTING

The practice of setting feature text slightly narrower than news, so that a full white, approximately a pica, takes the place of column rule, is long established. It makes a basic differentiation between the appearance of news and feature pages, aiding the readability of the longer feature items by the air it introduces. The value of this opening-up of the page can hardly be overestimated; hence the significance of the narrower measure for features. With normal column rules of 6 pt. or below it is worse than useless merely to substitute white for rule while continuing to set full news measure, though some papers have done this. So narrow a strip of vertical white is insufficient to separate the columns and the eye constantly tends to read across. This is why the white should approximate to a pica (10 pts. may be regarded as an absolute minimum), and feature single-column measure thus needs to be determined by subtracting from news measure the difference between the column rule measure and a pica.

Take a simple example. A newspaper with $11\frac{1}{2}$ em columns and 6 pt. column rule will need a feature measure of 11 ems (6 pts. being half an em, only another half is needed to make the full pica). If the newspaper worked with 3 pt. column rule ($\frac{1}{4}$ em) its feature measure should, strictly, be $10\frac{3}{4}$ ems. In practice, however, though the principle indicated here is correct it is not applied quite in this way. Actual measure is usually not changed for feature setting, in order to save time on the composing machines. Instead, news measure is indented by an appropriate space at the beginning of each line, the operators being instructed to use this indention for all feature setting; with most text types, and on newspapers using 6 pt. rule, an indention of 1 en ('nut indent') secures the approximate pica white desired.

For speed in subbing feature copy, and to ensure that the indention instruction will be followed even when the copy is divided into a number of takes, it is advisable to mark it with a bold line in coloured pencil right down each front margin. To ensure that proof corrections will also be set with the correct indention the readers should repeat this coloured stroke down all feature galleys. Adherence to these simple precautions will virtually eliminate the irritating error of an odd feature line set to news measure, though of course the only complete guarantee against this is a change of measure on the machine.

In addition to the variation in the basic single-column measure, feature pages offer wide scope for bastard measure settings. The most obvious is column-and-a-half setting, doubled up across three or across six columns, or used doubled up across three as the opening portion of a feature whose conclusion turns into single column. All-double-column setting, in larger-than-body sizes, will rarely be necessary or suitable for features; but there are more exotic measures capable of exploitation for occasional special settings—three columns making up across the normal four, four across five, four across seven, for instance. Or a feature made up shallow right across the top of the page could be set to make five or seven columns. Rarely is it possible here to adopt the American style of wider measure throughout on a feature page (e.g. an editorial page, devoid of advertising). When it can be applied to a leader page, however, it certainly helps to impart an acceptable note of distinction.

THE SINGLE-COLUMN INTRO.

While main feature *intros.* can on occasion be set across two or three columns, opening in the 12 pt. or 14 pt. used for main news intros.—or, if that is a bold style, preferably in a lighter version (e.g. Metrolite instead of Metroblack, Century instead of Century Bold)—it will be found that the single-column intro. is the most generally suitable for features of all weights. The method of treatment is simple. For main features one opening paragraph in 12 pt. is followed by one paragraph in the appropriate intermediate size (9 pt. or 10 pt.) and so into text (7 pt. or 8 pt.). Secondary features dispense with the opening 12 pt.

The value of this straightforward single-column intro. style for features is worth some stress, since it is the application of an important principle. That is: feature text typography should be unfussy, broken up to ease the eye, not to distract it; all the tricks should go into the headline display and illustration; when the reader has thus been attracted to the feature he should be able to read it more or less as he reads a magazine article or almost, might it be said, a book. The single-column intro. also accords well with the common device of a summary-cum-blurb, disposed in some eye-catching way at the head of the feature—heavily indented each end across two or three columns, set in not less than 12 pt. of a suitable display face and well leaded, sometimes boxed or panelled. Such summaries should not exceed one paragraph, set without the usual opening indention

But in fixing the day Dexter seems to have overlooked one point. On his wedding day the M.C.C. meet Surrey at Lord's, a fixture that will bring the England touring side against the champion county. It is a match in which Dexter was a possible for the M.C.C. team.

INTO BRITAIN yesterday with the most peculiar quote of the year came wealthy financier Ivar Bryce, backer of film-maker Kevin McClory. I asked: "Are you a millionaire?"

FIG. 108. The use of a portion of simple border to decorate a bold-face setting in a feature column. The border can also be used vertically down an indented bold paragraph.

and with the final line centred ('full out and centre break'); the breakline should not be too short. The incorporation of the writer's name in the summary, either to open or to close it, displayed in a larger size of type than the summary's text but lining up with it, obviates the need for a separate by-line.

Feature text, like news text, is set in the body size of the paper; but when that is below 8 pt. it is sound practice to set at least main features a size larger. A 7 pt. paper, for instance, should set its main features in 8 pt. Where space additionally permits the leading of main feature text, e.g. setting 8 pt. on 9-pt. slug, this is a further aid to readability. In any case, the two-point paragraph-leading mentioned in Chapter 8 as a sound procedure for main news stories is even more appropriate for features; a standing instruction can be given for this leading to be done on all feature matter as it is assembled on the random, before it goes to make-up.

Broadly speaking the principles of paragraphing news, discussed in Chapter 4, apply to features. The only qualification to be made is that feature paragraphs can with advantage be allowed to run somewhat longer. No sort of exact prescription is possible, since type size, measure, style of the paper, and the character of the particular feature have all to be taken into account. But it is reasonable to say that for normal feature articles, paragraphs may run a third longer than news paragraphs; the ability to judge whether they should on occasion be longer or shorter than that, and to what extent, is part of the finesse of feature sub-editing. In the case of the intro. paragraphs judgement must be exercised in the same way, though here it is wise to keep the lengths in general nearer to the news norm, certainly in 'popular' paper treatments. An over-long and lumbering large-type intro. paragraph is as deadening in features as it is in news. However, 'class' papers may run lengthy intros., running on from 9 pt. to 8 pt. (say) after the opening lines.

WHEN TO USE BOLD FACE

The view has been advanced above that feature text ought to be unfussy, and free from typographic tricks. It should in fact stick to roman. The use of 'black indent', already criticized as an outmoded and irritating device in news stories, is most undesirable. This is particularly so if the 'black' available is Doric, not Bold Face. As suggested for the news columns, the discreet use of roman indent is a better method of emphasis and column-breaking, though in feature text it will usually be found possible to dispense even with this indention.

If it is worse to spatter features with indented 'black' paragraphs than to disfigure news stories with them, there nevertheless remains a case for the controlled use of a suitable Bold Face—never Doric—on those occasions when a mass-circulation paper's big campaigning or sensational feature requires special emphasis on a summary or a series of key points. But this is not just a matter of casually marking odd paragraphs 'black indent'; it is the deliberate exploitation of Bold Face setting and indention for a specific purpose, always heightening the effect by the addition of some display ingredient. Thus the Bold setting may be all reverse indent, using drop figures for 1, 2, 3, 4 treatment, or signalling the opening of each paragraph with a black star or disk (a 'bullet' to the American newspaperman). An alternative modern fashion is to extra-indent the Bold, say 2 ems instead of 1, keeping the setting even without paragraph indention, cutting the slugs on the front, and placing a portion of fancy rule or border vertically in the resulting white. Some form of milled (simplex) rule is most favoured for this purpose; but any border, or strip of half-tone or mechanical tint, giving an effect of not too heavy shading, is suitable; it is important that the rule or border should not be too heavy, since it will then only draw attention to itself, instead of to the matter (Fig. 108).

On news pages entire stories may be set in Bold Face, with suitable indention, as explained in Chapter 4. The same technique is out of place in features, where such colour contrast in more or less lengthy portions of text could only be an irritant. Bold settings on feature pages should not exceed normal panel depth, averaging three to four paragraphs. On the other hand, there is no reason why features of the shorter kind should not be given, French fashion, the differentiation of setting in italic or a suitable light Sans or Egyptian. At any rate the style is worth some experiment; it requires, however, a new-style italic (e.g. Jubilee or Imperial) in not less than 8 pt. or, for the two alternatives, the same size in Metrolite or Memphis Light (Memphis Medium might be considered, but is probably a little too heavy).

DROPS AND DECORATIONS

Drop initials can play a much larger part in the typography of a feature page than simply opening the intro. paragraph. They offer wide scope for the opening up of feature articles and unobtrusively decorating the page. To secure the requisite variety and size—the intro. drop should be a three-liner, i.e. normally 36 pt. full face, to cover three lines of 12 pt.—these drops are usually not machine-set, but cut in by hand, using movable type or single Ludlow letters sawn from the slug.

The accurate setting of drop letters, fully covering flush lines of text, is even more necessary in features than in news where, as has been seen, the Victorian solecisms of insufficient cover and the ugly hanging indention are deep-rooted. While some bookwork refinements are out of the question, the book printer's standard device of mortising the letters A and L, to set the opening line of text close to the drop, is well worth following. His care in using only full-face 'titling' letters for drop initials is also to be emulated. Since there are few founts of true full-face titlings, it may be necessary to use a normal cap. letter with a beard; in this case the body-depth of the type will be ignored and the face-depth measured to secure the exact cover required; for example, the 36 pt. face needed to cover three lines of 12 pt. may be found in the caps. of a 42 pt. or 48 pt., or even larger-size fount. With movable type the beard must then be sawn off, or with Ludlow the bottom blank packing adjusted.

Feature drop letters should either accord in style with their main heading or be neutral (that is, they should in effect be some suitable, perhaps decorative, variety of Sans). The style accordance can be of a broad kind, e.g. a Caslon Old Face Titling drop would sort with a Goudy Bold main heading, both faces being old face in character. When decorative drops are employed they should, unless based on a Sans design, also broadly accord with the main heading style. Thus a face like Thorne Shaded (an open version of the Regency 'fat face', the letter now commonly called Ultra-Bodoni) should accompany a Bodoni Bold or Ultra-Bodoni heading; an open Egyptian like Rockwell Shadow (Monotype Series 175) should link with a Rockwell, Karnak, or other Egyptian-style heading.

BRITISH Soccer's most exciting tour — the 12,000 miles "dream holiday" to Brazil, Peru, Mexico and the United States—becomes a reality for 18 players tomorrow when England's party is named.

NOTHING is ever certain in Soccer—yet it looks a pretty safe bet that Coventry City, with three games to play, will win promotion from the Fourth Division. But manager Billy Frith is keeping his fingers tightly crossed—and trying not to think of what happened in 1937-38.

FIG. 109. Decorative drop letters.

Subject to what has now been said about style of setting there is nothing to add in the simple case of a feature opening with a drop letter, but relying on sub-headings, stars, or other decorative material to break up its text. That drop letter will be set full out to measure in the ordinary way; but when drop letters are used at appropriate points throughout a feature as the principal means of lightening and breaking up the text, the matter is not so simple. The text-breaking drop letter style, at its best in well illustrated features of some length, calls for the following:

1. The *position* of the drops should be carefully gauged in subbing so that they fall well in making up. This means subbing after the make-up has been determined; from the make-up the number of drops that should be employed—enough but not too many—can be estimated.

2. While the intro. drop letter should be set full out the succeeding drops—which may be three-liners, e.g. 24 pt. covering three lines of 8 pt. —should always be *indented*; 1 or 2 ems suffices on an $11–11\frac{1}{2}$ em column, though a 3 em indention is permissible on a column of 13 ems or more. The indention is necessary to emphasize the break made by the extra white at the side of the drop letter.

3. These drop letters should have some *decorative* quality. Outline, shaded, or three-dimensional faces are suitable, for example Gill Cameo, Gill Cameo Ruled, Umbra (Gill Shadow), Tempo Inline, Ludlow Cameo (Narciss), Rockwell Shadow, Thorne Shaded. Or the numerous modern pen or brush scripts could well be called on for the unusual occasion: Klang, Hauser, Studio, Mercurius, Mistral (Fig. 109; Figs. 136, 138).

4. Substantial white space should be carried over each drop-lettered section, broken by some simple form of *typographic decoration* rather than a crosshead. The plain five-pointed star, black or white (open), in a suitable size—12, 14, and 18 pt. will be found the most useful—is a sound choice. The choice can be single, double, or treble, well spaced in the line. Short lengths of border or fancy rule are a possible alternative. In any event the colour and style of the decorative item should not conflict with that of the drop letters.

One possible variant in the handling of text-breaking drop letters is to set them, not as drops at all, but, book-style, as cocked-up initials. This style is so rarely used that there is no need to give a detailed exposition here. The cock-up should be indented the same as the drop, the necessary text indention being on the first line only, with which the foot of the cock-up should line precisely. Justification calls for care, whether the initial is an individual type or machine-set to overhang on a blank slug (Fig. 110).

A concluding caveat may be entered to this discussion of the use of drop letters on feature pages. Throughout, the emphasis on decorative styles is directed to the 'popular' paper. The more serious journal, whether it regards itself as 'class' or not, would look overdressed with such styles. Its drops, even in the article-breaking indented style, should be of the plainer sort; indeed, it may often with advantage set them full out and use some discreet crosshead. The underlying point is the one made frequently in this book: the well-made paper is one that thinks out its typography as a proper expression of its character and thus as the proper mode of visual appeal to its readers.

SUB-HEADINGS IN FEATURES

The term 'sub-headings' may conveniently be used here to denote something more than it does in relation to the news columns (Chapter 6). For the display lines which break feature text are not only crossheads or side-heads; they include by-lines, summary or descriptive panels, subsidiary headings (which in news might be a deck to a main heading), any of which may be physically dropped into the text, overrun each end to cover them; typical is a double-column by-line centred across three columns, with half-column setting each end to cover.

Since the choice and treatment of type for feature display is much freer than it is for news it might appear that feature sub-headings require little discipline. This is not so. They should either agree typographically with their main headings, subject to necessary and appropriate variations in size and style, or be neutral (e.g. Sans), or contrast without clashing (e.g. Bodoni Bold italic sub-headings with a large Sans main heading). The typographic agreement prescribed here does not by any means necessarily imply typographic identity, especially when text crossheading is considered. Thus a feature headed in 60 or 72 pt. Goudy Bold might be subheaded in 14 pt. Goudy Bold (or 18 pt. of the medium weight Goudy Catalogue); but it could equally well be sub-headed in equivalent sizes of Caslon Old Face Heavy, Plantin Heavy, Times Bold—perhaps even better, because of the slight variation in cut and colour. The point is that the type faces last named, like Goudy Bold, fall broadly within the Old Face range, and therefore do not offend against the principle of typographic consonance.

Bitter

THOSE are just two expressions from the cryptic slang they use to describe the social disease from which they suffer.

☆ IN SCALE

ANOTHER Ritter hobbyhorse is the playhouse. "Have you ever realised how awesome a home is for

FIG. 110. An underscored feature crosshead (the wavy border of Fig. 108 could also be used) and a crosshead with star; note also the indented cock-up initial.

THE TEXT-BREAKING CROSSHEAD

Whatever the choice of type for feature sub-headings (agreement, neutrality, or contrast) the following specific crossheading factors have to be considered:

(i) *Size*: the general tendency is towards sizes one, or even two, steps above average news sub-headings. Length of feature and size of page have, of course, to be taken into account; but since there normally tend to be fewer sub-headings in a feature than a news story of comparable length, it is easy to comprehend that 14 pt. or 18 pt. will be called on, as against (say) 12 pt. in news. These size relationships should not be taken as a rigid prescription; it is in any event as necessary to avoid over-large and overweighty feature sub-headings as it is to avoid small and insignificant-looking ones. But the general tendency to go up on the news sizes will be found broadly true, varying mainly according to the smallness or otherwise of the chosen face.

(ii) *Style*: lower-case will be found preferable to caps. in almost all cases, especially in view of the size requirement. A cap. sub-heading in the larger sizes indicated tends to interrupt the flow of a feature. The choice of roman or italic is entirely a matter of taste, to be guided by the style of the main headings and the need to get some contrast on the page.

(iii) *Colour*: lightweight sub-headings are virtually useless, and the selection should normally be made from a Bold. The heavies usually go a little too far (if used, the size should be closely controlled) except in their condensed versions, e.g. Tempo Heavy Condensed, particularly its italic. Sledge-hammer letter like Ludlow Black or Linotype Pabst goes even further, and 14 pt. should be regarded as an effective ceiling here. The extra colour gained by condensation is nearly always useful, not least in a medium-weight Sans like Metromedium.

> A well designed paper explains itself at a glance. The typographical treatment distinguishes different kinds of news stories, and separates news from features. Further, it maintains interest throughout. There

FIG. 111. A feature panel showing the use of extra-large quotes.

(iv) *Decoration*: while this can range from simple underscoring in plain rule to broken-boxing in fancy border, it is sound practice to take the middle course—when any decorative treatment is thought necessary—and underscore in a fancy border of the more conventional sort, e.g. square-dot or heavy wavy. This simple decorative touch is quite enough for normal purposes; and even so it should not be used indiscriminately. Better too little decoration than too much. Alternatively a sub-heading may be opened with a star, circle, or other simple border unit, in this case setting full out as a sidehead; again, this should be kept as a decorative variant for special occasions, not made a general style (Fig. 110).

(v) *Number and placing*: as indicated in (i) above, a feature needs relatively fewer—though larger—sub-headings than a news story. The appropriate number for a main feature displayed across several columns usually falling unevenly, can only be effectively determined on the make-up sheet; this determination goes hand in hand with a proper placing of the sub-headings, which should break the columns evenly, none being too low or too high, and avoid any ranging with sub-headings in adjoining columns. The implication, it will be seen, is that sub-headings are not sent up with copy, but their position and size indicated on the make-up sheet. The stonehand can then allow for them and, after any final adjustments of placing have been made on the stone, they can either be written forthwith or on the first page-proof, whichever best suits edition requirements. The importance of constant care in this respect cannot be over-emphasized. If sub-headings are too few, or too many, and are badly placed, they can mar the appearance of the most attractively designed feature page.

BY-LINES AND OTHER SUBSIDIARY DISPLAY

So much for the detailed text-breaking or crosshead aspect of the feature sub-heading. Now for the other types of sub-heading—by-lines, summary panels, subsidiary lines. The point has already been made that any of these may be used to break text by dropping in and overrunning each end. The commonest style is to centre the line or lines on a measure one column more than its own—single column over two, two columns over three, and so on—resetting to approximately half-measure each end to cover, allowing for appropriate and even white. Ingenuity can easily suggest other arrangements, with bastard resettings, e.g. $1\frac{1}{2}$ columns over three, $2\frac{1}{2}$ columns over four, or any odd measure (a line set to whatever it makes, for example) centred over whatever number of columns allows the overrun to be not less than half-measure. Even half-measure, slow to set because of spacing difficulties, is a strain to read after more than a few lines, and dropped-in matter of any depth should therefore be handled with caution, if not avoided entirely.

In discussing the breaking of feature text by these dropped-in and overrun lines it is necessary to revert to the point stressed earlier in this chapter: namely, that once the display has attracted a reader to a feature he should be able to read it with the minimum of typographic interruption or distraction. Thus all forms of feature sub-heading need to be handled in a restrained fashion, the aim being to contribute to an agreeable and attractive overall page pattern without impinging on the straightforwardness and readability of text. Excessive, which often means confusing, break-up of feature text with sub-headings, particularly in their more elaborate forms, must be avoided.

The typography of by-lines, panels, and subsidiary lines is broadly determined by the principles of consonance, neutrality, and contrast already outlined in relation to feature crossheadings. But these three principles are not applied equally, as alternatives, to the three different types of sub-heading. Consonance is the better principle for by-lines and subsidiaries, the latter differentiating themselves from the main display by some simple style variation, e.g. italic, using a lighter weight if the main display is very heavy. Contrast is suitable for subsidiary lines when the main display is particularly powerful (e.g. a heavy Sans) and needs a clearly differentiated, as well as lighter, foil (e.g. a sufficiently large Bodoni italic, usually in lower-case). Neutrality, i.e. Sans, preferably in a medium or sometimes even light weight, scores with panels, whether these are summaries of the feature's main points, a quotation of a key passage, or a blurb on the writer. These panel-settings should always be leaded, not less than 2 pts., the type-size being not less than 10 pt. and not more than 14 pt., according to the measure and the amount of matter. Where the panel is a quotation the fashion of using extra-large, not to say monster, opening and closing single quotes (usually of the Ultra-Bodoni character) has been borrowed from the advertising typographers (Fig. 111).

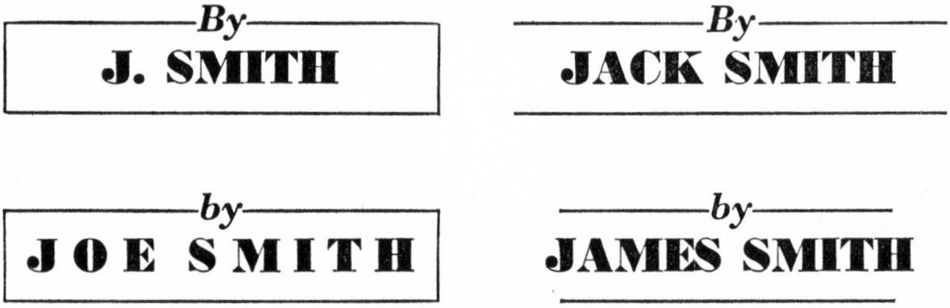

FIG. 112. Simple feature by-line styles, in box or panel; note the shortening of rules to range with type in the latter.

By-lines need a further word to themselves, especially in respect of their size. They need to be bold and sufficiently large, but not too large. An over-large by-line looks absurd. Given a type of sufficiently strong colour, and using caps. (normally most suitable for this purpose),[1] a by-line should only exceed 18 pt. in very rare cases, and frequently it will not need to be so large. With by-lines in caps. the value of letter-spacing can be duly exploited. A point of refinement to note is that the 'by' is better kept down (a cap. 'B' gives needless emphasis to the preposition) and can be set in italic. When by-lines are panelled or boxed it usually improves the appearance to cut the 'by' into the top rule, either centred or left. At the same time the line itself should be reasonably full, letter-spaced if necessary; a short by-line in a box with waste white each end has a very amateurish air. In panel treatments the top and bottom rules should range a trifle, say 6 pts. each end, inside the actual type line (Fig. 112).

[1] The contrary notion may be advanced here that novel and striking by-lines can be contrived in the lower-case of one of the modern Scripts, particularly the informal brush or pen Scripts, like Ludlow Hauser, Monotype Ashley Script (Series 574), even maybe the exotic Mistral: see Fig. 138.

GOUDY IS GOOD TYPE

Elegant Feature Headings

FINE FLOWING ITALIC

The best italic for features

TRY THIS VARIANT

U*se* Th*is for* V*ariety*

***B*ut Never *D*o *T*his**

FIG. 113. Ringing the changes on one type face, with its italic: an exercise in Goudy Bold.

THE CHOICE OF HEADLINE TYPES

The main factor differentiating a feature page from a news page is its headline typography; and the two must be quite distinct, the one from the other. The selection of a given type family as a paper's basic news headline style must bar it for features. Of course there are types which are in any case more suitable for news (e.g. Century Bold), but there are others suitable for either news or features (e.g. Bodoni, Caslon, Times); it is important, however, that they should not be used simultaneously for both.

In choosing a type for basic feature display regard should be paid to its range in both roman and italic—60 pt. and 72 pt. are vital, especially in lower-case—and to the availability of a variant weight. A full range of Bold or Heavy, with a selected range of Light or Medium, provides a main battery for any feature front. This primary approach can either be simplified or made more complex, according to the resources and needs of the paper, in this way:

(i) *One family, one weight*: one well-chosen Bold, with its italic, can be manipulated to provide at least six acceptable style variations—the four alphabets from roman and italic, caps. and lower-case respectively, plus the large initial line-up in roman caps. (giving a caps. and smalls effect) and in roman with italic lower-case (Fig. 113). Ringing the changes in this way is possible with any sound display type; but it is most successful when the type is one of some distinction, with a markedly 'feature' quality. In this class the 1917 vintage Goudy Bold, with its exceptional combination of elegance and strength, is still hard to beat; it is fully available in Monotype (Series 249), Ludlow (designated No. 11), and in a restricted Intertype range (up to 36 pt., with no italic after 14 pt.).

(ii) *Two families*: instead of complementing a full range of Bold with a selected range of its Light, it is supplemented with a selected range of an entirely different type, perhaps a shaded, and thus somewhat decorative one. Chisel, Ludlow Cameo, Monotype Gill Shadowline (Series 290), Imprint Shadow (Series 190) are all possibilities, providing a useful element of complete contrast; see Chapter 12. Quite different is the two-family specification which adds to the first full roman–italic range a second full roman–italic range in another face; here the purpose is not to provide contrast on the same page but a completely different dress for different pages.

(iii) *One family, many weights*: display types suitable for feature headlines are usually available in an extraordinary variety of weights, both roman and italic—Light, Medium, Bold, Heavy, Extra Heavy, plus Condensed and Extra Condensed variants. Not all these variants are happy; the extremes of thinness and fatness need to be treated with

Newspaper headlines are a signal

Newspaper headlines are a signal an

Newspaper headlines are a signa

Newspaper headlines are a signa

Newspaper headlines are a sig

Newspaper headlines are a sig

Newspaper headlines are

FIG. 114. Varying weights in Monotype Goudy: Oldstyle/Italic (291), Catalogue/Italic (268), Bold/Italic (269), Extra Bold (214).

ROCKWELL (371), Condensed (414), Bold (391), Bold Condensed (359), Extra Bold (424)

Newspaper headlines are a

Newspaper headlines are

Newspaper headlines are a signal and a sum

Newspaper headlines are

Newspaper headlines ar

Newspaper headlines are a signal a

Newspaper headlines

BODONI—Bold No. 2 (195), Ultra/Italic (120), Onyx (591)

Newspaper headlines are a sign

Newspaper headlines ar

Newspaper headlines a

Newspaper headlines are a signal and a summary

FIG. 115. Weight and style variations in an Egyptian face (Monotype Rockwell) with some extras in Bodoni and its associates (also all Monotype) to supplement the weights and styles in Fig. 53.

caution, and are sometimes too distorted for satisfactory use. Nevertheless, it is quite possible to devise suitable three-, four-, or even five-weight installations of, for example, Bodoni, Caslon, the Egyptians (Rockwell, Karnak, Memphis), Tempo or Gill Sans (Fig. 114). A Bodoni roman–italic specification might run as follows: *Monotype*—'Light', i.e. normal weight (Series 135), Bold (Series 260), Ultra (Series 120), Bold Condensed roman only (Series 529); *Ludlow*—Light or Modern, Bold, Black, Campanile (Extra Condensed, the italic is not recommended),

Bold Condensed roman only. Even on the minimum three-weight basis it is clear that most effective variation and colour contrast can thus be obtained within one type family (Fig. 115).

Let a word of warning be uttered here. There is a danger in expanding the feature pages' typographic repertory too richly; such riches bring embarrassment. A paper drawing on half a dozen different type families for the main lines on as many pages produces an effect of confusion rather than a contrast in effect. Often such procedures arise not from riches at all —not, that is to say, from the paper's possession of full ranges of all the types used—but from the bad old composing room practice of carrying a few sizes only of each of a large number of faces, instead of full ranges (always including italic) of one or two carefully selected faces. Sound feature typography starts there; the types available for feature display should be 'fit—but few', as Sir Francis Meynell once put it.

Today at Westminster MPs will be

BACK AT WORK

THE COMMONS RESUME TODAY: HERE IS A

Parliament Preview

FIG. 116. Right and wrong size and style for feature strap-lines.

'Fitness', implying fitness for purpose, can be interpreted in the general sense—as it has been so far in this chapter—of the suitability of a type face for overall feature display; it can be given another interpretation in the light of what may be called the evocative qualities of different faces. The point has long been familiar to commercial typographers, who would never think of using a heavy Egyptian to suggest femininity or a fancy Script to suggest structural strength.[1] It is a suggestive one for the newspaperman too, though he is in no position to pick what he may think the ideally fit face for a special feature from the scores stocked by the trade typesetter. But if his fitness-for-purpose approach is of this special kind it will help him in handling his feature display. For a woman's page he will turn to a large light italic, for entertainment to something colourful and lively (a heavy rounded italic or a large Sans lower-case), for Letters

[1] See the chapter 'Suitability—or fitness for purpose' in Geoffrey Dowding, *Factors in the Choice of Type Faces* (1957), p. 81.

to the Editor to a straightforward Bold roman. Pursuing this approach he may additionally appreciate the suitability of certain decorative treatments, for label and standing headings, strap-lines, and the like; these are discussed in more detail below.

FEATURE HEADLINE STYLE

Once a paper has selected and installed its feature types a heading sheet or card should be prepared, showing one line of each size and style, in both caps. and lower-case. The larger sizes (from 42 pt. upwards) are best shown across four columns, with the one-, two-, and three-column measures indicated. It is not usual to codify a feature-heading sheet in the letter or number style used for news headings. The size and type are specified, the last usually abbreviated—'Bod' for Bodoni, 'Gdy' for Goudy, and so on. Since there are far fewer feature than news headings, especially taking account of edition changes, a feature code is hardly necessary.

Since feature headlines, especially in the 'popular' papers, are much freer and less stylized than news headlines they cannot be brought within the framework of a formula to the same degree. Lower-case, especially in the largest sizes, is of prime importance; but the value of contrasting cap. treatments, particularly the 'caps. and smalls' line-up already mentioned, cannot be ignored. In the more complex pages the style of main headlines is largely determined by the designing of the make-up, including the relation of headline and illustration. Content can also determine form to a greater extent; measure, size, and style can be adjusted to a chosen wording. A sense of movement, and leading-in to the text, is important; hence the effectiveness of a turned main line—a heading across five columns turning to three is usually better than one of two lines across four.

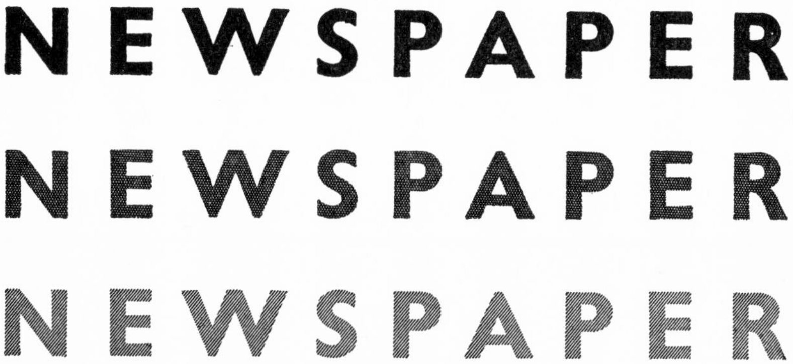

FIG. 117. The effect of stippling a line of type.

General principles for the treatment of subsidiary headlines have already been mentioned; the special case of strap-lines now demands a few words. The device of the strap is frequently even more useful in feature than in news headlining. Chapter 7's discussion of news strap-lines may be taken as a general guide for feature work, but some qualifications are necessary. The element of contrast is less necessary in a feature strap, which is often best executed in suitable smaller caps.—perhaps lightened by letter-spacing—of the face used in large lower-case for the main line. Some contrasting strap styles, e.g. condensed Sans caps., are ugly, ineffective, and word-wasting over a multi-column feature heading. The strap–main-line size relationship can be regarded somewhat more flexibly than in news, but still calls for a careful eye. A feature strap that is too tiny looks peculiarly grotesque, an over-large one unbalances the whole headline (Fig. 116).

TYPE-PROCESSING AND DECORATIVE HEADINGS

The three main methods of processing lines of type—reversing to white, type-on-tint, stippling—can all be usefully employed for varying the display of, and imparting a decorative note to, the feature pages. The reader may be reminded, in passing, that the first two at least have a certain value in news as well; and more particularly on the sports pages.

Stippling may be disposed of first, since it is generally the least often required. Its purpose is to reduce to grey the black of large and heavy lines, by reproducing them in tinted or shaded form. It has long been the practice in advertising when extra-large lines exceed the limits for solid black prescribed by the newspaper proprietors. With a machine called the Decorface stippled effects can now be produced on the actual type without blockmaking. Stippling will occasionally give just that out-of-the-ordinary note to a short, extra-large headline; but it is not often resorted to, even by the most ardent seekers after typographic novelty (Fig. 117).

The *reversal* techniques are perhaps the most valuable for newspaper use. White lettering on a black, ruled, or tinted ground of varying depths of greyness catches the eye instantly and contrasts admirably with accompanying display lines. The solid black ground is too heavy for reverses of any size, and tinted grounds are therefore usual. It is important to see that the tint (or 'half-line' ruling) is neither too light nor too dark; otherwise the white-letter contrast will be insufficient, or the ground may tend to fill in while printing. The lighter tints may be used if the reversed white lettering is to be black-shadowed, or 'black-cased';[1] but the process technique required here is of some complexity, and newspaper schedules

[1] See Chapter 13, pp. 257–8.

will rarely permit of its use, unless for some permanently standing section or department label heading.

Fine-seriffed types should be avoided for reverse blocks, especially with the broken outline that tint grounds give to letter. Sans types are the safest, and caps. are preferable to lower-case, since the border will then appear even, with no ascenders or descenders to break it. Caps. should also be letter-spaced, as the contrast of the extra portions of dark ground between the white lettering helps to give emphasis to the line. When lower-case is used it should always be of a big-bodied type with short ascenders and descenders. Watch that the border of ground, both top and bottom and at the ends, is kept both even and narrow. Excess ground each end looks clumsy; and horizontally there should be no more than suffices to give adequate tone contrast to the white lettering, from $\frac{1}{16}$ to $\frac{1}{8}$ in. usually being enough (Fig. 118).

WEEKEND SPORTS SUMMARY

DONCASTER RUNNERS, RIDERS

HURST PARK PROBABLES

BIRMINGHAM RACING GUIDE

FIG. 118. Reverse block treatments, squared-off, nicked, and rounded corners. Note the superiority of the Sans to the blunt-seriffed last line, a heavy face whose small counters practically disappear in reversing.

Type-on-Tint—the provision of a grey-tinted or light ruled ground for a normal black line—is the complementary technique of reversal and the same principles of style apply. The ground can be obtained by half-toning, by using a suitable mechanical tint, or by stripping a ruled cellophane transparency over a proof of the line of type and making a straight line block (Fig. 119).

Reversed or type-on-tint blocks can be finished in a number of ways. The edges of a tint ground can be left raw or fine black-ruled in process (this gives a slightly mannered appearance which is not generally recommended). The block can be squared off, given rounded ends (or corners), or a horizontal V-cut. Sometimes a ragged or torn edge effect can be

FIG. 119. Some type-on-tint treatments—the reverse of reverse.

striking (Fig. 120). Ingenuity can devise many variations of this kind, but great skill is needed if they are to succeed; otherwise it is always best to play for simplicity in processed-type treatments.

Type-processing can be combined with half-tone illustrations[1] or with line-drawings; and it can be used for the treatment of hand-lettering. The

FIG. 120. Plain and fancy finish reverse blocks; note that the large counters of Caslon Heavy avoid the defects seen in Fig. 118.

many variations possible along these lines can be exploited for the devising of the 'decorative headings for special features' praised by the 1957 Newspaper Design Award judges (their qualification 'we would have welcomed more enterprise in their invention and more skill in their designing' should be taken to heart). Decorative developments of this sort too often rely on hand-lettering, far below the superlative quality necessary to compete with type. When the skill of a first-class letterer is not available, it is best to apply one or other of the type-processing techniques described

[1] *The Times* (on the main feature page of 17 May 1958) has even reversed a 9 pt. caption and superimposed it on a half-tone block; that is to say, the appearing size of the white-lettered caption was 9 pt., no doubt reduced from a larger setting. Carrying the reversal technique to this fine point requires both caution and skill, in the machine-room as well as in process.

to a modern Script or other fancy letter. Often this will provide the best solution to the problem of distinctive—and, where possible, allusive—department or section headings. A reversed or light-grounded bold Script, for instance, would be apt for the Letters to the Editor columns, with its suggestion of handwriting; a similarly treated light Script or fancy shaded type could strike the right feminine note for the Woman's Page.

POINTS ON PICTURES

The main principles of picture-handling, discussed in Chapter 9 in relation to news pictures, apply also to the half-tone illustration of features. The difference is that the feature picture is illustrative, a pictorial point-scorer, rather than a news item, and it can have much freer block treatment in terms of shape, cutting-out and so forth. A well-sized, well-placed

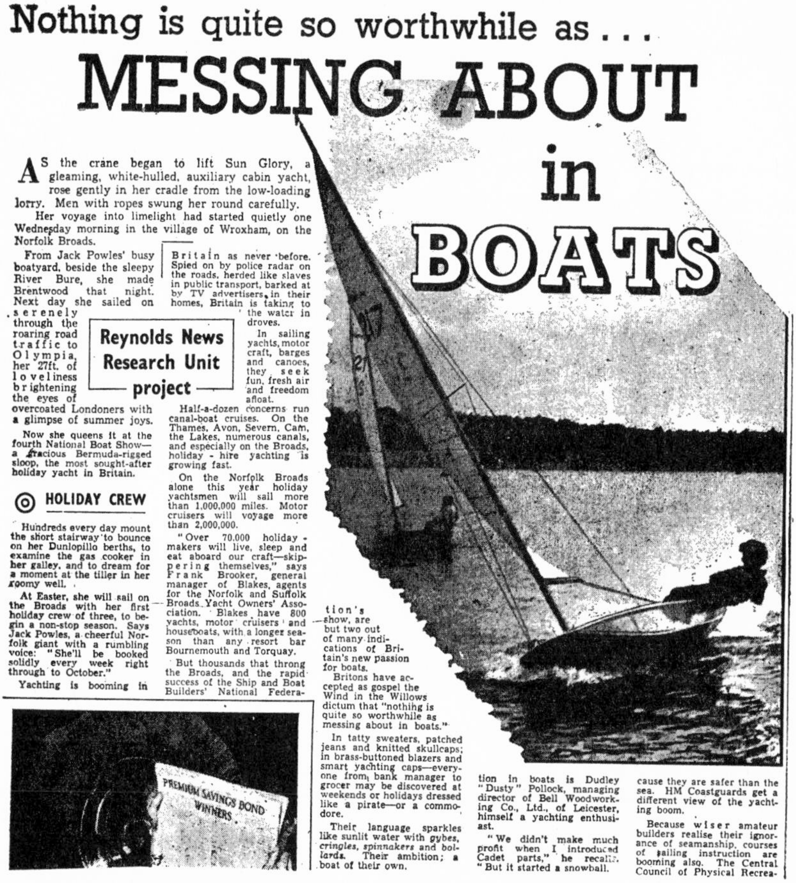

Nothing is quite so worthwhile as . . .

MESSING ABOUT in BOATS

AS the crane began to lift Sun Glory, a gleaming, white-hulled, auxiliary cabin yacht, rose gently in her cradle from the low-loading lorry. Men with ropes swung her round carefully.

Her voyage into limelight had started quietly one Wednesday morning in the village of Wroxham, on the Norfolk Broads.

From Jack Powles' busy boatyard, beside the sleepy River Bure, she made Brentwood that night. Next day she sailed on serenely through the roaring road traffic to Olympia, her 27ft. of loveliness brightening the eyes of overcoated Londoners with a glimpse of summer joys.

Now she queens it at the fourth National Boat Show—a gracious Bermuda-rigged sloop, the most sought-after holiday yacht in Britain.

Reynolds News Research Unit project

HOLIDAY CREW

Hundreds every day mount the short stairway to bounce on her Dunlopillo berths, to examine the gas cooker in her galley, and to dream for a moment at the tiller in her roomy well.

At Easter, she will sail on the Broads with her first holiday crew of three, to begin a non-stop season. Says Jack Powles, a cheerful Norfolk giant with a rumbling voice: "She'll be booked solidly every week right through to October."

Yachting is booming in Britain as never before. Spied on by police radar on the roads, herded like slaves in public transport, barked at by TV advertisers, in their homes, Britain is taking to the water in droves.

In sailing yachts, motor craft, barges and canoes, they seek fun, fresh air and freedom afloat.

Half-a-dozen concerns run canal-boat cruises. On the Thames, Avon, Severn, Cam, the Lakes, numerous canals, and especially on the Broads, holiday-hire yachting is growing fast.

On the Norfolk Broads alone this year holiday yachtsmen will sail more than 1,000,000 miles. Motor cruisers will voyage more than 2,000,000.

"Over 70,000 holiday-makers will live, sleep and eat aboard our craft—skippering themselves," says Frank Brooker, general manager of Blakes, agents for the Norfolk and Suffolk Broads Yacht Owners' Association. Blakes have 800 yachts, motor cruisers and houseboats, with a longer season than any resort bar Bournemouth and Torquay.

But thousands that throng the Broads, and the rapid success of the Ship and Boat Builders' National Federation's show, are but two out of many indications of Britain's new passion for boats.

Britons have accepted as gospel the Wind in the Willows dictum that "nothihg is quite so worthwhile as messing about in boats."

In tatty sweaters, patched jeans and knitted skullcaps; in brass-buttoned blazers and smart yachting caps—everyone from bank manager to grocer may be discovered at weekends or holidays dressed like a pirate—or a commodore.

Their language sparkles like sunlit water with *gybes, cringles, spinnakers* and *bollards*. Their ambition: a boat of their own.

PREMIUM SAVINGS BOND WINNERS

tion in boats is Dudley "Dusty" Pollock, managing director of Bell Woodworking Co., Ltd., of Leicester, himself a yachting enthusiast.

"We didn't make much profit when I introduced Cadet parts," he recalls. "But it started a snowball.

cause they are safer than the sea. HM Coastguards get a different view of the yachting boom.

Because wiser amateur builders realise their ignorance of seamanship, courses of sailing instruction are booming also. The Central Council of Physical Recrea-

FIG. 121. A porti on of a *Reynolds News* feature page showing a heading stripped over a block (combined line-and-tone).

14

Great Star-ACTION Programme

COLUMBIA PICTURES present A PAUL GRAETZ PRODUCTION

RICHARD BURTON
CURT JURGENS
RUTH ROMAN
RAYMOND PELLEGRIN

BITTER VICTORY

SEAN KELLY — NICHOLAS RAY

RANDOLPH SCOTT

DECISION AT SUNDOWN

TECHNICOLOR

JOHN CARROLL · KAREN STEELE · VALERIE FRENCH

ODEON TOTTENHAM COURT ROAD — STARTS TODAY — Metropole VICTORIA

ACADEMY AWARD WINNER

THE KING BROTHERS present

THE Brave One

introducing BRITAIN'S GREATEST BOY STAR MICHEL RAY as LEONARDO

Screenplay by HARRY FRANKLIN and MERRILL G. WHITE

Directed by IRVING RAPPER

Produced by MAURICE KING and FRANK KING

CINEMASCOPE TECHNICOLOR

CAMEO-Poly OXFORD CIRCUS LAN 1744

BRITISH GALA PREMIERE THURS. NEXT

6TH BIG WEEK!

The Horror film with the 'U' certificate for the whole family

LAUNDER & GILLIAT'S

Blue Murder at St. Trinian's

TODAY PROGS. 4.30 & 7.30

GAUMONT HAYMARKET

SPINE CHILLING NIGHTMARE TENSION..pluck up courage— AND GO!!'

THE NEWEST SCREEN DISCOVERY JULIETTE GRECO!

★ ★ ★ ★ ★ ★ ★ ★ ★ ★ ★ ★ ★ ★ ★ ★

★ *Mr. Laurence Harvey and h*

SIX-S

Miss

IT took just 10 mint
The conversation in
gentle, even sedate.

Miss Margaret Leighton
months now, appeared in a l
necklace and said, yes, wa
fun there, but it had been

Mr. Harvey, in Edwarc
hadn't been much of a hc
Then Miss Leighton reache
they were off.

"No," said Mr. Harvey. "It's the last one."

"Please," said Miss Leighton, "I'll pay you back."

"You always say that," said Mr. Harvey.

"I will, I truly will," said Miss Leighton. And she took the cigarette.

Mr. Harvey crumpled the packet and threw it disgustedly in the fire.

I reminded them that the last time we met they had been bickering.

"Over cigarettes," said Mr. Harvey.

"It's always over cigarettes," said Miss Leighton.

"I," said Mr. Harvey, who has a habit of beginning his sentences that way. "I smoke only American cigarettes because they don't make me cough."

He coughed.

Miss Leighton made a face.

"Well, they don't as a rule," said Mr. Harvey.

SCARCITY VALUE

He stood up. "But long, *long* before we were married I told my dear wife-to-be that they wouldn't make her cough either. Of course, she wouldn't believe me."

Mr. Harvey imitated Miss Leighton refusing to believe him. "Now she won't smoke anything

...The other Bardot

—this time the name is Mijanou.

Brigitte Bardot is her elder sister. Mijanou also wants to be a film actress, but says she wants to make her name alone, not as Brigitte's sister. She has already had screen tests. And the film offers are coming in.

FIG. 122. Ingenious curved shaping of a large half-tone by the *Sunday Express* to suit the theme and to stand the picture away from the advertising.

picture with a feature should attract as much attention as the headline to which it is linked—even physically linked in the sense that heading and picture are made as a composite block, with the type stripped in and perhaps partly reversed as well (Fig. 121). Any device to heighten the dynamic effect of a main picture is to be welcomed. Angle-placing, unusual shaping, cut-outs, can all be called on; it is worth recalling here the make-up point, made earlier in this chapter, that accurate tracings of cut-out blocks should always be used when preparing the page layouts, in order to visualize and gauge any bastard-measure heading or text setting that may be necessary.

THE SUNDAY EXPRESS LONDON FEBRUARY 23 1958

It's no wonder she loathed her wedding day

HAPPY *is the Bride*, at the **Ritz**, is dedicated to the proposition that nothing is more likely to undermine the marriage institution than the wedding itself. It has been said that marriage is a kind of friendship recognised by the police and this film shows that the marriage ceremony is as comforting as a pair of handcuffs.

Vaguely based upon Esther McCracken's play **Quiet Wedding**, it is a light-hearted investigation of the gruesome ritual by which middle-class English couples fondly imagine themselves made one.

Ian Carmichael and Janette Scott want to get married. But before they can do so they have to be harassed by relatives, besieged by tradesmen, mauled by dress-makers, swamped by useless presents, pestered by superstitions, admonished by vicars, and frightened by double beds. Otherwise the thing just isn't respectable.

FILMS by MILTON SHULMAN

"Who's that one?" whispers father, tripping over the body of one of the guests, sleeping on the landing, who has arrived for the wedding. "I don't know," whispers back mother, "but don't tread on him."

VINDICTIVE

With twittering aunts to the left of them and jittery in-laws to the right of them, the young couple crack. They quarrel, almost call the whole thing off, and then run away the night before the wedding.

Recognising, however, their duty to society, they return the next morning only to be arrested for knocking down a road sign and a bicycle.

With Terry-Thomas as a vindictive constable sombrely multiplying charges and Miles Malleson as a deaf magistrate mistakenly suspecting that he is trying a Yugoslavian named Moss Bros, this courtroom sequence is very, very funny.

Amiably directed by Roy Boulting, *Happy is the Bride* is a gentle, somewhat patchy, comedy that should please a good many past and future victims of the wedding ritual.

SO POIGNANT

WARTIME heroism has become almost the common coin of the cinema. We many permutations of courage, that its ability to move us is rather tarnished.

Stories of people like Violette Szabo, a young cockney girl whose valour won her the George Cross, tend to be over-sentimentalised tributes, stiff with phoney reverence for their theme.

Carve Her Name With Pride at the Leicester Square avoids these pitfalls. Some liberty has been taken with the romantic aspects of her story—there is little evidence that Violette actually fell in love with the Secret Agent portrayed by Paul Scofield—but there has been no need nor attempt to embellish her bravery.

What makes this film so poignant is the contrast between the humble origins of Violette Szabo, born Bushell, and the unflinching resolution with which she shouldered the ultimate demands of loyalty and courage.

DECISION

She was a 19-year-old shopgirl who wanted some day to be a hairdresser. Born of working-class parents, she spoke perfect French because it was her mother's native tongue.

In 1940 she married a Free French officer who was killed two years later in North Africa, leaving her with a baby daughter he had never seen.

As it does in wartime, the burden of decision was suddenly thrust upon her. She was asked to volunteer as a secret agent to be dropped in German-occupied France.

Miss McKenna . . . superbly moving as an agent tortured by the Gestapo in 'Carve Her Name With Pride.'

film makes its one lapse into false heroics. "I couldn't live the rest of my life knowing I failed to do my bit," the script has her declare as she accepts the job. I am sure someone as genuine as Violette would never have voiced so portentous a cliché.

The sequences in which she is trained as a female commando and parachutist are the usual blend of routine comedy and army acrobatics. But it is when she is dropped in France to discover what has happened to a broken Resistance group and excitement with commendable speed.

Her first mission successfully accomplished, she returns to London.

But with the coming of the Normandy invasion, more trained agents are needed. She is asked to go again. She has a premonition that luck is about to desert her. As she says good-bye to her parents and her baby, we share her forebodings and her agony.

Engaged in plans to delay the arrival of a German division to the battlefront, she and a Frenchman become involved in a running battle with hundreds of enemy troops. Covering his escape with a sub-machine-gun, she kills no fewer than 63 Germans before she is captured.

Tortured by the Gestapo, she refuses to divulge a secret code. Shipped to Ravensbruck, she is shot, with two other British female agents, by a firing squad.

Virginia McKenna, her fragile beauty lacerated into a skeletal mask in the prison scenes, 's superbly moving as a simple girl who did not know why Fate had chosen her to be a heroine, but knew only that courage was both her heritage and her duty.

FIG. 123. An elaborate half-tone cut-out from a *Sunday Express* feature page.

Broadly, these considerations apply not only to photographs but also to line-drawings and wash-drawings, the use of which for feature illustration is a matter of taste and of the quality of the illustrators at a paper's disposal. Artists' work has to be of a high order to compete with the camera when that and its product are well handled.

A word may be added here about the unusual shaping of blocks, by which is meant the cutting of the background to a shape perhaps symbolic or allusive in relation to the accompanying feature. Such shaping can be more effective than an elaborate cut-out. An ingenious example is given in Fig. 122, where a deep double-column half-tone illustrating a film feature has been given a curved cut suggesting a strip of film; this, it will be seen, at once gives movement to the block and breaks it off from the many half-toned advertisements in adjoining columns. Inspirations of this kind will not come every edition, of course, but they are worth watching for. The contrast with the full cut-out should be noted (Fig. 123).

FEATURE PAGE MAKE-UP

The pattern of a feature page must be attractive, attention-compelling, but simple. Complicated, over-elaborate, fussy make-up is always to be avoided. The page needs to have a sense of movement, to be dynamic; even more perhaps than a news page the disposition of its main headlines and illustrations has to be asymmetrical; squared-off, symmetrical

PRINCESS CHARMING'S NEW COIFFURE...

Good for your hair

IT'S tough having only males in your family—particularly at a time like this when the papers are full of pictures of Mr. Dior's "A-Line."

But money hasn't ceased to matter in these days of "equal educational opportunity for all."

Are parents making sacrifices to send their bright sons and daughters to university only to see them made unhappy because they can't "keep up" with wealthier students?

To answer this question—and others—I went to Oxford, where more than two-thirds of the 7,000 undergraduates now have some grant or other.

Full grant aid equals £370 to £385 for an arts student and £400 to £430 for a scientist—but most get less.

Those who win a full grant can get by and have a fairly good time as well. It's a tight squeeze, but they do it. The others, the majority, have to make many sacrifices—and so do their parents—to make ends meet.

● **Recent surveys show most grants are enough *(but only just)* for a careful student living free at home in the vacations and spending not more than £3 a term on pleasure and another £3 on clothes.**

Story" by Frank Colquhoun. *Hodder and Stoughton*, 10s. 6d.) does not claim that all these inquirers were converts.

"It must be stated quite clearly that no claim is made as to the number of conversions that took place during the crusade. That figure is known to God alone."

"I had to take my little boy, Richard, in his cot to the upper deck to sleep in the open from the time we were two days out of Hongkong until we reached Port Said, where it became too cold.

★ ★

"I complained but I was refused any help. An officer told me: 'I am not going to argue with you. I will do nothing.' Another said I was just a troublemaker and that he couldn't care less."

Mrs. Joan Rainford, of Benchill, Manchester, whose husband is a sergeant in the King's Liverpool Regiment, said: "The next cabin to us—another six-berther with me that this was too—was empty from Hongkong to Port Said."

Tthat was the question which led to her 67-year-old blind and crippled grandmother setting out alone on a 20-mile journey.

Mrs. Rainford wrote to Mrs. Bessie Braddock, Labour MP for the Liverpool Exchange Division, who was to have met the liner. But she was detained

● We must be ready to HOUSE bomb-burst, but wide tracks folow lwere given in the look like a piece of Brighton rock.

Among other places, the Bottoms' fairs will go to Putney and Battersea, London, and Great Yarmouth.

and bred among the caravans and lovely bunches of coconuts. **Just for the dash and devil-may-care of it.**

★ ★

Under the new agreement, the entitlement is protected during the first 12 months of employment in outside industry. This is as far as the Board will go.

Where the flood has struck and passed on it has left a mass of slime covering hundreds of square miles. Supplies of anti-typhoid serum were flown into

The union made every endeavour to securr the agreement of the Board to entitlement without date qualification Club, Hastings.

When all they need to do is say "Come on, ducks, have a go"—and then stand on the

MAKE YOUR CAKE NOW

TWO undergraduates I spent several hours with told me their parents make will be given an additional considerable sacrifices to simplest pleasures.

Benchill, Manchester, whose husband is a sergeant in the King's Liverpool Regiment, said: "The next cabin to us—another six-berther — was empty from Hongkong to Port aSid."

dent.

would not agree to the inclusion of widows of men who died from natural causes.

Employment in outside industry: Disabled men who cannot be employed in the mining industry and are absorbed into other employment, were generally speaking, not entitiled to house-coal under the old arrangements when they were not working.

ment to house-coal is governed by the cause of disability or death, and this is determined by the medical authorities.

The rents are so arranged now on two rent-free weeks a year, which they will not have to —about 70,000—who make and run Britain's fairs are still born and bred among the caravans

In fact, I worked myself to a frazzle on that razzle-dazzle

The bus has stopped for me at Greenford the escalator got the general school certificate right in front of the station, and keep them at Oxford, while they themselves have nothing left for more than the which took him to Oswestry High School for Boys. There he

WOMAN'S DAY

Dior atomises that H-Line

ALTHOUGH the oldest Daphne is still one of the most popular girls of any show in spite of the zooming competition of Whirls, Whips and Diving Jets.

How has Cardiff Rural District coveted prizes they are. Frank won one of them.

Frank now had a county grant and a college grant adding up to £210 a year. He went up in October, 1952.

to go up to Oxford, and the money. But even those did not give him a place. For that he . . . and got it.

He sits for his finals at the beginning of June.

had to sit for a commonership

Mr. Colquhoun says that in many of these cases there was no permanent conversion but claims that "there were multitudes of others for whom the crusade was a real means of spiritual ments Board, the middlemen

by NORA WILES

He sings in Oswestry church choir, enters with it for local Eisteddfods.

But under those fair curls, behind those laughing eyes, is a Brain with a capital B.

After all that she hopes to be a university lecturer—"I know that is ambitious, but it is what I want to be." And you know she will.

★ ★

Elaine is no Oxford blue stocking. She comes from Woolton, Liverpool.

Men, women and children were out all night putting up barricades in the path of the Westward-moving wall of water.

This is Elaine's fifth year at only a year and doesn't count in her educational career.

Mrs. Joan Rainford, of evacuated to the Lake District to secure the agreement of the Coal Board to extend the supply

education really began, and stayed there throughout the war.

She graduated there and took a Greats course before winning a scholarship to stay up and do the B Litt course.

"It would have been a struggle if my parents hadn't helped out with a few pounds each term.

£10 a term my parents manage Greats (ancient history, philosophy, Latin and Greek literature) and is now doing her B.Litt. in classics.

Turkey about 1600, were brought to Britain 200 years later, and have been called anything from Whirligigs to Razzle-Dazzles.

Many of the men and women with all the other little boys and blessing and yet whose names were never registered."

Cost of the crusade was about £148,000. Collections at meetings brought in **£56,626—which, considering the huge attendances, gives**

"I have the greatest respect for people who go into public houses and for publicans, but I cannot agree to those licences," he added.

The flats, varying from four to 13 stories, would provide amenities comparable with houses on the ground.

man. That was why he had been excluded.

There was no other public house for more than a mile. But "the licensee apparently wants to keep this a quiet country pub."

Both work in the vacations. So do most other undergraduates at Oxford with grants—as and to give the answer to the anxious question: "Are my relatives all right?"

He has cabled to friends in Sydney to make inquiries for him. The reply will take some time, and until then Mr. Nash and his wife—like hundreds of others—must wait for news to reach Australia House.

All kinds of streamlined trinkets will be on show

THERE was a leg of the octopus and the heart from the love tunnel. I dodged between the dodgems to get to them, but was asked to attend to the horses instead.

"Daphne's your girl," said Mr. Alfred Botton, one of the owners of the fair I was trying to work with in Farnborough, Kent.

Like all fairs in this country they hibernate for the winter, recolouring and rejigging their equipment. I joined them for a day.

Daphne was a grinning, golden horse from a roundabout, to whom I was supposed to give a face-uplift.

I poked her tentatively on the nose.

"Hoi, mask her eyes first," called foreman Jim Frost.

★ ★

I STUCK some brown paper over Daphne's glaring, glassy eyes to keep them clean and pure, and had a bash at her teeth.

But it was far more finicky than cleaning my own teeth.

I found the white paint kept dribbling down Daphne's bright scarlet tongue, which began to look like Brighton rock.

"Here, we can't have that," said Jim, as he expertly finished titivating Daphne himself, scrubbing behind her ears and giving her a bright new coat of gold and red paint.

In a few weeks, most fairs will emerge from their five months' rest and start hitting the roads again: about 250 travelling about Britain every week.

They have to be versatile, too: apart from repairs and painting, I was expected to knock about with carpentry, electrical repairs—and repartee.

You'll get the best - and a bargain - in LINGERIE IN 'Celanese Celshung'

Who says you have to pay a lot for luxury lingerie? Not you—when you discover the range of exquisite Lingerie in 'Celanese Celshung'. Here's everything your heart could wish for—beautiful nighties that stay so fresh looking, pretty panties, sleek-fitting slips, trimly tailored or aflounce with frills—all at prices that come as a happy surprise. A 'Celanese' Acetate Fabric, 'Celshung' has a soft luxurious texture. Easy to wash—long lasting too! There's a host of pretty pastels to choose from—and delectable floral prints.

FIG. 124. A dummy feature page using Ludlow Karnak, in the light and extra-condensed versions as more suitable for women's features. Hauser Script, with a Tempo Heavy Inline strapline, for contrast.

2 DAILY WORKER Friday June 15 1956

Government and Employers Hatch a New Plot Against YOUR WAGES

by J. R. CAMPBELL

THE OTHER OPERATION

Climbing to Power via a Sick Man

Republicans aim to use Eisenhower to win the election—then make Nixon President

by PHILIP BOLSOVER

Eisenhower and Dixon—President and sinister successor.

Training Tomatoes

GARDEN

L. M. Marshall

Give Us Automation in the Home

WASHING-UP

HOMEWORK

DUSTERS

Olga Jeans

TWO PLAYS YOU'LL SEE, LIKE, & ASK FOR MORE

RADIO & TV

by Alison Macleod

EARL CAMERON will be in "Petrified Forest."

Somewhere, over the Rainbow...

A Worker's Notebook

Walter Holmes

Today's Programmes

Daily Worker

FIG. 125. Feature page from the award-winning *Daily Worker* of 1956; praised by the judges for its 'masterly' use of Goudy Bold.

balance on a feature page makes it static and lifeless. This basic approach must constantly guide the correlation of those principles (already outlined in this chapter) which govern the handling of text, headlines, and pictures in effective make-up. A high degree of visualizing skill is obviously necessary, and hence, again, the importance and value of the full-size make-up sheet and precise page-planning described above.

Make-up procedure on feature pages differs from that on news in one obvious respect; it is generally less rushed, less liable to rapid and radical edition changes, and designed to stay through the whole of the run. Nevertheless, certain broad principles of news make-up apply, notably of 'strength below the fold' and of leading the page from the top left. The last point requires some modification, however. A feature page can be effectively led with the lead down page, immediately under, for example, a cartoon across four or more columns. Such make-ups need careful handling to avoid placing top left any subsidiary feature, with a heading across two or more columns, since this produces the anomalous effect of a competing lead. When in any doubt the safest line always is to lead top left (Figs. 124, 125).

12

★ IN PARIS IT'S A BLUE AND WHITE SUMMER

"Let's design a Gas Cooker that lights when you turn the taps!"

. . . said our Lady Consultant

Now we've improved even on the magnificent Flavel 'Envoy'! "Women want a cooker that lights *automatically*" said our Lady Consultant. That's why, in the new 'Envoy III' *every burner, including the oven*, lights at the turn of a tap. Automatic ignition *plus* all the famous 'Envoy' features makes the 'Envoy III' magnificent value at only £50.7.6 (terms available). *It's packed with ideas to make cooking easier, safer and quicker . . . because a woman designed it!*

● *Also available with tall splash-back and plate-rack*

THE ENVOY III

Lights at the turn of a tap!

'Only the 'Envoy III' gives you fully automatic lighting and the exclusive BAKE/WARM control *(which operates at the turn of a tap to keep food warm without drying)* plus all these luxury features:— Short splash-back has built-in timer; 'Glide-over' hotplate stops pans tipping; roomy, enclosed grill; oven big enough for the largest turkey; plate warming drawer

★ VERONICA PAPWORTH

A CERTAIN WINNER AT THE RACES

WELL maybe it was and maybe it wasn't a Black and White Ascot. What is certain is that it's a Blue and White Summer in Paris.

Yes BLUE . . . the colour the men like . . . the colour to match your

Even on Sark the money-bug gets you . . .

SCRATCH any serious City-bound gentleman waiting for the 8.15

Greatest Sale on Earth Begins TOMORROW

BARKERS SALE

FINEST VALUE FOR YEARS!

HANDWOVEN Harris Tweed COATS

Reduced to £6.6.0

TODAY'S VALUE £8.18.6

Generously cut. Swagger style. Fully lined. Lovely Blues, Greens, Brown or Grey Harris mixtures. Short and Average fittings. Hips: 36, 38, 40, 42, 44 and 46in.

ALL WOOL

FIG. 126. A dominating feature illustration which clashes with, and merges into, the display advertising.

The relationship of editorial to advertising display needs to be watched as closely as on news pages (see Chapter 8) and the case for the indication of illustration, particularly half-tones, in the advertising is at least as strong, if not stronger (Fig. 126). Even more than news pages, feature pages require generous whiting—in and around the headings and sub-headings, between stories, and so on—to secure the necessary airiness. On a feature page above all, where ease of reading is the prime need, overcrowding is death, decent white space the breath of life. Ample white is also necessary to accommodate the typographical decoration, a modicum of which undoubtedly helps to enliven a feature page. For what may be called 'area' decoration—the fencing off of a portion of the page, a heading, or a picture, either vertically or horizontally—the firm favourites are alternate black and white stars, in 12 pt. or 14 pt., wide-spaced. For cut-offs between stories, always shortened a few ems each end on the measure, some variant of wavy or dotted border, or the shaded 'simplex', will serve admirably (Fig. 127).

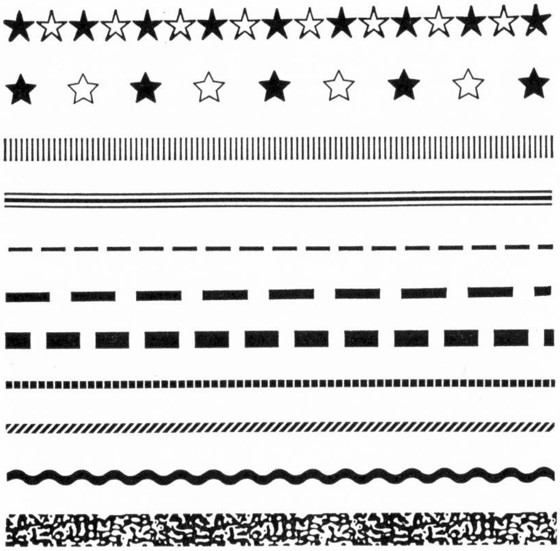

FIG. 127. Black and white stars, fancy rule and simple borders, suitable for feature-page decoration and cut-offs. Following the stars and the 'simplex' these are Monotype strip borders R12, CB 838, 854, 853, 748, 808, 805, 850.

Certain specific problems may be briefly touched on. The *leader page* of the 'class' paper—it is usually also the principal feature page—is much improved when set to a wider measure than the news pages, as is common practice in America. If advertising makes it impossible to change the whole page to wider measure, some convenient bastard measure can be employed at least for the leaders themselves and for the main features. It is understood, of course, that the leaders are set one or two sizes larger than normal text and judiciously leaded. Such pages depend on content rather than on form, and make-up variations from day to day can only be slight.

The *local weekly* frequently lacks the type and process resources, not to mention the editorial artistry, needed for the smart big-daily features styles. Nor is this to be regretted, provided the feature typography and make-up are purposely kept to simpler forms and somewhat more stylized (the *Worthing Herald*, discussed in Chapter 8, is an excellent example). Attempts to imitate the variety and elaboration of some nationals, even when the original is itself effective, range in their results from the unsatisfactory to the deplorable. The whole character of local weekly feature pages calls, in any event, for the simplest elements only of feature style—clear differentiation from news, straightforward and unfussy make-up, and good picture handling.

Special supplements, with an advertising tie-up, can be considered as a special case of feature treatment. Feature setting and make-up are most suitable for them. Display is best either in the paper's main feature style (rather than news style) or in a third style, if fully available. Type mixtures in supplement display are to be avoided; supplements need the uniting effect of single-family typography, ringing the changes on roman and italic, light and bold. It is normal for a supplement to have a distinctive page folio and its own pagination, using roman numerals. Supplements run as an even number of pages in the centre of the paper—the usual form—may be normal full-sheet format or half-sheet (folio or tabloid). The folio makes perhaps a better pull-out format for refolding and separate reading, when that is felt desirable; but the choice of format is principally dictated by the advertising. Though editorial men usually have little, if any, voice in the matter, the point is well worth stressing that consistent and controlled typography for the house-set advertisements in a supplement makes a vast difference to its appearance and further assists in the achievement of that typographical consonance which it requires.

12 · Periodical and Magazine Typography

A NEWSPAPER is a newspaper, typographically speaking; the possible, or desirable, style variations between a small country weekly, a big city evening, a 'popular' national morning, or a 'class' Sunday paper can be fairly closely defined, as the reader should by now have realized. Indeed in some respects these variations are more superficial than fundamental; and the mechanical factors, including the format, the entire printing process, and the paper used, are largely constant. To enter the luxuriant periodical and magazine field is to leave these constant factors behind. Instead we find every variety of format from pocket-size to large folio; every one of the three basic printing processes, letterpress, flat or rotary (and the latter either sheet or web-fed), gravure, litho-offset; every kind of paper from common newsprint to the highest-quality coated; every kind of illustration from simple line-drawings to photographs in full natural colour; every conceivable variation in the specification and combination of types for text and headlines.

The obvious conclusion to be drawn is that the techniques of newspaper typography have little, if anything, to do with the majority of our 4,000 commercial periodicals (weeklies, monthlies, quarterlies) and our 1,200 house journals. There is one exception. Of the periodicals there are nearly 700 trade and technical journals, some of which are done in newspaper style, as are some of the house journals. Here the general considerations advanced in the present book can be effectively applied. These newspaper-style journals usually approximate to tabloid format, though they are sometimes even smaller, and they tend to favour the heavy condensed Sans of classic tabloid technique. This is not always sound practice; for example when the journal is printed flat-bed on coated paper the dense black colour of the large sizes of Sans is too dazzling. Again, a number of these journals eschew the ultra-narrow tabloid column measure, making-up with four or five wider columns; here a condensed letter overweights the headings, which in, say, a five-column page, 12 em measure or thereabouts require a normal width letter as the basic heading style (Fig. 128).

St Michael NEWS

MARKS & SPENCER LTD.

VOL 6 No 7 JULY 1959

"FRIENDLINESS" AND "HIGH STANDARDS OF SERVICE" ARE PRAISED BY CHAIRMAN

St. Michael News Reporter

"THE friendliness which exists between sales staff and customers," and their "high standard of service,' were referred to by the Chairman at the 33rd Annual General Meeting held in the new head offices last month.

"It is with pleasure that I acclaim the fine spirit of service shown by our staff whether in head office or in dealing directly with the public in stores," said Sir Simon.

Before the meeting, those present stood for a moment in memory of Agnes Spencer, widow of the co-founder, Thomas Spencer.

Outlining the continuing work of our technologists and the great basic textile firms, on the wealth of materials, fabrics and finishes now available, Sir Simon drew attention in particular to Nylon, Terylene, Acrilan, Orlon and Tricel.

These new fabrics he said, "had added novelty and variety to the traditional fabrics, wool and cotton. They, in their turn have been given new properties which improve their performance in wear and have eased the burden of washing and ironing."

The Chairman then stressed the co-operation we had received from manufacturers in continuing the company's New Lower Price campaign.

Excellent progress had been made in the Food Division said Sir Simon, and here again "our executives and technologists had co-operated most effectively with some of the leading suppliers in the land."

The Chairman referred to the completion of our move into the new H.O. building and the opportunity it gave us of further streamlining operations.

Store Development

Of store development he said: "the size and character of the building projects we have evolved since the war are costly and take a considerable time to complete. They are important buildings and are notable landmarks in the shopping areas where they are situated."

During the year eleven major extensions involving considerable rebuilding had been completed, fifteen further substantial projects were in hand. New important schemes would be added to the list as soon as the necessary plans were completed.

Manufacturers

In paying tribute to manufacturers Sir Simon Marks said: "I am glad to pay tribute to our manufacturers for their splendid co-operation during the past year. They realise that our trade mark ST. MICHAEL, stands high in the esteem of the public as the symbol of good taste, quality and value.

"It is with satisfaction that I can say that our friends have helped us not only to maintain, but to enhance the prestige of ST. MICHAEL, which has become a household word. It is a source of great pride to us that we can state that 99 per cent of our goods and the materials used in them are of British manufacture."

NEW PACKS FOR OVER HALF MEN'S UNDERWEAR — SOON

St. Michael News Reporter

NEW polythene packs for all men's combed cotton underwear are planned.

Introduced into stores about 2½ years ago, combed cotton underwear accounts for well over half our total sales of athletic underwear.

The new polythene-packed lines will be extended to all stores running combed cotton lines, in the autumn, and will, it is claimed, considerably improve the appearance of the counter, as well as facilitating service.

At the same time a "double-knit" line will arrive, which is being made on exactly the same type of machine that produces the double jersey dresses. Good news for stores: there will be unlimited production of double-knit lines.

Three Knits

Customers will therefore have a choice, not only of three different knits—spring, mesh or double-but also possibly of colours. Blue has recently been tried out in a few stores with reasonable success, and other colours may follow in due course. No promises, but the future certainly looks brighter.

Artistry

★James Fitton, R.A., opening the Cookham Arts Club 18th annual exhibition, made reference to Cookham's distinguished painter son, Sir Stanley Spencer. Said Mr. F.: "To separate Spencer from Cookham in the art world is as impossible as separating Spencer from Marks in the business world."

★ FOR CHILLIER DAYS AHEAD ★

★All right then, so the summer can't last for ever. That's why SHE has a 39s. 11d. printed nylon umbrella to protect her 29s. 11d. wool-and-cotton blouse and her gorgeously reversible Acrilan-and-wool skirt she gave 59s. 11d. for. HE needs protection too, not only for himself but for his cotton twill 24s. 11d. shirt. He chose green, but could have had grey, salmon or brown. With it, a rust wool tie for 5s. 11d. He wears the trousers — they're linen and Terylene, and cost 55s. Colours: store, navy and blue.

Picture by Derrick Woolacott

★ ★ ★ ★ ★ ★ ★ ★ ★ ★ ★

This issue of St. Michael News has been produced under great difficulties by directors and apprentices.

We apologise for any delays or irregularities which may have occurred.

Sunday Pictorial's questions

News Reporter

LAST month, the *Sunday Pictorial* ran a fashion quiz, in conjunction with Marks & Spencer, to discover teen-age style and colour preferences.

Questions

Pictorial readers were invited to put in order of preference, fashion colours scarlet, pale blue, charcoal grey and lime green. They were asked: their favourite skirt style, whether they liked frilly petticoats, did they go shopping alone or with mother, did they prefer shirts or the more feminine blouses, and were they able to find clothes that were the right size?

And a few weeks later came these answers:

Top favourite colour is pale blue, followed by charcoal grey. Pleated skirts top the list of styles they buy, and frilly petticoats are top priority in every wardrobe.

Mother came too

Mother goes along in two cases out of three on clothes shopping expeditions she probably helps out with a little extra cash if its needed!

Shirt blouses please but pastel colours are more popular than bright shades.

Their biggest headache is finding clothes that will fit them, and this includes bras and girdles too.

Mary Welbeck

Says Mary Welbeck: *I take these findings with a fairly large grain of fashion salt. After all the teen-age group is inclined to be fickle in its enthusiasms. Their criticisms regarding suitable styles and lack of correct size ranges gets my sympathy they have a strong case here.*

DOUBLE-LIFER!

★This woman is leading a double life! Details page 4.

Store Site 'Paradise'

News Reporter

THE front-page story in the May issue of the NEWS continues to evoke considerable interest and comment in the building trade.

Among many letters received from contractors all over the country, is one from the President of the Building Surveyors' Institute (Midland Region). Mr. Lintern-Mole, who says: "I think this is a matter which is of great interest to all members in this area, and I would appreciate six further copies of ST. MICHAEL NEWS to pass on to others in the Midlands."

In Wales, the *South Wales Echo* visited the Charles Street, Cardiff, building site. Under the heading "Building Site is Workers' Paradise," was this story: "Men turn up in their best suits, change into their working clothes and leave after a hard day's work clean, tidy and well fed.

"For the contractors have installed a washroom, dining-room and a changing-room for the employees.

"Trade union officials are delighted at the scheme. 'This is well in advance of any other site for welfare conditions,' said a union official. 'If only other people would copy the idea.'

"It's all part of a new trend in building trade welfare, pioneered by the management of Marks & Spencer Ltd."

HOLD EVERYTHING!

★"Well, why not? You call it a hold-all, so surely that includes me? Not quite up to Pullman standards, I agree, but the service is excellent," says nine-month-old Susan Neal, snapped by a NEWS photographer when her mother brought her into Portsmouth, Commercial Road, last week.

TOP EMBROIDERERS WORKING FOR M & S

FROM the *Manchester Guardian* of June 12: "The firm of Forster Willi, who will work overnight to supply a few exclusive yards of guipure required by, say, Balenciaga or Hardy Amies, have on their books orders for thousands of yards of lingerie material for Marks & Spencer."

Comments Miss B. E. Werner: "As we use so much Swiss embroidery on our lingerie, it's interesting to know that Forster Willi, as well as supplying Balenciaga and Hardy Amies, are suppliers of Marks & Spencer!"

BRI-LON AND BRI-NYLON — BRITISH NYLON

TWO new names for British nylon—Bri-Nylon and Bri-Lon will be appearing on all Marks & Spencer ticketing, labels and other point-of-sale publicity, in September.

Initially, the Marks & Spencer ticket wording will be along the lines of: "Brushed nylon night-dresses in Bri-Lon," or "Nylons in Bri-Nylon."

The great point about the new names is that they give the correct connotation of "British." The names—it is claimed by British Nylon Spinners—are also easily pronounceable.

Extensive research by BNS reveals that the names have a very high "awareness figure"—representative age and income groups recognised the materials covered by the two words.

Provisionally, Bri-Nylon in Marks & Spencer will cover all lines in nylon, other than brushed nylon, which will be covered by Bri-Lon.

British Nylon Spinners are embarking on a major advertising campaign to popularise the two names.

FIG. 128. A house journal presented in newspaper style.

In short, there are often shortcomings in the application of newspaper techniques to this sort of periodical; but to overcome these defects needs no more than the proper application of those techniques; and there this matter may well be left. What, now, of the much wider field of the periodical or magazine proper, to which newspaper techniques do not apply? It is quite beyond the specialized scope of this book to examine this question in any detail; to do so would call for a separate work of at least equal length. All that can be attempted here is to indicate in broad outline the nature of the problem, or problems, and to suggest the sort of approach needed for its solution.

At the outset it is necessary to stress the duality in this chapter's title—'periodical and magazine'. All magazines are periodicals but all periodicals are not magazines. The dividing line is often fuzzy; there are not a few marginal cases; but the broad distinction can, and must, be made. By periodical is meant the special-interest professional, technical or trade (including trade union), and politico-literary journals. Their typography and make-up are simple and straightforward—functional, if you like—without needing to vary substantially. Their selective appeal is definitely based on their content. A two- or three-column format is normal, illustration is either at a minimum or only incidental, and a self-cover often suffices. If a coloured cover is provided, usually by way of the title-line in colour or a bold reverse treatment in colour incorporating all or part of the title-line, this is often the only colour in the journal. The *British Medical Journal* or the *Lancet*, the *New Statesman*, *Spectator*, *Economist*, or *Listener*, to name but a few at random, are characteristic of journals in this category (Fig. 129).

It is in fact wrong to regard a selective, limited, or specialized appeal as the essential criterion of these formalized and unvarying styles in periodical typography. Some of these publications have circulations far larger than some magazines whose styles are highly informal and constantly varying. The true criterion is one of function. If the function is to inform or instruct, rather than to entertain or distract, then some kind of fixed and formalized style is the most suitable. Nothing, after all, could be more highly formalized, or more calculatedly functional, than the typography of the periodical with the largest circulation of all—the *Radio Times*.

The typography of the periodicals indicated may be regarded in some respects as an extension of book typography. For text they use bookish types (Times, Monotype Plantin 110, Baskerville, Imprint) with a related Bold or some elegant display letter—the *New Statesman* was the first in the field with Linotype Minerva Bold—for headlines. A typographer skilled in bookwork is obviously well equipped to design a fitting and effective dress for periodicals of this type, and many indeed have done so. The typography of the *magazine*, on the other hand, is an extension, or perhaps more properly a special development, of commercial display (including advertising) typography. Its design is best entrusted to the typographer specially skilled in display, the graphic arts representative of the modern fraternity of 'industrial artists'. In designing a magazine such a typographer is functioning in the accepted sense of an industrial artist or designer—one who 'is concerned with the right choice and use of materials, with proportion, form, colour, tone and line, with fitness for purpose in the object to be produced and with the aesthetic satisfaction which it gives to those who see or use it'.[1]

NEW STATESMAN 12 SEPTEMBER 1959 295

those who do not gain admission – one suspects this would be a popular policy with university staff – or that university doors are opened fully, on the American pattern. In that case it would be essential to develop Oxford, Cambridge, London and other universities to a particularly high level and to expand organised graduate studies for examination as well as thesis. Until a Royal Commission has investigated the whole university system it is impossible to decide which of these policies offers the best alternative to self-determination, just as it is difficult to decide upon the best size for a university in a particular place, or where new colleges are to be built, how much say academic staff should have in university government, or if Oxford and Cambridge are to be permitted to occupy their special place in the system. Decisions taken now will influence university policy for years to come; but discussions taking place in the University Grants Committee and the universities are not an adequate substitute for an exhaustive enquiry into the whole system. Fears that setting up a Commission presents in some way a threat to academic freedom are groundless.

News from Our Own Correspondents

New Delhi

Menon Under Fire

Our Correspondent in Delhi writes: The Menon-Army defence crisis, it is generally agreed here, goes much deeper than a clash of personalities or temperaments. It is also felt that its real causes have not been disclosed. Army promotions do not explain the disagreement between Mr Krishna Menon and General Thimayya. The Prime Minister's statement in the Lok Sabha seemed to make it clear that army promotions with a few exceptions have been effected after consulting the Chief of Staff. But Mr Nehru gave no direct reply to the question, as one observer put it, 'whether or not the promotions in the army during Mr Menon's stewardship of the Defence Ministry had been fostered on grounds other than merit, and whether or not merit has been subordinated to Mr Menon's peculiar predilections'.

Mr Menon's 'peculiar predilections', and what is often termed his unconventional behaviour, have frequently been commented upon by his critics, sometimes unkindly—he was, for instance, once referred to as the 'ugly face' of India's foreign policy. His political leanings have been suspect even in his own party; it is considered significant that during parliament's discussion of the crisis he stood isolated from, by and large, his party as a whole, till Mr Nehru came to his rescue. Embarrassing support for Mr Menon came unstinted from the Communists. Apart from his publicly suspected political inclinations, Mr Menon's name has been associated with financial irregularities in the Ministry. Recently, the audit report on the country's defence services spoke of 'important financial irregularities', of 'avoidable expenditure', of 'infructuous purchases', and of 'fictitious financial adjustments'. The report complained that these irregularities had been pointed out with 'tireless regularity'. It is believed by many that the super-sessional promotions have been made by Mr Menon without consulting General Thimayya, and that these were dictated by political considerations primarily. Those who think this way point to the instance of Lieutenant-General B. M. Kaul, lately Major-General. He was on General Thimayya's staff in Korea, and the impression is that General Thimayya was not absolutely convinced of his personal loyalty. It is also alleged that, contrary to the traditions of the defence services, General Kaul keeps in touch with political leaders. He is known to admire the Chinese concept of mass armies, and is said to have strongly advocated it for the Indian army. Opinion in the army has little sympathy for him.

There is a general disposition to speculate on Mr Menon's real intentions. It is generally accepted that he has consistently shown sympathy for a certain kind of dictatorship. While it is unlikely that there is any immediate cause for concern, or that Mr Menon can easily maneouvre into a position of power (in any case he does not really appear to be the stuff that dictators are made of), the possibility cannot be ruled out of his introducing, even if unintentionally, a kind of confusion which others, inside or outside the army, might ambitiously attempt to use to their advantage. Doubts and fears in this respect in certain quarters in India arise from a number of factors. These include the emergence of dictatorships in some neighbouring countries; the mild discontent caused by delay in fulfilment of promises under the Five-year Plans and a too gradual unfolding of social development; and the existence of widespread corruption in the administration.

Meanwhile, whatever assurances Mr Nehru may or may not have privately given to General Thimayya, the problem of Menon is temporarily solved by his absence in New York as leader of the Indian delegation at the UN. During this time, Mr Nehru himself will take charge of the Defence Ministry. He will thus have ample opportunity to study the state of affairs for himself. In the meantime, conjectures are already being made on possible successors to Mr Menon.

Moscow

Red Riviera

Our Moscow Correspondent writes: This summer about 50,000 visitors from the People's Democracies, mainly Czecho-Slovakia, Poland and East Germany, have spent their holidays on a stretch of the Black Sea coast in Bulgaria, and plans to accommodate twice that number next year have been drawn up. Except for two or three hotels near the former royal palace outside Varna (the old name has been officially restored: for a short time it was known as Stalin), brand new buildings—'rest homes', hotels, motels and holiday camps—have housed these tourists. This new Red Riviera, created during the past three years, is, in short, becoming the main playground of eastern Europe, a powerful counter-attraction to the Adriatic littoral.

One is told by Bulgarians over glasses of *mastika* and sliced tomatoes that in the late Forties a premature-Krushchevite put forward a plan to develop the sandy shores of the Black Sea for international tourism, that he was severely criticised for it, and demoted. But later, the story runs, Krushchev himself, while on an unofficial visit to Bulgaria, pointed to the coast-line from the yacht on which he was discussing Bulgaria's economic problems and said: 'There is your gold'. The official was reinstated and his plan brought out of the files. The story may be apocryphal; the fact remains that, by developing this coast-line, Bulgaria has found a way of correcting its balance of payments with the lands from whom it imports the machinery so badly needed to modernise its food-processing industries and agriculture. One of the most striking signs of an improved foreign exchange position is the fact that during the past few months foreign cars, British, West German, and French as well as Skodas, Volgas and Warszawas have appeared on the market.

Most of the building along the coast between the Dubrudja town of Baltchik and the ancient Greek colony of Nassebar has been done to the designs of a group of young architects, who have never been abroad but who admit that their principal sources of reference are films of the Brussels Exhibition and American and French architectural journals. The result is a complete break with the Stalinist tradition in architecture. Unlike people working in other spheres of art in Bulgaria, the architects have been given a free hand and their solution is a wholly cosmopolitan one, although elements of national tradition may be found in a restricted use of local tufa and an occasional application of the abstract patterns of Byzantine art. It would be difficult to find a greater contrast with the Soviet resorts of Sochi, Gagra, Sukhumi etc., on the opposite shores of the Black Sea. Soviet holiday resorts, in the main, still aim at fulfilling the function of curing the workers' occupational diseases, and though the pattern is changing rapidly (one sees far fewer people in baggy, institutional pyjamas than two or three years ago), it is the sanatorium and the rest home that sets the tone.

One reason why the Bulgarian riviera is so different is, of course, that, while the inmates of Soviet holiday establishments are mostly factory workers, miners and farmers, the tourists in Bulgaria are party functionaries, intellectuals, office workers and professional people drawn to what has become known as the most *chic* series of beaches in eastern Europe. Polish and Slovak eyebrows rose when a generously-proportioned Russian woman removed an ankle-length satin gown on a Varna beach and sun-bathed in a pair of tight men's trunks and an elaborate pink bra. Soviet rest homes are 'dry', but light wines and strong spirits flow freely in Varna's Domino Bar and Neesebar's Casino. Excellent jazz is to be heard in the Bulgarian hotels and when a spell of accomplished jiving by Polish dancers in an international bar brought a smile of approval to the face of a visiting Mongolian, there was a general feeling that here at least Cold War prejudices were being shed. There are no portraits or busts of leaders, living or defunct, no exhortations to grow more maize or 'fight for peace' along the roads that have been driven through the littoral scrub, snake-infested until two truck-loads of hedgehogs were imported.

To this extent the Red Riviera offers an escape from the tensions and restrictions of eastern

ELECTION SPECIAL

During the coming weeks we shall be publishing a series of special articles designed to spotlight important issues on which the general election should be fought. Appearing next week will be

The Challenge of Africa

by Dingle Foot, QC, MP

FIG. 129. A typical inside page of the *New Statesman*.

[1] F. A. Mercer, *The Industrial Design Consultant* (1947), p. 22.

The difference between newspaper and magazine make-up, reduced to its simplest elements, has been expressed thus by an American authority: 'instead of a score of units to weave into a pattern that the newspaper designer has, the magazine make-up man has the headline, several pieces of art and only one block of type'.[1] The permutations and combinations of those three elements, however, can be most complex. Headline typography may vary from page to page, calling on all the tricks of type-processing, stripping, or reversing headings over pictures, which themselves may be disposed to make a vast variety of patterns and frequently 'bled-off' at one or other margin; text measure and style may freely change; and these are but a few of the items of typographical and pictorial flux out of which magazine pages emerge. This is to say nothing about the full colour effects available with the litho-offset and gravure processes, demanding great artistry for their effective and agreeable exploitation.

Further discourse on this infinite variety is really superfluous. Perusal of any half-dozen or dozen leading magazines is sufficiently instructive. It is enough to take two fields only: women, home, and fashion—ranging from the colourgravure mass weeklies like *Woman* and *Woman's Own* to the 'glossies' like *Vogue* and *Harper's*; and the picture weeklies, at a discount maybe in this country since the demise of *Picture Post*, but brilliantly exemplified—with studied typography and pictorial *panache*—in the American *Life* and *Look*, in *Paris-Match*, and the German *Quick*. In addition there is always the luxurious *Fortune* (Fig. 130).

Design and make-up of magazines like these demand a synthesis of artistic and typographic mastery. On that basis, and only on that basis, it is both possible and desirable to show some audacity, to be experimental. Once again an American authority may be cited: 'the magazines of the United States are a laboratory for continuous experiment in the graphic arts . . . in typography, illustration, the arrangement of diverse matter on the printed page . . . the art editor . . . can afford to be adventurous in the knowledge that his trial flights are not for the ages but can be superseded by others equally daring next week or next month'.[2] Experiment for experiment's sake, however, or experiment for the gratification of the designer's esoteric caprice, can be a sterile thing. Beware the epitaph once pronounced on a professional journal—'the patterns made by the pages are amusing to examine, almost impossible to read'. Magazine page patterns have to be, if not amusing, attractive; but never at the cost of the page's ease of reading.

At this point it is worth noting that the distinction drawn above between

[1] Arnold, op. cit., p. 276.

[2] Quoted in Dowding, op. cit., pp. 30–31. Mr. Dowding's own comments are well worth study.

A city of music and friendliness

by ANTHONY RHODES

THE GREATEST of all international conferences took place in Vienna, in 1814. And in July and August, for the first time in 150 years, another Congress of Vienna, on almost the same scale, took place, but of a different kind. At the end of July, 15,000 "delegates" from all the corners of the globe arrived in Vienna for the Communist sponsored "World Festival of Youth". But the Viennese, whose name is a byword for hospitality, have failed to live up to their tradition. The Viennese press boycotted the Festival by refusing to print a word about it, and other youth movements in the city arranged counter-attractions. Yet this Marxist jamboree in the city of the Habsburgs has aroused much amused interest among the Viennese. "It is not often" they said, "that we can hear a Burmese nose-flute player, a Ukranian Bandura player, and a fellow-travelling Scottish bagpipe player, all competing for the folk-lore prize in front of a Brazilian judge."

It was in the reign of Francis I, the emperor of the Vienna Congress, that this typical Viennese attitude was created. Frivolous, easy-going, above all non-political, this remark belongs to the picture the Viennese have, rightly or wrongly, drawn of themselves. It is described by the Viennese word, (unknown in other Teutonic lands), *schlamperei* implying amiability, politeness, nonchalance together with, on the debit side, a lack of endurance, an excessive, a light-hearted criticism of everything,

Schönbrunn - once the palace of Austrian Emperors, now open to the public. Today the grounds are still kept by three hundred gardeners. Photographs by Erich Lessing.

27

FIG. 130. Opening page of an illustrated feature in a 'glossy'—*The Queen.*

the periodical and the magazine in respect of the typographical qualifications their design demands—the first the book typographer, the second the display typographer—is not one that can be rigidly maintained. That is to say, any suggestion that the typography of the magazine is all display, with text as a secondary consideration, would be most misleading, precisely because of the basic ease of reading requirement already stressed. And the fundamentals of agreeable typography for continuous, or semi-continuous, reading are: good letter design in text sizes, the relation of type size to measure, the finer points of setting, the importance of leading, learnt from the typography of the book. The magazine, too, usually has better opportunity to follow the highest standards here than has the newspaper; among other things, it is frequently Monotype-set, enjoying the spacing refinements possible with that mode of composition.

If misapprehensions about the true relationship of book and magazine typography have now been corrected, emphasis may again be laid on the radical difference between the overall typography of the magazine and the book. It has been vigorously and authoritatively stated by John Farleigh, a noted designer, in these words:

> A magazine is not a book. The fundamental difference between a book and a magazine is that a book is a unit and a magazine is not. A book consists of a story by one author or stories and articles chosen from different authors, brought together with the idea of creating a unit. A magazine is a different proposition. . . . It is very similar to a street of shops; each shop window is as different from another as it can be, because each has something different to sell and something different to say. The individuality of each shop is the excitement of a street of shops. A magazine is consciously designed to appear as different on every opening as it can be; that is part of the structure of a magazine. Then there is the element of advertising running through it; each article that is being offered must be presented with the maximum variety. Therefore rules which apply to a book do not apply to a magazine. You can have a very formal page immediately followed by a drawing that is spreading, a different arrangement of type, paper of a different colour and type. The more variety there is, the more exciting is the magazine. This is the essence of magazine production.[1]

Variety as here extolled is limited typographically in two ways, technical and aesthetic; the first derives from the requirements of the printing process (including the desired and/or possible paper), the second from the doctrine of fitness for purpose, particularly germane to the multiplicity of magazine 'personalities', if it may be put that way.

Type behaves differently within the same process according to the paper upon which it is printed. In flat-bed letterpress, for example, antique, smooth, or coated papers are each suited to some types and not to others; broadly the distinction lies between the Old Face letter (best for the more absorbent antiques) and the fine-seriffed Moderns, from Bodoni and Walbaum onwards with their quality of contrast (best for the less absorbent smooth papers). Coated papers, the vehicle of the fine-screen

[1] John Farleigh, *It Never Dies*, p. 92. See also Herbert Jones, 'The Magic Power of Magazines', *Penrose Annual* (1958).

half-tone, need a strong-coloured letter like Plantin—or perhaps Times Roman, Monotype Ehrhardt (Series 453), Linotype Janson—to withstand the thinning effect of printing on their impervious surface. Rotary letterpress adds the complications of stereotyping, already considered in relation to newspaper production; many magazine rotaries, however, use plates of slight curvature only, and the distortion of mat shrinkage rarely arises. Rotary magazine printing presents certain differences of its own, however, in type reproduction; varying procedures—sheet-fed on high-grade surfaced paper, web-fed on newsprint (of differing degrees of finish) or on super-calendered mechanical printings—yield varying results.

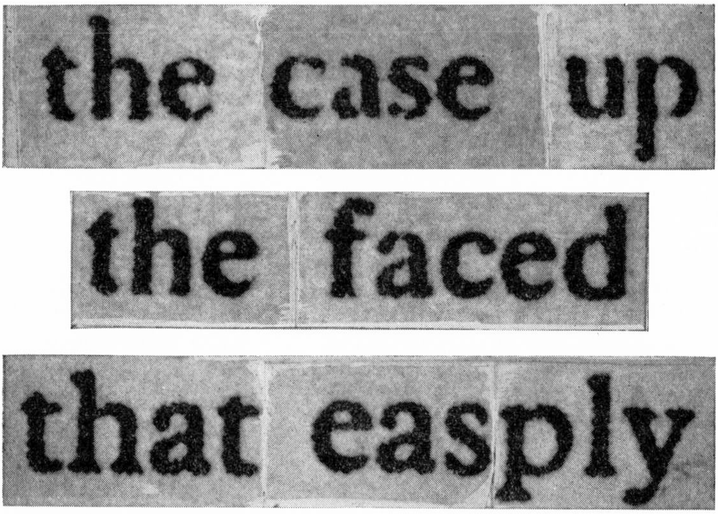

FIG. 131. Gravure-printed type, enlarged six times—respectively Perpetua, Times, Plantin 110. Note the differences in serif-reproduction.

Enough has been said to suggest the complex factors affecting the choice of type for a letterpress magazine job, factors which require close co-operation from the start between the printer and the designer. The complexities, or rather the limitations, do not lessen when we turn to the two other main processes, rotary photogravure and offset. Type, after all, is designed for letterpress, designed to be printed from as a relief surface impressed on to, or in to, paper. Gravure and offset, not being relief processes, only use type as a means of securing a 'reproduction proof', for photomechanical reproduction on a cylinder or plate; they are as well, or better, served by photocomposed film. Since both are 'impressionless' processes they cannot emulate the crisp typographic quality of letterpress. Both tend to soften the type outline, though gravure does so to a greater extent than offset; indeed, well-managed offset will give a very fair reproduction of most types, lacking merely the 'bite' of letterpress impression.

The development of high-speed web-fed offset may change the position; but at the time of writing (1960) rotary photogravure still dominates the mass-circulation, colour-illustrated, magazine field. The behaviour of type under gravure conditions is thus of particular importance. To the general softening effect of an impressionless process gravure adds a tendency to thicken or coarsen; and the gravure screen has an eroding effect on type outline and serifs. Thus bold faces are unsuitable, as are the more delicate Old Faces and the fine-seriffed Moderns. Faces of even but not heavy colour, open design, and stout serifs stand up best to gravure; a tentative list would include Linotype Jubilee, Electra, and Pilgrim (perhaps also Juliana), Monotype Plantin Light (Series 113), Ehrhardt (Series 453), and Bembo (Series 270), not forgetting the standard Old Styles which, though undistinguished, pass the gravure test well. Though not agreeable for lengthy text, the modern light Sans (Gill, Metro) or Egyptian (Rockwell, Memphis) faces also offer good gravure reproduction; and their heavier versions are useful for bold emphasis or subheading (Fig. 131).

So much for the technical limitations on choice of types for magazine work. They have been described from the basic standpoint of the text type; even given the problems of process and paper there is, for obvious reasons, more freedom with the larger display sizes. Here, however, the aesthetic, fitness for purpose limitation operates. The point has been touched on in Chapter 11, and clearly is of much more extensive and varied application in the periodical and magazine field than it can ever be in a newspaper.

The evocative qualities of display types are not, it need hardly be said, a matter of precise determination, but a matter of art. No one can present an exhaustive list of type faces certified suitable for a magazine of this or that character. The whole mystery of apt display typography, as applied here, is comprised in the practitioner's acquired ability to select—and properly handle—the types which effectively express a magazine's specific character and appeal. These few suggestions may illustrate the point:

Elegance. Slimblack, Onyx (Series 591), Corvinus Bold, Bell (Series 341) and italic, the lighter weights of the new-old German Grotesques (e.g. Standard, Venus), the revived Antiques (e.g. Consort).

Domesticity. Goudy Bold and italic, Caslon Old Face Heavy (with its colourful italic if in the Ludlow version).

Practicality. Sans (either modern or the Victorian Grots and Gothics) or the Egyptians; use the heavier weights.

Science and Art. Times Bold and Bold Titlings, Perpetua Bold (Series 461) with their respective light italics for contrast, Albertus (Series 481).

Entertainment (*including Sport*). Playbill or Figaro (Series 536), the Fat Faces—Ultra Bodoni, Falstaff (Series 323); including Thorne Shaded.

That these selections are in a sense arbitrary can be seen from the fact that, given a variation in weight, they are easily interchangeable. The heavier versions of the German Grotesques, for example, are suitable for practicality, not elegance. Goudy Old Style and its beautiful italic express elegance, not domesticity; the light modern Sans faces, with their italics, likewise evoke elegance, not practicality. The wider the selection the more it will be found that the weight (light, medium, bold, heavy) and style (roman, italic) are together factors at least as important in determining the evocative quality of a type face as the type design itself (Fig. 132).

GOUDY BOLD

Goudy Old Style italic

GILL EXTRA

Gill Sans Light italic

FIG. 132. Examples of bold/light, roman/italic contrast. Monotype Goudy Bold (269) with Goudy Oldstyle (291), Gill Extra Bold (321) with Gill Light (362).

Attention may here be drawn to the particular importance, in some cases for use on their own in magazine headlining, in others for combination with the types suggested above, of the faces falling into the categories —in the very broadest sense—of decorative types and scripts. In either category the more fancy the letter the greater the discipline and judgement required in its handling. Just as the correct dose of an exotic type can give the perfect finishing touch to a magazine headline, too much can reduce it to a bizarre jumble. Nor, in these cases, can the subtleties of setting be ignored. Judicious letter-spacing is more often than not a prime necessity; while the positioning—left, centre, right—the whiting, and ranging of lines require constant consideration.

The types properly described as 'decorated' are for the most part too ornate for use other than as occasional, and very special, initial letters. In this category are normally included Gill Floriated Initials (Series 431), Lilith, Raffia Initials, and Victoriana like Lettres Ornées or Scroll Shaded. Less fanciful letter like Fry's Ornamented or Vesta can be discreetly employed in headline display (Fig. 133).

NEWSPAP

Newspaper Headlines

NEWSPAPER HEADLINE

NEWSPAPER HEAD

NEWSPA

NEWSPAPER HE

FIG. 133. First of these decorated types is Monotype Gill Floriated (431), the others all typefounders—Lilith (Bauer), Vesta (Berthold), Scroll Shaded (Stevens, Shanks), Raffia (Amsterdam), Fry's Ornamented (Stephenson, Blake).

It is not in this restricted category, in any event, that the real repertory of decorative types is to be found, but in the large and extremely varied 'outline, shaded and three-dimensional' class. There are the *outline* types proper, like Bold Face Outline (Series 176), Champleve, Old Face Open, Moreau-le-Jeune (Gravure Open); the *shaded* types like Cameo, Goudy Handtooled, Imprint Shadow (Series 190), Caslon Old Face Heavy Open, Castellar Titling (Series 600), Gill Sans Shadowline (Series 290), and the fine-lined Prisma or Fatima (Atlas); the *inline* types like Chisel, Colonna (Series 225), Delphian, Tempo Heavy Inline, Phosphor; the *three-dimensionals* like Festival (Series 554), Umbra (Gill Shadow 406, Granby Shadow), Orplid (Gill Shadow Titling 304), Graphique, Profil, Sanserifs Shaded, Echo, Thorne Shaded, Elongated Roman Shaded, Rockwell Shadow (Series 175), Beton Open (Figs. 134, 135).

These lists look formidable, though in fact they only represent a selection of the more readily available types; the great range in character and style caters for every typographic-decorative *nuance*. To these 'decoratives' must be added the scripts. First come those non-script types which have a certain calligraphic quality (of pen or brush) in their design:

OS BOLD Outline featur

IMPRINT Shadow features

GILL Shadow Line features well

CASTELLAR FEATUR

COLONNA features well in you

CAMEO has its *italic too*

DELPHIAN CAPS ONLY

TEMPO HEAVY INLI

OLD FACE OPEN FE

CHAMPLEVE FEATURE

GRAVURE Open features w

CHISEL features well in

GOUDY Handtooled has its

ATLAS FEATURE

FIG. 134. Outline, shaded, and inline types: the Bold Outline (176), Imprint (190), Gill (290), Castellar (600), Colonna (225), all Monotype; the Cameo, Delphian, Tempo all Ludlow; rest typefounders.

GRAPHIQUE FEATURES WELL

PROFIL FEATURE

SANS SERIFS SHADED

ELONGATED ROMAN SHADED F

THORNE SHADED

ECHO FEATURE

FESTIVAL FEATURES

GILL SHADOW FEATU

GILL SHADOW TITLIN

ROCKWELL SHADOW

FIG. 135. Three-dimensional types: the first six typefounders—Graphique and Profil from Haas (Basle), Sans Shaded to Echo from Stephenson, Blake—the remainder Monotype, respectively Series 554, 406 (Ludlow Umbra is practically the same), 304 (comparable to Klingspor's Orplid), 175.

KLANG features well in your pa

MATURA features well in your

Allegro features well in your paper

Studio Bold features w

Post Roman features well in papers

FIG. 136. Some calligraphic or brush-script types: the first two Monotype (Series 593, 496 respectively); the rest typefounders—Allegro (Ludwig & Mayer), Studio (Amsterdam), Post (Berthold).

Allegro, Klang (Series 593), Cartoon, Post Roman, Studio, Steel, Matura (Series 496). The scripts proper range from the informal and usually bold brush scripts to the formalism of copperplate; they form one of the most luxuriant post-war type crops, and again only a representative selection is given here. Among the informal brush scripts are Ashley Script (Series 574), Balzac, Beta, Choc, Flash (Series 473), Holla, Hauser, Mercurius (Series 584), with Swing Bold (Series 583) and Scribe somewhat more calligraphic; the informal pen scripts include Mistral—the most notable for the present purpose—Legend and Reiner Script; the semi-formal Trafton Script and Coronet (particularly its Bold) have marked elegance,

Monoline Script features well in

Coronet Bold has its place in your fea

Mercury features well in your pa

Palace Script features well in your

FIG. 137. Scripts of semi-formal or formal character—Monotype (351), Ludlow, and two typefounders (Palace Script is also available as Monotype 429).

Ashley Script features well in your

Mercurius features well in

Swing Bold features well in your pape

Pepita features well in your paper

Hauser Script has its place in your features

Mistral features well in your pap

Choc features well in your paper

Balzac features well in your paper

Beta features well in your paper

Scribe features well in paper

Legend features well in your paper

Reiner Script features well in your paper

FIG. 138. 'Informal' scripts: the first four Monotype (574, 584, 583, 613), Hauser Ludlow; the rest typefounders—Mistral (Amsterdam), Choc (Olive), Balzac (Stempel), Beta (Bauer), Scribe (Deberny & Peignot), Legend (Bauer), Reiner Script (Amsterdam).

which is not a feature of the monotone formal scripts Monoline (Series 351) and Mandate; two typical copperplates are Marina Script and Palace Script (Series 429) (Figs. 136–8).

Enough has now been said to indicate the embarrassingly rich typographic resources available to provide the variety which, as John Farleigh emphasized above, is essential to a magazine. The kind of thematic variation in headlining practised, for example by the *Readers' Digest*, or the more fanciful variegations in page make-up suitable for the larger-format 'glossies' or gravure journals, can both be assisted by a deft admixture of the decoratives and the scripts. The deftness is the thing; for the effective combination of widely differing type faces is not easily attained.[1] It is important to evaluate correctly the size relationship and to avoid the mating of extremes (e.g. a fat-face main line and an extra-condensed subsidiary; or a light three-dimensional like Festival with a heavy brush script like Ludlow Hauser). The simple device of using a fancy roman initial, usually one or two sizes larger, to a display line in lower-case italic, will further illustrate the point. Suppose the italic is Caslon Old Face or Gara-

MODEL HO

Exhibition excites buyers

REPRODUCTION

Old Masters seen perfectly

UNFAIR MIXTURE

This too heavy

FIG. 139. Three decorative combination headline-settings: (i) Thorne Shaded/Ashley Script, (ii) Fry's Ornamented/Caslon Old Face italic are both agreeable, while (iii) Festival/Mercurius is an example of an unsuitable and ugly combination.

[1] Dowding, op. cit., pp. 75–78.

mond Bold (but any other old face could be specified), an initial like Fry's Ornamented will look far more elegant than one much removed from the spirit of the italic, e.g. Gill Floriated or Lilith (Fig. 139).

Magazine work offers particular scope for the decorative effect of good hand-lettering, even in the simple form of decent calligraphy in chalk or charcoal reproduced as a straight line block for a standing heading. Equally, magazine illustration calls for every complexity of artistic technique, ranging from the wash-drawing to scraper-board, and the full range of process techniques, including combination line and tone, line and tone colour, and so on. When to this is added the elaboration of a coloured cover, with title-line, the important role of the graphic artist–designer in magazine work is again demonstrated.

13 · Title-piece, Seal, and Fudge

A NEWSPAPER'S title-piece is one of the most important items in its typography; yet more often than not it is the most sadly neglected. Papers which re-dress themselves with agreeable headline and text types, effectively made up, retain hanging over their now smart shop window—the front page—the ancient and grotesque sign which accompanied the spindly news titling heads (complete with full points) and the muddy minion text of their founding fathers. It is a position that no ordinary self-interested shopkeeper would tolerate for a moment, and for obvious reasons. That these reasons seem often not to be obvious to newspaper proprietors and managements is a curiosity of trade conservatism quite out of place in the second half of the twentieth century.

Let terms be defined: by *title-piece* is meant the title-line itself as made up with all its trimmings—number, date, price, edition indication, and any other subsidiary lines, ears (if any), seal (if used), cut-off rules—at the head of Page One. These incidentals, whose handling and make-up are vital to the whole title-piece, will be considered in detail later on. To start with, the typography of the *title-line* itself demands attention, since it is the dominant feature of the title ensemble. Not for nothing do the Americans call the title-line the nameplate or flag;[1] it requires just their qualities—to draw attention like a well-designed nameplate, to rouse interest and to rally supporters like a distinctive flag. To draw a commercial analogy, it may fairly be said that a newspaper title-line calls for as much care as that normally given nowadays to the styling of a product name on a package label.

There is the evident importance of association. A distinctive title-line, like a good trademark, helps to build a positive association in the minds of readers and potential readers; and to develop this association it should be used, enlarged or reduced according to circumstances, wherever the paper's title appears—from letterheadings to the office façade. Here one word of warning; sometimes this association argument is stood on its head and used to justify the retention of an antiquated and poor title-line.

[1] The erroneous use of *masthead* for title-line may be disposed of here; its only correct use is for the name and other information (ownership, publication details, and so on) appearing either boxed, or over the first leader, on the leader page.

The line has existed for so long, it is averred, that it has acquired an association-value which will be lost if it is changed. This, however, is merely to cling to antiquity for antiquity's sake, which amounts to saying that there should be no change, that is no improvement, in a newspaper's graphic presentation.

THE FINE OLD ENGLISH TITLE-LINE

Customarily the ancient title-line is some form of Blackletter, usually white-lined. Even now it is still commonly believed that the Blackletter (or Gothic or Old English) style is truly traditional, although more than a quarter of a century ago Stanley Morison proved this to be untrue. There had, certainly, been a genuinely traditional use of Blackletter; but that was either in the largest size of plain Text (used as the best available bold face) or the elegant calligraphic text initiated by Ichabod Dawks in his *News Letter* at the end of the seventeenth century. Both forms were rare as against the normal title-style of large-size roman caps. or lowercase in union with a discreet subsidiary use of italics. The white-lined, over-elaborated, Blackletter title-line was never seen before New Year's Day 1787, when it appeared over No. 1 of *The World and Fashionable Advertiser*, launched by that famous printer and newspaper promoter, John Bell (Fig. 140).

FIG. 140. The 'Strawberry Hill Gothic' adopted by *The Times* in 1788.

Bell's 'mock-antique', said Morison, was a 'Blackletter entirely without precedent . . . "old-world" or rather "Ye Olde Tudor Tea-Shoppe" in connotation. . . . Tricked out with a white line drawn or "tooled" upon every letter—thus making a namby-pamby, artificial affair of it. The mannerism was consistent with, if not inspired by, Strawberry Hill. Unfortunately, *The World* became an immediate vogue—a rage, in fact—it was copied everywhere, in every detail . . . Strawberry Hill Gothic and all.'[1]

This 'namby-pamby' Gothic was soon replaced by a less flimsy letter. By the second decade of last century newspapers were changing their title-lines from a white *inlined* to a white *outlined* Blackletter. Instead of a white line being tooled into an existing Blackletter, it was added to one;

[1] Morison, op. cit., p. 181.

FIG. 141. The 'fat Blacks'—No. 1 of the *Sunday Times* (1822), No. 1 of the *Sunday Worker* (1925), the *Selby Times* (1959) with a typical solid version of this Regency style, Caslon's Original Black; the Minster Black of Stevens, Shanks was slightly less heavy.

thus the Blackletter strokes were not weakened, the white appearing as a shading. This stouter-than-Bell white outlined Blackletter was shown in the Caslon specimen of 1808; while during the next decade there was a further development, which returned to the white inlining, or tooling, in a different form; the Fat Face vogue spread to Blacks, starting with Figgins in 1815. By 1821 Figgins, Caslon, and other founders as well were offering these new Blacks in various degrees of fatness, with or without the white inline—the 'opening' of them by the latter still leaving a sturdy face. What might be called the half or three-quarter fats of this vintage, white-lined, provided some of the best newspaper titles up to mid-century; one authority has called them 'refreshing'[1] and they were notably sharp and free from tricks in drawing or decoration. The most obese of these Blacks —for example, Caslon's Original Black, which continued in their specimen books until 1925—had a jovial, Falstaffian quality well suited for the title-line of a vigorous newspaper; but in this extreme form they were not often used. White-lined letter of this sort made the title of the *Sunday Times* and the *Standard* in the 1820's and a hundred years later that of the short-lived *Sunday Worker* (1925–9) (Fig. 141).

[1] Nicolette Gray, *Nineteenth Century Ornamented Types*, p. 26.

FIG. 142. Top is a line in the typefounders' early Victorian white-lined Germanic Black (this is Anglo-Saxon Open), weak and fussy. Below are examples in this original form or thickened-up, but without losing the ugly over-elaboration.

VICTORIAN GERMANIC GOTHIC

If Blackletter had remained at this Regency stage things might have been different. But the Victorian Gothic revival was to mark a decisive change for the worse. Under German influence—might it have been part of the Germanic vogue associated with the Prince Consort?—a Blackletter quite out of the English tradition, and oddly named Anglo-Saxon, appeared in 1847. It was even more angular and spiky than its German progenitors Kanzlei, Textura, and Gotisch.[1] Excessive scrolling and hairlining, the addition of extraneous perpendicular strokes descending below the x-line to a preposterous blob, made a usually too condensed letter look as fussy as it was weak. Often it was taken as the direct model for a title-line (Fig. 142), and apart from this exercised a debasing influence on Blackletter in general. This Germanic degeneration was substantially reflected in the stock patterns of Blackletter for newspaper title-lines which the typefounders exhibited in their catalogues, offering them as mounted electros or hand-cut in brass.

While these variants of the white-lined Blackletter principally prevailed, a minority of newspapers preferred the solid style. Sometimes, though not always, this plain Blackletter was better than the whited versions, though it was subject to comparable eccentricities in design. In general, however, a decently executed solid Black is clearly preferable to a tasteless white-lined specimen; and there is a modern tendency for newspapers, when they

[1] Gray, op. cit., pp. 55–56.

prefer a Blackletter title, to adopt simplified solid forms (Fig. 143). This was done by the *Daily Mail* some years ago, with a thickening of the fine lines and careful letter-spacing, though its weekend companion the *Sunday Dispatch*, after an unprecedented series of public trials of varying Blackletter in 1957, decided in March 1958 to go over to an elegant lower-case line in Times Roman blown up to 84 pt., later slightly reducing the size and thickening the strokes (Fig. 144).

FIG. 143. Solid Blacks: the simplified current version of the *Daily Mail* (compared with its previous reverse title), an admirable design from Dumfries, and two still over-fussy versions from Plymouth and Streatham.

THE USES OF BLACKLETTER

At this point it will be as well to draw certain practical conclusions about the continued use of Blackletter for title-lines. That Morison's demolition of the 'tradition' is valid there can be no doubt; nor can we dispute the significance of the movement away from Blackletter, which he himself initiated when he romanized *The Times* title-line in 1932. Yet the total anathema formerly pronounced on Gothic by the present writer among others needs some qualification. Perhaps such a qualification was always implicit in the remark that 'it is not enough to become convinced of the vices of Gothic and summarily to eject it. The title-space may thus be swept and garnished for seven far worse devils';[1] later, and explicitly, 'it

[1] Hutt, 'The Gothic Title-piece and the English Newspaper' (*Alphabet and Image*, no. 3, Dec. 1946, pp. 13–14).

FIG. 144. The most remarkable public experiment in title-design ever practised by a newspaper. Top is the long-standing Blackletter of the *Sunday Dispatch*, changed to the second line on 21 April 1957; the succeeding lines followed on 28 April, 5 May, 19 May, 21 July; then in March 1958 the Blackletter was abandoned for Times Roman, natural state, itself to be slightly reduced in size and thickened-up for the final version in September of that year.

would be foolish to imagine that the problem is solved by the mere scrapping of Gothic and substituting, say, a hand-lettered title. There are not a few newspapers with old-standing roman title-pieces which are absolute shockers, devised in the worst traditions of debased commercial sign-writing or late Victorian typefounders' trickery. In comparison a simplified and fairly stout Gothic, like the title of the London *Daily Telegraph*, is a positive relief.'[1] These quotations evade the central point, however,

[1] Hutt, *An Outline of Newspaper Typography* (1950), p. 43.

which is that Blackletter had and has a functional value; it is distinctive and cannot clash with—or worse still, merge with—any editorial display. This functional value is enhanced by simple improvements in the style of the Blackletter—mainly through the excision of the more exaggerated letter-forms—or, at the least, by cleaning-up and respacing the line (Fig. 145).

FIG. 145. Improving the white-lined Black: the *Daily Telegraph*'s notable simplification, a clean-up and respacing from Wolverhampton, a sound line from Taunton, and a novel design from Exmouth.

The word *cleaning-up* needs particular emphasis. A title-line, whatever its design and whatever its printing surface, must always be clean and sharp. Hand-cut brass is not really necessary; an electro or a stereo regularly renewed, before it shows any signs of serious wear, from a master zinco or type-line, serves perfectly well. Particularly in Blackletter a worn and muddy title-block sheds an aura of shabbiness over the whole front page, not to say the whole paper.

The relevance of the central point, stressed above, is not confined to Gothic. It is, indeed, the touchstone of all title-lines, which must always be distinctive in themselves—the unmistakable sign manual of their newspaper—and clearly differentiated from the matter over which they hang; or, to put it briefly, they must be distinctive in a dual sense. Choice of a title-line will thus always be related to the character of the front page, whether all-advertising (smalls or display) or, if news, to the weight and style of the editorial display. Obviously, heavy 'popular' make-up with extra-bold large cap. leads demands sharper differentiation in the title-line than does restrained 'class' make-up, with no cap. heading larger than 30 or 36 pt.

That distinctiveness, in the dual sense indicated, is the criterion of a sound title-line has to be borne in mind in considering the persistent non-Gothic tradition of certain sections of the British Press. The critics of Gothic have rightly emphasized the persistence of the roman title-line in the mass-circulation Sunday papers of the early and mid-nineteenth century—the solid or shaded fat faces of the *Weekly Dispatch* and *Bell's Life in London*, the bold or condensed romans of *Reynolds News* and *Lloyd's News*—and the later evening papers like the *Pall Mall Gazette*, *St. James's Gazette*, the, *Echo* and the *Westminster Gazette* (Fig. 146). But

FIG. 146. The old roman tradition: the *Weekly Dispatch*, now the *Sunday Dispatch* (1801), *Reynolds News* (1886), the *Hereford Times* (1956). Note the use of a Blackletter tag-line.

the virtues of these title-lines did not simply lie in the fact that they were roman; they were well differentiated from the style of pages over which they appeared. Of two, the *Pall Mall* and *St. James's*, this could perhaps hardly be said; adopting Old Style for their text, a startling innovation for those days, they used Old Style roman caps. for their titles; the size differentiation sufficed but the general effect was one of harmony rather than distinctiveness. The point is rather academic, since these two gentlemanly sheets were *sui generis*; in any event the *Pall Mall*, in its later years, combined Caslon Titling and Antique in a three-line arrangement to secure a bolder result.

THE VALUE OF LOWER-CASE

The Gothic controversy may now be left; but in turning to consider the wide field from which to choose a non-Gothic title-line, one aspect of the title-use of Blackletter should not be forgotten—namely, that it must be run in lower-case. There is hardly need to stress the importance of this when main headline display is normally in caps., up to 60 pt. and 72 pt. in 'popular' make-up. Against heavy cap. display the use of lower-case

FIG. 147. Type treatments in upper- and lower-case. Norwich goes from Black to Ludlow Caslon Bold (the 'ears' were reduced from 22 to 17½ ems each, thus giving the title much more air), Reading to Falstaff, the *Worker* to Ultra-Bodoni italic, Crawley to Times Bold (note the great improvement on the previous indifferent design), Hastings to Times Bold also (from the Black in Fig. 142). The 1959 Hastings change to caps.—Perpetua Bold Titling—with the excellent redesign of the subsidiary lines, is significant. Crawley has now adopted a reverse-block treatment.

for the title-line is a means of differentiation not to be neglected. It seems curious that there are, on the whole, so few lower-case non-Gothic title-lines; when they have been introduced they appear to be entirely satisfactory. The only argument against them is that they require a size somewhat larger, and thus a little more space-consuming, than a cap. line.

Of the three sources of title-lines—(*a*) *type*, (*b*) *processed type*, (*c*) *hand-lettering*—the first is particularly fruitful when a lower-case line is sought. Attention has already been drawn to the *Sunday Dispatch*'s blown-up Times Roman; here the element of contrast between the medium weight, as well as the character, of the title and the heavy Century-Bodoni display of the page is most marked. Contrast again, though of character rather than weight, marks lower-case title-lines like the Ludlow Caslon Bold of the *Eastern Daily Press* (Bodoni Bold display), the Monotype Ultra Bodoni italic of the *Daily Worker* (Caslon-Bodoni-Sans), the Monotype Falstaff of the *Reading Standard* (Caslon), the Monotype Times Bold of the *Crawley Courier* (Sans) (Fig. 147).

It may be noted that while the lines described derive directly from an actual type, they are not always achieved by straight setting. Apart from photographic blowing-up, they may require special spacing and fit-up which cannot be done in metal and which need careful lining-up of letters cut from a proof or an enlarged photostat. This last was the case, for example, with the *Daily Worker*'s title-line. It should also be noted that since individual letter peculiarities (and not necessarily disagreeable ones) are often more marked in lower-case, the actual wording of the title is important. It should always be set in the selected type or types and proofed for inspection before the final choice is made. It is by no means enough merely to glance at a type specimen which may not contain all the letters of a given title.

County Express

Times

FIG. 148. Lower-case italic title-lines which will not conflict with any normal seriffed news display—Ludlow Tempo Heavy italic and Karnak Heavy italic.

The comparative rarity of lower-case title-lines is exceeded by the rarity of their italic variant (the *Daily Worker* is the only national example). Yet the use of italic will usually assist still further the differentiation of the title. The Cheshire *County Express* shows how this can be done in Sans, by blowing-up a judiciously spaced line in Tempo Heavy italic to 84 pt.; and in the same extra-bold field a heavy Egyptian italic might be found very suitable (Fig. 148). But there has so far been no serious exploitation of the rich resources available among the modern calligraphic and informal script type faces, some of which have been shown in Chapter 12. Here are sloped lower-case letters—only one or two of the brush-scripts like Cartoon were designed for cap. setting—which are as decisively differentiated as Blackletter from any possible news display. A small selection of large-size lines from these ranges will illustrate the point (Figs. 149, 150).

Turning now to plain type treatment for title-lines in caps., the basic principle of contrast remains paramount. This can be seen in the Times Bold Titling No. 2 of the *Bridgwater Mercury* (Bodoni Bold display); the Times Semi-Bold of the *Surrey Comet* (Century-Bodoni), a striking example of a change-over from Blackletter, which included the elimination of advertising ears; the Times Roman of the *Camberley News* (Times Bold); the Perpetua Bold Titling of the *Manchester Guardian* (Century); the *Luton News* (Bodoni Bold); or the *Worthing Herald* series (Tempo Heavy-Century) (Figs. 151, 152).

Perpetua Bold Titling (Series 200) deserves a few words to itself. It is matchless as a heavy monumental letter, as indeed, in the lighter weight, is its prototype Perpetua Titling (Series 258). The present writer has frequently specified it, from the 72 pt. size for *Reynolds News* in 1936 (suggested by Stanley Morison) to the 42 pt. size for the *Manchester Guardian* in 1952; the former newspaper lost distinction by a subsequent retreat, via

FIG. 149. Some founders' types of calligraphic character suitable for title-lines: Gillies Gothic Bold (Bauer), Ritmo (Nebiolo), Goudytype (A.T.F.), Allegro (Ludwig & Mayer).

Daily News

Daily News

Daily Ne

Daily News

FIG. 150. Monotype faces similarly suitable: Klang (593), Matura (496), Mercurius (584), Ashley Script (574).

WORTHING HERALD

No. 1969 FRIDAY, JANUARY 24, 1958 FOURPENCE

THE LUTON NEWS

BRIDGWATER MERCURY
and County Press

CAMBERLEY NEWS

BAGSHOT OBSERVER AND FRIMLEY, SANDHURST & BLACKWATER CHRONICLE
AND WOKING OPINION

FIG. 151. Type title-lines in caps. (all Monotype faces): two arrangements of Perpetua Bold Titling (200), Times Bold Titling No. 2 (328), Times Roman (327).

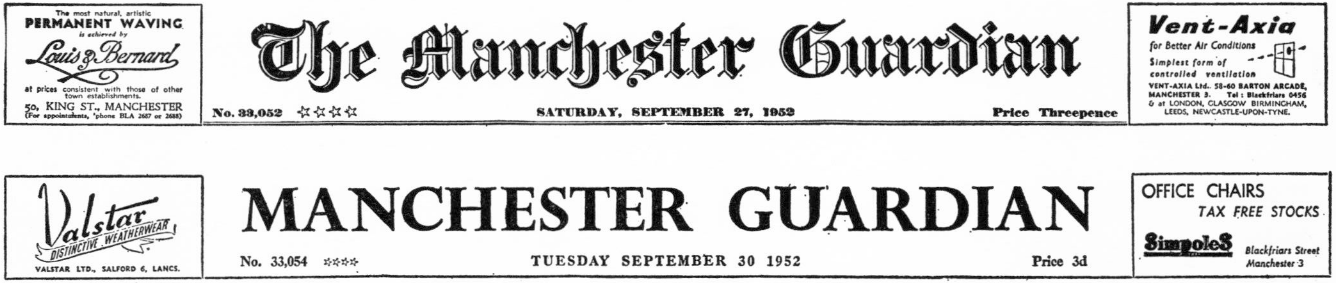

FIG. 152. Two interesting change-overs from Blackletter to roman caps.—the *Guardian* to Perpetua Bold Titling, the *Comet* to Times Semi-Bold (421)—one retaining ears, the other not

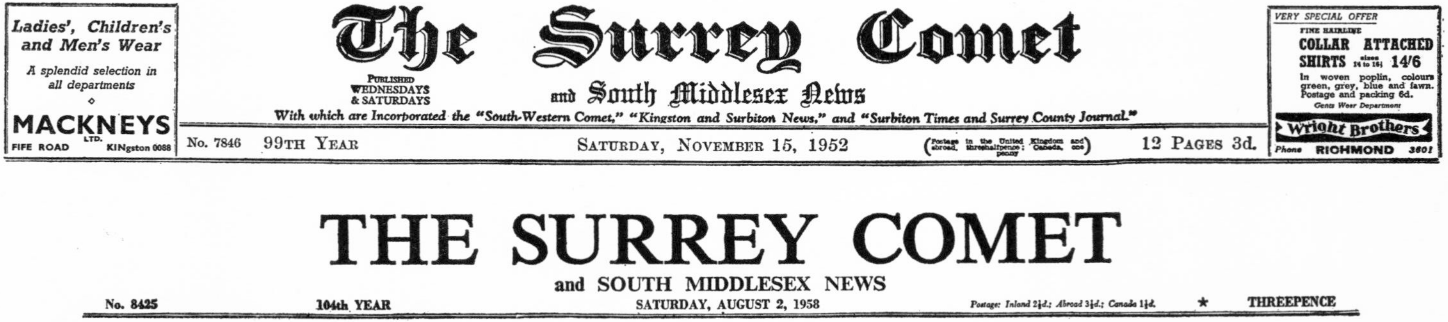

a version in Goudy Heavy to its present hand-lettered facsimile of the *Daily Express* line (Fig. 153). For a distinguished daily or Sunday newspaper, or for a local weekly with solidly rooted authority in its community, Perpetua Bold Titling can hardly be bettered as a straightforward cap. title-line. Subtle differences, if desired, can be secured by using the caps. of Perpetua Bold (Series 461), which have certain slight design variations, e.g. the J, N, Q, T, U; it should be remembered that this is a small-bodied type, whose 72 pt. caps. are slightly smaller than the full-face 48 pt. caps. of the Bold Titling (Fig. 154). If a fine monumental letter of an entirely different character is sought, Albertus Titling (Series 324) or Bold Titling (Series 538) is well worth consideration. Its near-Sans character—it has 'thickened terminals rather than serifs' says the *Encyclopaedia of Type Faces*—coupled with its square but elegant cut, combines that necessary title-line note of distinction and difference (Fig. 155).

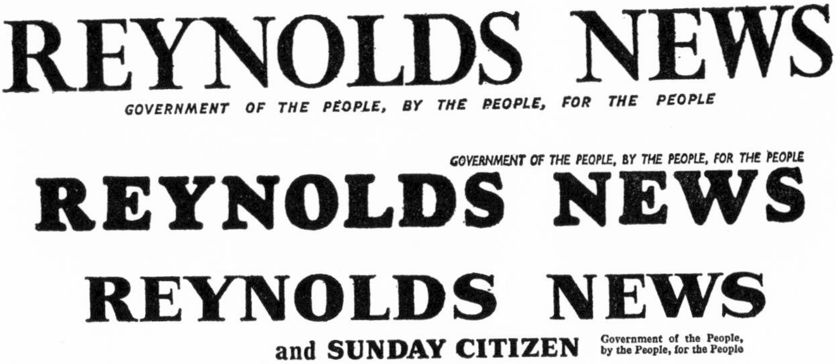

FIG. 153. Title-line changes by *Reynolds News*: Perpetua Bold Titling, originally in 72 pt. (1936), Goudy Heavy (1948), and currently *Express*-style hand-lettering.

THE DECORATIVE NOTE

So far all the title-line type-treatments discussed have been strictly plain and solid; the possibilities of processing the lines, or of introducing colour, are dealt with later. Throughout, the importance of the distinctiveness and differentiation of the title-line has been stressed; but the achievement of these qualities has been explained within the limitations of the selection and handling of plain type. Now the field can be extended by considering the wide range of more decorative types, in the shaded and outline category, which are possible title-line material (Fig. 156). By the character of their design such types solve the problem of differentiation from the editorial display as completely as Blackletter, for they are distinctive, and they impart a certain decorative note to the title. On the

JNQTU

JNQTU

FIG. 154. Letter-differences to note between the caps. of Perpetua Bold (461) and Perpetua Bold Titling (200); respective sizes shown here are 72 pt. and 48 pt.

other hand, and in terms of a given paper, some of them may be thought too decorative, or too exotic. They nevertheless repay examination, as a brief research in the Berry–Johnson–Jaspert *Encyclopaedia* will disclose; some have already been shown in Chapter 12. It is convenient to group them for title-line purposes as follows (Figs. 156, 157, 158, 159).

1. *Three-dimensional*: varying greatly in colour and impact, this all-caps. group is perhaps more effective in its seriffed than in its Sans letter. Among the first are the powerful Profil, Thorne Shaded, Elongated Roman Shaded or the slightly wider Regina, Rockwell Shadow (or equivalent three-dimensional Egyptian like Beton Open). The second include Graphique, Echo (but its lower-case must be avoided), Sans Serifs Shaded, Umbra (Ludlow) or the equivalent Gill Shadow No. 1, Gill Shadow Titling or Orplid.

2. *Shaded*: from the wide range of the usual white-lined display romans only Ludlow Cameo (or the more elegant original German typefounder's Narcissus, if available) is worth selecting for its effectiveness in the 60 and 72 pt. sizes needed for title-lines, with Goudy Handtooled (its original version had a magnificent 84 pt. and 96 pt.) as a possible alternative. The

Daily News

DAILY NEWS

FIG. 155. Monotype Albertus (481) and Albertus Bold Titling (538) have a differentiation from normal display which gives them marked title-line utility.

HARLOW CITIZEN

NUMBER 13 FRIDAY 24 JULY 1953 TWOPENCE

THE ONLY PAPER PRINTED AND PUBLISHED IN HARLOW

Largest circulation in Harlow

HARLOW CITIZEN

ESSEX & HERTS BORDER ADVERTISER

Supreme for HARLOW Small Ads.

NUMBER 273 FRIDAY 18 JULY 1958 Registered for transmission by post. Postage 2½d. THREEPENCE

EMPIRE NEWS

NEW TIMES

FIG. 156. Some actual three-dimensional titles. For type (Thorne Shaded) the *Harlow Citizen* has substituted a drawn letter of comparable character. The *Empire News*, a drawn letter, recalls the Victorian Ornamented No. 6 (Reed) or its later German derivative Diamant. Regina (Berthold) may be compared with Elongated Roman Shaded (Fig. 135).

unusual and heavy Atrax (caps. only) is worth looking at, and so is Bauer's Bodoni Open.

3. *Inline*: here the long-popular Chisel is outstanding (it has even crossed the Atlantic and appeared in Mid-Western newspaper title-lines). Its Expanded variant is of more limited use. Two Sans faces in this group deserve attention—Ludlow Tempo Heavy Inline and Phosphor (the in-lined version of Erbar).

4. *Decorative shaded*: the sturdy Motor and the vivacious Paris Flash have possibilities, though perhaps they betray a little too much their respective German and French origins. The same may be said of Kombinette (whose fine white horizontal scoring probably needs discreet opening-up, to avoid the danger of filling in on the run) and Eclair.

5. *Stencil*: a needlessly neglected group, represented by Stencil (Ludlow), a square version, with Tea Chest (Stephenson, Blake) more condensed. Allegro does not really belong here, but it is admissible because the nature of its drawing and its unclosed bowls give it a certain stencil quality. Best in lower-case, it has the advantage of being available up to 96 pt.

6. *Grey shaded*: not of frequent utility, but helpful if it is desired to

Times

NEW TIMES

Times

NEW TIMES

Times

Times

FIG. 157. Shaded (inlined) and stencil types with title-line possibilities. Stephenson, Blake's Chisel Expanded and Tea Chest, Ludlow Cameo (72 pt.) and Stencil, Monotype Cooper Tooled or Hilite (582), Goudy Hand-tooled.

lighten the overall colour of the title-line (when the stippling or half-line shading of a solid face might be in mind). The first favourite would be the Sans Prisma—a multi-lined version of Koch's Cable—with the more fanciful Floride (not to be used under 72 pt.) as an outsider. The (American) Lanston Monotype Bodoni Bold Shaded is an acceptable half-lined version of this face.

REVERSE AND OTHER BLOCK TITLES

The second source of title-lines, *processed type*, ranges from the stippling of solid type to reduce its colour—a rarely useful practice, as already suggested—to one or other of the reversal techniques. Under the latter head many effects can be obtained by ingenuity in the process department; the straight reverse to white lettering on a tint ground of varying pattern and density is only the first and the simplest of several variants. Black-casing or

FIG. 158. These more decorative shaded types may solve some title-line problems—Motor (Ludwig & Mayer), Stop (Bauer), Paris Flash (Fonderie Typographique Française), Eclair (Deberny & Peignot), contrasting with plain inline Phosphor (Ludwig & Mayer). See also Figs. 133, 134, 135.

FIG. 159. Grey-shaded types that contrast well with heavy editorial display—Prisma (Klingspor) and Floride (Deberny & Peignot).

white-casing of lettering, black or white shadow effects, doubled black and white reversed shadow, shadow-outlining of a solid letter in black or tint, can all be contrived without special artwork.[1] It should be said at once, however, that reverse block newspaper titles rarely seem permanently acceptable, except when they are short-measure cornerpiece titles for a tabloid (then often run in colour, with a solid ground) (Fig. 160).

Three leading national newspapers, the *Daily Mail*, *Daily Herald*, and *News Chronicle*, have all tried reverse block title-lines, only to abandon them eventually; the fact that each one was hand-drawn, and not reversed from actual type, does not affect the argument. A shallow reversed strip at the head of a broadsheet seems to look more like a label than a

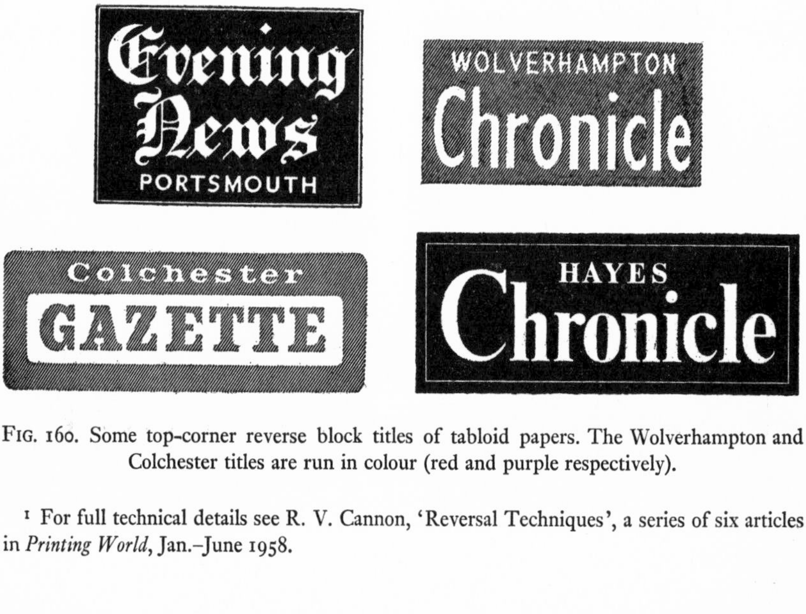

FIG. 160. Some top-corner reverse block titles of tabloid papers. The Wolverhampton and Colchester titles are run in colour (red and purple respectively).

[1] For full technical details see R. V. Cannon, 'Reversal Techniques', a series of six articles in *Printing World*, Jan.–June 1958.

FIG. 161. The famous decorative title-line of *The Scotsman* (top) as redesigned and relettered in April 1957. The first redesign—known in the Edinburgh office as the 'paintbrush' version, from the solid drawing of the thistle flowers—was shortly succeeded by No. 3, with the national emblem more normally represented, and in June 1959 by No. 4, relettered with a redrawn, simplified background.

FIG. 162. The basic 'music-hall' letter of the *News of the World* scroll has changed little since 1843; below are three other current titles in the same genre.

title, apart from any technical printing problems that a substantial area of close-tinted ground may present.

Since they must necessarily be processed as line blocks, the highly decorated or partially illustrated titles, rare in this country, may be disposed of here. The only one with a claim to distinction is the classic thistle-backed scroll of *The Scotsman*, recently redrawn (with lettering now still further improved) (Fig. 161). Of the *News of the World* block, with its enrayed Britannia and symbolic tomes, Morison's remark in 1932 remains true: 'the ornamental lettering on a waved ribbon has been slightly simplified, but the style is still what it was in 1843, namely, a common sign-writer's lettering such as would have been familiar to the patrons of the old London music halls'.[1] The *News of the World* is, after all, an institution and its title-piece has a peculiar institutional significance; no one will ever imitate it. Only one comparable period piece is known to the present writer, that of the West Cumberland *Whitehaven News*, though there are other examples of 'music-hall' lettering (Figs. 162, 163).

FIG. 163. Our most splendid surviving Victorian decorative title-piece. The original wood-engraving is still in the office of the *Whitehaven News* (founded 1852), and is reproduced above from a press proof; the reproduction below of the present block shows no change save a slight reduction in width of the title-scroll.

THE USE OF HAND-LETTERING

Hand-lettering, the third source of title-lines, has of course the advantage of complete flexibility, with the fullest opportunity for originality and freedom in design. But this freedom has obvious dangers unless the letterer is a scholarly, skilful, and disciplined artist. Local newspapers in particular tend to accept any reach-me-down job of the poorest commercial art standard. The result is worse than the most mediocre conventional Gothic. This is not the way to achieve a satisfactory title-line; for of few items in a newspaper's typography can it more truthfully be said that 'cheapness is

[1] Morison, op. cit., p. 255.

death'. Since a successful title-line is a permanent and valuable investment it is worth every penny of what it costs to get a first-class letterer to execute it.[1]

There is no need to discuss in detail here the question of the encouragement and development of good lettering, with which calligraphy is so intimately connected, although it is a subject of great interest, both aesthetic and educational. Reference may be made to authoritative expositions such as those in the Studio publication *Lettering and Calligraphy* (1954), or to recent contributions by calligraphers and typographers in *Penrose Annual*.[2] The high value already placed in these pages on scripts and types of a broadly calligraphic quality should suggest that there is room for an approach to title-line design in terms of sheer calligraphy. But bold main strokes must keep the colour strong; lightness or delicacy, which may suit some periodical titles, are out of place in the normal newspaper title-line.

FIG. 164. The Blackletter title-line of *The Times*, displaced in 1932 by the roman cap. line shown second; third is the current design, by Reynolds Stone, introduced in 1953.

The letterer-calligrapher has also to cope with the by no means easy task of providing a simplified, sound, and strong Blackletter for those papers which prefer Gothic; and when he is called upon for a roman letter, usually with the depth limitations clearly indicated, he has to produce one which, however evocative it may be in its inspiration, emerges as an individual design, achieving its distinctive aim as a title in a way that no line of type could do. The second is currently the principal demand made

[1] Advice on securing a good letterer can be had from the Guild of Lettering Craftsmen, 6 Queen Square, London, W.C. 1.

[2] *Penrose Annual* references include: (1954) Will Carter, 'An Opportunity for Penmen'; (1955) Arnold Bank, 'The Craft of Lettering'; Walter Tracy, 'Why should Lettering be Neglected?'; (1956) Frederick A. Horn, 'Lettering and the Advertising Message'; John Brinkley, 'On the Teaching of Lettering'.

DAILY EXPRESS

News Chronicle

DAILY HERALD

The Birmingham Post

ESSEX COUNTY STANDARD

EAST ANGLIAN
DAILY TIMES

FIG. 165. Some hand-lettered titles of sound quality and mainly of recent design. The *Birmingham Post*, however, is virtually the same as the paper's original line of 1857; the *Express* line was a wartime (1942) innovation.

by newspapers on the letterer. Two outstanding designs may be mentioned. In April 1953 *The Times* introduced the noble title-lettering that it has today, replacing what Printing House Square officially describes as the 'compromise' of 1932—when a roman letter based on the original title of 1788 was substituted for the Gothic—and thus realizing the 'completion of the original design' for the paper's revolutionary re-dress. The new title-line was 'designed without reference to any precedent in the newspaper's history' and satisfies to perfection the requirements named above (Fig. 164).[1] So, in a different way, does the fat but elegant title designed for the *Daily Express* by Stanley Morison as a wartime space-saver in 1942—it was nearly $\frac{3}{4}$ inch shallower than its Gothic predecessor—and permanently retained with only slight adjustments in the letter-spacing. It has been flattered by frequent imitation. To the expert eye the *Express* title may seem to combine something of the colour of Corvinus Bold and something of the letter-structure of Metropolis; but such elements as there may be here are fused, or synthesized, into an individual and original letter (Fig. 165). It should be noted that the *Express* has always used strap-lines to separate the cap. title from the cap. streamer.

Of the other titles illustrated here the *Birmingham Post* faithfully

[1] *Printing The Times 1785–1953*, p. 171.

continues the tradition of the shaded roman lower-case line with which that newspaper, most unusually for the period, graced its first number in 1857. Neither the *Daily Herald* nor the *News Chronicle* are fully satisfactory. The *Herald* appears to be a vertically compressed version of the *Express* title, differentiated by an abnormal extension of the serifs; apart from stronger colour it is hard to see why it should be preferred to the Baskerville Bold Titling—another Morison design—which had been the most

FIG. 166. These hand-lettered titles are of varying degrees of demerit. The Hull *Daily Mail* is quite indefensible and the Blackpool *Gazette* little better. Note the *Northamptonshire Evening Telegraph*'s cleaning-up operation and Scarborough's sensible turn to type (Old Style No. 5).

stable (1944–57) of the *Herald*'s series of title-line experiments that began in 1940. The *News Chronicle* title looks like an Ultra-Bodoni line with an Old Face stress and serif-bracketing; the device is not enough to give real originality. At local level the varied title-lettering of the *West Sussex County Times*, the *Brighton and Hove Herald*, and the *Barnsley Chronicle* is worth noting (Fig. 170); the last is virtually Cooper Black, but by introducing an element of condensation that the original type never possessed it gives an effect of novelty, unfortunately removed in a later redrawing.

The survival of indefensible lettering, together with attempts at improvement, is illustrated in Fig. 166. It will be noted that the *Evening Telegraph* (Kettering) still clings to its enlarged initials and underscore, while the Scarborough paper prefers good type to bad drawing. The *Express & Echo* (Exeter) just fails through slips in detail, e g. the weight of the down-strokes varies too much, the curled tail of the R is out of character and the ampersand a trifle too fussy.

THE MAKE-UP OF THE TITLE-PIECE

The opening paragraphs of this chapter listed the various items that make up with the title-line to form the whole title-piece; their arrangement has now to be considered. First, however, it is necessary to determine the overall measure. For broadsheet papers this is assumed to be the full width of the page, with or without 'ears'. British experience, at any rate, has been quite decisive on this point. In 1941–2 the *Daily Herald* experimented with three different double-column reverse block titles, centred or cornered left, and then abandoned the whole thing; as, later, it did in 1957 after a brief trial of a three-column boxed title-piece cornered right.[1] The full measure does not, incidentally, exclude the riding up of the first or the last column to the head of the page if required. Shorter measure, as noted earlier in respect of reverse block titles, is nowadays normally adopted only by tabloids—and often they prefer full measure; double-column cornered left is usual, though with short-titled papers like the *Star* single-column may suffice. The additional, but highly important, point should be noted that unless the definite article is an essential part of the title (e.g. *The Times*) its omission improves the display.

[1] From its revival as a daily paper in 1919 to 1957 the *Daily Herald* had no fewer than twelve title-lines, including three pen-drawn versions, with or without the famous chanticleer (1919–30), Gothic (1930–40), four reverse blocks (1940–2), an extremely poor semi-Egyptian (1942–4), Baskerville Bold Titling (1944–57), the three-column box (1957), and the expanded roman caps. (1957). A full documentation and illustration, with the exception of two of the three double-column reverse blocks, will be found in an article by James Moran in *Printing News*, 18 April 1957. See also Fig. 10, p. 42.

Middlesex Advertiser and County Gazette

BUCKINGHAMSHIRE ADVERTISER
THE UXBRIDGE GAZETTE
ESTABLISHED IN 1840 AS "BROADWATER'S JOURNAL"
The Old-Established
MIDDLESEX
HARROW & WATFORD JOURNAL
RUISLIP-NORTHWOOD COURIER
County Newspaper
REGISTERED AT THE GENERAL POST OFFICE AS A NEWSPAPER

HAVE YOUR EYES Examined Periodically
P. C. HIRST.
Consulting Optician
42a SOUTH STREET ROMFORD Tel.: 1312
Hours: 9.30 a.m. - 6 p.m. Thurs. 12.30 p.m.
Also Friday evenings by appointment

ROMFORD RECORDER

FRIDAY, APRIL 5th 1957 ★ 32 PAGES FOR THREEPENCE ★ No. 3051

★COLLIER ROW
★HORNCHURCH
★HAROLD HILL
★UPMINSTER
BRENTWOOD★
DAGENHAM★
RAINHAM★

WEST KENT MERCURY

Incorporating the Bromley & West Kent Mercury,
The Orpington, Petts Wood & District Journal,
The Bromley Chronicle, The Bromley & West Kent Telegraph,
The Beckenham & Shortlands Chronicle,
and The Chislehurst & Mottingham Chronicle.

Established
— 1865 —

The Newspaper for Bromley, Hayes, Sundridge Park,
Bickley, Shortlands, Keston, Beckenham,
West Wickham, Eden Park, Chislehurst, Petts Wood, Downham,
Orpington, The Crays, Farnborough, Chelsfield, Downe,
Green Street Green, Biggin Hill, etc.

Richmond and Twickenham Times

A JOURNAL OF LOCAL NEWS, SOCIETY, ART AND LITERATURE.
Circulating in Richmond, Kew, Petersham, Ham, Barnes, Mortlake, East Sheen, Kingston, &c. (Surrey), and Twickenham, St. Margaret's, Whitton, Isleworth, Hounslow, Hanworth, Teddington, the Hamptons, Brentford, Sunbury, &c. (Middlesex).

VOL. LXXXIII. No. 9,040 SATURDAY, NOVEMBER 2, 1957 Telephones RIChmond 0063, 0064 Telegrams "TIMES" Richmond Surrey PRICE FOURPENCE

FIG. 167. Local weeklies cling to their subsidiary titles and/or circulation area details; the first three title-pieces above show how these lines can be reasonably handled, while the fourth is an object lesson to the contrary—now transformed (see Preface).

There are only three essential items to carry with the title-line: the number, date, and price—and it may be argued whether the number, a formality to most people, may not be adequately accommodated at the end of the imprint. By custom these items are set left, centre, and right respectively, and there is no reason to depart from custom, though minor adjustments can be made. In size they should be clearly perceptible but not prominent (10 pt. or 12 pt. is a maximum); in style they should harmonize with the text or main headings of the paper, or be neutral (e.g. a medium Sans). Edition lines, if run in the forme, need careful relating to the title-piece typography as a whole.

To these essentials many newspapers add an extraordinary medley: a tag or slogan line ('The County Paper of —'), a list of incorporated titles and/or circulation areas, telephone numbers of branch offices, postal details, the weather, lighting-up times, and the like. While it is possible, if need be, to display conveniently one short line like the weather, the clutter that the other items usually entail should be seriously pondered. Under today's conditions they are often completely meaningless and may

FIG. 168. Evolution of a title-piece: the *Sunday Times*, still Blackletter in 1949, introduced its first roman title-line in May 1953 but by August of that year this was changed for the Times Extended Style, first without, then with, advertising ears.

FIG. 169. Title-pieces with emblems, symbolic or local; the latter are usually county arms or crests, except for Reading, whose *Mercury* exhibits an ancient version (*c.* 1810) of the borough's arms with their mysterious five heads.

be entirely dispensed with, to the great advantage of the title-piece. If it is really necessary to retain them, they must be well laid out in agreeable typography, with the recognition that the depth of the title-piece will inevitably be increased. The point is established by contrasting the cramped chaos of the *Richmond and Twickenham Times* with the orderly arrangements of the *Middlesex Advertiser*, *Romford Recorder*, and *West Kent Mercury* (Fig. 167).

The rulework of the title-piece should be simplified to one full cut-off in plain column rule, the number, date, price, and so on being no longer cut off between page-width double-fine or even thick and thin rules. The evolution of the *Sunday Times* title-piece (Fig. 168) illustrates this, as well as the important matter of the presence or absence of advertising 'ears'. There can be no question that newspapers which dispense with 'ears' invariably secure a much more impressive title-piece; when retained their measure should be restricted to single column, or very little more, to avoid crowding the title. Emblems can give a decorative note to a title-piece; the traditional use of the Royal Arms[1] is one example, but many local papers make effective use of a city, county, or other local device (Figs. 169, 170).

[1] Introduced early in the eighteenth century, this usage has never had any official authority (Morison, op. cit., p. 78).

Colour gives great impact to a title-line, but in this country of rotary-printed papers only tabloids as a rule use it, since they can run the title in colour from the seal head, without the expense of a colour unit or other special attachment. Cossar-printed papers can also run their titles in colour, given an extra attachment. It is important to see that colour titles are kept plain and simple, bold and unadorned lettering or straight white-on-solid reverse (cf. the *Daily Mirror* and the *Sunday Pictorial*). Muddying up a colour title with ruled backgrounds, or anything that obscures the colour white paper contrast, nullifies the purpose of colour. A clean, bright red tending to scarlet is the best colour, though an equally bright green can be very effective. It is hard to make blue sufficiently bright without making it too light; the contrast with black is in any event less striking.

THE SEAL AND THE FUDGE

Most rotary presses have a seal head, which can be fixed to print a small block of colour, usually not more than single column in width, in any selected column of a broadsheet paper. The depth of the seal can be

FIG. 170. More emblems, with varied lettering; that of Barnsley, an acceptable approximation to Cooper Black, has not been improved by recent redrawing.

increased according to the circumference of the seal cylinder, and so on a tabloid (half-sheet) paper a long strip of colour can be run. It is common practice to use the seal as an edition indicator, particularly with evening papers, but some morning papers prefer symbols (the *Express* Crusader, the *Herald* chanticleer), slogans, or simple decoration (the plain blue circles of the *Daily Mail*).

The conventional shields, serrated circles, and other odd shapes bearing rather battered reverse lettering are blots on a decent page. Plain type properly chosen can be very effective; but a reverse block, if it is desired, should be in clean Sans caps. on a plain circle, oval, round-cornered square or oblong ground. The colour should be kept clean and bright always; nothing looks worse than a dirty pinkish-red on a seal.

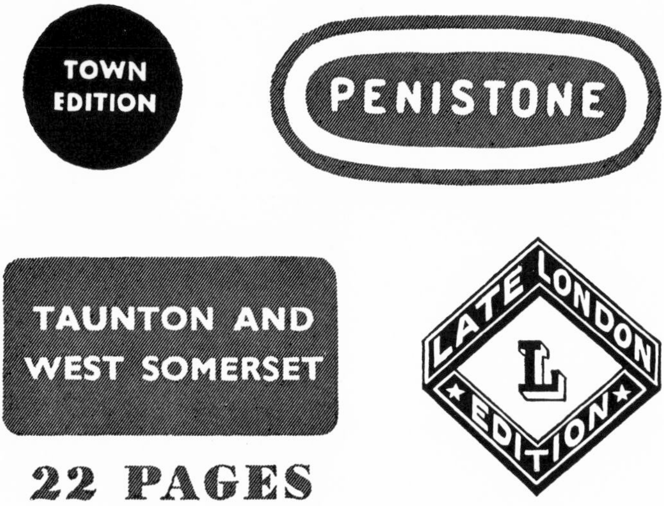

FIG. 171. Colour seals (edition lines) from the *Bournemouth Times*, *Barnsley Chronicle*, *Somerset County Gazette*, with a prewar *Reynolds News* design.

Permanent seals are often engraved in brass or gun-metal. By using stereos, nickel-faced if the run is long, it is possible to change the seal at will, using it to signal some main feature on an inside page. These stereos are cast in a special small box resembling the box for casting plate fudges.

An edition seal, or any other edition indication, has a dual function; it is presumed to be a guide to the customers and it certainly is a guide to the packers and to the newspaper's staff in general. From this latter point of view, of course, any conventional code will suit; for instance the white or black stars reducing by one for each edition or replate. But typographic designers have mostly ignored the possibility of treating the seal, in respect of both its functions, as something both decorative and useful. *Reynolds News* made an attempt before the war with a three-dimensional quadrangular device, bearing the edition's title in reverse lettering round its rim, and within a reversed Rockwell Shadow letter—L for Late London, N for National, S for Scottish, and so on (Fig. 171). The field is probably worth more exploration than the lack of interest would suggest.

The 'fudge', or late-news device, is commonly regarded as a utilitarian portion of the paper where any pretence at typographic quality is of no consequence; indeed, where the word may as well rhyme with smudge. This is a mistaken view, even though the printing quality of the fudge can never equal that of the page. The fudge position on the page should always have a good standing heading—'Latest News' or whatever the chosen wording may be—according with the general typography of the paper, and given prominence by reversing or other processing. The headings to the fudge items should be uniform in style; if it is a slug fudge they will have to be uniform in size too.

The plate fudges used by large papers both give scope for variation in heading size and take their text matter solid. Slug fudges of the modern sort take normal slug-lines; but the line-separating wedges give the effect of heavy leading; and when the fudge is run in colour—it is technically more satisfactory to run the fudge in the same colour as the seal—it will be found better to use the Bold face of the text rather than the normal roman. The slug fudge will not normally take slugs of more than 8 pt. body; for headings therefore it is necessary to select as large a cap. letter as can be got on that body. A 10 pt. in the extra-bold range will be found suitable—Pabst or one of the keyboard versions of Ultra-Bodoni.

14 · Other Countries Other Styles

NEWSPAPER make-up styles vary in the same way national characteristics vary. The point can be over-stressed, of course, and it would be foolish to apply it in any automatic or mechanical way. It will be conceded, however, that the exuberance of French newspaper typography can hardly be divorced from the Gallic temperament, that the German passion for *ordnung* is reflected in the stiff make-up of their sheets, and that the clean and open look of the Scandinavian journals exemplifies the *petit-bourgeois* virtues typical of those Northern lands. The genius of the language has something to do with it. Thus French seems well suited to a headline which is a series of sentences, each in a different size and style of type; certainly those Paris papers which have sought to model themselves on the sparer and more disciplined English or American style have only succeeded in making themselves look un-French.

The existence of a national newspaper style does not mean that newspapers, or journalists, should regard themselves as functioning in a species of national vacuum. There is no virtue in the type of newspaper chauvinism which regards anything done by 'the foreigners' as grotesque or suspect. To note and understand the differences in national style enhances an understanding of one's own style, and may encourage useful self-criticism. It is not so much a question of literally translating a particular make-up notion, which can rarely be possible, but rather of broadening the comprehension of make-up problems by observing how they are solved elsewhere, of understanding the essential approach of the newspaperman overseas and thus discovering some point of principle which may with advantage be adapted to the national idiom.

It is instructive, for instance, to note the use of colour in newspapers in other countries besides the United States, which is notably colour-conscious. Full-colour half-tones of remarkable quality are regularly produced as far apart as Finland and Greece, and Scandinavian pioneering in this field is well known. Editorial and advertising line-and-tint colour is featured in leading German newspapers, while editorial colour—headlines, titles, underscoring, box rules, and decorative treatments—has been

EDITION **

Le Parisien libéré

20

124, rue Réaumur, PARIS (2e)
Tél. : GUT. 75-20 (lignes groupées)
Publicité générale : 114, Champs-Elysées

LE PLUS FORT TIRAGE DES QUOTIDIENS FRANÇAIS DU MATIN

15e ANNEE — No 4254
Vendredi 16 mai 1958

CE SOIR
COURSES - 20 heures
à
VINCENNES
PROCHAINES SOIREES : 19 23 et 27 MAI

DE GAULLE : "Je me tiens prêt a assumer les pouvoirs de la République"

DEVANT "LA DÉGRADATION DE L'ÉTAT ET LA DISLOCATION NATIONALE"

Celui qui en 1944 restaura la République s'est adressé hier au pays

Cette déclaration capitale aussitôt diffusée à Alger y a suscité l'enthousiasme

L'APPEL DU 15 MAI

« La dégradation de l'État entraîne infailliblement l'éloignement des peuples associés, le trouble de l'armée au combat, la dislocation nationale, la perte de l'indépendance. Depuis douze ans, la France, aux prises avec des problèmes trop rudes pour le régime des partis, est engagée dans un processus désastreux.

» Naguère, le pays, dans ses profondeurs, m'a fait confiance pour le conduire tout entier jusqu'à son salut.

» Aujourd'hui, devant les épreuves qui montent de nouveau vers lui, qu'il sache que je me tiens prêt à assumer les pouvoirs de la République. »

UN COMITÉ ALGÉRIEN DE SALUT PUBLIC *est sur le point d'étendre* SON AUTORITE A TOUTE L'ALGERIE

Au balcon du gouvernement général, à Alger, le général Salan s'adresse à la foule. (RADIOPHOTO)

Sur la place du Forum, devant 15.000 manifestants le général Salan s'écrie : *"Vive la France ! Vive l'Algérie française ! Vive le général de Gaulle !"*

1 tonne 328! SPOUTNIK III A ÉTÉ LANCÉ HIER EN U.R.S.S.

Véritable observatoire evoluant à 1.880 km. du globe (à son apogée)
le plus lourd satellite du monde renferme 968 kilos *d'instruments scientifiques*

IL N'Y A PAS D'ANIMAUX A BORD

VOIR NOS INFORMATIONS A LA PAGE 18

— Ben vrai, ce qu'il a forci depuis sept mois !
(Dessin de Pol FERJAC)

Sous les acclamations des Algérois, le général Salan quitte le gouvernement général. La foule bloque sa voiture (RADIOPHOTO)

Échec du remaniement ministériel
M. PIERRE PFLIMLIN N'A PU OBTENIR QUE LE CONCOURS DE M. GUY MOLLET
tandis que M. Pinay se récusait

UN CONSEIL DES MINISTRES EXTRAORDINAIRE S'EST TENU CETTE NUIT

Voir pages 8, 9 et 10 :
- l'article de Paul LE GALL ;
- les câbles de nos envoyés spéciaux à Alger : Gérald TILLY et J. PAILLARDIN ;
- nos informations

LES SPORTS
Sensation à Forli où **ANQUETIL CONCÈDE PRÈS DE 5' A L'ITALIEN BALDINI** contre la montre

Le Tour d'Espagne s'est terminé par la victoire de Jean STABLINSKI

Le double sera décisif à Roland-Garros
FRANCE ET CHILI A ÉGALITÉ : 1 A 1
VOIR PAGES 16 ET 17

Ercole Baldini en pleine action

Mystère macabre à Saint-Ouen-l'Aumône
LE CADAVRE D'UN INCONNU ÉTRANGLÉ EST DÉCOUVERT FICELÉ DANS UN SAC
au fond d'une carrière désaffectée (VOIR A LA PAGE 5)

La carrière abandonnée, à Saint-Ouen-l'Aumône, où le cadavre a été trouvé. (Photo « LE PARISIEN libéré »)

LE BILLET DU PARISIEN
de Marc BLANCPAIN

Nouveaux incidents hier à Beyrouth: **10 morts**
VOIR A LA PAGE 3

FIG. 172. The Gallic ultimate; other Parisian and French provincial dailies have some text on *la une*.

used in many European countries since well before the war. Over twenty years ago it was common for Athens papers to combine red and blue in front-page headlines. It is appropriate to recall the point, made in Chapter 2, that this colour work is usually done on short-run papers with minimum plate requirements.

So much by way of introduction. Let us now survey the European newspaper scene, beginning with *France*. The French journalist maintains the distinction between the 'opinion' paper (*journal d'opinion*) and the 'news' paper (*journal d'informations*). The fact that the first carries plenty of news and the second a good deal of opinion does not invalidate the distinction. It is a question of the front page, not of the overall content of the paper; and here the difference is between a paper which always puts on the front page one, two, or more signed editorial articles, not to mention signed major news stories which combine comment with news, and a paper which devotes its front page exclusively to the main news, and news pictures, of the day.

Thus, though the *journal d'informations* accords in principle with British ideas of journalism, in presentation it may be very different, as can be seen from the morning circulation leader *Le Parisien Libéré* (Fig. 172). Its headings-and-pictures-only make-up, cross-referring to the texts of stories variously distributed through the paper, was a pre-war Parisian evening-paper device. In this extreme form it is not general; but a maximum of headlines with a minimum of text on the front page, with such devices as a boxed news précis referring to other pages, stories turning inside and so on, has become common form even with the *journaux d'opinion* (except for their most refined representative, *Le Monde*) (Fig. 173).

A French authority claims that this front-page style brought the chief sub-editor 'freedom from the tyranny of metal' and enabled him 'to visualize the front page as a kind of poster'.[1] It will be observed that this poster-style page presents in its most extravagant form the typographic anarchy which has marked French papers since they first developed big editorial display; a typical *Parisien Libéré* front page in 1958 exhibited thirteen different type families or, with their variants, eighteen series. The reason is simple. These headlines are not written to any specified style;[2] the compositor, given the measure and a notion of the prominence required, selects the types that will make the copy fit these requirements. The resulting make-up is the last word in what the Americans call 'circus' or 'razzle-dazzle'. Yet, as suggested earlier, it appears to suit the French temperament and the French language.

With this front-page turmoil has gone a development of the back-page as the second main news page; a great increase in illustration, both half-tone and line (strips, cartoons, picture-serials); the regular publication of a pull-out 'paper within a paper', printed to fold to quarto, containing

[1] Raymond Manevy, *L'Evolution des formules de présentation de la presse quotidienne* (Paris, 1956), p. 77.

[2] Some of the more sober Parisian 'populars', like the *Figaro*, do work to a heading style, duly specified on copy.

QUINZIEME ANNEE. — Nº 4228. **12 PAGES — DERNIÈRE ÉDITION** JEUDI 28 AOUT 1958.

LIRE EN PAGE

Le Monde

Rédaction, Administration : 5, r. des Italiens, Paris-IXᵉ. — Directeur : Hubert BEUVE-MÉRY.

ABONNEMENTS

	3 mois	6 mois	1 an
France et Un. Fse	1 700 f.	3 300 f.	6 300 f.
Etranger	2 400 f.	4 880 f.	9 750 f.
Af. du Nord (messageries-avion)	1 840 f.	3 580 f.	6 760 f.

Les abonnements partent des 1er et 16 de chaque mois

LE NUMÉRO : 25 fr.

Tun., Mar. : 30 f. Bel.-Lux. : 3 f. Ital. : 50 L.

Adr. télégraphique JOURMONDE PARIS
TÉL. : PRO. 91-29 ; TAI. 70-60
CHÈQUE POSTAL : PARIS Nº 4207-23

BULLETIN DE L'ÉTRANGER

Les missions de M. « H »

M. Hammarskjœld commence aujourd'hui une tournée de trois semaines dans les capitales arabes du Proche-Orient avec mission de déterminer les moyens qui permettraient d'appliquer la résolution adoptée le 21 août dernier par l'Assemblée générale des Nations unies.

Présentée par les dix pays arabes membres de l'O.N.U., cette résolution invite le secrétaire général des Nations unies à s'attaquer aux problèmes politiques, militaires et économiques qui se trouvent à l'origine de la tension qui ne cesse de menacer la paix dans cette région.

M. Hammarskjœld doit en premier lieu chercher la formule qui garantirait l'indépendance et l'intégrité territoriale des pays en cause, et mettrait fin aux ingérences étrangères qui visent à renverser les régimes établis.

La présence des troupes américaines au Liban et celle des forces britanniques en Jordanie sont intimement liées à ce problème. Les gouvernements de Beyrouth et d'Amman estiment, en effet, que l'assistance militaire étrangère leur est indispensable face au danger que fait peser sur eux la République arabe unie du président Nasser.

Enfin M. Hammarskjœld est habilité à engager des pourparlers avec l'ensemble des Etats arabes en vue de l'établissement d'une institution régionale de développement économique. Les Nations unies ont estimé, à juste raison, que l'instabilité politique de l'Orient arabe est due en grande partie à la misère qui y règne et à la concurrence qui s'est engagée entre les grandes puissances pour porter aux pays de la région une aide économique qui n'est pas toujours dépourvue d'arrière-pensées politiques.

Le secrétaire général de l'O.N.U. entreprend sa délicate mission avec un mandat qui lui a été décerné unanimement par les membres des Nations unies. Ceux-ci ont accepté avec satisfaction la résolution arabe, pour des raisons différentes. Le bloc de l'Est et les gouvernements arabes pro-nassériens y ont vu le moyen d'obtenir l'évacuation des troupes anglo-américaines du Proche-Orient. Les puissances occidentales, et en tête les Etats-Unis, espèrent que M. « H » réussira en premier lieu à maintenir le « statu quo » actuel, première condition à l'endiguement de l'expansionnisme nassérien.

Y réussira-t-il ? Au Liban on peut espérer que la situation ne tardera pas à se stabiliser avec le départ, le 23 septembre prochain, du président de la République, M. Chamoun, et la prise du pouvoir par le général Chehab, élu à la fois par les voix de l'opposition et des loyalistes. En revanche à Amman, où il est arrivé ce matin, M. « H » se trouve en présence d'un véritable « casse-tête ».

On sait, en effet, que le roi Hussein s'oppose au remplacement des « bérets rouges » britanniques par des forces de l'O.N.U. Il ne veut pas davantage d'un régime libéral qui ferait appel aux hommes politiques qu'il a congédiés en avril 1957. Il n'est assuré en outre ni de la loyauté de son peuple ni de la bienveillance des pays voisins. Il est difficile dans ces conditions d'accorder à la Jordanie le secours financier dont elle a absolument besoin, et il ne reste plus guère au roi Hussein qu'à se démettre ou à tenter une nouvelle opération de rapprochement avec le camp nassérien, qui pourrait alors l'épargner provisoirement, comme c'est actuellement le cas pour le souverain d'Arabie Séoudite.

Dans l'immédiat la tâche de M. Hammarskjœld semble donc réduite à combler la brèche entre la Jordanie et la République arabe unie, et à préconiser une nouvelle ère de collaboration au sein d'une Ligue arabe rénovée.

C'est seulement après avoir franchi ce premier obstacle que le secrétaire général pourrait atteindre ses deux autres objectifs : obtenir le retrait des forces anglo-américaines du Proche-Orient et instaurer une organisation régionale d'assistance économique.

LE ROI PAUL ET LA REINE FREDERIKA VOGUENT VERS LA FRANCE

Athènes, 27 août (A.P.). — Le roi Paul de Grèce, la reine Frederika, le prince-héritier Constantin et la princesse Sophie ont quitté hier Athènes à bord du destroyer *Polemistis*, de la marine royale grecque. Les souverains grecs se rendent en visite officielle en Suisse.

Un communiqué de la cour indique que la famille royale se rendra d'abord à Paris, puis en Belgique, où elle séjournera trois jours et sera l'hôte de la famille royale de Belgique. Les souverains visiteront l'Exposition internationale de Bruxelles et les mines belges employant des ouvriers grecs.

AVANT SON TROISIÈME SÉJOUR EN ALGÉRIE

Le général de Gaulle a confirmé le choix proposé à l'Afrique noire

Le général de Gaulle, qui a quitté ce matin mercredi Dakar, était attendu à 15 heures à Alger, où l'avaient précédé MM. Guillaumat, ministre des armées, et Buron, ministre des travaux publics. Aucune cérémonie n'a été prévue pour son arrivée. Le général doit s'absenter d'Alger jeudi et vendredi, mais le programme de ses déplacements n'a pas été publié.

Malgré l'accueil désagréable qui lui avait été réservé à Dakar par les représentants de l'Union générale des travailleurs d'Afrique noire et du Parti africain de l'indépendance, le président du conseil a réaffirmé, dans les mêmes termes qu'à Brazzaville, les options les plus larges qui sont offertes aux Africains.

Il est trop tôt pour dégager les répercussions que le voyage du général de Gaulle en Afrique noire aura sur le vote des populations appelées à se prononcer le 28 septembre. Néanmoins certains courants se sont affirmés qui permettent d'établir un premier inventaire. L'accueil réservé au général par les mouvements politique locaux a été, comme on pouvait s'y attendre, chaleureux à Tananarive et à Brazzaville, enthousiaste à Abidjan, mitigé à Conakry, discourtois de la part d'une partie de la population à Dakar.

Dès Brazzaville, et dans l'intention sans doute de prévenir les critiques qu'il prévoyait aux étapes suivantes, le président du conseil a défini avec netteté les options qui sont offertes aux territoires d'outre-mer : communauté franco-africaine, avec les avantages mais aussi les limitations de souveraineté qu'elle implique, ou indépendance — immédiate ou à terme — avec les risques d'isolement qu'elle comporte.

Le choix est assez clair pour que de nombreux leaders africains n'aient pas cru devoir attendre de connaître le texte définitif du projet constitutionnel pour se prononcer. C'est ainsi que M. Houphouet-Boigny, chef de file des partisans de la communauté, a apporté l'adhésion de la plupart des sections R.D.A. d'A.-O.F. et de celles d'A.-E.F., et que M. Tsiranana, à Madagascar, a confirmé au général de Gaulle l'accord qu'il lui avait déjà exprimé à Paris.

D'autres dirigeants locaux ont formulé des critiques, souvent de manière peu explicite, et réservé leur réponse jusqu'à la publication du texte constitutionnel. Cette opposition virtuelle, qui s'est exprimée plus vivement dans la rue que dans les discours, se groupe autour de la section guinéenne du R.D.A. et du Parti du regroupement africain (P.R.A) aussi bien en A.-E. F. que dans son fief du Sénégal. Bien que divergeant sur le programme — l'un prônant la fédération avec la France, l'autre s'en tenant à la confédération, — ces deux courants se rejoignent en une revendication commune, nettement formulée ces derniers jours : l'inscription dans le texte constitutionnel du droit des territoires africains à l'indépendance.

M. Sekou Touré comme M. Senghor ne se contentent pas de l'engagement solennel pris par le général de Gaulle de ne pas s'opposer à la sécession ultérieure des territoires qui n'auront pas trouvé dans la communauté les avantages qu'ils en attendent.

PHILIPPE HERREMAN.

(Lire la suite en 2e page, 5e colonne.)

Des leaders sénégalais déplorent les incidents de Dakar

De notre envoyé spécial JEAN LACOUTURE

Dakar, 27 août. — Cette journée que nous venons de vivre, tumultueuse et irritante, s'inscrira au passif des adversaires de la coopération franco-africaine. Quelles que soient les intentions des leaders politiques locaux, les témoins français ne leur sauront pas gré d'avoir permis, par leur action ou par leur absence, de laisser vulgairement et bêtement « chahuter » le représentant de la France, alors que pour une fois notre pays offrait une révision courageuse et réaliste de la politique africaine.

Quand on pense aux flots de paroles vaines que le régime colonial fit naguère écouter patiemment par les populations, on enrage de voir aujourd'hui des hommes qui ont justement pour objectif la restauration de la dignité africaine opposer des hurlements au programme novateur qui leur est offert.

L'affaire avait mal commencé. Le général de Gaulle et sa suite, à leur arrivée à Dakar, se trouvèrent en présence d'une foule dont les slogans et les banderoles, où il était très naturellement question d'indépendance, étaient moins inquiétants que son attitude de défi. Pour avoir sillonné bien souvent les cités nord-africaines en effervescence révolutionnaire, nous pouvons témoigner que nous y sentîmes bien rarement à ce degré la rancœur raciste. Il est vrai que cette foule provenait du quartier de Médina, où règne une navrante misère. Mais ce que nous entendions était moins l'irrécusable protestation des pauvres qu'une mise en demeure d'un nationalisme qui se cherche dans le sarcasme.

Une atmosphère de meeting

Sur la vaste place Protet, au centre de Dakar, une estrade avait été dressée. Etant donnée l'atmosphère de politisation frénétique qui règne à Dakar, en proie aux clubs pré-révolutionnaires, il était facile de prévoir que la manifestation tournerait au meeting. La place avait été « faite ». Les abords de la tribune étaient occupés surtout par les anciens combattants et traditionalistes. Plus loin se dressaient des pancartes du P.R.A., réclamant l'indépendance et l'unité africaine, tandis que des activistes d'extrême gauche du Parti africain de l'indépendance agitaient des drapeaux rouges au fond de la place, venant d'un meeting rival organisé au stade et qui groupa trois ou quatre mille manifestants aux cris d' « A bas de Gaulle ! »...

Avant le chef du gouvernement divers orateurs prirent la parole, notamment M. Valdiodio N'Diaye, ministre de l'intérieur du Sénégal, qui parlait au nom du président du conseil, M. Mamadou Dia, dont l'absence était sévèrement commentée par les observateurs africains. Cet avocat de Kaolak formula sans aménité les plus intelligentes critiques que nous ayons entendues pendant le périple africain contre les méthodes du référendum. Il n'avait réservé qu'une seule phrase à l'évocation de l'amitié franco-africaine : il est regrettable qu'elle ait été précisément couverte par les vrombissements des avions survolant à ce moment le rassemblement.

Avant même que le général de Gaulle se soit levé, des hurlements rageurs montaient du fond de la place, tandis que des drapeaux rouges frappés de l'étoile noire s'agitaient frénétiquement. Le chef du gouvernement ne tenta pas de faire taire les perturbateurs. La veille, face à M. Sekou Touré, il n'avait pas dissimulé sa mélancolie d'homme de la vieille Europe bousculé par les impatiences africaines. Face au puéril « emboîtage » des agitateurs de Médina il préféra recourir à une furieuse truculence, lançant sa lourde voix contre le flot de cette invincible clameur : « *Messieurs les porteurs de pancartes, si vous voulez l'indépendance, prenez-la !* »

(Lire la suite en page 2, 4e colonne.)

NOUVEAUX ATTENTATS F.L.N. A PARIS

Trois agents et un sous-officier blessés

Le gouvernement prend d'importantes mesures de protection

Les terroristes nord-africains ont de nouveau frappé, la nuit dernière, les représentants de l'ordre. Trois agents de police parisiens ont été atteints par des coups de feu, avenue Denfert-Rochereau, et un sous-officier grièvement blessé dans le couloir du métro Bonne-Nouvelle.

Le F.L.N. est donc décidé à poursuivre et à aggraver son action terroriste sur le territoire métropolitain. Autant que ces nouveaux attentats, les déclarations qu'a faites au Caire M. Ferhat Abbas ne laissent aucun doute. S'il assure que des instructions ont été données aux membres du F.L.N. « pour que les civils soient épargnés », il affirme en même temps la volonté du F.L.N. d'atteindre sur le sol national même « le potentiel économique et militaire de la France ».

Le gouvernement n'a pas sous-estimé la menace. Des mesures ont été prises mardi pour préserver « la sécurité des personnes et des biens » au cours d'une réunion à laquelle ont pris part MM. Guy Mollet, qui assure l'intérim de la présidence du conseil, Emile Pelletier, ministre de l'intérieur, et Guillaumat, ministre des armées. La troupe participerait désormais à la surveillance des installations essentielles à la vie du pays.

L'EXPANSION RUSSE EN AFRIQUE

Le tentacule oriental

L'expansion russe, commencée à la fin du XIXᵉ siècle, momentanément arrêtée entre les deux guerres mondiales pour permettre à la nouvelle U.R.S.S. de forger son organisation politique et de créer de toutes pièces cette puissance industrielle et économique dont le développement extraordinaire s'est tout dernièrement mis en évidence, a retrouvé toute sa vigueur depuis l'écrasement de l'Allemagne hitlérienne. Se montrant les champions de toutes les « idées-forces » qui naissent à travers un monde en pleine transformation, les Soviets ont étendu leur zone d'influence à la moitié de l'Europe et à la quasi-totalité de l'Asie. Aujourd'hui leur objectif est l'Afrique, et ils ne l'ont pas caché lors de la conférence du Caire qui s'est réunie en décembre 1957.

Le moment est particulièrement bien choisi pour s'attaquer à un continent qui, hier encore, était la paisible chasse gardée des grandes puissances européennes ; les tempêtes du nationalisme et de l'anticolonialisme, après avoir, dès l'après-guerre, balayé l'Asie, soufflent aujourd'hui sur l'Afrique. Du Caire, Nasser s'efforce de contrôler et d'orienter une partie de ces courants par le « panarabisme » et le « panislamisme ». Le premier, comme un immense tentacule, recouvre la partie nord de l'Afrique, atteint l'Atlantique, se recourbe vers la Mauritanie pour se terminer, menaçant, aux frontières du bloc noir islamisé. Le second descend le long de la mer Rouge, aborde l'océan Indien, contourne le bassin éthiopien qu'il isole, et, par les Somalis, s'allonge jusqu'au sud de l'Equateur.

Trop absorbée par les dangers du nationalisme panarabe nord-africain, la France a tendance à ne pas suffisamment voir le péril que représente, pour elle et pour ses territoires de l'océan Indien, le tentacule oriental qui s'apprête à faire de la mer Rouge une mer arabe avant d'en faire une mer soviétique : or ce sont les communications entre l'Europe et l'Asie, c'est tout le ravitaillement en hydrocarbures en provenance du Moyen-Orient, c'est l'avenir immédiat de Djibouti et de Madagascar, c'est le sort de l'Ethiopie qui sont en jeu.

Les forces en présence

On ne saurait parler de l'Afrique orientale sans y englober l'immense péninsule arabe, son prolongement naturel.

Par ses richesses considérables en pétrole, ce désert, politiquement morcelé, est devenu l'une des régions les plus importantes du globe, le vaste réservoir énergétique de l'Europe. Les Anglais, en tenant Aden et en contrôlant la frange côtière jusqu'au fond du golfe Persique ; les Américains par leurs concessions pétrolières, avaient fait de cette région une « zone d'influence » chèrement acquise, âprement disputée, perpétuellement convoitée.

Il semble qu'actuellement la double domination anglo-saxonne soit tout particulièrement menacée.

Le Yémen, violemment antibritannique, s'est rallié à la République arabe unifiée de Nasser et se trouve en état de guerre larvée contre Aden ; il constitue déjà, aux yeux des nationalistes égyptiens, la base de départ des offensives militaires et de propagande qui doivent chasser les Anglais d'Aden et libérer les petits Etats arabes de l'Hadramaout, d'Oman, de Mascate que le Colonial Office britannique tente en vain de fédérer sous la forme d'un « Etat d'Arabie du Sud » affilié au Commonwealth. Tout dernièrement même, le sultan de Lahej, le plus puissant du protectorat occidental d'Aden, et dont le territoire jouxte la « colony » d'Aden, ne cachait pas son intention d'adhérer à la R.A.U.

« C'est à Aden que Nasser attend les Anglais », déclarait dernièrement la radio du Caire. Cette menace laisse présager des jours sombres pour les Britanniques, car la guérilla déjà existante peut dégénérer, avec les armes russes et les instructeurs égyptiens chargés d'encadrer les troupes yéménites, en une véritable guerre encouragée et appuyée indirectement par l'aviation et les moyens militaires de la R.A.U. Déjà le correspondant du *Times* à Aden signale que des travaux sont prévus à Hodeida pour en faire une base navale et une base pour les sous-marins soviétiques.

Mais à l'intérieur de la péninsule le problème est aussi grave ; les difficultés du roi Séoud, plus ou moins supplanté par son frère Feyçal, indiquent une évolution pronassérienne, dont les Américains s'inquiètent à juste titre. Certes, pour lutter contre le panarabisme anti-occidental, les Américains disposent de leurs dollars et d'installations apparemment solides. Mais leur prestige a baissé au profit de celui des Russes ; à leur orgueilleuse puissance financière les Russes, lors de la conférence du Caire en particulier, opposent les résultats foudroyants de leur industrie lourde, et au « mercantilisme » des premiers les seconds opposent un désintéressement qui se dit amical.

Or, la perte par l'Europe des pétroles du Moyen-Orient aurait des répercussions immenses pour toute l'économie du vieux continent. A moins que le Sahara ne puisse prendre la relève. Ce à quoi Nasser et Moscou s'efforceront de l'empêcher. Mais « cela est une autre histoire ».

Retournons dans l'Afrique proprement dite : il nous suffit d'enjamber le canal de Suez pour être dans l'Egypte nassérienne, jeune nation bruyante, fière de sa vigoureuse adolescence, enivrée de se voir choyée par une Russie tendrement amicale et une Amérique craintive et perplexe.

Un des grands mérites de Nasser est d'avoir su ranimer les vieux idéaux du « panarabisme » et du « panislamisme » ; mieux, il les a personnifiés, et son portrait, tiré à des milliers d'exemplaires, trône dans les foyers non seulement arabes, mais encore musulmans, comme le symbole d'une ère nouvelle où les disciples de Mahomet de toutes les races prendraient conscience de leur solidarité pour sortir de leur médiocrité, de leur servitude et assurer le triomphe de leur religion et de leurs concepts de vie.

ALBERT DUQUET.

(Lire la suite en 2e page, 2e colonne.)

AU JOUR LE JOUR

LE LANGAGE DES PIERRES

Les murs du passage souterrain de l'Etoile qui conduira à la tombe du Soldat inconnu doivent être revêtus d'inscriptions destinées à magnifier le sacrifice de celui qui repose sous la dalle et de ses compagnons. Or il paraît que ces inscriptions ne seraient pas de la meilleure qualité littéraire. Un conseiller municipal, ayant eu connaissance des textes projetés, vient d'inviter le préfet de la Seine à relire ses auteurs et à réviser son choix.

Il est à craindre qu'il ne soit pas très aisé de le satisfaire. L'épigraphe est un genre difficile. Si la postérité n'avait pour se faire une idée du génie de Paul Valéry que les maximes qu'il a composées pour le palais de Chaillot, son jugement risquerait de manquer d'indulgence.

Au surplus est-il nécessaire de couvrir les murs du souterrain de l'Etoile de citations, fussent-elles excellentes ? La nudité de la pierre a aussi son éloquence. En un pareil endroit toute littérature n'est-elle pas inutile ?

Aussi bien, à une époque où l'architecture propose systématiquement des surfaces lisses et refuse à l'œil la distraction d'ornements jugés superflus, à quoi bon solliciter l'attention par des phrases, même belles ? Mieux vaut laisser chacun à sa méditation, à ses souvenirs...

Et si l'on tient absolument à graver quelques paroles, ne suffit-il pas de « ceux qui pieusement... ». Vous savez, comme moi, la suite par cœur. A-t-on dit mieux ?

ROGER DARDENNE.

FIG. 173. French 'class' style; an echo of *Le Temps* of other days.

radio programmes and the like; and exploitation of the 'skyline' streamer, sometimes a reverse block, over the title-line to announce forthcoming features or to signal a big inside story.

Text in an eight-column page is usually 7 pt. (or under). Signed articles are by custom set in a different type face from that of the body of the paper —a roman or an italic of an entirely different fount (maybe an Old Face or some form of book letter) or a light Egyptian—and each article is often set in a different face. There is something to be said for this custom.

As for title-lines, France is understandably enough the country where the Anglo-German Gothic style has never taken root (*Le Monde* is an exception in following its predecessor *Le Temps* in this respect). Some form of heavy slab-seriffed Egyptian, frequently in lower-case, is the favourite style, and very effective it is. Perhaps this is why radical style changes in French title-lines are practically unknown. The title of the *Figaro* has not changed since the paper's birth as a bi-weekly in 1856; that of *l'Humanité* is merely a reduced version of the line that Jean Jaurès approved for its first issue in 1904.

France has always been simply a market, not a manufacturing base, for the international composing machine monopolies. All machine-set headlines—and French newspaper printers are Ludlow enthusiasts—are therefore in American or British faces, duly provided with accents. French faces only appear when, for size or style reasons, founders' type is used; perhaps for a main streamer above the Ludlow limit, or for a special feature calling for the light fantastic. It is a curious point to note, especially in the light of the great traditions, and sensitive style, of French type design. Much the same has come to apply to text; when the *Parisien Libéré* restyled its text in 1958 it chose a British news-text, Linotype Jubilee.

The position in *Germany*, West or East, is exactly the reverse. The native type foundries are the most famous, and the most prolific, in the world; the German subsidiaries of the slug machine monopolies design and manufacture their own matrices; and as a result, since the Ludlow is not commonly used in Germany, the typography of the German newspaper is as exclusively national as its make-up. This may be described as formal horizontal, the main accent on the page being a series of double-column headings, squared-off with their stories under each other, or stepped-off with alternate three-column headings. The headings are normally two lower-case single-line decks, each as a rule written short of measure, the first deck in a bolder or contrasting letter, the second deck half or less than half the body of the first. An entire page will have its headings in identical size and style.

The effect is orderly but stiff, offering no scope for variations in emphasis on news. Pictures and colour, both well handled, help to give some

Größte deutsche Abendzeitung

Hamburger Abendblatt

UNABHÄNGIG — ÜBERPARTEILICH

Nr. 279/Jahrgang 10/Preis 35 Pf (ausw. 40 Pf)

Hamburg, Sbd./Stg., 30. Nov./1. Dez. 1957

Briefe an das Rote Kreuz - Sie rufen uns alle! (Siehe Seite 32)

Professor Thielicke stellt fest:

Urteil gegen Leipziger Pfarrer schmähliche Rechtsbeugung

Parteien protestieren

Kollision vor Brunsbüttelkoog

Sonntag ist 1. Advent

Lesen Sie heute:

2500 Abiturienten

Menschlich gesehen:

Pastor mit „New Look"

Bundeskanzler fliegt Mittwoch nach London

Vorbereitungen trotz Erkältung Adenauers

Mit 1500 Mann gesunken?

Unbestätigte Meldung über sowjetische Schiffskatastrophe 1955

Das Sowjet-Schlachtschiff „Noworossiisk"

Der tödliche Speerwurf

Unterpflasterbahn

Doch nach Brüssel

Eisenhower auf der Farm

Schnelle Besserung / Nixon leitet Kabinettssitzung

Auch Bahnsteigkarten

Frost

Vorhersage fürs Wochenende:

FIG. 174. This leading German evening always has colour on its front page; here the reverse block banner is in red.

life particularly to front pages (Fig. 174). There are three standard newspaper formats in Germany of which the most popular, the Berlin format, is slightly deeper and wider than our normal half-sheet or tabloid; the Berlin cut-off is approximately 18½ inches, accommodating five 12-em (cicero) columns with em whites, or sometimes four 15-em columns. The large format is approximately the width of our standard format, its cut-off about an inch less (22½ in.). The maximum number of columns is seven, but six is more usual, and there is a widespread tendency to abandon column rules for em whites. Thus the German practice, compared with British, is to have fewer but wider columns; the red-splashed Hamburg 8-column tabloid-style broadsheet, the *Bild Zeitung*, is an exception.

Anno 83 - N. 204 - L. 30 (Arretrato L. 40) — IL NUOVO — Milano, Giovedì 28 agosto 1958 - L. 30

CORRIERE DELLA SERA

STEVENSON NARRA IL SUO VIAGGIO NELL'U. R. S. S.

Basata su strane pretese la "buona volontà" di Kruscev

Egli non ammette che gli Stati Uniti si interessino di quanto avviene nel mondo comunista, ma pretende che gli sforzi di penetrazione comunisti nel mondo libero non vengano intralciati

CONFERENZA-STAMPA ALLA CASA BIANCA

L'importanza di Quemoy rilevata da Eisenhower

Un terzo delle forze di Ciang Kai-scek è impegnato nelle isole davanti a Formosa - Il Presidente conferma che l'atomica sarebbe usata solo su suo ordine

COLPI DI SCENA NELL'INCHIESTA SULL'« ANONIMA »

GIUFFRÈ SI RIFÀ VIVO

E DICHIARA CHE PAGHERÀ TUTTI

Soldati di Ciang Kai-scek preparano sbarramenti di filo spinato sulle coste dell'isola di Quemoy. (Telefoto al «Nuovo Corriere della Sera»).

Giovanbattista Giuffrè, con il figlio, ieri, a Bologna.

GLI ATTENTATI TERRORISTICI IN FRANCIA

I piani di sabotaggio del F.L.N. erano stati preparati a Ginevra

Nel corso della riunione gli interventisti ebbero la meglio sugli attendisti - Le ipotesi sulla provenienza degli esplosivi impiegati dagli algerini - 4 agenti feriti da "fellaga" a Parigi

L'incendio minaccia un altro serbatoio a Marsiglia

Il generale De Gaulle, nella sosta a Dakar del suo viaggio, è stato accolto dai notabili. (Telefoto).

FIG. 175. Typical of Italy—squared-off multi-column headings, rare crossheads and one main story set all in italic.

POLITIKEN

POLITIKENS SPORT med 6 SIDER FOR SIG IDRÆTS BLADET

KØBENHAVN, MANDAG 25. AUGUST 1958

Afgørende møde om 12 mile begynder i dag

Stor spænding omkring drøftelserne, som foregaar under hele verdens opmærksomhed

Engelsk regerings-communiqué udsendt i aftes ★ Hvad man er villig til ★ Islands stilling

Tre cyprioter dræbt under ildkamp med engelske tropper

Atom-ubaaden „Skate" til Oslo i dag

Islands afhængighed af fiskeriet

6 + 6 mil med dispensationer

Aksel Larsen slaas som „arg" titoist

Kampen i kommunist-partiet fortsatte endnu i aftes – Forberedelser til partikongres

Kamp om politisk kursændring

USA-drabant sporløst forsvundet i rummet

Alle fire trin i raketten eksploderet i rigtig rækkefølge – men ingen lyd fra drabanten

Skulle udforske det radioaktive bælte

Større fare for rumrejser end hidtil troet

Inde i bladet

Kroniken:

Annonce-register:

Opfordring ikke nødvendig:

Fransk interesse for vaaben-leverancer til Vesttyskland

Indien søger økonomisk støtte i Vesten

Jane Horney-filmen:

„En lang kæde af løftebrud"

Jørn Jeppesen gaar imod dir. Malmströms reklamemetoder ★ „Vi har ikke søgt den historiske sandhed", siger filmens forfatter

Usmageligt og urigtigt

Premièren væk fra 29. august

Sovjet bryder aftale om hvede til Jugoslavien

Ooouuuggg trrr-æ-æ-kk — oouuuuuuuugg trrr-æ-æ-ekh:

FIG. 176. The Scandinavian (Danish) style, in Sanserif.

The systematization and good house-setting of display advertisements, as well as the clear styling and disposition of the 'smalls', deserve remark. Title-lines, though now often in bold hand-drawn roman lettering, offer an excellent selection of crisp and well-spaced Gothic of various styles.

The *Italian* style is even more horizontal than the German; that is to say, it runs to four- or five-column headlines; but it is not formal (Fig. 175).

It might be called informal horizontal, since the three or four main headings on a page will each, French fashion, be in a different type-style. The only common feature is that the headings are all two-line, all lower-case, and both lines are driven full out to measure. Light-weight strap-lines or decks may be used. Format is eight or nine column and crossheads are rarely employed even in lengthy stories, of which at least one per page will be set entirely in italic.

Scandinavia's newspapers, whether Danish, Norwegian, or Swedish, have a broad general style quite unlike any other, which might be described as architectural. These pages have the air of being constructed, built, rather than made up (Fig. 176). Type mixtures are generally avoided and contrast secured by varying style—roman/italic, light/bold—with devices like the careful letter-spacing of caps. Flush-left or neatly stepped headings in lower-case read into leaded text; the Swedes favour Bodoni (normal weight) while the Danes tend to prefer Sans. Page make-up is a well-planned exercise in asymmetrical balance. The multiplication of stories on the front page, however, often produces a substantial number of turns.

Two exotics, that is newspapers of countries not using the Latin alphabet, may conclude this brief sketch of European newspaper styles. The example from *Greece* (Fig. 177) is simply intended to show the

Τετάρτη, 22 Ἰουλίου 1959 ΑΚΡΟΠΟΛΙΣ

ΕΔΗΜΟΣΙΕΥΘΗΣΑΝ ΧΘΕΣ ΑΙ ΣΥΜΦΩΝΙΑΙ ΠΕΡΙ ΤΩΝ ΑΤΟΜΙΚΩΝ ΟΠΛΩΝ ΜΕΤΑΞΥ ΕΛΛΑΔΟΣ, ΑΜΕΡΙΚΗΣ ΚΑΙ ΑΛΛΩΝ ΧΩΡΩΝ

ΟΙ ΠΥΡΗΝΙΚΟΙ ΚΩΝΟΙ ΥΠΟ ΤΟΝ ΕΛΕΓΧΟΝ ΤΩΝ ΗΠΑ

ΣΑΦΗΣ ΟΜΟΛΟΓΙΑ ΠΕΡΙ ΙΔΕΟΛΟΓΙΚΗΣ ΚΡΙΣΕΩΣ ΕΙΣ ΤΟ ΣΤΡΑΤΟΠΕΔΟΝ ΤΟΥ

Ο ΚΡΟΥΤΣΕΦ ΕΙΣ ΒΙΑΙΟΝ ΛΟΓΟΝ ΕΣΤΡΑΦΗ ΕΜΜΕΣΩΣ ΚΑΤΑ ΤΟΥ ΤΙΤΟ ΕΠΙΚΡΙΝΩΝ ΔΡΙΜΥΤΑΤΑ ΤΟΥΣ ΡΕΒΙΖΙΟΝΙΣΤΑΣ ΚΑΙ ΔΟΓΜΑΤΙΣΤΑΣ

ΠΑΡΕΔΕΧΘΗ ΟΤΙ «ΤΟΙΑΥΤΑ ΣΤΟΙΧΕΙΑ» ΥΠΑΡΧΟΥΝ ΗΔΗ ΚΑΙ ΕΙΣ ΤΗΝ ΣΟΒ. ΕΝΩΣΙΝ ΚΑΙ ΔΙΕΚΗΡΥΞΕΝ ΟΤΙ «ΘΑ ΑΓΩΝΙΣΘΩΜΕΝ ΜΕ ΣΤΑΘΕΡΑ ΜΕΤΡΑ ΕΝΑΝΤΙΟΝ ΤΩΝ»

ΙΣΧΥΡΙΣΘΗ ΟΤΙ ΕΝΙΣΧΥΟΝΤΑΙ ΑΠΟ ΤΑΣ ΔΥΤΙΚΑΣ «ΑΝΤΙΔΡΑΣΤΙΚΑΣ» ΔΥΝΑΜΕΙΣ

ΔΙΗΠΕΙΡΩΤΙΚΟΣ ΠΥΡΑΥΛΟΣ «ΑΤΛΑΣ» ΕΞΕΤΟΞΕΥΘΗ ΕΠΙΤΥΧΩΣ ΕΚ ΚΑΝΑΒΕΡΑΛ ΔΙΗΝΥΣΕΝ ΑΠΟΣΤΑΣΙΝ 5.500 ΜΙΛΛΙΩΝ

Ο ΚΩΝΟΣ ΤΟΥ ΠΕΡΙΣΥΝΕΛΕΓΗ ΚΑΙ ΘΑ ΕΞΕΤΑΣΘΗ

ΚΑΤΑΣΚΕΥΑΖΕΤΑΙ ΗΔΗ ΦΟΡΗΤΟΣ ΠΥΡΑΥΛΟΣ ΔΥΝΑΜΕΝΟΣ ΝΑ ΦΕΡΕΤΑΙ ΕΙΣ ΩΜΟΝ ΣΤΡΑΤΙΩΤΟΥ

ΑΥΡΙΟΝ ΘΑ ΛΗΦΘΟΥΝ ΟΡΙΣΤΙΚΑΙ ΑΠΟΦΑΣΕΙΣ ΔΙΑ ΤΗΝ ΑΝΑΔΙΑΡΘΡΩΣΙΝ ΤΩΝ ΚΑΛΛΙΕΡΓΕΙΩΝ

ΕΥΡΕΙΑ ΣΥΣΚΕΨΙΣ ΤΩΝ ΑΡΜΟΔΙΩΝ ΠΑΡΑΓΟΝΤΩΝ

Ο ΝΙΞΟΝ ΑΝΑΧΩΡΕΙ ΣΗΜΕΡΟΝ ΕΙΣ ΤΗΝ ΡΩΣΙΑΝ

ΜΕΤΑΦΕΡΕΙ ΕΙΣ ΤΟΥΣ ΗΓΕΤΑΣ ΤΟΥ ΚΡΕΜΛΙΝΟΥ ΤΗΝ ΑΠΟΦΑΣΙΝ ΤΗΣ ΑΜΕΡΙΚΗΣ ΝΑ ΔΙΑΠΡΑΓΜΑΤΕΥΘΗ ΜΕ ΕΛΑΣΤΙΚΟΤΗΤΑ, ΑΛΛΑ ΑΝΕΥ ΟΥΔΕΜΙΑΣ ΑΔΥΝΑΜΙΑΣ

ΚΑΘΕΙΛΚΥΣΘΗ ΤΟ ΠΡΩΤΟΝ ΑΤΟΜΟΚΙΝΗΤΟΝ ΦΟΡΤΗΓΟΝ ΣΚΑΦΟΣ ΕΙΣ ΤΑΣ ΗΝΩΜ. ΠΟΛΙΤΕΙΑΣ ΜΕ ΜΙΚΡΑΝ ΠΟΣΟΤΗΤΑ ΟΥΡΑΝΙΟΥ ΘΑ ΕΙΝΕ ΔΥΝΑΤΟΝ ΝΑ ΚΙΝΗΤΑΙ ΕΠΙ 3 ΕΤΗ ΣΥΝΕΧΩΣ

ΜΕΤΕΚΛΗΘΗΣΑΝ ΞΕΝΟΙ ΚΑΘΗΓΗΤΑΙ, ΕΙΔΙΚΟΙ ΔΙΑ ΤΗΝ ΑΞΙΟΠΟΙΗΣΙΝ ΤΩΝ ΑΓΡΟΤΙΚΩΝ ΕΡΓΩΝ

Ο κ. ΒΕΝΙΖΕΛΟΣ ΔΗΛΟΙ ΟΤΙ Η ΡΟΥΜΑΝΙΑ ΕΠΙΘΥΜΕΙ ΝΑ ΑΥΞΗΣΗ ΤΑΣ ΣΥΝΑΛΛΑΓΑΣ ΜΕ ΤΗΝ ΕΛΛΑΔΑ

Ο ΚΡΟΥΤΣΕΦ ΔΕΝ ΠΗΓΑΙΝΕΙ ΕΙΣ ΣΚΑΝΔΥΝΑΥΪΑΝ ΔΙΟΤΙ ΦΟΒΕΙΤΑΙ ΟΤΙ ΘΑ ΤΟΝ ΑΠΕΔΟΚΙΜΑΖΟΝ ΕΒΑΡΥΝΘΗ ΚΑΙ ΤΟ ΠΡΟΓΡΑΜΜΑ ΔΕΞΙΩΣΕΩΝ...

ΕΨΗΦΙΣΘΗ ΚΑΤ' ΑΡΧΗΝ ΤΟ Ν.Δ. ΠΕΡΙ ΑΝΩΤΑΤΩΝ ΣΧΟΛΩΝ

ΑΥΞΑΝΟΥΝ ΤΑ ΤΜΗΜΑΤΑ ΣΠΟΥΔΩΝ, ΔΗΜΙΟΥΡΓΟΥΝΤΑΙ ΝΕΑ ΕΡΓΑΣΤΗΡΙΑ ΚΑΙ ΕΞΑΣΦΑΛΙΖΕΤΑΙ ΑΡΤΙΟΝ ΕΠΙΣΤΗΜΟΝΙΚΟΝ ΠΡΟΣΩΠΙΚΟΝ

ΘΑ ΚΑΤΑΡΓΗΘΟΥΝ ΤΑ ΠΙΣΤΟΠΟΙΗΤΙΚΑ ΤΩΝ ΚΟΙΝΩΝΙΚΩΝ ΦΡΟΝΗΜΑΤΩΝ

Ο κ. ΒΟΓΙΑΤΖΗΣ ΑΝΑΛΥΕΙ ΤΟ ΝΟΜΟΣΧΕΔΙΟΝ

ΑΝΑΧΩΡΕΙ ΕΙΣ ΑΓΚΥΡΑΝ ΣΗΜΕΡΟΝ Ο κ. ΜΠΙΤΣΙΟΣ

ΟΛΟΚΛΗΡΩΣΙΣ ΕΛΛΗΝΟΤΟΥΡΚΙΚΩΝ ΣΥΝΟΜΙΛΙΩΝ

Ο ΔΡ. ΑΝΤΕΝΑΟΥΕΡ ΑΠΕΔΕΧΘΗ ΤΗΝ ΠΡΟΣΚΛΗΣΙΝ

FIG. 177. An Athenian news page; note the predominance of caps. and the Italianate squared-off headings.

Пролетарии всех стран, соединяйтесь!

ВЕЧЕРНЯЯ МОСКВА

27 АВГУСТА 1958 г. СРЕДА № 202 (10.568) ЦЕНА 20 КОП.

Газета Московского городского комитета Коммунистической партии Советского Союза и Моссовета

В честь великого Октября

Когда берегут драгоценные секунды

На уровень 1960 года!

НАМ СЕГОДНЯ СООБЩИЛИ:

МИРОВОЙ РЕКОРД ФЛОРЫ СОЛДАДЗЕ

По пути технического прогресса

НА КОНГРЕССЕ ФИДЕ

Лаборантка Е. Кузнецова—чемпионка спартакиады

ТУРИСТЫ ВЫЕХАЛИ В ЧЕХОСЛОВАКИЮ

ОХОТНИКИ ФИНЛЯНДИИ

Спутник в полете

ПОГОДА

ИСКУССТВЕННЫЕ ЗАМЕНИТЕЛИ КОЖИ

Незаконные действия английских властей в Гонконге

Рост экономики социалистических государств

За рубежом

Китайские фильмы под запретом

Американская печать о положении пуэрториканцев в США

В странах народной демократии

ВЫСОКИЕ УРОЖАИ В РУМЫНИИ

ВНЕШНЯЯ ТОРГОВЛЯ ВЕНГРИИ

ОСВОЕНИЕ ПУСТУЮЩИХ ЗЕМЕЛЬ В АЛБАНИИ

НОВАЯ ТОПЛИВНАЯ БАЗА БОЛГАРИИ

Ветераны революционного движения Австрии горячо приветствуют москвичей

Встреча на Ленинградском вокзале

FIG. 178. Moscow's evening paper, the *Vechernaya Moskva*, pioneer in 'popular' make-up (Russian style) with a seven-column page.

influence of language on typographic display. It will be noted that all the headlines are in caps., banked in several single-line decks; the reason for the exclusive use of caps. is to avoid the complication of the many accented sorts Greek requires in lower-case. It will be observed that the columns are narrow.

In the *Soviet Union* the Germanic broad gauge is still usual, and

ВОТ ОНО—НАСТОЯЩЕЕ ДЕЛО ДЛЯ СЕРДЕЦ БЕСПОКОЙНЫХ И СМЕЛЫХ

ПРОЛЕТАРИИ ВСЕХ СТРАН, СОЕДИНЯЙТЕСЬ!

Орган Центрального Комитета ВЛКСМ

КОМСОМОЛЬСКАЯ ПРАВДА

Год издания 35-й № 146 (10471)

Среда, 24 июня 1959 года

Цена 20 коп.

Сегодня начинает свою работу Пленум Центрального Комитета Коммунистической партии Советского Союза.

ОБГОНЯЯ ВРЕМЯ

Автомат—хозяин скважины

Рязанские «спутники»

Н. С. Хрущев принял А. Гарримана

На каждого—два станка

ИСКАТЕЛИ

ДОСРОЧНО!

FIG. 179. The Soviet youth daily, *Komsomolskaya Pravda*, brightens its six-column page with narrow-measure settings and free headlining. Note the two-line banner—a slogan—over the title-piece.

Russian make-up tends to the horizontal German style (Fig. 178). There is a good deal more type variation in headlining, however, and the make-up style is sometimes pressed to greater extremes; a one-line two- or three-column heading will have doubled under it a story of only half a dozen lines. It would be wrong to imagine, however, that the heavy six-column make-up of *Pravda* is typical of the whole Soviet Press, where in fact a great deal of experimentation is going on. The official *Izvestia*, now seven columns, is brisker in its typography than the Party organ, while the principal youth paper, *Komsomolskaya Pravda*, is displaying a very lively spirit in page make-up (Fig. 179).

The *United States* is a country, or rather a continent, which has no national daily newspapers in the British sense. Even the metropolitan papers are local. Yet the American newspaper leads the world in conforming to a national style, and a style which is not, like our own, mainly empirical. The typography and make-up now normal from the 49th Parallel to the Gulf, from Atlantic to Pacific, were worked out in a generation of theoretical exposition and discussion of general principles initiated by the late John E. Allen, to whom reference was made in Chapter 3. Allen's long editorship of the *Linotype News*, earning it the title 'the nation's typographic laboratory', and the three textbooks he published between 1936 and 1947, transformed the newspapers of a nation.

Allen revolted against the traditional, highly formalized style of American newspaper headlining and make-up, with its elaborate decker headings alternating main decks in caps. (either full out to measure or closely stepped) with over-wordy, inverted-pyramid, lower-case decks. The style, with its corollary of perfect symmetry in make-up, survives in classical perfection in the *New York Times* to this day (Fig. 180). The essentials of Allen's revolutionary doctrine were simple: (1) lower-case is more legible in display than caps. and therefore makes a better news headline; (2) headlines should be set flush-left and abandon the old strict and stiff justification to the column.

For many years now the annual Ayer Cup contest for newspaper design—instituted by the N. W. Ayer advertising agency in 1931—has shown how these doctrines have become the accepted practice of the best-produced United States newspapers. It may be claimed that the old formalism persists more in the newspapers which do not enter for the contest; but the number and distribution of the entries suggest that they are a fair, if not an exact, cross-section of America's over 2,500 English-language dailies (the entry figure for 1960 was 859). Frequently the fidelity to Allen's textbook specimen headlines is complete. The 1958 Cup winner, the tabloid *Gazette and Daily* of York (Pa.), adopted as its main single-column style his suggested three lines of 34 pt. Erbar Light Condensed set flush-left (Fig. 181); so did the *Goshen News*, 1959 winner.[1]

The *Gazette and Daily*, first tabloid to win the coveted Cup, well exemplifies the American use of the term in its format sense only, that is

[1] John E. Allen, *Newspaper Designing* (New York, 1947), p. 77.

"All the News That's Fit to Print"

The New York Times.

LATE CITY EDITION

VOL. CVIII. No. 36,767. NEW YORK, TUESDAY, SEPTEMBER 23, 1958. FIVE CENTS

SHERMAN ADAMS RESIGNS; SEES 'VILIFICATION' DRIVE; PRESIDENT VOICES SADNESS

AIDE GOES ON TV

Tells Nation He Was Innocent of Wrong in Goldfine Case

By RUSSELL BAKER

CONFERENCE IN NEWPORT: President Eisenhower accompanies Sherman Adams to helicopter after talk at summer White House. The Assistant to the President had flown there early yesterday to confer on his resignation.

U. S. SAYS PEIPING IS 'SHOOTING' AWAY TAIWAN SOLUTION

Holds Red China's Attacks on Offshore Island Bar Entry as U. N. Member

GROMYKO IN NEW THREAT

Asserts Washington Must Stop 'Playing With Fire' Before It Is Too Late

By THOMAS J. HAMILTON

U.N. Votes 61-10 to Debate Hungarian Killing of Nagy

Assembly Overrides Soviet's Protests —Budapest Minister Says Discussion Till 'Doomsday' Won't Alter Things

By KATHLEEN TELTSCH

GOV. COLLINS ASKS U.S.-STATE BOARDS FOR INTEGRATION

Tells Southern Governors Congress Should Move Quickly on Problem

By CLAUDE SITTON

CITY HALL AWAITS PUBLIC REACTION TO OFF-TRACK TAX

But Mayor Stresses Need for Funds—Talk of Sales Levy Rise 'Very General'

By CHARLES G. BENNETT

No Decision on Cease-Fire, New Warsaw Meeting Set

By A. M. ROSENTHAL

TAIWAN BIDS U. S. BACK AIR ATTACK

Chiang Said to Ask Approval for Raiding Red Guns—Effectiveness Doubted

By ROBERT TRUMBULL

Birth Control Rule Says 2 Physicians Must Certify Need

By PETER KIHSS

REPUBLICANS SEE GOVERNMENT LOSS

Nixon and Alcorn Extol Aide —Others Say Resignation Is for Good of Party

BEIRUT SEETHING ON EVE OF CHANGE

Chehab Takes Office Today —Shooting Erupts in City

By SAM POPE BREWER

Israel Getting Arms From U.S. and Allies

By DANA ADAMS SCHMIDT

Van Buren Peaceful as Negroes Return to School

Three of the eight Negro students who returned to Van Buren High School enter building.

6 HOURS OF SCHOOL GIVEN ON TV HERE

State Starts Program Aimed at Classes and Homes

By LEONARD BUDER

Mary Roberts Rinehart Is Dead; Author of Mysteries and Plays

FIG. 180. The super-symmetrical *New York Times* sometimes makes concessions like this to asymmetrical make-up.

The Weather—
Hot, humid through tomorrow with scattered showers tomorrow. High 85-93. Details on Page 30.

The Gazette and Daily

The news all the time without fear or favor, bias or prejudice.

Vol. 144—No. 23084 | York, Pa., Saturday Morning, July 18, 1959 | Price 5c—25c a Week

Conferees OK Foreign Aid Bill Slashing Military

Senate-House group cut $200 million from Eisenhower's $1.6 billion arms aid request. Conferees call on President to have specific plans next year on how to cut foreign grants. Both houses to act soon on measure.

Washington (UP)—A bill putting a $3,556,200,000 ceiling on foreign aid this year—$353,200,000 less than President Eisenhower asked—won approval yesterday from a Senate-House Conference committee.

The conferees, fitting together the versions passed by the Senate and House, also called on the President to come up with specific plans next year on how to start cutting off foreign grants.

The biggest cut in the adjusted version was $200 million from Eisenhower's request for $1.6 billion in military aid. This was achieved by those who argue that the administration is relying too much on arms aid, rather than economic.

The legislation is to be called up in the House Wednesday, and in the Senate soon thereafter. It provides only an authorization for foreign aid in the fiscal year which began July 1; the actual appropriation must be voted later and it could be under the authorized ceiling.

In addition to holding the military aid total to $1.4 billion, the compromise bill eliminates a Senate earmarking of $893,670,000 for countries in the North Atlantic Treaty Organization (NATO). This would permit more to be spent on non-NATO countries, including Korea and Formosa.

It also provides that no more than $67 million may be spent on military assistance to Latin American countires, the same amount as last year.

(Continued on Page Thirty-One)
See Foreign Aid Bill

City Will Allot $21,500 To Hire Planners Directly

A bill introduced in city council yesterday appropriated $21,500 to complete center city planning by hiring planners directly. The money will come from a loan made in 1958.

The plan of hiring the planners directly was devised by City Solicitor John W. Heller III after he had ruled that council under state law could not channel the money through York Redevelopment authority, which is handling the project.

Heller's new plan has been upheld by the city's bond counsel, Townsend, Elliott and Munson, according to Mayor Fred A. Schiding.

Planners Maurice Rotival and Dr. Ernst Jurkat are to handle the final phases of blueprinting.

Navy Admits It Made Mistakes Costing Millions

General Accounting Office says errors in negotiating contracts contained more than $12 million in excess charges.

Washington (UP) — The Navy admitted yesterday mistakes were made in negotiating contracts which, the General Accounting Office says, contained more than $12 million in excess charges.

"We made mistakes both in these cases, and in our relations with the GAO," Asst. Secretary of the Navy Cecil P. Milne told the House Armed Service Investigations subcommittee.

Milne said a number of the contracts dated back to the rush and pressure of Korean war days. He said negotiating methods have been vastly improved since then.

But the Navy stood firm in its refusal to give the GAO, the ac-

(Continued on Page Thirty-One)
See Navy Mistakes

Barton Introduces Bill To Demolish Park Farmhouse

Parks director proposes to raze architecturally historic structure in Memorial park unless some civic group will finance restoration.

Demolition of the architecturally historic farmhouse in Spring Garden Memorial park is authorized in a bill introduced into city council yesterday by Parks Director Jack H. Barton.

Barton told council that before having the building torn down he would wait a "reasonable" length of time to see if any civic group decides to finance the cost of restoring the two-story brick building.

Barton made the statement in reply to Mayor Fred A. Schiding, who asked Barton if he would be willing to give "people interested in restoring the building" sufficient time to make proposals.

The bill authorizing the destruction of the farm house is scheduled to come up for final passage when council meets next Friday. Barton told a reporter he is willing to wait even beyond that date before beginning demolition.

The Junior Service League of York has given up the idea of taking on the project of restoring the house, league spokesmen indicated yesterday after hearing of council's action.

"But the community should do something to prevent things like this from happening in the future," one of the spokesmen said.

"We recognize the architectural significance of the farmhouse but we could not restore it ourselves," she explained, adding: "We feel that as one of the early American farmhouses it should be preserved."

Restoration of the two-story brick building has been recommeded by Pennsylvania Bureau of Museums, Historical Sites and Properties and by the City Planning commission.

(Continued on Page Thirty-One)
See Farmhouse

Castro Quits Post, Accusing Urrutia Of Failing Revolt

Cuban Prime Minister and leader of revolution tells nation President Urrutia became hostile because he was denied leave of absence and neglected his duties. Castro criticizes U.S. Senate committee for calling Diaz Lanz to testify.

BULLETIN

Havana (UP)—President Manuel Urrutia resigned last night.

The council of ministers immediately named Osvaldo Dorticos, a lawyer in his 40's, as Cuba's new president. Dorticos, a relative unknown in Cuban politics, was made minister of revolutionary laws in last month's cabinet shakeup.

Havana (UP) — Fidel Castro resigned as prime minister of Cuba last night, accusing President Manuel Urrutia of immobility and of failing to discharge his duties.

This in turn, Castro told a television audience, has created "discrepancies of moral order."

Urrutia was not available for comment. At the presidential palace he refused to receive newsmen.

"In the midst of the Diaz Lanz blackmail game," Castro declared, "The President suspiciously pictures himself as the champion of anti-communism."

(Castro referred to the escape to the United States of former Air Force chief, Maj. Pedro Luis Diaz Lanz, who testified this week before a Senate committee headed by Sen. James O. Eastland (D-Miss.). Diaz Lanz called Castro a Communist and his government a Communist dictatorship.)

Plans Defamation Drive

Castro said Urrutia had begun "an elaborate plan of defamation against the government similar to the one of Pedro Diaz Lanz."

Castro also criticized a U. S. Senate committee in connection with the Diaz Lanz case. He said the committee, which heard Diaz Lanz testify in Washington, "descended to the low of calling a traitor to testify."

"Our enemies abroad, those sinister personages in the Senate or who knows where, these reactionary interests were poised for the blow against us," Castro said.

"I have always rejected Communist support and I believe all true revolutionaries should reject Communist support," Castro said.

"In the U.S.A. itself there is a Communist newspaper (the New York Daily Worker). Why then are we expected to go after the Communists? No, sir. We recognize freedom of all.

"We mobilized the forces of the nation to free man from fear of political dogma without dictatorship or terror of any kind. Capitalism kills a man with hunger. Com-

(Continued on Page Thirty-One)
See Castro Quits

Racial Unit May Act On Bunche Discrimination

Although Nobel Prize winning Negro considers West Side tennis incident closed, city race commission may force private clubs to make membership lists public.

New York (UP)—Dr. Ralph J. Bunche was ready yesterday to drop his complaint against the West Side Tennis club. But a city racial commission was less willing to forgive and forget.

After hearing the Nobel Prize-winning Negro, the city's Commission on Intergroup Relations said it may seek to force private clubs to make their membership lists public.

The commission also went ahead with plans to interrogate representatives of the tennis club, which operates the Forest Hills arena in Queens where many championship matches are held.

Dr. Bunche, a United Nations undersecretary, originally inquired about the possibility of joining the tennis club so his 15-year-old son would have a place to practice the game.

Bunche said he was told by club president Wilfred Burglund that Negroes and Jews were not eligible for membership.

Earlier this week, Burglund restatement saying it considers membership applications without regard to race, creed or color.

The club invited Bunche and his son to submit formal applications and promised them every consideration. Bunche said he is interested now in joining. His son still is thinking the matter over.

Before yesterday's meetng with the commission, Bunche said:

"This has not been a pleasant experience and I am glad it is over. But I will never give aid and comfort and religious intolerance whenever and wherever I encounter it, by withholding from the public information that it is entitled to have.

"In this community, happily, bigotry cannot long stand the heat of public exposure.

"So far as I am personally concerned, that statement (by the club), which is admirably to the point of all counts, winds up the West Side tennis story. Should I be asked, I will inform the commission to that effect."

After the meeting, the commis-

(Continued on Page Thirty-One)
See Racial Unit

—Photo by The Gazette and Daily

'I WANNA GO HOME,' cried six-year-old Kevin Carroll, tightly clutching his tennis shoes and plastic airplane. He arrived at the bus depot here with 36 other "fresh air" kids who came from New York City for two-week vacations with York county families. But Kevin was not in a holiday mood. He cried bitterly for his mother and his home in the Bronx. For the outcome, see page three.

State Seeks To Halt $900,000 Tax Refund For Manu-Mine Co.

Washington (UP) — The Pennsylvania Turnpike Commission yesterday appealed to the Supreme Court in its effort to keep a $900,000 federal income tax refund from going to the Manu-Mine Research & Development Co.

The commission asked the court to review a circuit court of appeals decision that the case is one for state court rather than federal court. jurisdiction.

In the appeal, counsel for the commission noted that the president of the Reading, Pa., firm, had been convicted of conspiracy to defraud and obtaining money by false pretenses in connection with a large mine-filling contract for the northeastern extension of the Pennsylvania turnpike.

"The defrauding corporation . . . obtained possession of the money by fraud, used it to pay the income taxes on the money so obtained, and then applied for the refund which the defendant district director was about to make," the commission's appeal said.

Censorship Lifted For Reports On Nixon's Soviet Trip

Washington (UP) — The Soviet government has agreed to lift censorship for newsmen accompanying Vice President Richard M. Nixon on his good will visit to Russia this month.

Nixon's office disclosed this yesterday after weeks of backstage negotiation with Moscow on the issue.

Some 80 American reporters are assigned to cover Nixon's activities when he arrives in Moscow next Thursday for a two-week tour.

About 50 will accompany him from Washington, leaving Wednesday in a brand new jet airliner which is to make the first American nonstop flight to Moscow.

Nixon said the Soviet government has agreed that newsmen may file dispatches "freely and without delay" from Moscow and a half dozen other Russian cities he will visit.

State Senate To Vote Monday On Reform Of Minor Judiciary

(By a Staff Reporter)

Harrisburg — Pennsylvania's 50 state senators face Monday the squeamish job of taking a final vote on proposed constitutional amendments to reduce in number and put on a salaried basis the state's fee-collecting magistrates.

Their votes will, in effect, indicate the senators' choice between advancing the cause of justice for their constitutents and Pennsylvanians as a whole or yielding to the pressure of the small, but politically powerful minor judiciary.

Through their state-wide organization, the magistrates — aldermen and justices of the peace — have been lobbying aggressively in Harrisburg for defeat of the amendment.

When they act on the amendments, the senators will be weighing also political pressure against a recommendation of experts for better government. The experts were members of the Commission on Constitutional Revision which was set up by an act of the legislature. They included some sena-

(Continued on Page Thirty)
See State Senate

FIG. 181. The first U.S. tabloid to win the Ayer Cup (1958).

a folio or half-sheet paper irrespective of its typography and make-up. The persistence of the American tradition of the right-hand lead will also be noted; and while the restriction of the lead headline to a deep double column is unusual there is a general trend away from the full-page banner to four- or five-column banked headings in lower-case for the lead.

American text treatments are conservative compared with ours. Mainly single-column intros. (when two- or three-column intros. are used they are only one or two sizes above text, and usually in roman), no drop letters, very little indented setting—these are constant features. Text is rarely set solid, the body usually being ½, 1, or even 1½ pts. above face size; the reason has been indicated in Chapter 4's discussion of the Ionic group of news texts. Crossheads are sparingly used, sometimes not at all, even in main stories.

The possible patterns of page make-up are reduced to six 'basic' styles in the American textbooks.[1] These are the *symmetrical* (see the *New York Times*); the *informal balance* (sufficiently self-explanatory); the *quadrant* (which means having a heavy and striking headline—a 'stopper' —or a picture in each of the four quarters of the page); the *brace* (a multi-column heading supporting or bracing the lead head, which reads into single-column); the *circus* or *razzle-dazzle* (see the reference under France above); and the *horizontal* (all main headings three columns and over, giving multiple horizontal splitting of the page). To these six Edmund C. Arnold, Allen's successor, adds a seventh—the *functional*, 'based on presenting the day's news in the way that will be most appealing and convenient to the reader'; he urges, for instance, the value of the left-hand rather than the right-hand lead, more multi-column intros., more 'skyline' streamers and stories, more special foot-of-page treatments.

The eight-column page, of 12-em or 11½-em columns, is still the standard, although a substantial group of papers have gone over to nine columns, dropping their column measure by half an em (rarely an em) and getting down to plate width by super-shrinkage of stereotype mats, with 3 pt. or 4 pt. column rules. The aim of the nine columns is to save newsprint and increase advertising revenue, also keeping within the page capacity of the rotary.

Bodoni headline styles have been growing in favour (Fig. 182) and the 1960 Ayer winners showed Bodoni leading seven to two over Sans (here the condensed Erbar shares the field with Spartan, the wide-ranged Mergenthaler modern Sans mentioned in Chapter 7 above). The Gothic or Blackletter title-line continues, but plain roman styles are in the ascendant; the 1958 Ayer winners rated three Gothic titles, eight roman; the 1959 score was four and seven; in 1960 Gothic had vanished.

[1] Arnold, op. cit., pp. 165–85.

The Allen revolution has certainly brought to American news pages a sense of movement that they lacked in the old decker days; nevertheless they retain a definite formality, compared with our own informal style. The discipline of American newspaper typography is admirable and the overall effect more economical than that in this country; the greater daily variation of treatment and page pattern in the English style at its best is more dynamic, however.

THE SUMTER DAILY ITEM

VOL. 64 NO. 283 FOUNDED OCT. 15, 1894 SUMTER, S. C., SATURDAY AFTERNOON, SEPTEMBER 13, 1958 10 PAGES TODAY FIVE CENTS A COPY

Little Rock Tense And Fearful Today

Faubus Orders Schools Closed As Of Monday

WARREN SCHOOL CLOSED

Virginia Employs Ultimate Weapon

N.C. Federal Judge Tosses Out Case

INSTEAD OF DENOUNCING U.S.

Dissuade China, Soviet Told

U.S. Demanding News Of Airmen

FOR TROOPER SLAYERS

Speedy Trial Being Sought

MANNING STARTS FUND FOR FAMILY

Pal Day Set November 19

16-Year Minimum For Driving Urged

Advance Solicitation To Begin

Southern Solons Ready To Fight

Smathers Invokes Moderation

LITTLE LIZ

FIG. 182. A South Carolina example of the all-Bodoni style, growing in popularity in the U.S. No cap. headings—and no crossheads.

LATE EDITION PRICE, 5d

The Sydney Morning Herald.

No. 37,611 TELEPHONE: B0944 ONE HUNDRED AND TWENTY-EIGHTH YEAR OF PUBLICATION 60 PAGES SYDNEY, SATURDAY, JULY 5, 1958

THREAT OF NATIONAL WATERFRONT STRIKE OVER HURSEYS

From Our Industrial Roundsman

MELBOURNE, Friday.—A decision today by the executive of the Australian Council of Trade Unions on the Hursey issue could lead to a national waterfront strike.

With the object of bringing the whole matter to a head, the executive has sent certain instructions to Hobart waterside union officials.

The instructions were not made public, but it is understood that if the Hurseys again seek work on the waterfront the entire Hobart work force will walk off the wharves.

There is general agreement that if the dispute develops to this extent most branches of the Waterside Workers' Federation would decide to make common cause with the Hobart men and cease work.

The executive today expressed the hope that the Hurseys would seek leave of absence from the waterfront until their legal actions for damages have been settled.

"Unco-operative" Charge

HYDE PARK CEREMONY IN MEMORY OF HUNGARIAN REVOLT VICTIMS

To the sounds of Beethoven's Fifth Symphony, Hungarian migrants place lighted candles around a black cross in Hyde Park last night at the end of a ceremony in memory of the victims of the 1956 Hungarian revolt.

U.N. Told Lebanon Rebellion Internal

NEW YORK, July 4 (A.A.P.-Reuter). — The U.N. observer group says it has found no evidence of "outside" rebels fighting in Lebanon.

COLUMN 8

T.A.A. is flying 35 gallons of sweet white wine to London to test the market.

It will be the most expensive wine to reach there, I should think.

The cost of flying it from Adelaide via Sydney is £350.

Death Of Mary Grant Bruce In England

STAFF CORRESPONDENT AND A.A.P.-REUTER

LONDON, July 4.—Mary Grant Bruce, author of the "Billabong" series of Australian stories, died at Bexhill, Surrey, on Wednesday, aged 80.

WIFE-DESERTION HAS DOUBLED SINCE 1947 —GRAVE VIEW TAKEN

CANBERRA, Friday.—The number of deserted wives in Australia receiving pensions has more than doubled since 1947 to nearly 10,000.

Announcing this today, the Minister for Social Services, Mr H. S. Roberton, said the increase was evidence of a social problem which could have grave implications for the future.

Freedom Fighters Honoured

More than 400 Hungarian migrants commemorated the deaths of Hungarian freedom fighters in the 1956 revolt in a ceremony in Hyde Park last night.

Man, Woman Killed By Car

LATE NEWS

COOPER WINS IN FOUR SETS

STAFF CORRESPONDENT

WIMBLEDON, July 4.—Ashley Cooper beat fellow Australian Neale Fraser 3-6, 6-3, 6-4, 13-11 in the Wimbledon men's singles final today.

MASKED MEN KILL GREEK CYPRIOT

Cool, Windy Day Expected

A cool, windy day with a few showers is expected in Sydney today.

NEW SERIAL TODAY

THE "Herald's" exciting new serial, "Gideon's Night," begins today on page 9.

North Sydney P.O. Transfer

Shoebridge Says Rear Bus Signs Not Needed

The Transport Commissioner, Mr A. A. Shoebridge, said last night that he did not consider the restoration of destination signs at the rear of buses justified.

JAPANESE M.P.s RETURN VISIT

The Curtin Of The Years Between

WHEN John Curtin entered Federal Parliament in 1928 he was a comparative unknown from Western Australia.

This gripping instalment of a fascinating story tears aside the curtain from one of the most obscure periods of the wartime Prime Minister's life.

On Other Pages

FIG. 183. Ten-column broadsheet, this leading Australian daily.

What has been said of American style applies to the newspapers of *Canada*, while those of *South Africa* and *India* (English language) approximate broadly to the English style. In the Antipodes the position is somewhat different; there the newspapers, particularly those of *Australia*, have evolved a style of their own, combining both English and American features. The most striking aspect of Australian newspapers is their use

JAGUAR
BRYSON INDUSTRIES LTD.

BUREAU FORECAST: City. — A little rain tomorrow. Page 14.

The Herald

No. 25,300 MELBOURNE, WEDNESDAY, JULY 2, 1958 Phones: MF0211 32 PAGES 3d.

HOME EDITION

Orlando SHERRY

TV TONIGHT

PLOT FAILED IN JORDAN: REPORT

King asks Irak for army aid

Australian Associated Press

LONDON, Tues. — Jordan is reported to have asked Irak for immediate military aid following an attempted coup d'etat by military officers.

Details of the plot are shrouded in mystery. The authorities in Jordan's capital, Amman, have clapped a complete ban on news being sent out.

All the authorities there will say is that comment must wait until they have finished their investigations.

Similar plot a year ago

Holds vital position

Police chase car at 90 mph

Troops swim under guard

You can't live at 80

Woman, 72, dies in fire

Club snubbed him—so he bought it

Herald Special Service, London

Features

Ike's anniversary

HE PUT OUT BOTTLES AND VANISHED

Police and relatives are seeking a man who has not been seen by his family since he put out the empty-milk bottles three weeks ago today.

ALFRED BELLOTS

Tatts results —Page 21

CAR ROLLS OVER

'DREADFUL,' SAY DENTISTS

Flavoring in milk "threat to teeth"

The Australian Dental Association today warned that flavored milk—soon to be on sale in Melbourne — could increase dental decay.

Last straw

Best possible

HERALD MAN REPORTS ON NZ

JOHN EDDY

32.3 —That's why you shivered

IT FROZE

South Africa builds a car

EASY WASH FOR COASTAL SHIP CREWS

Herald Shipping Reporter

Major Australian shipping companies are going to install washing machines in their coastal ships — for the use of officers and crew.

Boy's art shook the Queen

RADIOLA

FEDERAL
PETROL DIESEL
COMMONWEALTH MOTORS PTY. LTD.

WANTED 200 RADIOS
T.V. 21 in. 169 Gns.
FREE TEST
IN YOUR HOME TONIGHT!
FB1156
FB3939
Packard Radio
267 SWANSTON STREET

FIG. 184. This Australian metropolitan evening is also a 10-column broadsheet—on news pages; the feature pages are 9 column.

of the abnormally narrow tabloid column measure of 9 or 9½ ems in broadsheet papers, making up to ten-column pages. This is common to both the metropolitan morning and evening papers shown here (Figs. 183, 184).

The *Sydney Morning Herald*, while recalling American style in the straightforwardness of its text treatment (in 8 pt. Times) and in its multi-line single-deck headlines, is more English in the type mixture of its headings (Century Bold, Cheltenham Bold and Bold Condensed, Bodoni Bold) and in its contrasting-type intros. in Century and Cheltenham. The *Melbourne Herald* heads in American-style Sans faces (Gothic No. 16, Tempo of various weights, Metroblack) but occasionally uses Century Bold italic, English fashion, for contrast; its use of black and heavy large-size crossheads in its Ionic text is also English rather than American.

Both papers are dominated by display advertising, notably local store advertising, which they tend to place in American pyramidal or 'well' fashion. The style of headline writing is more American than English. On the other hand, the indifferent Gothic title-lines are only too evidently English in their inspiration. Points of detail like whiting of headings, rule-joins, story-division, tend to be ignored. The *Sydney Morning Herald*, for instance, uses a strange abnormally spaced half-double, of a fortunately unique style, to separate stories, with a double-fine for full cut-offs.

15 · The Future of Newspaper Design

PACKAGE your product well and it can be sold well—if it is a product that consistently satisfies the consumer. That is the essence of newspaper design in its relationship to the newspaper, as the introductory chapter of this book has already argued. Thus newspaper design has no future apart from the future of newspapers; but the proposition may well be put contrariwise—the future of newspapers, involving wide questions of editorial policy beyond the scope of this discussion, is inseparable from the future of newspaper design. In broad terms the link has been expressed by Sir William Haley, Editor of *The Times*, who is reported as follows:

> He thought the newspaper maker had to decide on which front he was to meet the challenge of television. The weakest front was following television. In newspapers the practice of 80 per cent. being taken up with headlines was on its way out, and Picasso-like make-up would also go.[1]

It is not necessary to accept the implications of Sir William's references to Picasso or to make-up to see that a sound point of principle has been made.

American newspapermen, facing the problem of wooing an entire 'viewing and listening generation' now replacing the reading generations, lay even greater emphasis upon the question of design. Howard N. King, of the Intertype Corporation, addressing newspaper proprietors in conference at Chicago, discussed the need for 'new format designs', including page-size and column-measure (he made the 'revolutionary' suggestion of wide 15-em columns with text set in 10/12 pt.), to get a 'clean, easy-to-read, contemporary paper'.[2] Edmund C. Arnold devotes an entire chapter to 'The Teen-agers' Page', stressing the importance of 'creating the early habit of reading the newspaper . . . It is sheer self-interest on the part of the newspaper to acclimate children to regular readership rather than relinquish them to competing media without a struggle.'[3] King's

[1] *The Times*, 2 May 1958.
[2] *Printing World*, 21 August 1957.
[3] Arnold, op. cit., p. 243.

conclusion was particularly interesting; every newspaper, he told the American proprietors, should have a director of design and typography:

> It will be his business constantly to improve the appearance of your paper. He will be concerned not only with the layout and typography of your news columns but with the improved appearance of your advertising pages as well. On the editorial side your director of design and typography will simplify the headings of your newspaper in such a way that you will need just a few sizes of a good modern headletter type in both roman and italic. He will avoid the big, bold streamer headlines because it will no longer be necessary for the paper to scream at the top of its voice.

The directorial title should deter no one. It is the function that counts; and this amounts to no more than some extension of what has already begun to be recognized on a number of newspapers with the creation of the post of production editor. What is obvious is that among newspapermen there needs to be more specialization, more training (both theoretical and practical) in typography and design. Here is a problem that the newspaper industry will have to face and solve collectively. It is interesting that in a country like the United States, where the organized teaching of journalism is so extensive, the Mergenthaler Linotype Company found it valuable in 1955 to appoint Gilbert P. Farrar, a veteran newspaper typographer, as its consultant on newspaper design and to send him round the country conducting one-week seminars in newspaper typography and make-up.

More specialization should go hand in hand with a general widening of interest, throughout the editorial department, in typography and make-up. A French authority has well said that 'a journalist—even if occupied in what are commonly considered the superior lines of political reporting, dramatic or literary criticism—cannot pretend to know his job if he has never seen his copy going into type and if he has never taken part in its make-up in the page'.[1] Nor must this general interest, this heightened consciousness of the importance of the look of the paper, be limited to the editorial department. Every mechanical department, including dispatch, is concerned. Typography does not end with a page dummy, nor with the forme going to the foundry, nor even with the papers coming up the conveyor into the publishing room. It ends only when a well-made, well-printed, clean copy reaches the reader.

There is really little more to be said. Whatever the refashioning of newspapers dictated by changing circumstances, the point made by the late John E. Allen remains fundamental:

> The basic principle of modern newspaper make-up, typographically, is

[1] Manevy, op. cit., p. 5.

simplicity. The big idea is to present the story as clearly as possible; to strip it of typographic affectations and superfluities, to free it from physical devices that may intrude on the consciousness of the reader—that may get between him and the story itself.[1]

The extension of departmentalizing or sectionalizing, the development of the 'daily news magazine', the exploitation of various devices to present the gist of the news in condensed fashion and give more space to the 'news behind the news', all demand the good design which—to quote the 1957 Design Award judges—can 'reinforce the readability of the text and the aesthetic appeal of the page'.

[1] Allen, op. cit., p. 399.

Glossary

Agate: American name for $5\frac{1}{2}$ pt., used as the unit for U.S. advertising linage.

Ampersand: the typographical sign for 'and' (&).

A.P.: the Associated Press (news agency).

Autoplate: the usual machine for casting curved stereotype plates for rotary presses.

Bank: *see* Random.

Banner: a main headline right across the top of the page.

Black: carbon copy of a side of editorial matter: also bold-faced text type.

Bourgeois: pronounced 'burjoyce', old name for 9 pt.

Box: an item ruled off on all four sides, usually with heavy rule or border.

Brevier: old name for 8 pt.

Brief: news item of a few lines.

Broadsheet: a page the full size of a rotary press plate.

B.U.P.: British United Press (news agency).

Caption: the descriptive matter accompanying an illustration; sometimes loosely, and incorrectly, used as a synonym for headline.

Casting-off: calculating how much space a given amount of copy will take in a given type size and measure.

Catchline: word or phrase written at the top right hand of succeeding sides of copy, with the page folio, for easy identification.

Chase: the steel frame in which type is assembled to make a page.

Column rule: the light-faced rule used to separate columns.

Comp.: usual abbreviation for compositor.

Copy paper: newsprint offcuts made into blocks and used for editorial copy.

Cossar: a newspaper press, printing from reels but not rotary; correctly web-fed flat-bed, *not* 'flat-bed rotary'.

Creed: the fast telegraphic printer used by news agencies for communication of their news service to editorial offices: usually applied to the provincial transmission of the Press Association.

Crosshead: a centred sub-heading in text.

Curtain: a headline ruled off on three sides only.

Cut: a deletion from matter, in copy or type.

Cut-off: a full rule across one or more columns; also the depth of sheet of a rotary-printed page.

Deck: a separate portion or section of a headline, usually applied to its subsidiary second section.

Delete: to cut a word or phrase from copy or proof: indicated by the letter 'd' with a loop (i.e. the Greek delta).

Drop letter: usually indicated 'dp' or 'dp ltr', an initial letter covering two or three lines of text type.

Duplex: an American newspaper press resembling the Cossar.

Ear: the advertising space (or spaces) beside the front-page title-line.

Elrod: a rule- and lead-casting machine.

Em: the width of the lower-case letter 'm' in any type-size, i.e. the square of the body depth, usually taken as the 12 pt. or pica em, which is the unit of measure in setting, and called a 'mutton' in composing-room jargon.

Embargo: fixed time for publication of a pre-released story.

En: half an em—i.e. the width of the lower-case 'n': called a 'nut', and used for indicating ordinary indentions (e.g. 'indent nut each end') and as a measure of compositors' output (e.g. a linotype operator will be said to have an output of so many ens, say 9,000 or 10,000 an hour).

Exchange or Extel: the Exchange Telegraph Company (news agency).

Flong: the sheet of papier mâché used to make a mould from a forme for casting a stereotype plate.

Folio: a side of copy; the running headline of a page; a tabloid (q.v.) sheet.

Forme: the completed page of type locked up in a chase.

Fount: pronounced 'font'—the complete set of type of one particular face and size: applied also to the set of matrices in a composing machine magazine.

Fudge Box: the attachment for running stop press news on a rotary press.

Galley: the metal tray on which type is assembled and proofed.

Half-double: the rule or dash half the width of the column used to indicate the end of a story: traditionally a double rule, thick and thin, but now usually a single rule (formerly differentiated as a 'half-single').

Half-stick: small portrait block half the column measure; also called thumbnail.

Hanging indent: an indented setting where the first line of each paragraph is set full out to the column measure and the remaining lines indented 1 em; thus this setting is sometimes indicated as '0 and 1'.

Hood: see Curtain.

Indention: any setting short of the column measure, e.g. for panels, normally indented 'nut each end', or for black or italic paragraphs indented in text, which are set with the appropriate indention on the front only (indicated as '2 and 1', i.e. 2 ems indent the first line, then 1 em).

Intertype: composing machine similar to the Linotype.

Keep up: use capital letters. *Per contra*, 'keep down', use lower-case letters.

Klischograph: an electronic engraving machine (German).

Lead: the main news story in the paper or the opening paragraph of any news story.

Lead: pronounced 'led'—the strips of type metal or brass used to space out headings and text. Normal sizes in newspaper work are 1½ pt. ('thin'), 2 pt., and 3 pt. ('thick').

Lift: use existing type matter. Marking on proof or clippings when making changes between editions.

Linotype: composing machine which sets solid lines of type from matrices assembled by keyboard operation.

Literal: any primary error in setting, e.g. incorrect spelling, use of wrong letter, transpositions, &c.

Long Primer: old name for 10 pt.

Lower-case: the small letters in a fount of type.

Ludlow: Machine which casts large sizes of type on a slug from hand-assembled matrices.

Magazine: the case holding the matrices on a Linotype or Intertype.

Make-up: the sheet indicating the placing of the various items on a page; the process of actual assembly of the page.

Mangle: the stereotyper's moulding machine, either cylindrical (whence the name) or hydraulic direct pressure (the more modern form).

Masthead: loosely, and incorrectly, used for the front-page title line. Of American origin, the term properly means the newspaper's title and other house matter displayed on the editorial page over the first leading article.

Mat: short for matrix, meaning (*a*) the stereotypers' flong after moulding; (*b*) the individual brass letter moulds on a composing machine.

Minion: old name for 7 pt.

Monotype: composing machine which casts single types.

N.F.: 'no fly'—compositors' slang meaning that an instruction is cancelled.

Nonpareil: old name for 6 pt., used as an indicator for measure or spacing, indicating half a pica (12 pt.) em.

Overmatter: matter set but superfluous to the requirements of a given edition or issue.

Overrun: resetting of lines to insert omitted matter or to change measure (e.g. to run round a block.)

Overset: more matter than is required to fill the paper.

P.A.: Press Association (principal home news agency).

Page proof: proof of a made-up page of type.

Panel: a short item indented either side, usually in bold-face or italic type, with a rule or border top and bottom.

Pearl: old name for 5 pt.

Pica: pronounced 'pieker', old name for 12 pt. The pica em is the unit for measurement in setting, e.g. a 14-em column means a column 14 picas wide.

Plate: the curved metal plate cast from a stereotype mat for printing on a rotary press.

Point: the standard unit of type size, 0·01383 in. or approximately 72 to the inch (British-American system). Common newspaper text sizes are 5, 5½, 6, 7, 8, 9, 10, 12 pt. and display sizes 14, 18, 24, 30, 36, 42, 48, 60, 72 pt. The continental (Didot) point is differently calculated.

Proof correction: the marking of errors or changes on a galley or page proof, employing the conventional proof reader's signs. Correction should always be in ink. Reader's marks are exemplified and explained in many textbooks or in a publication of the British Standards Institution, 2 Park Street, W. 1 (*Printers' and Authors' Proof Corrections*, price 2*s*. 6*d*.).

Pull: a proof of set matter, usually applied to a galley proof.

Quad: the larger spacing units—en, em, and upwards: thus 'nut quad', 'mutton quad'.
Quire: the unit of newspaper distribution, usually 26 copies.

Random: the surface where type matter is assembled on galleys for proofing and make-up.
Reader: a corrector of the press.
Rejig: any editorial changes in matter already set.
Replate: page changes for urgent news made during an edition run.
Reuter: the principal British agency for foreign news.
Reverse indent: *see* Hanging indent.
Revise: a proof of set matter after corrections have been made.
R.O.P.: run-of-paper, applied to colour printing in a newspaper.
Rotary: a newspaper press printing from the reel and with cylindrical printing surfaces.
Ruby: old name for 5½ pt.
Run: the period of printing an edition.
Run-on: where matter is not to be broken into paragraphs.

Scan-a-graver: an American electronic engraving machine.
Screen: the number of dots to the square inch of a half-tone process block; the lower the number the coarser the reproduction. Usual newspaper screens are 55 or 65 for rotary and 85 for flatbed or Cossar.
S.G.: the signal that a service message, as distinct from news copy, is being telegraphed.
Side: a sheet of teleprinter tape or editorial copy.
Sidehead: a sub-heading in text set flush left.
Slug: a line of type or a blank line set on a Linotype, Intertype, or Ludlow.
Slug machine: generic term for Linotypes and Intertypes.
Space: the non-printing graded units for spacing out a line of type, classified as hair, thin, mid, thick.
Spaceband: the metal wedge which automatically spaces lines on a Linotype.
Splash: the main story leading the front page of the paper.
Stereo: a flat plate made by stereotyping from type or blocks, usually applied to advertisements supplied in plate form.
Stick: about 2 inches of type matter (the depth of the hand composing stick.)
Stone: the smooth iron or steel surface on which pages are made up: originally of marble, hence the name.
Stonehand: a compositor employed on page-make-up.
Story: common term for any editorial item other than a leading or feature article.
Strap: subsidiary headline placed over a main headline.
Streamer: a multi-column headline leading a page, but not necessarily across its full width: *see* Banner.
Style: the special requirements of a given newspaper for the preparation and setting of copy in respect of capitalization, punctuation, contractions, variant spellings, and the like.
Supercaster: a Monotype machine which casts large sizes of type for headlines, rules, borders, and leads.

Tabloid: a page half the size (the folio or single fold) of a broadsheet.
Tag: a short line in smaller type following a main heading, e.g. '— Court Told'; the agency acknowledgement at the end of a foreign message, e.g. A.P., Reuter, &c.
Take: a portion of copy as divided among compositors for speedy setting.
Tape: newsagency copy, nowadays normally in teleprinter sheets.
Text: solid matter as opposed to display; also used as synonym for broadsheet.
Titling: a headline type available in capitals only.

Upper-case: the capital letters in a fount of type.

White: generic term for space, i.e. the non-printing portion of a page.

Index

(Names of types are in *italic*)

Newspapers Cited

PRINTED IN GREAT BRITAIN
AT THE UNIVERSITY PRESS, OXFORD
BY VIVIAN RIDLER
PRINTER TO THE UNIVERSITY